STATE OF THE
WORLD
1994

Other Norton/Worldwatch Books

Lester R. Brown et al.

State of the World 1984

State of the World 1985

State of the World 1986

State of the World 1987

State of the World 1988

State of the World 1989

State of the World 1990

State of the World 1991

State of the World 1992

State of the World 1993

Vital Signs 1992

Vital Signs 1993

ENVIRONMENTAL ALERT SERIES

Lester R. Brown et al.

Saving the Planet

Alan Thein Durning

How Much Is Enough?

Sandra Postel

Last Oasis

STATE OF THE WORLD

1994

A Worldwatch Institute Report on Progress Toward a Sustainable Society

PROJECT DIRECTOR
Lester R. Brown

ASSOCIATE PROJECT DIRECTORS
Christopher Flavin
Sandra Postel

EDITOR
Linda Starke

CONTRIBUTING RESEARCHERS
Lester R. Brown
Alan Thein Durning
Christopher Flavin
Hilary F. French
Nicholas Lenssen
Marcia D. Lowe
Ann Misch
Sandra Postel
Michael Renner
Peter Weber
John E. Young

W·W·NORTON & COMPANY

NEW YORK   LONDON

The text of this book is composed in Baskerville, with the display set in Caslon.
Composition and manufacturing by the Haddon Craftsmen, Inc.

First Edition

ISBN 0-393-03578-6 (cloth)
ISBN 0-393-31117-1 (paper)

W. W. Norton & Company, Inc., 500 Fifth Avenue, New York, N.Y. 10110
W. W. Norton & Company Ltd., 10 Coptic Street, London WC1A 1PU

1 2 3 4 5 6 7 8 9 0

This book is printed on recycled paper.

Acknowledgments

By now, *State of the World* is taken for granted by much of the world, something people look forward to that simply appears automatically every year. Yet getting it out is anything but simple. Each annual edition—and this is the eleventh—demands long hours and meticulous research pulling together all the materials that become 10 new chapters on the world's progress toward a sustainable society. We wish to acknowledge here the many people whose names are not on the cover but without whom *State of the World* would not appear, including our ever-supportive Board of Directors, the foundations and individuals who fund our research, and those who help us by generously taking the time to review draft chapters.

Core funding for the research and writing of *State of the World* comes from the Rockefeller Brothers Fund. The Turner Foundation, with its interest in carrying capacity, funded both Chapters 1 and 10. Chapter 4 draws on our research on energy, which is funded by the Energy and Joyce Mertz-Gilmore foundations. The Curtis and Edith Munson Foundation helped us with Chapter 3, on oceans. In addition, we are grateful to the following for their continuing general support of Worldwatch Institute: the Geraldine R. Dodge, W. Alton Jones, John D. and Catherine T. MacArthur, Andrew W. Mellon, Edward John Noble, Surdna, Wallace Genetic, and Frank Weeden foundations, the Pew Charitable Trusts, and the Lynn R. and Karl E. Prickett Fund.

Something else often taken for granted is a dedicated research and support staff. Worldwatch's is second to none. Researching everything from aboriginal land rights to zooplankton, the chapter authors have been more than ably assisted this year by their colleagues Nancy Chege (for Chapter 2), Derek Denniston (Chapter 1), Hal Kane (Chapter 10), Anne Platt (Chapter 3), David Malin Roodman (Chapter 4), Megan Ryan (Chapter 9), and Aaron Sachs (Chapters 6 and 7). Besides helping channel information to all researchers, Worldwatch Librarian Lori Baldwin gave special assistance to Chapters 5 and 8.

The most fascinating research results in the world would go unnoticed without our dedicated outreach team. Responsibility for disseminating the results of the research in *State of the World* rests with Worldwatch Paper Editor Carole Douglis, Communications Associate Steve Kaufman, and Assistant Director of Communications Denise Byers Thomma.

As *State of the World* advances through the research and writing phases, moving toward staff review and then external review, independent editor Linda Starke joins us. At some point, this manuscript becomes *her* manuscript as she shepherds it through the tight, demanding cycle of editing and production. Her capacity to work long days and nights as well as weekends permits us to produce this book in record time. At one of those make-or-break phases of the schedule near the end, she is joined by Julie Phillips, who produces the detailed index. Also playing key roles in the production are Iva Ashner and Andrew Marasia, our understanding colleagues at W.W. Norton & Company.

It continues to be something of a marvel that six issues of *World Watch* magazine appear each year—with their bimonthly deadlines—amidst the flurry of *State of the World* and other Worldwatch activities. This is thanks to the hard work, skill, and patience of *World Watch* Editor Ed Ayres and Senior Editor Carla Atkinson.

On the administrative side of the Institute's work, Worldwatch runs smoothly because of its outstanding support staff. Vice President and Treasurer Blondeen Gravely, Executive Assistant to the President and Computer Systems Administrator Reah Janise Kauffman, Assistant Treasurer Barbara Fallin, Publication Sales Manager Gloria Grant, and Executive Assistant to the Vice Presidents for Research Kari Whealen (who also assembles the data from all our publications for the Worldwatch Database diskette) adeptly handle an extraordinary array of administrative work. They are joined by Receptionist Suzanne Clift, Publications Assistants Joseph Gravely and Millicent Johnson, Communications Administrative Assistant Shirley Page, and Library Assistant James Porter.

As usual, we prevailed on colleagues outside the Institute to review chapter drafts at short notice and with scant time to reply. The list of people we are indebted to this year for giving us that assistance includes Kent Anger, Nicholas Ashford, Husna Rozana Baksh, Mark Bennett, A.N. Bleijenberg, Gerald Braun, Peter Breysse, Leslie Byster, Ralph Cavanagh, John Clark, Armond Cohen, Gretchen Daily, Herman Daly, Devra Davis, Rita Diehl, Sylvia Earle, S. David Freeman, Stephen Gasteyer, Robert Ginsberg, Robert Goodland, Deborah Gordon, Judith Gradwohl, Jan Hamrin, Amanda Hawes, Don Hinrichsen, Eric Hirst, Richard F. Hirsh, Paul Hyland, Nural Islam, Catherine J. Karr, Kaye Kilburn, Reinhard Loske, Alair MacLean, William Mansfield III, Marcia Marks, Claudia Miller, David Moskovitz, Norman Myers, Robert Paarlberg, Andy Palmer, Patti Petesch, Michael Philips, David Pimentel, Per Pinstrup-Andersen, Gregory Pitts, Glenn Prickett, David Rall, Maria Rapuano, Howard Rheingold, Bruce Rich, Donald Robadue, Jr., Vernon Ruttan, Louis Scarano, Jr., Kristen Schafer, Ted Smith, Michael Stein, Boyce Thorne-Miller, Frederik van Bolhuis, Amy Vickers, Michael Weber, Carl Weinberg, John Whitelegg, and Stephen Wiel.

At the risk of sounding like a proud parent, we are pleased to announce the birth of an offspring organization—Northwest Environment Watch (NEW). Designed to be a regional Worldwatch, NEW is being founded by Alan Thein Durning—a seven-year veteran of Worldwatch—in his new home in Seattle. We look forward to following its progress as Alan and his colleagues devise a strategy for the environmental sustainability of the region.

And finally, we welcome and celebrate the arrival of several fledgling Worldwatchers: Alexander (better known as Zan) Lowe-Skillern, born to Marcia Lowe and Peter Skillern; Michael Lenssen, born to Nick and Maureen; Jack Thomma, born to Steve and Denise; and Kathryn Thein Durning, born to Alan and Amy. Each new arrival in the midst of our small Worldwatch family reminds us of the urgency of moving the world onto an environmentally sustainable path of progress.

Lester R. Brown, Christopher Flavin,
and Sandra Postel

Contents

List of Tables and Figures

LIST OF TABLES

LIST OF FIGURES

Foreword

In September of this year, people from around the world will gather in Cairo for the International Conference on Population and Development. Since the first such U.N.-sponsored gathering two decades ago in Bucharest, much has changed in the demographic landscape. The number of people on the planet has risen by 1.5 billion—nearly 40 percent. The balance of demographic power has shifted increasingly to the developing world, where 78 percent of the world now lives. And poverty has spread, with more than 1 billion people today surviving on less than a dollar a day.

In *State of the World 1994*, we examine some of the critical issues confronting the delegates at Cairo through the lens of the earth's "carrying capacity." Together, population growth, high rates of resource consumption, and poverty are driving the global economy toward ecological bankruptcy—a process that can only be reversed if their root causes are eliminated. We have filled up the planet's ecological space, and it will take reducing excessive consumption, redistributing wealth and resources, accelerating the development of more environmentally sustainable technologies, and slowing population growth to achieve a world in which all people may have a decent and secure life.

This year also marks the fiftieth anniversary of the creation of the Bretton Woods institutions—the World Bank and the International Monetary Fund. In this *State of the World* we examine how the World Bank, the largest single lender to the Third World, might be redirected toward the world's most pressing priority today: achieving a sustainable society.

State of the World continues to play a vital role in shaping environmental thinking and policy. The United States now has a president and vice president who have both read earlier editions of this book. Whether this played a small part in Bill Clinton's decision to sign the Biodiversity Convention in the spring of 1993, we may never know—but we would like to think so. Certainly, Worldwatch's thinking is well represented in Vice President Gore's best-selling book, *Earth in the Balance*.

In an ideal world, *State of the World* would be produced at U.N. headquarters in New York, but since it is not, the Institute's report has become semiofficial, used by governments, U.N. agencies, and the international development community. When Vice President Gore announced that the U.S. government's annual report, *Environmental Quality*, was being discontinued, he explained that if private groups could produce better annual reports, there was no need for the government to do so.

A primary goal of Worldwatch since its founding has been to raise the level of environmental literacy worldwide. *State of the World* has helped us do this in many ways. College and university course adoptions in the United States alone have averaged more than 1,000 annually in recent years. At a time when global challenges are more pressing than ever, we derive some satisfaction from this and hope that, because of *State of the World*, the next generation of leaders will have a greater understanding of environmental issues.

The book has also helped us in our goal to expand environmental literacy through its translation into 27 languages, which makes it accessible to most people who desire to read it. In some languages, the book is published in more than one location, thereby spreading its reach. The English edition, for example, is published in New York, London, and New Delhi. And the Spanish version is published in Barcelona, Mexico City, and Buenos Aires. Among the various editions, the English is still the largest by far, with a first printing of 100,000 copies.

In 1993, several of the foreign language editions were launched within a few weeks of the English one. The Nordic versions, for example, were released in January and early February with press conferences and media interviews in Copenhagen, Helsinki, Oslo, and Stockholm. The Dutch edition was launched in Brussels the same week as the U.S. edition. And we again briefed the European Parliament in Strasbourg, where copies of *State of the World* were distributed.

We continue to appreciate the extraordinary effort that many individuals make to translate *State of the World* quickly into various languages. Others put their time or financial resources into helping get *State of the World* into the hands of key decisionmakers. In the United States, Ted Turner distributes copies to the Fortune 500 CEOs, to members of Congress, and to state governors, a practice he began a decade ago. When he was Governor of Arkansas, Bill Clinton regularly received a copy of *State of the World* as part of the Turner distri-

bution. In addition, Turner buys 700 copies each year for distribution to CNN editors and reporters.

In Europe, Izaak van Melle, the CEO of the Dutch-based Van Melle corporation, purchased advance copies of *State of the World* for each of the executives participating in the World Economic Forum's annual conference in Davos, Switzerland. This distribution to 1,100 of the world's most prominent corporate leaders was a major step forward.

This past year also saw publication of a children's edition of *State of the World* in Japanese under the leadership of Soki Oda, the head of Worldwatch Japan. In addition, Magnar Norderhaug, the director of Worldwatch Institute Norden, is working on a children's version of *State of the World* for use by teachers in the Nordic countries.

For the first time, the data in the charts and graphs in *State of the World 1994* are now available on diskette. This Worldwatch data base diskette also includes all the data in the tables and graphs in all other Worldwatch publications released during the past year: *Vital Signs*, the Institute's new annual report; Worldwatch Papers; the Environmental Alert series of books; and *World Watch* magazine. For researchers, professors, and managers in both the public and private sectors, this diskette provides an up-to-date global environmental data base. Ordering information appears at the end of the table of contents.

As always, we welcome your suggestions.

Lester R. Brown
Christopher Flavin
Sandra Postel

Worldwatch Institute
1776 Massachusetts Ave., NW
Washington, DC 20036

December 1993

STATE OF THE
WORLD
1994

1

Carrying Capacity: Earth's Bottom Line

Sandra Postel

It takes no stretch of the imagination to see that the human species is now an agent of change of geologic proportions. We literally move mountains to mine the earth's minerals, redirect rivers to build cities in the desert, torch forests to make way for crops and cattle, and alter the chemistry of the atmosphere in disposing of our wastes. At humanity's hand, the earth is undergoing a profound transformation—one with consequences we cannot fully grasp.

It may be the ultimate irony that in our efforts to make the earth yield more for ourselves, we are diminishing its ability to sustain life of all kinds, humans included. Signs of environmental constraints are now pervasive. Cropland is scarcely expanding any more, and a good portion of existing agricultural land is losing fertility. Grasslands have been overgrazed and fisheries overharvested, limiting the amount of additional

Units of measure throughout this book are metric unless common usage dictates otherwise.

food from these sources. Water bodies have suffered extensive depletion and pollution, severely restricting future food production and urban expansion. And natural forests—which help stabilize the climate, moderate water supplies, and harbor a majority of the planet's terrestrial biodiversity—continue to recede.

These trends are not new. Human societies have been altering the earth since they began. But the pace and scale of degradation that started about mid-century—and continues today—is historically new. The central conundrum of sustainable development is now all too apparent: population and economies grow exponentially, but the natural resources that support them do not.

Biologists often apply the concept of "carrying capacity" to questions of population pressures on an environment. Carrying capacity is the largest number of any given species that a habitat can support indefinitely. When that maximum sustainable population level is surpassed, the resource base begins to decline—and sometime thereafter, so does the population.

A simple but telling example of a breach of carrying capacity involved the introduction of 29 reindeer to St. Matthew Island in the Bering Sea in 1944. Under favorable conditions, the herd expanded to 6,000 by the summer of 1963. The following winter, however, the population crashed, leaving fewer than 50 reindeer. According to a 1968 study by biologist David R. Klein of the University of Alaska, the large herd had overgrazed the island's lichens, its main source of winter forage, and the animals faced extreme competition for limited supplies during a particularly severe winter. Klein concluded that "food supply, through its interaction with climatic factors, was the dominant population regulating mechanism for reindeer on St. Matthew Island."[1]

Of course, human interactions with the environment are far more complicated than those of reindeer on an island. The earth's capacity to support humans is determined not just by our most basic food requirements but also by our levels of consumption of a whole range of resources, by the amount of waste we generate, by the technologies we choose for our varied activities, and by our success at mobilizing to deal with major threats. In recent years, the global problems of ozone depletion and greenhouse warming have underscored the danger of overstepping the earth's ability to absorb our waste products. Less well recognized, however, are the consequences of exceeding the sustainable supply of essential resources—and how far along that course we may already be.

As a result of our population size, consumption patterns, and technology choices, we have surpassed the planet's carrying capacity. This is plainly evident by the extent to which we are damaging and depleting natural capital. The earth's environmental assets are now insufficient to sustain both our present patterns of economic activity and the life-support systems we depend on. If current trends in resource use continue and if world population grows as projected, by 2010 per capita availability of rangeland will drop by 22 percent and the fish catch by 10 percent. Together, these provide much of the world's animal protein. The per capita area of irrigated land, which now yields about a third of the global food harvest, will drop by 12 percent. And cropland area and forestland per person will shrink by 21 and 30 percent, respectively.[2]

The days of the frontier economy—in which abundant resources were available to propel economic growth and living standards—are over. We have entered an era in which global prosperity increasingly depends on using resources more efficiently, distributing them more equitably, and reducing consumption levels overall. Unless we accelerate this transition, powerful social tensions are likely to arise from increased competition for the scarce resources that remain. The human population will not crash wholesale as the St. Matthew Island reindeer did, but there will likely be a surge in hunger, crossborder migration, and conflict—trends already painfully evident in parts of the world.[3]

Wiser and more discriminating use of technology offers the possibility of tremendous gains in resource efficiency and productivity, helping us get more out of each hectare of land, ton of wood, or cubic meter of water. In this way, technology can help stretch the earth's capacity to support humans sustainably. Trade also has an important, though more limited role. Besides helping spread beneficial technologies, it enables one country to import ecological capital from another. Trade can thus help surmount local or regional scarcities of land, water, wood, or other resources.

In these ways, technology and trade can buy time to tackle the larger challenges of stabilizing population, reducing excessive consumption, and redistributing wealth. Unfortunately, past gains in these two areas have deluded us into thinking that any constraint can be overcome, and that we can therefore avoid the more fundamental tasks. And rather than directing technology and trade toward sustainable development, we have more often used them in ways that hasten resource depletion and degradation.

The roots of environmental damage run deep. Unless they are unearthed soon, we risk exceeding the planet's carrying capacity to such a degree that a future of economic and social decline will be impossible to avoid.

DRIVING FORCES

Since mid-century, three trends have contributed most directly to the excessive pressures now being placed on the earth's natural systems—the doubling of world population, the quintupling of global economic output, and the widening gap in the distribution of income. The environmental impact of our population, now numbering 5.5 billion, has been vastly multiplied by economic and social systems that strongly favor growth and ever-rising consumption over equity and poverty alleviation; that fail to give women equal rights, education, and economic opportunity—and thereby perpetuate the conditions under which poverty and rapid population growth persists; and that do not discriminate between means of production that are environmentally sound and those that are not.

Of the three principal driving forces, the growing inequality in income between rich and poor stands out in sharpest relief. In 1960, the richest 20 percent of the world's people absorbed 70 percent of global income; by 1989 (the latest year for which comparable figures are available), the wealthy's share had climbed to nearly 83 percent. The poorest 20 percent, meanwhile, saw their share of global income drop from an already meager 2.3 percent to just 1.4 percent. The ratio of the richest fifth's share to the poorest's thus grew from 30 to 1 in 1960 to 59 to 1 in 1989. (See Table 1–1.)[4]

This chasm of inequity is a major cause of environmental decline: it fosters overconsumption at the top of the income ladder and persistent poverty at the bottom. By now, ample evidence shows that people at either end of the income spectrum are far more likely than those in the middle to damage the earth's ecological health—the rich because of their high consumption of energy, raw materials, and manufactured goods, and the poor because they must often cut trees, grow crops, or graze cat-

Table 1–1. Global Income Distribution, 1960–89

Year	Share of Global Income Going to		Ratio of Richest to Poorest
	Richest 20 Percent	Poorest 20 Percent	
	(percent)		
1960	70.2	2.3	30 to 1
1970	73.9	2.3	32 to 1
1980	76.3	1.7	45 to 1
1989	82.7	1.4	59 to 1

SOURCE: United Nations Development Programme, *Human Development Report 1992* (New York: Oxford University Press, 1992).

tle in ways harmful to the earth merely to survive from one day to the next.[5]

Families in the western United States, for instance, often use as much as 3,000 liters of water a day—enough to fill a bathtub 20 times. Overdevelopment of water there has contributed to the depletion of rivers and aquifers, destroyed wetlands and fisheries, and, by creating an illusion of abundance, led to excessive consumption. Meanwhile, nearly one out of every three people in the developing world—some 1.2 billion people in all—lack access to a safe supply of drinking water. This contributes to the spread of debilitating disease and death, and forces women and children to trek many hours a day to collect a few jugs of water to meet their family's most basic needs.[6]

Disparities in food consumption are revealing as well. (See Table 1–2.) As many as 700 million people do not eat enough to live and work at their full potential. The average African, for instance, consumes only 87 percent of the calories needed for a healthy and productive life. Meanwhile, diets in many rich countries are so laden with animal fat as to cause increased rates of heart disease and cancers. Moreover, the meat-intensive diets of the wealthy usurp a disproportionately large share of the earth's agricultural carrying capacity since producing one kilogram of meat takes several kilograms of grain. If everyone in the world required as much grain for their diet as the average American does, the global harvest would need to be 2.6 times greater than it is today—a highly improbable scenario.[7]

Economic growth—the second driving force—has been fueled in part by the introduction of oil onto the energy scene. Since mid-century, the global economy has expanded fivefold. As much was produced in two-and-a-half months of 1990 as in the entire year of 1950. World trade, moreover, grew even faster: exports of primary commodities

Table 1–2. Grain Consumption Per Person in Selected Countries, 1990

Country	Grain Consumption Per Person
	(kilograms)
Canada	974
United States	860
Soviet Union	843
Australia	503
France	465
Turkey	419
Mexico	309
Japan	297
China	292
Brazil	277
India	186
Bangladesh	176
Kenya	145
Tanzania	145
Haiti	100
World Average	323

SOURCES: Worldwatch Institute estimate, based on U.S. Department of Agriculture, *World Grain Database* (unpublished printout) (Washington, D.C.: 1992); Population Reference Bureau, *1990 World Population Data Sheet* (Washington, D.C.: 1990).

and manufactured products rose elevenfold.[8]

The extent to which the overall scale of economic activity damages the earth depends largely on the technologies used and the amount of resources consumed in the process. Electricity generated by burning coal may contribute as much to economic output as an equal amount generated by wind turbines, for example, but burning coal causes far more environmental harm. A similar comparison holds for a ton of paper made from newly cut trees and a ton produced from recycled paper.

Unfortunately, economic growth has most often been of the damaging variety—powered by the extraction and consumption of fossil fuels, water, timber, minerals, and other resources. Between 1950 and 1990, the industrial round-wood harvest doubled, water use tripled, and oil production rose nearly sixfold. Environmental damage increased proportionately.[9]

Compounding the rises in both poverty and resource consumption related to the worsening of inequality and rapid economic expansion, population growth has added greatly to pressures on the earth's carrying capacity. The doubling of world population since 1950 has meant more or less steady increases in the number of people added to the planet each year. Whereas births exceeded deaths by 37 million in 1950, the net population gain in 1993 was 87 million—roughly equal to the population of Mexico. (See Figure 1–1).[10]

Aside from the late fifties, when the massive famine caused by China's Great Leap Forward led to a sharp drop in annual population growth, the only interval of sustained reductions in the yearly addition to population during the last 40 years occurred in the seventies. Fairly widespread improvements in living standards then and the introduction of family planning programs in a number of countries caused birth rates to drop. This translated into a decline in the growth rate. If the trend of the seventies

had continued along roughly the same path, world population would have stabilized in 2030 at 6.7 billion.[11]

Instead, the population growth rate stopped declining in the late seventies and remained stalled through much of the eighties. This initiated another period of record-setting additions to world population. The U.N. medium population projection now shows world population reaching 8.9 billion by 2030—2.2 billion more people than if the slow-down of the seventies had continued—and levelling off at 11.5 billion around 2150.[12]

Rarely do the driving forces of environmental decline operate in isolation; more often they entangle, like a spider's web. Where people's livelihoods depend directly on the renewable resource base around them, for example, poverty, social inequity, and population growth fuel a vicious cycle in which environmental decline and worsening poverty reduce options for escaping these traps. This is plainly evident in the African Sahel, where traditional agricultural systems that depended on leaving land fallow for a time to restore its productivity have broken down under population pressures.[13]

On Burkina Faso's Mossi Plateau, for instance, some 60 percent of the arable land is under cultivation in a given year, which means it is not lying idle long enough to rejuvenate. The reduced organic content and moisture-storage capacity of the soil lowers crop productivity and makes farmers more vulnerable to drought. In addition, with firewood in scarce supply in many Sahelian countries, families often use livestock dung for fuel, which also robs the land of nutrients. The result is a lowering of the land's carrying capacity, reduced food security, greater poverty, and continued high population growth.[14]

To take another example, the U.S. government protects domestic sugar producers by keeping sugar prices at

Million

Figure 1-1. Annual Increase in World Population, 1950–93

Source: Census Bureau

three to five times world market levels. Because of the lost market opportunity, low-cost sugarcane growers in the Philippines produce less, putting cane-cutters out of work. The inequitable distribution of cropland in the Philippines combines with rapid population growth to leave the cutters little choice but to migrate into the hills to find land to grow subsistence crops. They clear plots by deforesting the upper watershed, causing increased flooding and soil erosion, which in turn silts up reservoirs and irrigation canals downstream. Poverty deepens, the gap between the rich and poor widens, and the environment deteriorates further.[15]

THE RESOURCE BASE

The outer limit of the planet's carrying capacity is determined by the total amount of solar energy converted into biochemical energy through plant photosynthesis minus the energy those plants use for their own life processes. This is called the earth's net primary productivity (NPP), and it is the basic food source for all life.

Prior to human impacts, the earth's forests, grasslands, and other terrestrial ecosystems had the potential to produce a net total of some 150 billion tons of organic matter per year. Stanford University biologist Peter Vitousek and his colleagues estimate, however, that humans have destroyed outright about 12 percent of the terrestrial NPP and now directly use or co-opt an additional 27 percent. Thus, one species—*Homo sapiens*—has appropriated nearly 40 percent of the terrestrial food supply, leaving only 60 percent for the millions of other land-based plants and animals.[16]

It may be tempting to infer that, at 40

percent of NPP, we are still comfortably below the ultimate limit. But this is not the case. We have appropriated the 40 percent that was easiest to acquire. It may be impossible to double our share, yet theoretically that would happen in just 60 years if our share rose in tandem with population growth. And if average resource consumption per person continues to increase, that doubling would occur much sooner.

Perhaps more important, human survival hinges on a host of environmental services provided by natural systems—from forests' regulation of the hydrological cycle to wetlands' filtering of pollutants. As we destroy, alter, or appropriate more of these natural systems for ourselves, these environmental services are compromised. At some point, the likely result is a chain reaction of environmental decline—widespread flooding and erosion brought on by deforestation, for example, or worsened drought and crop losses from desertification, or pervasive aquatic pollution and fisheries losses from wetlands destruction. The simultaneous unfolding of several such scenarios could cause unprecedented human hardship, famine, and disease. Precisely when vital thresholds will be crossed, no one can say. But as Vitousek and his colleagues note, those "who believe that limits to growth are so distant as to be of no consequence for today's decision makers appear unaware of these biological realities."[17]

How have we come to usurp so much of the earth's productive capacity? In our efforts to feed, clothe, house, and otherwise satisfy our ever-growing material desires, we have steadily converted diverse and complex biological systems to more uniform and simple ones that are managed for human benefit. Timber companies cleared primary forests and replaced them with monoculture pine plantations to make pulp and paper. Migrant peasants torched tropical forests in order to plant crops merely to survive. And farmers plowed the prairie grasslands of the U.S. Midwest to plant corn, creating one of the most productive agricultural regions in the world. Although these transformations have allowed more humans to be supported at a higher standard of living, they have come at the expense of natural systems, other plant and animal species, and ecological stability.

Continuing along this course is risky. But the flip side of the problem is equally sobering. What do we do when we have claimed virtually all that we can, yet our population and demands are still growing?

This is precisely the predicament we now face. Opportunities to expand our use of certain essential resources—including cropland, rangeland, fisheries, water, and forests—are severely limited, and a good share of the resources we have already appropriated, and depend on, are losing productivity. And unlike energy systems, where we can envisage a technically feasible shift from fossil fuels to solar-based sources, there are no identifiable substitutes for these essential biological and water resources.

Between 1980 and 1990, cropland area worldwide expanded by just 2 percent, which means that gains in the global food harvest came almost entirely from raising yields on existing cropland. Most of the remaining area that could be used to grow crops is in Africa and Latin America; very little is in Asia. The most sizable near-term additions to the cropland base are likely to be a portion of the 76 million hectares of savanna grasslands in South America that are already accessible and potentially cultivable, as well as some portion of African rangeland and forest. These conversions, of course, may come at a high environmental price, and will push our 40-percent share of NPP even higher.[18]

Moreover, a portion of any cropland gains that do occur will be offset by losses. As economies of developing countries diversify and as cities expand to accommodate population growth and migration, land is rapidly being lost to industrial development, housing, road construction, and the like. Canadian geographer Vaclav Smil estimates, for instance, that between 1957 and 1990, China's arable land diminished by at least 35 million hectares—an area equal to all the cropland in France, Germany, Denmark, and the Netherlands combined. At China's 1990 average grain yield and consumption levels, that amount of cropland could have supported some 450 million people, about 40 percent of its population.[19]

In addition, much of the land we continue to farm is losing its inherent productivity because of unsound agricultural practices and overuse. The Global Assessment of Soil Degradation, a three-year study involving some 250 scientists, found that more than 550 million hectares are losing topsoil or undergoing other forms of degradation as a direct result of poor agricultural methods. (See Table 1–3.)[20]

On balance, unless crop prices rise (which in turn depends on economic conditions in developing countries and on whether purchasing power rises sufficiently to push up the demand for food), it appears unlikely that the net cropland area will expand much more quickly over the next two decades than it did between 1980 and 1990. Assuming a net expansion of 5 percent, which may be optimistic, total cropland area would climb to just over 1.5 billion hectares. Given the projected 33-percent increase in world population by 2010, the amount of cropland per person would decline by 21 percent. (See Table 1–4).

Pasture and rangeland cover some 3.4 billion hectares of land, more than twice the area in crops. The cattle, sheep,

State of the World 1994

Table 1–3. Human-Induced Land Degradation Worldwide, 1945 to Present

Region	Over-grazing	Defores-tation	Agricultural Misman-agement	Other[1]	Total	Degraded Area as Share of Total Vegetated Land
	(million hectares)					(percent)
Asia	197	298	204	47	746	20
Africa	243	67	121	63	494	22
South America	68	100	64	12	244	14
Europe	50	84	64	22	220	23
North & Cent. Amer.	38	18	91	11	158	8
Oceania	83	12	8	0	103	13
World	679	579	552	155	1,965	17

[1]Includes exploitation of vegetation for domestic use (133 million hectares) and bioindustrial activities, such as pollution (22 million hectares).
SOURCE: Worldwatch Institute, based on "The Extent of Human-Induced Soil Degradation," Annex 5 in L.R. Oldeman et al., *World Map of the Status of Human-Induced Soil Degradation* (Wageningen, Netherlands: United Nations Environment Programme and International Soil Reference and Information Centre, 1991).

goats, buffalo, and camels that graze them convert grass, which humans cannot digest, into meat and milk, which they can. The global ruminant livestock herd, which numbers about 3.3 billion, thus adds a source of food for people that does not subtract from the grain supply, in contrast to the production of pigs, chickens, and cattle raised in feedlots.[21]

Much of the world's rangeland is already heavily overgrazed and cannot continue to support the livestock herds and management practices that exist today. According to the Global Assessment of Soil Degradation, overgrazing has degraded some 680 million hectares since mid-century. This suggests that 20 percent of the world's pasture and range is losing productivity and will continue to do so unless herd sizes are reduced or more sustainable livestock practices are put in place.[22]

During the eighties, the total range area increased slightly, in part because land deforested or taken out of crops often reverted to some form of grass. If similar trends persist over the next two decades, by 2010 the total area of rangeland and pasture will have increased 4 percent, but it will have dropped 22 percent in per capita terms. In Africa and Asia, which together contain nearly half the world's rangelands and where many traditional cultures depend heavily on livestock, even larger per capita declines could significantly weaken food economies.

Fisheries—another natural biological system that humans depend on—add calories, protein, and diversity to human diets. The annual fish catch from all sources, including aquaculture, totalled 97 million tons in 1990, about 5 percent of the protein humans consume. Fish account for a good portion of the calories consumed overall in many coastal regions and island nations. (See Chapter 3.)[23]

The world fish catch has climbed rapidly in recent decades, expanding nearly fivefold since 1950. But it peaked at just above 100 million tons in 1989. Although catches from both inland fisheries and aquaculture (fish farming) have been rising steadily, they have not offset

Table 1–4. Population Size and Availability of Renewable Resources, Circa 1990, With Projections for 2010

	Circa 1990	2010	Total Change	Per Capita Change
	(million)		(percent)	
Population	5,290	7,030	+33	–
Fish Catch (tons)[1]	85	102	+20	−10
Irrigated Land (hectares)	237	277	+17	−12
Cropland (hectares)	1,444	1,516	+5	−21
Rangeland and Pasture (hectares)	3,402	3,540	+4	−22
Forests (hectares)[2]	3,413	3,165	−7	−30

[1]Wild catch from fresh and marine waters; excludes aquaculture.   [2]Includes plantations; excludes woodlands and shrublands.
SOURCES: Population figures from U.S. Bureau of the Census, Department of Commerce, *International Data Base,* unpublished printout, November 2, 1993; 1990 irrigated land, cropland, and rangeland from U.N. Food and Agriculture Organization (FAO), *Production Yearbook 1991* (Rome: 1992); fish catch from M. Perotti, chief, Statistics Branch, Fisheries Department, FAO, Rome, private communication, November 3, 1993; forests from FAO, *Forest Resources Assessment 1990* (Rome: 1992 and 1993) and other sources documented in endnote 30. For explanation of projections, see text.

the decline in the much larger wild marine catch, which fell from a historic peak of 82 million tons in 1989 to 77 million in 1991, a drop of 6 percent.[24]

With the advent of mechanized hauling gear, bigger nets, electronic fish detection aids, and other technologies, almost all marine fisheries have suffered from extensive overexploitation. Under current practices, considerable additional growth in the global fish catch overall looks highly unlikely. Indeed, the U.N. Food and Agriculture Organization (FAO) now estimates that all 17 of the world's major fishing areas have either reached or exceeded their natural limits, and that 9 are in serious decline.[25]

FAO scientists believe that better fisheries management might allow the wild marine catch to increase by some 20 percent. If this could be achieved, and if the freshwater catch increased proportion-

ately, the total wild catch would rise to 102 million tons; by 2010, this would nonetheless represent a 10-percent drop in per capita terms.[26]

Fresh water may be even more essential than cropland, rangeland, and fisheries; without water, after all, nothing can live. Signs of water scarcity are now pervasive. Today, 26 countries have insufficient renewable water supplies within their own territories to meet the needs of a moderately developed society at their current population size—and populations are growing fastest in some of the most water-short countries, including many in Africa and the Middle East. Rivers, lakes, and underground aquifers show widespread signs of degradation and depletion, even as human demands rise inexorably.[27]

Water constraints already appear to be slowing food production, and those

restrictions will only become more severe. Agricultural lands that receive irrigation water play a disproportionate
role in meeting the world's food needs:
the 237 million hectares of irrigated land
account for only 16 percent of total
cropland but more than a third of the
global harvest. For most of human history, irrigated area expanded faster than
population did, which helped food production per person to increase steadily.
In 1978, however, per capita irrigated
land peaked, and it has fallen nearly 6
percent since then.[28]

There is little to suggest that this disturbing trend will turn around soon. The
rising cost of building new irrigation
projects, growing competition for scarce
water, mounting concern about the social and environmental effects of large
dams, and the steady loss of perhaps 2
million hectares of irrigated land each
year due to salinization suggest that the
pace of net irrigation expansion is not
likely to pick up any time soon. Indeed,
it may slow further. Assuming, perhaps
optimistically, that the irrigation base
spreads at an average rate of 2 million
hectares a year for the next two decades,
irrigated area would climb to 277 million
hectares—a 17-percent gain over 1990,
but a 12-percent loss in per capita
terms.[29]

Forests and woodlands, the last key
component of the biological resource
base, contribute a host of important
commodities to the global economy—
logs and lumber for constructing homes
and furniture, fiber for making paper,
fruits and nuts for direct consumption,
and, in poor countries, fuelwood for
heating and cooking. More important
even than these benefits, however, are
the ecological services forests perform—
from conserving soils and moderating
water cycles to storing carbon, protecting air quality, and harboring millions of
plant and animal species.

Today forests cover 24 percent less

area than in 1700—3.4 billion hectares
compared with an estimated 4.5 billion
about 300 years ago. Most of that area
was cleared for crop cultivation, but cattle ranching, timber and fuelwood harvesting, and the growth of cities, suburbs, and highways all claimed a share as
well. Recent assessments suggest that
the world's forests declined by about
130 million hectares between 1980 and
1990, an area larger than Peru.[30]

Most of this clearing occurred in the
tropics, which lost 154 million hectares
of natural forests but gained 18 million
hectares of plantations. (See also Chapter 2.) Among temperate countries, substantial losses occurred in China (some
13 million hectares). Other temperate
areas, however, including the former Soviet Union, experienced a net gain. For
the world as a whole, if the average net
loss of 3.7 percent per decade continues,
by 2010 the world's forested area will
shrink by an additional 7 percent; per
capita forest area will drop by an astonishing 30 percent.[31]

Tragically, much tropical forest is
being cleared in order to cultivate soils
that cannot sustain crop production for
more than a few years. Yet the species
extinguished in the process are gone forever. And the associated environmental
destruction will have repercussions for
generations.

REDIRECTING TECHNOLOGY

Advances in technology—which is used
broadly here to mean the application of
knowledge to an activity—offer at least a
partial way out of our predicament. The
challenge of finding ways to meet the
legitimate needs of our growing population without further destroying the natural resource base certainly ranks among
the greatest missions humanity has ever

faced. In most cases, "appropriate" technologies will no longer be engineering schemes, techniques, or methods that enable us to claim more of nature's resources, but instead systems that allow us to benefit more from the resources we already have. As long as the resulting gains are directed toward bettering the environment and the lives of the less fortunate instead of toward increased consumption by the rich, such efforts will reduce human impacts on the earth.

The power of technology to help meet human needs was a critical missing piece in the world view of Thomas Malthus, the English curate whose famous 1798 essay postulated that the growth of human population would outstrip the earth's food-producing capabilities. His prediction was a dire one—massive famine, disease, and death. But a stream of agricultural advances combined with the productivity leaps of the Industrial Revolution made the Malthusian nightmare fade for much of the world.

Without question, technological advances have steadily enhanced our capacity to raise living standards. They not only helped boost food production, the main concern of Malthus, they also increased our access to sources of water, energy, timber, and minerals. In many ways, however, technology has proved to be a double-edged sword. Take, for example, the chlorofluorocarbons that at first appeared to be ideal chemicals for so many different uses. It turned out that once they reached the upper atmosphere they began destroying the ozone layer, and thus threatened life on the planet.

Likewise, the irrigation, agricultural chemicals, and high-yielding crop varieties that made the Green Revolution possible also depleted and contaminated water supplies, poisoned wildlife and people, and encouraged monoculture cropping that reduced agricultural diversity. Huge driftnets boosted fish harvests but contributed to overfishing and

the depletion of stocks. And manufacturing processes that rapidly turn timber into pulp and paper have fueled the loss of forests and created mountains of waste paper.

As a society, we have failed to discriminate between technologies that meet our needs in a sustainable way and those that harm the earth. We have let the market largely dictate which technologies move forward, without adjusting for its failure to take proper account of environmental damages. Now that we have exceeded the planet's carrying capacity and are rapidly running down its natural capital, such a correction is urgently needed.

As a society, we have failed to discriminate between technologies that meet our needs in a sustainable way and those that harm the earth.

Meeting future food needs, for instance, now depends almost entirely on raising the productivity of land and water resources. Over the last several decades, remarkable gains have been made in boosting cropland productivity. Between 1950 and 1991, world grain production rose 169 percent despite only a 17-percent increase in the area of grain harvested. An impressive 131-percent increase in average grain yield—brought about largely by Green Revolution technologies—allowed production to expand so greatly. If today's grain harvest were being produced at 1950's average yield, we would need at least twice as much land in crops as today—and pressure to turn forests and grasslands into cropland would have increased proportionately.[32]

Whether technological advances continue to raise crop yields fast enough to meet rising demand is, at the moment, an open question. Given the extent of cropland and rangeland degradation and the slowdown in irrigation expansion, it may be difficult to sustain the past pace of yield increases. Indeed, per capita grain production in 1992 was 7 percent lower than the historic peak in 1984. Whether this is a short-term phenomenon or the onset of a longer-term trend will depend on what new crop varieties and technologies reach farmers' fields and if they can overcome the yield-suppressing effects of environmental degradation. Another factor is whether agricultural policies and prices encourage farmers to invest in raising land productivity further.[33]

A portion of our current food output is being produced by using land and water unsustainably.

Currently, yields of the major grain crops are still significantly below their genetic potential, so it is possible that scientists will develop new crop varieties that can boost land productivity. They are working, for example, on a new strain of rice that may offer yield gains within a decade. And they have developed a wheat variety that is resistant to leaf rust disease, which could both increase yields and allow wheat to be grown in more humid regions.[34]

Gains from biotechnology may be forthcoming soon as well. According to Gabrielle Persley of the World Bank, rice varieties bioengineered for virus resistance are likely to be in farmers' fields by 1995. Wheat varieties with built-in disease and insect resistance, which could reduce crop losses to pests, are under development. And scientists are genetically engineering maize varieties for insect resistance, although no commercial field applications are expected until sometime after 2000. It remains to be

seen whether these and other potential gains materialize and whether they collectively increase yields at the rates needed. The recent cutback in funding for international agricultural research centers, where much of the work on grain crops takes place, is troubling.[35]

Parallelling the need to raise yields, however, is the less recognized challenge of making both existing and future food production systems sustainable. A portion of our current food output is being produced by using land and water unsustainably. Unless this is corrected, food production from these areas will decline at some point.

For instance, in parts of India's Punjab, the nation's breadbasket, the high-yielding rice paddy-wheat rotation that is common requires heavy doses of agricultural chemicals and substantial amounts of irrigation water. A recent study by researchers from the University of Delhi and the World Resources Institute in Washington, D.C., found that in one Punjab district, Ludhiana, groundwater pumping exceeds recharge by one third and water tables are dropping nearly 1 meter per year. Even if water use were reduced to 80 percent of the recommended level, which would cause yields to drop an estimated 8 percent, groundwater levels would still decline by a half-meter per year. Given the importance of the Punjab to India's food production, the authors' conclusion is sobering, to say the least: "Unless production practices are developed that dramatically reduce water use, any paddy production system may be unsustainable in this region."[36]

Indeed, in many agricultural regions—including northern China, southern India (as well as the Punjab), Mexico, the western United States, parts of the Middle East, and elsewhere—water may be much more of a constraint to future food production than land, crop yield potential, or most other factors. Developing and distributing technologies and practices that improve water management is critical to sustaining the food production capability we now have, much less increasing it for the future.

Water-short Israel is a front-runner in making its agricultural economy more water-efficient. Its current agricultural output could probably not have been achieved without steady advances in water management—including highly efficient drip irrigation, automated systems that apply water only when crops need it, and the setting of water allocations based on predetermined optimum water applications for each crop. The nation's success is notable: between 1951 and 1990, Israeli farmers reduced the amount of water applied to each hectare of cropland by 36 percent. This allowed the irrigated area to more than triple with only a doubling of irrigation water use.[37]

Whether high-tech, like the Israeli systems, or more traditional, like the vast canal schemes in much of Asia, improvements in irrigation management are critical. At the same time, technologies and methods to raise the productivity of rainfed lands are urgently needed. Particularly in dry regions, where land degradation and drought make soil and water conservation a matter of survival, improvements on many traditional methods could simultaneously raise local food production, reduce hunger, and slow environmental decline.[38]

In the Burkina Faso province of Yatenga, for example, farmers have revived a traditional technique of building simple stone lines across the slopes of their fields to reduce erosion and help store moisture in the soil. With the aid of Oxfam, a U.K.-based development organization, they improved on the earlier technique by constructing the stone walls along contour lines, using a simple water-tube device to help them determine a series of level points. The technique has raised yields by up to 50 percent, and is now being used on more than 8,000 hectares in the province.[39]

Matching the need for sustainable gains in land and water productivity is the need for improvements in the efficiency of wood use and reductions in wood and paper waste in order to reduce pressures on forests and woodlands. A beneficial timber technology is no longer one that improves logging efficiency—the number of trees cut per hour—but rather one that makes each log harvested go further. Raising the efficiency of forest product manufacturing in the United States, the world's largest wood consumer, roughly to Japanese levels would reduce U.S. timber needs by about a fourth, for instance. Together, available methods of reducing waste, increasing manufacturing efficiency, and recycling more paper could cut U.S. wood consumption in half; a serious effort to produce new wood-saving techniques would reduce it even more.[40]

With the world's paper demand projected to double by the year 2010, there may be good reason to shift production toward "treeless paper"—that made from nonwood pulp. Hemp, bamboo, jute, and kenaf are among the alternative sources of pulp. The fast-growing kenaf plant, for example, produces two to four times more pulp per hectare than southern pine, and the pulp has all of the main qualities needed for making most grades of paper. In China, more than 80 percent of all paper pulp is made from nonwood sources. Treeless paper was manufactured in 45 countries in 1992, and accounted for 9 percent of the world's paper supply. With proper economic incentives and support for technology and market development, the use of treeless paper could expand greatly.[41]

These are but a few examples of the refocusing of technology that is needed. A key policy instrument for encouraging more sustainable and efficient means of production is the institution of environmental taxes, which would help correct the market's failure to include environmental harm in the pricing of products and activities. In addition, stronger criteria are needed within development institutions and aid agencies to ensure that the projects they fund are ecologically sound and sustainable. (See Chapter 9.)

The many past gains from technological advances might make concerns about resource constraints seem anachronistic. But as Dartmouth College professor Donella Meadows and her coauthors caution in their 1992 study *Beyond the Limits*, "the more successfully society puts off its limits through economic and technical adaptations, the more likely it is in the future to run into several of them at the same time." The wiser use of technology can only buy time—and precious time it is—to bring consumption and population growth down to sustainable levels and to distribute resources more equitably.[42]

THE ROLE OF TRADE

Consider two countries, each with a population of about 125 million. Country A has a population density of 331 people per square kilometer, has just 372 square meters of cropland per inhabitant (one seventh the world average), and imports almost three fourths of its grain and nearly two thirds of its wood. Country B, on the other hand, has a population density less than half that of Country A and nearly five times as much cropland per person. It imports only one tenth of its grain and no wood. Which country has most exceeded its carrying capacity?[43]

Certainly it would be Country A—which, as it turns out, is Japan—a na-

tion boasting a real gross domestic product (GDP) of some $18,000 per capita. Country B, which from these few indicators seems closer to living within its means, is Pakistan—with a real GDP per capita of only $1,900. By any economic measure, Japan is far and away the more successful of the two, so how can questions of carrying capacity be all that relevant?[44]

The answer, of course, lies in large part with trade. Japan sells cars and computers, and uses some of the earnings to buy food, timber, oil, and other raw materials. And that is what trade is supposed to be about: selling what one can make better or more efficiently, and buying what others have a comparative advantage in producing. Through trade, countries with scarce resources can import what they need from countries with a greater abundance. If those reindeer on St. Matthew Island had been able to import lichens, their numbers might not have crashed so drastically.

Imports of biologically based commodities like food and timber are, indirectly, imports of land, water, nutrients, and the other components of ecological capital needed to produce them. Many countries would not be able to support anything like their current population and consumption levels were it not for trade. To meet its food and timber demands alone, the Netherlands, for instance, appropriates the production capabilities of 24 million hectares of land—10 times its own area of cropland, pasture, and forest.[45]

In principle, there is nothing inherently unsustainable about one nation relying on another's ecological surplus. The problem, however, is the widespread perception that all countries can exceed their carrying capacities and grow economically by expanding manufactured and industrial goods at the expense of natural capital—paving over agricultural land to build factories, for example, or clear-cutting forest to build new homes. But all countries cannot continue to do this indefinitely. As economist Herman Daly observes, "One country's ability to substitute man-made for natural capital depends on some other country's making the opposite (complementary) choice."[46]

In other words, globally the ecological books must balance. Many economists see no cause for worry, believing that the market will take care of any needed adjustments. As cropland, forests, and water grow scarce, all that is necessary, they say, is for prices to rise; the added incentives to conserve, use resources more productively, alter consumption patterns, and develop new technologies will keep output rising with demand. But once paved over for a highway or housing complex, cropland is unlikely to be brought back into production—no matter how severe food shortages may become. Moreover, no mechanism exists for assuring that an adequate resource base is maintained to meet needs that the marketplace ignores or heavily discounts—including those of vital ecosystems, other species, the poor, or the next generation.

Trade in forest products illuminates some of these trends. East Asia, where the much-touted economic miracles of Japan and the newly industrializing countries have taken place, has steadily and rapidly appropriated increasing amounts of other nations' forest resources. In Japan, where economic activity boomed after World War II, net imports of forest products rose eightfold between 1961 and 1991. (See Table 1–5.) The nation is now the world's largest net importer of forest products by far. Starting from a smaller base, South Korea's net imports have more than quadrupled since 1971, and Taiwan's have risen more than sevenfold.[47]

China is a big wild card in the global forest picture. According to He Bochuan, a lecturer at Sun Yat-sen University in Guangdong, China's consumption of raw wood—some 300 million cubic meters per year—exceeds the sustainable yield of its forests and woodlands by 30 percent. During the last decade alone its net forest product imports more than doubled. With one fifth of the world's population, economic growth rates that have averaged around 12 percent in recent years, only about 13 percent of its land covered by trees, and its own limited stocks undergoing depletion, China could fast become the leading importer of wood. If its per capita use of forest products were to rise to the level of Japan's today, China's total demand would exceed Japan's by nine times—and its import needs would place enormous pressure on forests worldwide.[48]

Thus, like technology, trade cuts both

Table 1–5. Net Imports of Forest Products, Selected East Asian Countries, 1961–91

Country	1961	1971	1981	1991
		(thousand cubic meters)[1]		
Japan	8,800	45,000	50,000	70,100
South Korea	500	2,900	4,700	12,700
Taiwan	0	1,200	6,700	8,800
China	200	200	3,100	6,800
Hong Kong	900	1,300	2,000	2,500
Singapore	200	1,600	1,400	1,100

[1]All forest products are expressed in equivalent units of wood fiber content.
SOURCES: Worldwatch Institute, based on sources documented in endnote 47.

ways. It can help overcome local or regional carrying capacity constraints by allowing countries to bring in resources to meet their needs. But it can also foster unsustainable consumption levels by creating the illusion of infinite supplies. And because trade allows environmental damage to be done in a land far from where the products are used, it encourages what Stanford University biologists Gretchen Daily and Paul Ehrlich call "discounting over distance"—placing a lower value on environmental harm done far from home.[49]

Trade can foster unsustainable consumption levels by creating the illusion of infinite supplies.

East Asia's appetite for wood, for instance, has done just that—depleting and degrading Southeast Asia's species-rich tropical forests. Although logging is directly responsible for only a small portion of tropical deforestation (clearing for agriculture is the biggest cause), the construction of logging and access roads provides peasants, migrants, and land speculators a gateway into the forest that often initiates a chain reaction culminating in the clearing and burning of large forest tracts.[50]

The last several decades have seen the rise and fall of one Southeast Asian timber exporter after another. The wave pattern began with the Philippines during the sixties, followed by Indonesia and Thailand during a good bit of the seventies, and then by Malaysia during the eighties—with most of the shipments going to Japan. Having experienced extensive forest losses, Thailand and the Philippines are now net importers. Indonesia, with a bigger forest base, remains a significant net exporter. But the largest exporter of tropical wood products is now Malaysia—which shipped the equivalent of nearly 26 million cubic meters in 1991. With timber cutting in Malaysian forests estimated to be up to four times the sustainable yield, a decline in exports appears inevitable there as well.[51]

Like technology, trade is neither inherently good nor bad. One of its strengths is its ability to spread the benefits of more efficient and sustainable technologies and products, whether they be advanced drip irrigation systems, nontimber products from tropical forests, or the latest paper recycling techniques. Trade can also generate more wealth in developing countries, which conceivably could permit greater investments in environmental protection and help alleviate poverty. So far, however, the potential gains from trade have been overwhelmed by its more negative facets—in particular, by its tendency to foster ecological deficit-financing and unsustainable consumption.

In light of this, it is disturbing, to say the least, that negotiators involved in the eight-year-long Uruguay Round of the General Agreement on Tariffs and Trade (GATT) seem barely interested in the role trade plays in promoting environmental destruction. While the reduction of government subsidies and other barriers to free trade—the main concern of the GATT round—could make international markets more efficient and increase the foreign exchange earnings of developing countries, that offers no guarantee that trade will be more environmentally sound or socially equitable.

Since environmental taxes, regulations, or other means of internalizing environmental costs would help redirect products and activities toward those that are less damaging to the earth's natural systems, they would also help make trade—which is merely the exchange of those goods and services—more sustainable. For this to work, however, countries would need to adopt such measures more or less simultaneously to avoid placing some of them at a competitive disadvantage. And developing countries would likely participate only if they received substantial financial and technical assistance from wealthier nations, which for decades have benefited from having the environment absorb the damages caused by their activities. Unfortunately, the reluctance of rich countries to agree at the 1992 Earth Summit to any sizable transfer of funds to poorer nations does not bode well for such an initiative.[52]

There is talk that the next series of GATT negotiations may be a "green round" that would address the trade-environment nexus more directly, although probably not as broadly as is needed. Moreover, with short-term considerations such as slow economic growth and high unemployment taking precedence over long-term concerns, a coordinated effort to make trade more sustainable through cost-internalizing measures is not high on the agenda. If action is delayed too long, however, the future will arrive in a state of ecological impoverishment that no amount of free trade will be able to overcome.

Lightening the Load

Ship captains pay careful attention to a marking on their vessels called the Plimsoll line. If the water level rises above the Plimsoll line, the boat is too heavy and is in danger of sinking. When that happens, rearranging items on the ship will not help much. The problem is the total weight, which has surpassed the carrying capacity of the ship.[53]

Economist Herman Daly sometimes uses this analogy to underscore that the scale of human activity can reach a level that the earth's natural systems can no longer support. The ecological equivalent of the Plimsoll line may be the maximum share of the earth's biological resource base that humans can appropriate before a rapid and cascading deterioration in the planet's life-support systems is set in motion. Given the degree of resource destruction already evident, we may be close to this critical mark. The challenge, then, is to lighten our burden on the planet before "the ship" sinks.

More than 1,600 scientists, including 102 Nobel laureates, underscored this point in collectively signing a "Warning to Humanity" in late 1992. It states that "No more than one or a few decades remain before the chance to avert the threats we now confront will be lost and the prospects for humanity immeasurably diminished. . . . A new ethic is required—a new attitude towards discharging our responsibility for caring for ourselves and for the earth. . . . This ethic must motivate a great movement, convincing reluctant leaders and reluctant governments and reluctant peoples themselves to effect the needed changes."[54]

A successful global effort to lighten humanity's load on the earth would directly address the three major driving forces of environmental decline—the grossly inequitable distribution of income, resource-consumptive economic growth, and rapid population growth—and would redirect technology and trade to buy time for this great movement. Although there is far too much to say about each of these challenges to be comprehensive here, some key points bear noting.

Wealth inequality may be the most intractable problem, since it has existed for millennia. The difference today, however, is that the future of both rich and poor alike hinges on reducing poverty and thereby eliminating this driving force of global environmental decline. In this way, self-interest joins ethics as a motive for redistributing wealth, and raises the chances that it might be done.

Important actions to narrow the income gap include greatly reducing Third World debt, much talked about in the eighties but still not accomplished, and focusing foreign aid, trade, and international lending policies more directly on improving the living standards of the poor. If decision makers consistently asked themselves whether a choice they were about to make would help the poorest of the poor—that 20 percent of the world's people who share only 1.4 percent of the world's income—and acted only if the answer were yes, more people might break out of the poverty trap and have the opportunity to live sustainably.[55]

Individuals in wealthier countries can help lighten humanity's load by voluntarily reducing their personal levels of consumption.

Especially in poorer countries, much could be gained from greater support for the myriad grassroots organizations working for a better future. These groups constitute a powerful force for achieving sustainable development in its truest form—through bottom-up action by local people. In an October 1993 address at the World Bank, Kenyan environmentalist Wangari Maathai noted that among the great benefits of the Green Belt Movement, the tree planting campaign she founded, was the understanding it gave people that "no progress can be made when the environment is neglected, polluted, degraded and over-exploited. Many people have also come to appreciate that taking care of the environment is not the responsibility of only the Government but of the citizens as well. This awareness is empower-

ing and brings the environment close to the people. Only when this happens do people feel and care for the environment."[56]

A key prescription for reducing the kinds of economic growth that harm the environment is the same as that for making technology and trade more sustainable—internalizing environmental costs. If this is done through the adoption of environmental taxes, governments can avoid imposing heavier taxes overall by lowering income taxes accordingly. In addition, establishing better measures of economic accounting is critical. Since the calculations used to produce the gross national product do not account for the destruction or depletion of natural resources, this popular economic measure is extremely misleading. It tells us we are making progress even as our ecological foundations are crumbling. A better beacon to guide us toward a sustainable path is essential. The United Nations and several individual governments have been working to develop such a measure, but progress has been slow.[57]

Besides calling on political leaders to effect these changes, individuals in wealthier countries can help lighten humanity's load by voluntarily reducing their personal levels of consumption. By purchasing "greener products" for necessities and reducing discretionary consumption, the top 1 billion can help create ecological space for the bottom 1 billion to consume enough for a decent and secure life.

In September 1994, government officials will gather in Cairo for the International Conference on Population and Development, the third such gathering on population. This is a timely opportunity to draw attention to the connections between poverty, population growth, and environmental decline—and to devise strategies that simultaneously address the root causes. Much greater efforts are needed, for instance, to raise women's social and economic status and to give women equal rights and access to resources. Only if gender biases are rooted out will women be able to escape the poverty trap and to choose to have fewer children. In the realm of family planning, an essential step is to meet the needs of more than 100 million couples who want to limit or plan their families but who lack access to the means to do so safely and effectively. To succeed, such programs must also meet women's reproductive health needs as they perceive them.[58]

Progress in these areas was set back during the eighties when population-related issues were politicized under the Reagan and Bush administrations and when the United States stopped funding the U.N. Population Fund and the International Planned Parenthood Federation. Fortunately, funding has been restored under the Clinton administration. And at a May 1993 preparatory meeting for the Cairo conference, State Depart-

ment Counselor Tim Wirth indicated a major course correction in U.S. policy when he noted that "advancing women's rights and health and promoting family planning are mutually reinforcing objectives," and that "all barriers which deprive women of equal opportunity must be removed."[59]

The challenge of living sustainably on the earth will never be met, however, if population and environment conferences are the only forums in which it is addressed. Success hinges on the creativity and energy of a wide range of people in many walks of life. The scientists' Warning to Humanity ends with a call to the world's scientists, business and industry leaders, the religious community, and people everywhere to join in the urgent mission of halting the earth's environmental decline.

Everyone is aboard the same ship. The Plimsoll line carries the same meaning for all. And time appears short to accomplish the challenging task of lightening the human load.

2

Redesigning the Forest Economy

Alan Thein Durning

Imagine a time-lapse film of the earth taken from space. Play back the last 10,-000 years sped up so that a millennium passes by every minute. For more than seven minutes, the screen displays what looks like a still photograph: the blue planet Earth, its lands swathed in a mantle of trees. Forests cover 34 percent of the land. Aside from the occasional flash of a wildfire, none of the natural changes in the forest coat are perceptible. The Agricultural Revolution that transforms human existence in the film's first minute is invisible.[1]

After seven-and-a-half minutes, the lands around Athens and the tiny islands of the Aegean Sea lose their forest. This is the flowering of classical Greece. Little else changes. At nine minutes—1,000 years ago—the mantle grows threadbare in scattered parts of Europe, Central America, China, and India. Then 12 seconds from the end, two centuries ago,

the thinning spreads, leaving parts of Europe and China bare. Six seconds from the end, one century ago, eastern North America is deforested. This is the Industrial Revolution. Still, little has changed. Forests cover 32 percent of the land.[2]

In the last three seconds—after 1950—the change accelerates explosively. Vast tracts of forest vanish from Japan, the Philippines, and the mainland of Southeast Asia, from most of Central America and the horn of Africa, from western North America and eastern South America, from the Indian subcontinent and sub-Saharan Africa. Fires rage in the Amazon Basin where they never did before. Central Europe's forests die, poisoned by the air and the rain. Southeast Asia looks like a dog with the mange. Malaysian Borneo is scalped. In the final fractions of a second, the clearing spreads to Siberia and the Canadian north. Forests disappear so suddenly from so many places that it looks like a plague of locusts has descended on the planet.

An expanded version of this chapter appeared as Worldwatch Paper 117, *Saving the Forests: What Will It Take?*

The film freezes on the last frame. Trees cover 26 percent of the land. Three fourths of the original forest area still has some tree cover, but just one third of the initial total—12 percent of the land—retains a mantle of intact forest ecosystems. The rest consists of biologically impoverished stands of commercial timber and fragmented regrowth. This is the present: a globe profoundly altered by the workings—or failings—of the human economy.[3]

On the ground, this planetary wave of deforestation has been accompanied by surging growth in gross national product and by catastrophic losses to human welfare and ecological health. The litany of destruction documented by social scientists includes wrenching costs overlooked by the money economy. Logging towns in the northwest of the United States, on the bust side of a boom-and-bust cycle, are showing the social signs of economic decline long evident in inner cities: rising alcoholism and drug abuse, domestic violence and broken homes, homelessness and emigration. Indigenous cultures in the forests of the tropics are wracked by the violence, disease, and alienation that have long haunted the frontiers of the world economy. Ancient villages in the woods of Africa and Asia suffer diminishing yields of farm crops and shrinking supplies of game, fruits, and the other wild foods that insure them against starvation.

Damages detailed by natural scientists include extinctions of thousands of species, exacerbation of droughts and floods, release of heat-trapping carbon dioxide into the atmosphere, greater variation in local temperatures, release of new pests into agricultural lands, hemorrhaging of topsoil, sedimentation of rivers and hydroelectric reservoirs, and loss of productive fisheries.

Yet all of this is known; indeed, it has been thoroughly studied by specialists and widely reported by the global media. What is not known—and what we desperately need to know—is what to do. Already, numerous well-meaning initiatives have failed to arrest the loss of forests. The Tropical Forestry Action Plan, the International Tropical Timber Agreement, the International Tropical Timber Organization, and the U.N. Statement of Forest Principles have each been launched with fanfare and high hopes, and have each proved disappointing, if not fruitless. Deforestation rates in much of the world have only risen.[4]

The crucial question is, What would it really take to save the forests? It would take going beyond quick fixes and easy solutions. Past efforts have foundered largely because they have set their sights on the proximate rather than the ultimate causes of deforestation. They have sought to halt the commercial cultivators and ranchers, real estate speculators and developers, loggers and miners, and legions of impoverished slash-and-burn farmers who fell the trees. Yet these are merely the leading edge of a far larger force. They are the teeth of the saw, but the saw is a money economy blind to its ecological roots. Arresting deforestation requires changing three structural features of that economy: tenure, price, and power.

RIGHTS TO THE FORESTS

Four decades ago, the city of Udaipur in the Indian state of Rajasthan was the center of a vast forested zone of small villages, where tigers roamed and water flowed in streams year-round. Today, Udaipur's hinterlands—the Aravali hills—are barren. Its tigers are gone, its streams flood and parch with the seasons, its farms are less productive, and thousands of its able-bodied sons and daughters spend their time far from home, drifting from city to city as migrant laborers. "Our region is a case study in ecological decline," says Jagat Mehta, president of Seva Mandir, a voluntary development organization that has worked in the area for 30 years.[5]

In the early eighties, Seva Mandir began helping villagers plant trees. Sadly, as in all too many such initiatives, few of the seedlings survived. The immediate problem was goats, which ate the seedlings before they could take root. But there was a deeper problem as well. Most of the villages were surrounded by land that, however devoid of trees it might be, was classified as forestland and, consequently, was under the exclusive jurisdiction of the state forest department. Indeed, if a tree ever were to grow there, regardless of who planted or cared for it, it would belong to the forest department. No wonder the seedlings ended up as goat fodder.

Next, Seva Mandir tried to convince the government to give villagers a stake in managing the denuded forestland. It petitioned for a joint forest management agreement, an innovative approach to resource management pioneered in eastern India under which governments continue to own forestlands but villagers get long-term rights to use them, along with responsibilities to protect them. Seva Mandir's pleas initially fell on deaf ears, for the state government—hidebound by bureaucracy—had no procedure for granting joint forest management agreements. Eventually, however, Seva Mandir's persistence paid off, and it gained several experimental agreements. Villagers, the government allowed, could cut trees and harvest other products grown on forestland.

By 1991, the results were drawn in patches of dark green on the hills around villages such as Dolpura. Trees were growing again. They were shoulder-high and surrounded with thick grass. Barriers of dried thor, a type of cactus, were

the first defense against goats, and a thousand eyes of villagers scanned the perimeter for breaches in the line, ever vigilant to protect their trees. This "social fencing" was the only kind that worked against both the indefatigable goats and their owners, who otherwise might seek fuelwood and fodder from the regenerating plots. The return of forests to their hills was received with such appreciation that the people of Dolpura had already declared the first restored hill a sacred grove, forbidding any felling there.

Success in places like Dolpura has been so striking that forest departments have had little choice but to accept the concept of sharing rights to forest products with villagers. By late 1993, 13 Indian states had issued official orders in support of joint management. As many as 10,000 villages were sharing management responsibilities in an area of perhaps 1.5 million hectares. Elsewhere in Asia and Africa the same concept has gradually been gaining credence. In the Philippines, for example, 171,000 hectares of upland and mangrove forest are managed by those who live there. And villagers have been negotiating informal agreements with local foresters across Southeast Asia.[6]

The spread of joint management programs is full of historical irony. It is a tacit admission that forest policies in the tropics are ill founded. In India, as elsewhere, under the guise of conservation, colonial powers nationalized forests to expedite the extraction of timber. Deeming forest dwellers incompetent to care for the lands they had inhabited for centuries, colonial authorities established forest departments on the model earlier devised in Europe: guards to keep commoners out of royal hunting reserves. In the space of just 150 years, 80 percent of the world's tropical forests passed from the hands of local communities—the

Dolpuras of the world—to the hands of such authorities. The transfer never gained the assent of most forest dwellers, of course. Linka Ansulang, a tribal woman from the southern Philippines, speaks for many of them when she says, "The government calls us squatters, but the government is the real squatter."[7]

After independence, Third World leaders continued with the centralized model of forest management, believing, as had their predecessors, that modern nations could not entrust illiterate villagers with the fate of the forests. Over time, a theory of resource use—the tragedy of the commons—developed that provided a convenient justification for this policy of state control. A tragedy of the commons arises when the lack of clear property rights leads individuals to overexploit shared resources or risk losing out while others do the same. In such a situation, so the reasoning goes, only a central authority can reconcile individual and social interests. That is usually interpreted to mean the state.

What the theory overlooked was that under village control, forests were not unregulated commons. In Dolpura, as in most of the world's thousands of forest communities, villagers had elaborated systems to control use of their shared forests. In Borneo, for example, generations of the Galik people have carefully conserved ironwood trees. Ironwood, the heaviest known wood in the world, is exceptionally durable and insect-resistant, making it highly valuable in the rural economy. Use of the wood has traditionally been governed by an ethic that required broad sharing along kinship lines. Sadly, the failure of national policy to recognize the Galik people's rights to their village forest reserves, hastened by the entry of state-sanctioned loggers into the Galik area, has undermined traditional restraints. Afraid of losing the ironwood to the loggers, the Galik have raced to sell it themselves, endangering both the resource and the village economy.[8]

In Borneo, as elsewhere, nationalizing the forests sabotaged traditional management, creating the free-for-all it purported to avert. It became a crime to impose the effective, albeit not foolproof, local penalties for overuse of forests by insiders and cut-and-run exploitation by outsiders. Yet national penalties for the same transgressions, even if written in law, proved unenforceable.

By late 1993, 13 Indian states had issued official orders in support of joint management.

Across the Third World, forest departments are hopelessly inadequate to the problem at hand. Their guards number in the hundreds or thousands in most tropical countries, while tropical forest inhabitants number in the millions. (See Table 2–1.) In Zaire, for instance, the forest department's staff of about 800 is charged with protecting 100 million hectares of jungle inhabited by perhaps 15 million people. That is tantamount to patrolling the state of New York with the police force of the city of Rochester.

The kind of joint forest management in force in Dolpura is a halting but welcome step toward reversing the centralization of control over forests. A few nations in the American tropics have taken more decisive steps. Under intense grassroots pressure, they have recognized the land rights of tribes that have inhabited and conserved forests since time immemorial. Since 1989, Bolivia, Brazil, Colombia, Ecuador, and Venezuela have demarcated vast areas of little-disturbed forests in the Amazon Basin as

Table 2–1. Forest Area, Residents, and Forestry Staff, Selected Countries, Late Eighties

Country	Closed Tropical Forest Area	Estimated Forest Residents	Estimated Forest Department Staff
	(million hectares)	(million)	(number)
Indonesia	114	15	17,000
Zaire	100	15	800
Peru	70	2	1,000
Papua New Guinea	36	3.5	400
Cameroon	16	0.4	800
Ecuador	14	2.2	800
Thailand	9	6	7,000

SOURCE: Nels Johnson and Bruce Cabarle, *Surviving the Cut: Natural Forest Management in the Humid Tropics* (Washington, D.C.: World Resources Institute, 1993).

homelands for indigenous peoples. Sadly, these boundaries are difficult to protect against encroachment.[9]

Still, the recognition of indigenous homelands in the Amazon has been the most hopeful sign for the world's forests in years. History will likely show that indigenous peoples and their supporters in human rights organizations saved more tropical forest than all the world's conservation groups put together. The forested homeland of the Yanomami in Brazil and Venezuela, for example, is as big as Uruguay, and far larger than any forested park or reserve in the world.[10]

If African and Asian nations would follow this precedent, the prospects for tropical forests would improve markedly. Unfortunately, the rights of traditional peoples in most of the world are observed only in the breach. All but powerless in national politics, Asian forest tribes have minimal legal rights, and African tribes have even fewer. The pygmies of central Africa—the most ancient of all the world's forest dwellers—have absolutely no enforceable rights to the forests they have inhabited for perhaps 40,000 years.[11]

One step that outside organizations can take to help forest dwellers secure recognition of their rights is to assist them in developing accurate maps of

their territories. On the Atlantic Coast of Honduras, the Miskito Indians have recently completed this task. Community leaders met to review scores of hand-drawn charts for accuracy before compiling them, with the help of trained cartographers, into a master map of the Miskito territory. The mapping project even caught the interest of the Honduran military, which like most of the national government had previously viewed the Miskito Coast as empty land, ripe for settlement. Maps are not rights, but they often help in national politics.[12]

In the world's remaining intact temperate and boreal forests—concentrated in North America and Siberia—the social context of the forest economy is different, but the issue of who controls the forest is equally important. In these places, governments control forests not only in principle but in fact, because forest dwellers are far fewer and governments are better staffed than in the tropics. Where indigenous forest communities' rights remain unrecognized, as in parts of Canada and Russia, securing those rights is a priority, just as in the tropics. Elsewhere, however, the challenge is to establish tenure rules that encourage forest managers, most of whom are government officials, to protect the land's ecological integrity.

Along these lines, economist Randal O'Toole of Cascade Holistic Economic Consultants in Oak Grove, Oregon, proposes a radical redesign of the U.S. Forest Service, which he believes would better align forest management decisions with protection of forests' full range of ecological services. Large organizations, O'Toole argues, act first and foremost so as to maximize their budgets—a thesis supported by research on bureaucratic behavior. The Forest Service is no different. It favors commodity extraction over recreational, nonconsumptive uses because peculiarities of its legal structure allow it to retain most of the proceeds from timber sales. Its budget does not benefit, however, from camping, fishing, hunting, hiking, skiing, or any other nonconsumptive use. Nor does the Forest Service budget benefit from the water its forests provide to farmers and cities downstream, or from the fish and wildlife that depend on its forests for habitat.[13]

O'Toole contends that the Forest Service will behave as a prudent manager of all the national forests' functions only when it can itself benefit from them. To do that, he recommends that the agency be reorganized to charge user fees for everything from camping to mining in national forests. The Service's own budget would come exclusively from those user fees. Because the nonconsumptive benefits of forests greatly exceed the consumptive ones in value, O'Toole believes the Forest Service would allow little timbering, mining, or other high-impact activities on the lands it controls. Charging visitors as little as $3 a day would generate more revenue than selling timber now does, leading forest managers to favor nonconsumptive uses over consumptive ones.[14]

Forests in some industrial countries, notably the United States, are less concentrated in the hands of the state than is the norm in the tropics. Indeed, U.S. timber production is overwhelmingly concentrated on private forestlands, largely in the southeast and northwest. Small landowners in these regions are plagued by a set of perverse incentives that work against sustainability. Inheritance taxes, for example, turn the death of a family member into a must-cut situation. As a shield against these forces, private and public institutions have created conservation easements—legally binding additions to the title deed that forbid certain activities, such as clear-cut logging and urban development. Conservation easements ensure that lands cannot be taxed as if they were in commodity production.

Another approach with great promise is to increase involvement of local communities in management of forestlands through community land trusts. In the logging and mining town of Revelstoke in British Columbia, Canada, for instance, 20 citizens sued the owner of a tree farm license—effectively, a timber concession—for cut-and-run practices that violated the terms of the license. In late 1992, after winning in court, the Revelstoke Resource Development Committee borrowed enough money from commercial banks to buy the license. The committee is developing a multicentury plan for logging, tourism, nontimber forest products, and value-added wood processing businesses. Meanwhile, scores of volunteers are working in the forest to close logging roads and restore eroded stream banks.[15]

That tenure is a key determinant of the sustainability of forest economies is supported by reams of scholarly studies and economic analyses. Yet both politicians and the mass media have tended recently to focus instead on the prospects of a new, or newly popularized, category of forest output: nontimber products. The enormous economic potential of these goods suggests to many that developing markets for them is a substitute for resolving the bitter questions of control over forests. In fact, the potential of nontimber forest products merely augments the importance of tenure issues, as examining one widely reported case makes clear.

In late 1991, Merck & Company, the world's largest pharmaceutical firm, sent a $1-million check to a small Costa Rican organization called the National Institute for Biodiversity (INBio). Merck also signed a contract that committed it to training Costa Rican researchers and paying INBio a share of the profits from products it might develop in the future. In exchange, all INBio had to do was supply the pharmaceutical giant with a steady stream of leaves, bugs, and microscopic goo from the country's tropical forests.[16]

Not a single country extends intellectual property rights to indigenous knowledge.

Why would Merck enter such an agreement? To discover new medicines. In the eighties, researchers developed automated chemical screening techniques that allowed them to test compounds by the thousands for medicinal properties. The technology made it economical to begin exploring the great chemical factory of the natural world: tropical forests. In this stable, warm, and wet environment, plants, animals, insects, and microorganisms have evolved in millions of varieties, each equipped for the evolutionary battle with its own weaponry. Much of that weaponry is chemical, and some of it has already proved enormously valuable to humans. Leech saliva, for example, contains a substance called hirudin that prevents clotting, allowing leeches to extract more blood from their victims. Inspired by the leech, modern medicine uses hirudin in skin transplants and to treat rheumatism, thrombosis, and contusions.[17]

The economic value of medicines taken from forests is staggering. Forty percent of prescription drugs dispensed by U.S. pharmacies have active ingredients derived from wild plants, animals, or microorganisms, many of them from forests. Given that the global pharmaceuticals industry is worth $200 billion, that the use of biologically derived medicines probably exceeds 40 percent of prescriptions outside the United States, and that a disproportionate share of biologically derived medicines originate in forest species, it is likely that annual sales of drugs with active ingredients derived from forests total more than $100 billion. Forests also provide most of the herbal medicine used by some 80 percent of developing-country residents.[18]

Furthermore, scientists have so far evaluated just a few thousand of the world's estimated 10 million species—perhaps half of which dwell in tropical forests. Harvard University biologist Edward O. Wilson conveys the magnitude of the potential: "A newly discovered species of roundworm might produce an antibiotic of extraordinary power, an unnamed moth a substance that blocks viruses in a manner never guessed by molecular biologists. . . . An obscure herb could be the source of a sure-fire blackfly repellant—at last. Millions of years of testing by natural selection have made organisms chemists of superhuman skill, champions at defeating most of the kinds of biological problems that undermine human health." Shamans and other traditional healers have experimented with many of the species unknown to scientists. Tragically, their knowledge is disappearing even faster than forest ecosystems are, as indigenous cultures are overrun and assimilated by the expanding world economy.[19]

For Merck, signing the contract with INBio was a shrewd investment, a way to gain access to Costa Rica's estimated 12,000 species of plants and 300,000 species of insects. But it was also a principled decision, because it implicitly recognized that Costa Rica's biological resources were its own. It was not until a year later, in fact, that the government declared all wild plants and animals to be "national patrimony."[20]

Even that minimal principle of tenure—that untamed nature belongs to the state—is rarely recognized by collectors of biological samples. Organizations ranging from Merck's competitors in the pharmaceutical industry to crop breeders in search of fresh genetic traits consider plants, animals, and microorganisms free for the taking. The Merck-INBio agreement was, in this light, a remarkable step. It also had clear and substantial benefits for Costa Rican forest conservation: INBio designated one tenth of the original Merck payment for the country's national parks budget, and similarly committed half the royalties it is entitled to if Merck develops any products based on INBio's samples. Along the way, INBio will compile a national inventory of biological diversity and train a network of "para-taxonomists."[21]

Impressive as these results are, however, the terms of the agreement also demonstrate just how far tenure arrangements are from those required for a sustainable forest economy. By assuming that the living resources of Costa Rica's forests were the state's to dispose of as it sees fit, Merck and INBio ignored the possibility that the rightful owners of those forests were the communities that live there. The government of Costa Rica—one of Latin America's most democratic and progressive—clearly confirmed this position when it claimed for itself absolute ownership of all wild plants and animals, effectively voiding the claims of citizens, some of whom had served as the primary stewards of those living resources for generations.

Worse, neither Merck nor INBio stipulated that local lore used to guide the selection of samples be treated as intellectual property, with ownership vested in the communities and tribes that have developed it over long years of experimentation. The government of Costa Rica has not done any better, offering no protection under intellectual property law—the category that governs patents, copyrights, breeders' rights, and trade secrets—for forest dwellers' vast body of knowledge of the properties and uses of natural substances.

Around the world, not a single country extends intellectual property rights to indigenous knowledge; they treat it as if it were a national resource to be mined by the modern economy for whatever benefit it might offer. If a traditional healer knows how to cure a skin disease with an herbal remedy, it is called folklore. If a pharmaceutical company isolates and markets the active chemical in the healer's herbs, it is called a medical breakthrough, protected with a patent, and rewarded with international monopoly power. Among biodiversity collectors, only the most ethical practitioners—notably the handful of ethnobotanists who study the plant uses of traditional cultures—adhere to codes of conduct that include negotiations with local communities to ensure that they benefit from any commercial products their knowledge helps create.

Under prevailing laws, then, forest dwellers in much of the world own neither their lands nor their knowledge of that land. In the absence of such tenure, biological diversity prospecting—the "gene rush"—is likely to yield the same results as past resource booms in the tropics: more poverty, less forest.

The same is true of the other nontimber forest products, ranging from fruits and nuts to industrial fibers, that are now recognized as offering better livelihoods for many forest dwellers than timber extraction or slash-and-burn farming. In Belize, for instance, expert gatherers of forest products can earn between two and ten times as much per hectare as farmers who clear the forest for crops. Without secure control of these resources, however, their potential as engines of sustainable development will be lost.[22]

And that potential is large. Southeast Asian sales of rattan, for example, the stems of palm used to make wicker furniture, are worth $3 billion annually. These economic returns, moreover, are spread far more equitably than timber returns because of the labor intensity of harvesting them. Three times as many Indonesians work in the rattan industry as in the timber industry. Of course, gathering any forest product on a commercial scale can degrade forest ecosystems if it is not done conservatively. Collectors of *xate* palm in Guatemala, for instance, have overharvested the plant in wide regions. But tenure is the main problem.[23]

Extractive reserves offer one contemporary model of local control. Owned by the government but managed by forest dwellers, extractive reserves were conceived in Brazil, which has now created 14 of them, covering close to 1 percent of its Amazon forests. Others have been created in Guatemala and Peru. In many ways, extractive reserves are a variation on joint forest management, distinct from the Asian form primarily in an emphasis on commercial harvesting of nontimber products rather than on subsistence uses of the forest. More important,

both are actually just a new version of an ancient and pervasive form of land management.[24]

Under traditional law in much of the world, villages, clans, and other indigenous local institutions set aside broad areas for gathering forest goods. The Galik who conserved ironwood, for example, also reserved forests for the collection of nuts, incense, fruit, and fuel. This latticework of local forest management systems still exists—though in a dilapidated, disempowered state—in much of its original range. No one knows what share of the globe's forests are managed as extractive reserves under this unofficial regime. But the best way to expand opportunities for nontimber forest products is to get nation-states to decentralize legal authority, returning at least a share of it to local, traditional forest managers.[25]

The need for decentralization is as great in industrial countries as it is in the Third World, although the reasons are different. Collecting goods from the woods is a large, little-noticed industry, even in the world's richest nations. Karen Hobbs of Forks, Washington, for example, supplies florists with strange and beautiful mosses, lichens, and driftwood—all of it collected in the coastal temperate rain forests of the Pacific Northwest. Yet government managers see scant returns to their own budgets from sales of nontimber forest products. They consequently tend to favor timber, at the expense of low-impact forest products and no-impact forest services.[26]

Whether the resource is land, timber, floral supplies, or indigenous knowledge, secure tenure is the first necessary condition of a sustainable forest economy. Without it, the people who actually manage the world's forests will have little reason, and less authority, to safeguard forest health.

ECOLOGICAL PRICING

Ecological pricing is the second necessary condition of a sustainable forest economy. Under prevailing prices, the world economy works against ecological integrity, making forest conservation an uphill battle. This point is perhaps best made by examining two recent advances in protecting forests: wood certification and new forestry.

In December 1991, B&Q, a leading U.K. chain of hardware stores, announced it was phasing out all products containing wood not harvested from sustainably managed forests. The company promised to be exclusively a "good wood" outlet by the end of 1995. The decision was a victory for European environmentalists who had been targetting the timber trade for almost a decade. Their efforts had already succeeded in convincing hundreds of local authorities in Austria, the Netherlands, Germany, and the United Kingdom to forbid the purchase of tropical timber for use in government offices.[27]

The trouble with the campaign was that it threatened to merely displace destructive logging from tropical forests to temperate and boreal ones. By the late eighties the European activists and their North American counterparts had realized the importance of certifying sustainably produced wood—whatever its region of origin—so that consumers had a clear choice. Supplying B&Q, and competitors that followed its lead, added urgency to that goal.

Unfortunately, despite concerted efforts on both sides of the Atlantic, there is little wood that meets high standards of sustainability. In the tropics, just one tenth of 1 percent of all wood is logged on a sustained-yield basis (where the annual harvest equals annual regrowth). And sustained-yield principles are frequently violated elsewhere as well. Worse, even sustained-yield timbering has proved unsustainable, because maintaining the wood output can be accompanied by the wholesale replacement of vibrant ecosystems and the extinction of species.[28]

Meanwhile, as wood certification efforts proliferated, a loose cluster of foresters began developing a new forestry, predicated on the notion that sustained yield is not enough. The new forestry is germinating in North America, which is fitting, since the region is the world's largest timber producer. Indeed, North America and the other timber superpower—the republics of the former Soviet Union—together account for 54 percent of world production of industrial roundwood, the term foresters use to encompass all wood products except fuelwood and charcoal. (See Table 2–2.)

Specifically, most new forestry initiatives have originated in the Pacific Northwest of North America, one of the few remaining temperate regions to possess old-growth forests of any size. New forestry is not a finished technique, and it varies in application from one ecosystem to the next. Its principles include striving to leave elements of the forest's ecological structure intact—such as its canopy layers, its patterns of plant succession, and its cycling of nutrients—and safeguarding biological diversity by, for example, protecting riparian habitats with broad undisturbed corridors. New forestry generally requires minimizing road building, and often mimics natural forces that disturb forests, such as fire and wind.

New forestry is not necessarily selective logging, although it is not indiscriminate clear-cutting either. Indeed, in the tropics it means harvesting little-used and even little-known species along with the few lucrative trunks. Selective logging in tropical forests has typically meant knocking over or damaging half the trees, partly because of the tangle of vines that connect many of them and

Table 2–2. World Production of Industrial Roundwood, Top 20 Nations and World, 1991

Country	Industrial Roundwood	Share of Total
	(million cubic meters)	(percent)
United States	410	26
Soviet Union	274	17
Canada	171	11
China	90	6
Brazil	74	5
Sweden	47	3
Germany	40	3
Malaysia	40	3
France	34	2
Finland	31	2
Indonesia	29	2
Japan	28	2
India	25	2
Australia	18	1
Spain	15	1
Czechoslovakia	15	1
Poland	14	1
New Zealand	14	1
Austria	14	1
South Africa	13	1
Others	200	13
World	1,599	100

SOURCE: U.N. Food and Agriculture Organization, *Forest Products Yearbook, 1991* (Rome: 1993).

partly because of the extra roads needed to reach the coveted species. Two species of mahogany have been so meticulously plucked from the forests of Central and South America that they are now listed for protection under the Convention on International Trade in Endangered Species of Flora and Fauna.[29]

Forest ecosystems are so complex that new forestry will undoubtedly continue to evolve for decades. Until 10 years ago, for example, scientists had little appreciation of the role that underground webs of micorrhyzal fungi play in forest eco-systems. Now those webs are thought indispensable; they enable tree roots to absorb phosphorus and other nutrients. Sustainable forestry, we now know, protects micorrhyzal fungi. What will we add to the definition in the next decade?[30]

Wood certification programs and new forestry initiatives arose independently, but they complement one another, and together they could demonstrate powerfully the possibility of low-impact timbering. More immediately, they could meet B&Q's supply needs.

They cannot, however, shift the bulk of timbering away from the high-impact ways of the present. Likewise, they cannot reduce demand for wood overall, as is clearly necessary given the strain that forest ecosystems are under. Nor do they address the other driving forces of deforestation, such as the felling of forests for pasture and suburban subdivisions. Under prevailing economic values, certified "good" wood will always cost extra because new forestry is more expensive than old forestry. But that relationship is an artifact of faulty economics.

Old forestry is only less expensive because it externalizes many of its costs. The price of teak does not reflect the costs of flooding that rapacious teak logging has caused in Myanmar. The price of old-growth fir does not include the losses suffered by the fishing industry because logging destroys salmon habitat. For example, the estimated present value of a wild chinook salmon in the Columbia River is $2,150 when future benefits to sports and commercial fishers are counted. Yet chinook currently sell for about $50 in local markets. If prices told the truth—if they accurately reflected all the environmental costs of production—good wood would be a bargain. But until prices equal costs, only the conscientious minority of consumers will opt for good wood.[31]

The full costs of forest loss are unknown but clearly enormous. (See Table 2–3.) Deforestation, for instance, eradicates plant varieties with potential as crops. The fruits of the babassu palm yield more vegetable oil per hectare than any plant ever measured, yet babassu is all but unknown outside its wild range in the Brazilian Amazon. Deforestation releases climate-changing gases. The carbon storage function of one hectare of Malaysian forest is worth more than $3,000 in "net present value"—a measure of future benefits expressed at their present worth.[32]

Table 2–3. Economic Services Provided by Intact Forest Ecosystems

Service	Economic Importance
Gene pool	Forests contain a diversity of species, habitats, and genes that is probably their most valuable asset; it is also the most difficult to measure. They provide the gene pool that can protect commercial plant strains against pests and changing conditions of climate and soil and can provide the raw material for breeding higher-yielding strains. The wild relatives of avocado, banana, cashew, cacao, cinnamon, coconut, coffee, grapefruit, lemon, paprika, oil palm, rubber, and vanilla—exports of which were worth more than $20 billion in 1991—are found in tropical forests.
Water	Forests absorb rainwater and release it gradually into streams, preventing flooding and extending water availability into dry months when it is most needed. Some 40 percent of Third World farmers depend on forested watersheds for water to irrigate crops or water livestock. In India, forests provide water regulation and flood control valued at $72 billion per year.
Watershed	Forests keep soil from eroding into rivers. Siltation of reservoirs costs the world economy about $6 billion per year in lost hydroelectricity and irrigation water.
Fisheries	Forests protect fisheries in rivers, lakes, estuaries, and coastal waters. Three fourths of fish sold in the markets of Manaus, Brazil, are nurtured in seasonally flooded *varzea* forests, where they feed on fruits and plants. The viability of 112 stocks of salmon and other fish in the Pacific Northwest depends on natural, old-growth forests; the region's salmon fishery is a $1-billion industry.
Climate	Forests stabilize climate. Tropical deforestation releases the greenhouse gases carbon dioxide, methane, and nitrous oxide, and accounts for 25 percent of the net warming effect of all greenhouse gas emissions. Replacing the carbon storage function of all tropical forests would cost an estimated $3.7 trillion—equal to the gross national product of Japan.
Recreation	Forests serve people directly for recreation. The U.S. Forest Service calculates that in eight of its nine administrative regions, the recreation, fish, wildlife, and other nonextractive benefits of national forests are more valuable than timber, grazing, mining, and other commodities.

SOURCES: Compiled by Worldwatch Institute from sources documented in endnote 32.

Deforestation destroys nontimber forest products that do not register fully in the money economy. Fruits, nuts, fibers, and wild game are mostly consumed in the subsistence economy of the poor, never entering the realm of cash transactions where they would show up in national accounting systems and count in the deliberations of those who make policy. Wildlife sold on the black market may reach national and even international markets, but when there is no compensation to local people or national authorities, it too is invisible to the official economy.

No one knows the full magnitude of the nontimber forest-products industries endangered by deforestation. Yet the harder researchers look, the larger they find them to be: Mater Engineering, Ltd., investigated markets for four obscure plants—bear grass, huckleberries, salal, and sword fern—that grow in profusion in national forests near their offices in Corvallis, Oregon, and discovered global sales worth $72 million. Likewise, they learned that foraging for wild mushrooms from the forests of the Pacific Northwest is an industry with sales in the hundreds of millions of dollars. The market value of nontimber forest products may exceed that of solid wood harvested from U.S. national forests—$1 billion in 1992.[33]

Deforestation also destroys scenery with real, economic value, both for the world's huge nature tourism industry and in subtler ways. Economists Ed Whitelaw and Ernest Niemi of Eugene, Oregon, have demonstrated that the scenic beauty of their state, including its mountains, forests, streams, and beaches, has an enormous value to Oregonians. By comparing pay scales nationwide in "footloose" industries—those that can be located anywhere—they have shown that people will work for less pay for companies in Oregon than in less beautiful locales. Oregon-

ians, they argue, receive a "second paycheck" from nature worth about $500 apiece. Totalled statewide, these second paychecks almost equal the combined payrolls of all the state's lumber and wood-products firms.[34]

Few attempts have been made to calculate the prices of forest products under ecological pricing, but the prices of high-impact goods would undoubtedly be astronomical. The full value of a hamburger produced on pasture cleared from rain forests is about $200, according to an exploratory study conducted at New York University's School of Business, and a mature forest tree in India is worth $50,000, estimates the Center for Science and Environment in New Delhi. These figures are, of course, speculative. Calculating them requires making assumptions about how many dollars, for instance, a species is worth—perhaps an imponderable question. But the alternative to trying—failing to reflect the loss of ecological functions at all in the price of wood and other forest products—ensures that the economy will continue to destroy forests.[35]

Nature-blind pricing not only biases production toward high-impact techniques, it also boosts consumption to unsustainable levels by encouraging inefficiency. Most notably, it promotes waste of forests' main commodity product—wood. In 1991, the world economy used 3.4 billion cubic meters of wood. That is 2.5 times as much wood as was used in 1950—one third more per person. Consumption rates per person are far higher in industrial nations than in developing ones, but recent growth in total and per capita consumption has taken place mainly in the Third World.[36]

Half the wood is burned as fuel, mostly in developing countries; the other half is cut as timber and milled into boards, plywood, veneer, chipboard, paper, paperboard, and other products, mostly in industrial countries. (The gathering of fuelwood is a hardship for Third World women and children and taxes open woodland ecosystems; it rarely threatens closed forests, however, and is therefore omitted from this chapter.)

The conventional wisdom among foresters counsels that "people demand wood." Much as energy producers once believed their product was an irreplaceable input to industrial production, most timber producers treat wood as an end in itself; they assume demand for it is bound to grow. In the words of a 1974 public relations brochure published by the U.S. Forest Service, "We harvest timber because it is needed for man's survival." The U.N. Food and Agriculture Organization and the U.S. Forest Service have both consistently overestimated future demand for wood, based largely on this assumption.[37]

In the energy industry, many have now learned that energy consumption is sensitive to price, and that enormous opportunities exist for cost-effective savings through efficiency improvements. Some among them now profit from these opportunities. The wood products industry—aside from a few of its most astute members—is largely stuck in the old commodity mindset. It focuses on quantity over quality, on volume over value. Yet there is abundant evidence that people do not demand wood. They demand houses, tables, chairs, printed information, and other useful amenities. Wood is simply a means to an end—a means that will be used more or less frugally depending on its price.

In fact, per capita wood consumption has been declining in industrial nations for most of a century, first as fuelwood was replaced with fossil fuels and later as lumber was replaced with metal, plastics, and other materials. There is no reason to think this trend will abate. Better technologies continue to trim losses in the milling process. New materials, meanwhile, keep edging into the traditional realm of solid wood. Chipboard—fibers of wood waste pressed and glued together—has replaced lumber in a substantial share of furniture manufacturing worldwide. This opens new supply options: fiber can come from recycling, from tree species such as alder that were previously regarded as weeds in temperate zones, from thousands of little-known species currently bulldozed aside to reach mahogany and teak in tropical forests, from agricultural crop wastes such as rice straw, and from fast-growing crops such as kenaf.

Nature-blind pricing boosts consumption to unsustainable levels by encouraging inefficiency.

Ecological pricing would accelerate such technological advances and discourage the waste that is rife in the world's consumer societies. A principal use of solid lumber around the world is for construction of new houses; in North America, it is the leading use. Already, some manufacturers of housing components and furniture are recognizing the wood savings they can achieve. Anderson Window, the world's largest window maker, plans to collect old sashes in the trucks they use to distribute their windows. They will remanufacture the recycled sash into new, better insulated products. TrusJoist International's I-beams—high-strength structural lumber manufactured from wood wastes and second-growth timber—are quickly replacing solid, old-growth lumber for roof framing in North American home building. And Herman-Miller, Inc., plans to begin collecting, repairing, refinishing, and reselling used furniture from its product line.[38]

The scale of the wood-efficiency po-

tential stands out clearly in the home
Steve Loken of Missoula, Montana, built
in 1991. Loken sought opportunities to
save wood—and other natural resources—at every step. His house is con-
structed to high specifications of quality,
appearance, and safety, but it required
just half as much solid wood as a typical
house of its size. For homebuilders, ecological pricing would turn Loken's house
from a curiosity into a model. For consumers, it would divulge the costs of
their choices.[39]

At present, unfortunately, housing
trends have worked strongly against sustainability, especially in North America.
There, while family size has fallen
sharply, house size has ballooned. In
1949, the average new house in the
United States was 100 square meters; by
1993, it was 185 square meters. On average, North Americans have half again as
much residential space per person as
West Europeans, nearly twice as much as
Japanese, and more than three times as
much as Russians. Ecological pricing
would help people select a dwelling size
that not only they but the planet can afford.[40]

Ecological pricing would also expose
paper markets to a healthy dose of ecological reality. Per capita paper consumption is soaring worldwide, a dis-
heartening trend for the environment
because the pulp and paper sector is the
biggest polluter among wood products
industries. It is a heavy user of energy
and water, and a major source of toxic
water pollutants such as dioxin. Paper
production has grown rapidly throughout the twentieth century, increasing its
output twentyfold since 1913. (See Figure 2–1.)[41]

Rising literacy around the world accounts for some of this growth, but the
largest share of paper and paperboard is
used in industrial countries as boxes and
other forms of packaging. Other major
factors driving the growth of paper con-

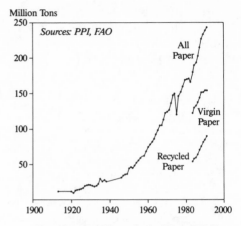

Figure 2-1. World Paper Consumption, 1913–91,
and Recycled Paper Consumption, 1983–91

sumption have been increasing advertising and office automation. As of 1992,
for example, the world had more than 19
million photocopiers, a device only introduced in 1948. Since 1955, world
consumption of printing and writing
paper, including photocopying paper,
has increased sevenfold. In the United
States alone, the spread of office printers, photocopiers, and fax machines
drove the near doubling of office paper
consumption during the eighties.[42]

Recycling rates are rising in many of
the major paper-consuming nations.
From 1983 to 1991, the share of all
paper and paperboard worldwide that
was manufactured from recycled fibers
rose from 30 percent to 37 percent. Still,
during that period recycling had yet to
dent the world's appetite for virgin-fiber
pulp, merely slowing its growth. As with
wood, the efficiency of paper use would
improve markedly under ecological pricing. Newspapers might shift their classified advertising sections onto electronic
databases available by telephone. Pack-
agers would trim the excess. Catalog
distributors would better hone their
mailings. Wholesalers would reuse cor-
rugated boxes meticulously. The long-
awaited paperless office might finally arrive. (See Chapter 6.)[43]

How can we move toward ecological pricing? The answers lie in changing government policies. A primary responsibility of governments is to correct the failures of the money economy, and global deforestation is surely a glaring one. Yet forest policies in most nations do the opposite: they accelerate its loss. The first order of business for governments, therefore, is to stop subsidizing deforestation. The second is to use tax and trade policies to make ecological costs apparent in the money economy.

In April 1993, the U.S. Forest Service proposed that it would stop selling timber from 62 of the 156 national forests it administers because those forests had consistently lost money on timber sales. The announcement represented a capitulation after a decade of pressure from conservation and taxpayer organizations, but it fell far short of ending the subsidized sale of logs from U.S. federal lands.[44]

Randal O'Toole of Cascade Holistic Economic Consultants calculates that 109 national forests, accounting for 80 percent of national forest wood output, lost money on their timber sales in 1992. The loss to U.S. taxpayers was $499 million. The effect was to subsidize the logging of public forests, a disproportionate share of which are pristine and fragile high-country ecosystems, thereby shifting production away from more-productive, already-disturbed lowland sites on private land. It also lowered the price of wood overall.[45]

Most governments in tropical countries award timber concessions through a political process rather than competitive bidding, with the result that logs go at fire-sale prices. In 1992, the Indonesian state took in just 17 percent of the "economic rent"—the earnings they could have made from sales—of timber concessions, and studies in other countries show few capture more than half

the economic rent. Because the timber is sold at rock-bottom prices, the price of the wood on the world market is artificially low.[46]

Once governments stop subsidizing destruction, they can begin to implement ecological pricing. The most powerful approach is to impose environmental taxes on goods produced at high ecological cost. Specifically, governments can shift the tax burden away from income and savings and toward "throughput"—the inputs of raw materials into the economy and the outputs of pollution and waste from it. For example, timber felled in intact, primary forests could be taxed at the highest rate, timber from secondary forests at a lower rate, and timber certified by an accredited independent monitor as produced with the most sustainable practices available at the lowest rate. Of course, such taxes would need to be introduced across the board—not simply on forest products—or else businesses that use wood might substitute higher-impact commodities, such as aluminum and steel, for wood. Indeed, comprehensive ecological pricing would likely increase consumption of wood for some uses, because the alternatives are sometimes harder on the earth.

Because some forest products are traded internationally, governments would also have to impose tariffs on goods from countries that did not employ ecological pricing. Industrial countries might assess tariffs on beef from pastures in Central American rain forests and palm oil from plantations that replaced Southeast Asian forests, for example, while developing countries might impose tariffs on goods from industrial countries that fail to stem the loss of forests to suburban sprawl. Without ecological trade policies, forest destruction would be shifted abroad rather than halted.

A QUESTION OF POWER

Designing tenure and price policies for sustainability is not difficult. The problem is meeting the third necessary condition of a sustainable forest economy: political change. Past reform attempts have mostly foundered. When implemented through national forest agencies, reform-oriented programs have been diluted, distorted, and dissected to the point where more often than not they have simply reinforced the status quo.

And the status quo has enormous staying power. The world's forest economy functions—or malfunctions—as it does because its current structure benefits powerful groups. They can be expected to fight tenaciously in defense of their privileges. Overcoming their concentrated economic and political power will require concerted campaigns, tireless grassroots organization, and ingenious political strategies. Unless the disenfranchised groups who depend on forests for sustenance gain greater influence over their fate, there is no hope for saving the forests. In particular, unless the viselike grip of big timber interests—and miners, ranchers, and related resource extractors—can be broken, all bets for forest conservation are off.

Malaysia is the extreme case and illustrates the point clearly. The largest exporter of tropical timber in the world, Malaysia is stripping its Borneo provinces of trees at a breakneck pace. Work in some operations continues around the clock, with gigantic floodlights illuminating the forests. The ruin of local ecosystems, the destruction of indigenous homelands, and the economic folly of mining a potentially renewable resource—all have been thoroughly documented and publicized in Malaysia and abroad. The government has no excuse for continuing along this path. But continuing is just what it is doing, and the prospects for reform are slim.[47]

The explanation is that logging in Malaysian Borneo is driven by the collusion of power and money. By tradition, elected leaders in Malaysian provinces have authority to distribute contracts to exploit public resources, notably timber, according to their whims. This prerogative has become a crucial part of their power base. They distribute logging concessions to loyal supporters who mine them for quick profits—estimated in the hundreds of millions of dollars—a share of which they use to keep their patron in office. The officials usually end up millionaires as well.[48]

To varying degrees, this bond between timber money and political power is found in all the world's major timber economies. Indonesian timber magnate Prajogo Pangestu, who owns concession rights and wood products industries worth an estimated $5 billion, continues to expand his control of the nation's forests with the help of those at the highest levels of government. Similarly, the Philippine Congress is packed with loggers and members of logging families.[49]

The political influence of timber money is not confined to the Third World. In 1993, the provincial government of British Columbia agreed to allow MacMillan Bloedel, the province's largest logging firm, to log in the watershed of Clayoquot Sound, an intact coastal temperate rain forest. Just five weeks earlier, a different part of the government bought 4 percent of the company's stock, although no evidence was found linking the two decisions.[50]

In the U.S. timber states of Washington and Oregon, the wood products industry outspent environmentalists six to one in contributions to congressional candidates between 1985 and 1992; grateful members of Congress from these states almost every year set higher logging targets for national forests in their districts than the Forest Service itself recommended. Only the intervention of federal courts in 1990 lowered timber sales to levels compatible with national laws on forest management and species protection.[51]

Garden-variety corruption is also widespread in the disposition of the world's forests. Papua New Guinea appointed a commission to investigate the enforcement of national forestry laws, particularly on foreign timber companies, in New Ireland Province. The commission reported that foreign timber companies were "roaming the countryside with the self-assurance of robber barons; bribing politicians and leaders, creating social disharmony and ignoring laws in order to gain access to, rip out, and export the last remnants of the province's valuable timber."[52]

In Indonesia, a study conducted by the environmental organization Walhi found that concessionaires commonly bribe forest inspectors so they will not enforce forestry rules. Just 22 of 578 concessionaires followed the rules, and 70 percent of the timber harvest was taken illegally in some provinces. In the Philippines, the illegal timber trade is perhaps four times the size of the legal trade.[53]

Challenging the collusion of power and money is, in the best cases, a monumental test. In the United States, one of the most democratic societies in the world, it took five years of a nationwide grassroots campaign and a court injunction to arrest the clear-cutting of primary forests in the Pacific Northwest—even though such logging was patently illegal under both the National Forest Management Act and the Endangered Species Act.[54]

In less democratic countries, those who question the prerogatives of economic power all too often end up as murder statistics in human rights reports. On July 17, 1993, to cite just one case, three men hacked to death Filipino development worker William Rom—a researcher documenting the economic and educational needs of the Mamanua tribal people. His apparent transgression was to work for a nongovernmental organization that exposed illegal logging on tribal lands. What hope there is in such grim situations lies only in the courage of citizens like Rom who, despite the odds, bear witness to injustice.[55]

The world's forest economy functions—or malfunctions—as it does because its current structure benefits powerful groups.

Again, Linka Ansulang speaks for many of these unsung heroes. An aged tribal woman from Mindanao—the same island where Rom was killed—Ansulang led 31 Manubo families in reclaiming tribal forestland from state corporations. Long ago, the government made a verbal agreement with her people to provide farm tools and employment in exchange for a 35-year lease of the tract. Although the state never fulfilled its promises, the Manubo left the land for 35 years. When the contract expired— on May 25, 1990—they returned, greeted by a local mayor's threats to bury them there. The standoff continues. Through it all, Ansulang and her people have remained committed to a peaceful reoccupation of what is rightfully theirs. "All we have to defend ourselves with," she says with a smile, "are carabao [water buffalo] and grass."[56]

FORESTS FOREVER

In April 1993, the government of Indonesia bought large advertisements in influential American newspapers touting the ecological sensitivity of its forest policies. "Forests Forever," proclaimed the ads. About the same time, the Canadian government launched a $6-million public relations effort in Europe, aiming to polish an image tarnished by media coverage of clear-cutting on the Pacific Coast. The premier of British Columbia vowed to "battle the campaign of misinformation bombarding our international customers."[57]

In fact, neither Indonesia nor Canada has much to brag about. Rates of primary forest clearing are high in both countries. Indonesia certainly will not have "forests forever" if it continues as it has—trampling on the rights of forest dwellers, serving up national resources to an oligopoly of the president's cronies, and doing it all at fire-sale prices. By the same token, some Canadian provinces have yet to recognize indigenous peoples' land rights. Many provinces subsidize timber extraction. And most cater to politically powerful logging, pulp, and paper industries.

Still, these publicity campaigns are backhanded compliments to the advocates of sustainability. That the two governments would feel it necessary to defend their forest policies says that consumer perceptions of environmental stewardship matter. They do not yet matter enough to change government policy and redesign the forest economy. But they matter. The challenge is make them matter more.

In the end, the fate of the earth's wooded lands is tied to the fate of their inhabitants. They will rise or fall together. Either rights to ancestral lands will be defended with the full force of the law, or the forest will fall. Either they will be accorded a share of the economic worth of the ecological services their forests provide, or the forests will fall. Either they will be allowed into the corridors of power where policies are made, or the forests will fall. Other things can help save forests, but these things are fundamental. Tenure, price, and power. As they are currently structured, there is no hope for a close to the epoch of sweeping deforestation that has gripped the world since 1950.

If those who manage forests can be made to benefit from sustaining them in the full vigor of their ecological functioning—through reforms in tenure, price, and power—the future need not repeat the recent past. We can envision a world of regenerated forests and healthy economies: one where forest dwellers, with their intimate practical knowledge of forests, join forces with ecologists to plan the use of their lands. We can hope for a landscape designed for ecological health and economic productivity. We can expect an economy that thrives on value rather than volume, rewards thrift, and aims for permanence. And we can imagine a time-lapse film of the earth from space, showing forests gradually growing thicker, spreading outward, returning to health.

3

Safeguarding Oceans

Peter Weber

For centuries, sailors feared travelling too far from shore lest they be eaten by sea monsters or fall off the edge of the earth. Poseidon, Neptune, and other gods and mystical forces—not humanity—ruled the watery depths. People did not even think about managing or protecting the marine environment. Oceans were infinite, too vast to explore let alone defile.

They may appear invulnerable, but oceans are subject to the same basic pressures that are undermining the terrestrial environment—rapid population growth, industrial expansion, rising consumption, and persistent poverty. The resulting pollution, habitat destruction, and overfishing are causing economic and biological losses in oceans, and global atmospheric changes could bring even greater deterioration in the future.

Degradation in oceans' biological systems is most immediately visible in the human industries that directly depend on the seas. Marine fishing, which supplies the world with more animal protein than any other source including pork, beef, or poultry, is facing a global crisis. According to the U.N. Food and Agricul-

ture Organization (FAO), fish stocks around the world are at their limits. At the same time, the multibillion-dollar coastal tourism industry has been hit by polluted beaches, marred coral reefs, and otherwise degraded coastal waters.[1]

Although fundamental oceanic systems appear less vulnerable, these too are threatened by continued degradation. In addition to providing the basis for economic uses of the marine environment, they have irreplaceable roles in global climate and biological diversity. Marine photosynthesis is of particular interest in this era of accumulating greenhouse gases because it drives the "biological pump" that moderates carbon dioxide levels in the atmosphere.

Despite the economic and ecological services of the marine environment, societies are reluctant to make its protection a priority. In some ways, people seem to cling still to the archaic notion that oceans are limitless and somehow beyond humanity's influence. Public outcry over catastrophic spills of oil tankers, the fouling of beaches, the killing of whales, and other high-profile issues have prompted some promising actions—yet these are not the biggest problems. Less dramatic but more pervasive and ultimately more destructive are the slow, persistent incursions of

An expanded version of this chapter appeared as Worldwatch Paper 116, *Abandoned Seas: Reversing the Decline of the Oceans.*

coastal habitat destruction, chronic overfishing, and pollution from land-based sources.

If the ecological needs of oceans are ignored, the deteriorating state of the marine environment will become an impediment to sustainable development rather than a resource. As Rachel Carson put it in her classic *The Sea Around Us*: "It is a curious situation that the sea, from which life first arose, should now be threatened by the activities of one form of that life. But the sea, though changed in a sinister way, will continue to exist; the threat is rather to life itself."[2]

OCEAN SYSTEMS

Since the dawn of life on earth, oceans have been the ecological keel of the biosphere. Stretching from the brackish waters where rivers flow into the sea to the depths of the ocean, the marine environment constitutes roughly 90 percent of the world's habitat. Oceans cover nearly 71 percent of the earth's surface, and their deepest trenches plunge farther below sea level than Mount Everest climbs above it. They contain 97 percent of the water on earth, and more than 10,000 times as much as all the world's freshwater lakes and rivers combined.[3]

The oceans' seminal contribution to the planet was life itself. Scientists believe that the very first organisms were bacteria that developed in the depths of the seas some 4 billion years ago. These were the evolutionary forerunners of all subsequent organisms, and helped create the conditions under which life as we know it could evolve. The early biosphere was inhospitable to other life forms partly because the atmosphere was deficient in oxygen. In the process of synthesizing simple sugars from carbon dioxide, photosynthetic strains of marine bacteria created the oxygen-rich atmosphere in which more advanced life forms could develop.[4]

Time and evolution have distanced us from these origins, but we still bear the traces of saltwater heritage in our blood. And the almost universal human fascination with the timeless procession of waves, the smell of salt water, and the call of seabirds also bespeaks a deep-seated psychological connection with the sea. Do we inherently understand that oceans continue to serve a critical role in the biosphere?

Arguably, the oceans' most important function is the regulation of global climate through both physical and biological processes. Their huge mass, for instance, moderates local temperatures by absorbing heat in the summer and releasing heat in the winter. Oceanic currents even out temperatures further by absorbing heat near the equator and releasing it as they approach the poles. The Gulf Stream, for instance, transports warm water from the Gulf of Mexico to northern Europe, moderating the climate to such an extent that lemon trees can grow along the coast in western Ireland at nearly the same latitude as Moscow. Shifts in oceanic currents—a potential consequence of global warming—would bring drastic changes in regional climates. On a global level, temperatures might average between one and two degrees Celsius higher if not for the heat absorbed by oceans.[5]

In the process of producing a third to half of the global oxygen supply, oceans help regulate the primary greenhouse gas, carbon dioxide, through a mechanism known as the biological pump. Carbon dioxide enters the churning upper layer of oceans, where phytoplankton and other marine plants use it in photosynthesis to make simple sugars. Although 90 percent of the carbon is recycled through the marine food web, some falls into oceans' deeper layers as the detritus of decaying phytoplankton and other sea plants or animals. There, the organic matter is oxidized and stored as dissolved carbon dioxide in deep ocean currents. It takes about 1,000 years for these slow-moving currents to bring the carbon back to the surface.[6]

The biological pump is the successor to the primitive process that initially created the oxygen-rich atmosphere a few billion years ago. Today, by slowing the buildup of greenhouse gases, this process is credited with helping forestall a predicted increase in global temperatures. The rise in greenhouse gases is driven by such human activities as burning fossil fuels and clearing forests, which add 7 billion tons of carbon to the global carbon cycle each year. About half of the excess over what is produced by nature ends up in the atmosphere, while one third is retained in oceans.[7]

Although the carbon cycle is poorly understood, oceans are clearly an important link, if only because they contain more than 20 times as much carbon as all the world's forests and other terrestrial biomass combined. Because oceans hold so much carbon, a disruption to their systems could not only slow the uptake, but also release additional amounts of carbon dioxide into the atmosphere, accelerating the buildup of greenhouse gases in the atmosphere.[8]

Beside driving the biological pump, marine photosynthesis is at the foundation of the oceanic systems that yield 80 million tons of seafood per year. Globally, the marine catch accounts for 16 percent of animal-protein consumption and is a particularly important source of protein in developing countries. (See Table 3–1.) In Asia, 1 billion people rely on fish as their primary source of protein, as do many people in island nations and the coastal nations of Africa.[9]

Marine biological diversity is crucial to maintaining the health and stability of the food web and the biological pump.

Table 3–1. Contribution of Fish to Diet, Circa 1988

Region	Fish as Share of Animal Protein Consumed
	(percent)
North America	6.6
Western Europe	9.7
Africa	21.1
Latin America and Caribbean	8.2
Near East	7.8
Far East	27.8
Asian Centrally Planned Economies	21.7
World	16

SOURCE: U.N. Food and Agriculture Organization, "Marine Fisheries and the Law of the Sea: A Decade of Change," Fisheries Circular No. 853, Rome, 1993.

Organisms from bacteria to great blue whales occupy necessary ecological niches. Copepods, for instance, are minute crustaceans that eat phytoplankton and are thought to be the most numerous animals in the oceans. They fill a critical link between oceans' primary producers and the rest of the food chain. If ecological conditions change such that copepods can no longer perform this function, their disappearance would have damaging effects.[10]

Oceans' biological storehouse is also of global scientific importance. About 90 percent of the history of life on earth took place in salt water, making the oceanic gene pool an invaluable resource. Its species are the descendants of the 3.5 billion years of evolution that predated the appearance of life on dry land some 450 million years ago. Many of them have no evolutionary counterparts on land. The total species count may be higher on land, but if biodiversity is measured in terms of physical disparities between species as classified by fundamental body characteristics in phyla, it is greater in oceans than on land. (Humans and bony fish, for instance, are both members of the phylum *chordata*, whose fundamental characteristic is a flexible spinal cord and complex nervous system.) Of the 33 animal phyla, 15 exist exclusively in oceans—whereas only 1 lives exclusively on land. Another 5 phyla are at least 95 percent marine.[11]

Ninety percent of the marine fish catch comes from the third of oceans near land.

Scientific researchers are increasingly turning to the sea in their search for medical cures and unique compounds. They have derived antileukemia drugs from sea sponges, bone-graft material from corals, diagnostic chemicals from red algae, anti-infection compounds in shark skin, and many more useful agents. Because marine life is relatively unstudied compared with terrestrial life, oceans are a vast new frontier for research.[12]

In trying to understand the diversity of life on land, we look at the enormous variations of terrestrial environments—marshes, deserts, grasslands, mountains, rain forests—and note radical differences in conditions for growth and survival. In contrast, to the untrained eye the sea may seem much the same everywhere. But ocean habitats vary from glacially cold plains and mountain ranges thousands of meters below sea level to shallow, brilliant coral reefs in coastal waters.

In general, coastal waters teem with more life than the open ocean or the deep sea because they contain the most abundant food sources. Twenty percent of oceans' plant production occurs in the 9.9 percent of the ocean area that lies over continental shelves. Here, microscopic phytoplankton and bottom-dwelling plants thrive on the nutrients that rivers deliver from land. Continental shelves extend an average of 70 kilometers from shore, with more extensive ones in such areas as the North Atlantic and Southeast Asia. Phytoplankton, which account for the bulk of marine productivity, also concentrate near the continents where coastal winds drive off the surface waters, allowing deep-sea currents laden with nutrients to come to the surface. These "upwelling" zones, such as off the western coasts of South America and southern Africa, cover 0.1 percent of the oceans and are some of its most productive waters. But it is where oceans touch land that the most fertile areas can be found: the nutrient-rich brackish waters of river estuaries, mangrove swamps, and salt marshes are thought to produce more organic material per square meter than any other habitat on earth.[13]

Coastal ecosystems are thus the centers of ocean fishing. Ninety percent of the marine fish catch comes from the third of oceans near land. Estuaries and wetlands, because of their extreme abundance of food, are the nurseries for many species of juvenile fish. About two thirds of all commercially valuable fish species spend the first—and most vulnerable—stages of their life in these waters.[14]

In contrast, the productivity of the open ocean has often been compared with that of a desert. Although both have low plant production, the connotation of barrenness is misleading because neither is devoid of life. The low density of phytoplankton leaves the open waters clear and blue, allowing photosynthetic activity to occur at greater depths than in coastal waters. The total mass of phytoplankton, dispersed across 90 percent of the ocean surface, accounts for 80 percent of marine productivity. Although barren by comparison to coastal areas, the open ocean is the engine that drives the biological pump. Its food web also supports such important migratory species as tuna, dolphins, and salmon, which graze on the dispersed animal life there.[15]

Below 1,000 meters, in the realm of perpetual night, no plants grow at all. Organisms there rely primarily on a slow rain of food particles falling from above. Only at the occasional geologic fissures in the ocean floor do deep-sea communities have their own source of primary food production. At these thermal vents, thought to be the font of all life on earth, bacteria still consume the inorganic molecules synthesized in the intense heat from the volcanic activity below. The crabs, starfish, and other organisms that have adapted to the noxious chemicals and heat of these primordial environments contrast sharply with the more dispersed and smaller life forms of the extensive deep-sea floor because of the immediate source of food.

Though devoid of plants, the deep ocean is not the biological graveyard that scientists once thought. Remarkably, deep-sea dredges indicate that the ocean floor may contain as many species as do tropical rain forests, generally regarded as the most species-rich ecosystems. Many of the species brought to the surface cannot be identified because they have never been seen before, and successive dredges are unlikely to repeat previous finds. The density of unique species in the deep ocean is not thought to be high, but because half the earth's surface is 3,000 meters or more below sea level, the total count is likely to be extraordinary.[16]

In contrast, coral reefs are believed to contain the highest density of unique species in oceans. Because they form in the nutrient-poor waters of the tropics, these coastal ecosystems rely on their complex food web to efficiently recycle nutrients. The heart of coral diversity lies in Southeast Asia, with decreasing diversity spreading out into the Indian and Pacific Oceans. The Caribbean Sea is the center of biological diversity for the Atlantic Ocean, although it ranks a distant second behind Southeast Asia.[17]

While these distinctions between regions are instructive, they should not obscure the underlying interdependence of the marine environment. Nutrients cycle from the coasts to the deep ocean and back, species migrate between continents, and the biological miracle of the deep thermal vents continues to build the genetic diversity of oceans over the eons. Oceans are even connected, like a single global organism, by great currents that slowly flow from hemisphere to hemisphere. The essential value of understanding these interconnected systems is to provide a means of protecting them—and ourselves—from degradation of a magnitude we can barely imagine.

LIVING ON THE EDGE

If we were to declare war against oceans, our best offensive strategy would be to target the coasts, the regions of most highly concentrated biological activity. Tragically, that is what human activity is already doing—not by deliberate attack, of course, but through the prevailing pattern of economic development. These waters are under the greatest environmental stress because coasts are the natural crossroads between human activity and the sea. Here is where agricultural and urban wastes flow in from the land, smoggy clouds pour out their contaminants, ships flush their tanks, and cities bulldoze wetlands to extend their land seaward. Because oceans' vital processes are heavily concentrated in coastal waters, disruptions there have a disproportionate effect on the whole ocean ecosystem.

About three quarters of the pollution entering oceans worldwide comes from human activities on land. (See Table 3–2.) Ironically, human industries and settlements are choking oceans with the very rivers that make coastal waters productive. Most nutrients, sediments, pathogens, persistent toxicants, and thermal pollution come from land-based sources. Even oil pollution, which is typically associated with accidents at sea such as the Exxon Valdez, actually comes as much from land as from the sea. Of the major sources of pollution, only the introduction of alien species (genetic pollution) originates primarily from sea-based sources. (See Table 3–3.)[18]

The flow of nutrients into oceans has at least doubled since prehistoric times, and sediments have nearly tripled as a result of human activity. Together, these pollutants degrade estuaries and coastal waters by prompting algal blooms, blocking sunlight, suffocating fish and coastal habitats, and importing pathogens and toxicants. Globally, nutrients and sediments have contributed to the decline of estuaries, coastal wetlands, coral reefs, seagrass beds, and other coastal ecosystems. They have also contributed to the increased incidence of "red tides"—blooms of algae that release deadly toxicants into surrounding waters.[19]

A large share of the nutrients entering coastal waters come from the ubiquitous problem of city sewage. Eutrophying nutrients, however, are only part of the trouble associated with this waste. Sewage sludge at concentrations as low as 0.1 percent is toxic to herring and cod eggs. Untreated sewage—including overflow during rain storms—endangers the health of unwitting swimmers and people who eat contaminated seafood. Cities also commonly mix wastewater from small industries with street runoff and sewage, thereby contaminating the water with oil, heavy metals, and other toxicants that threaten health and the environment.[20]

A surprising amount of the pollutants entering coastal waters originate not from nearby communities but from farther away. Of the nutrients, at least half come from inland. In the eastern United States, for instance, the Chesapeake Bay has been overwhelmed by nutrients from distant sources. Farmers are the source of one third and air pollution another one quarter of the nitrogen pollution that has contributed to the decline of this estuary—the largest in the United States and once one of the most productive in the world. The oyster catch in the Chesapeake fell from 20,000 tons in the fifties to less than 3,000 tons in the late eighties, at least partly as a result of pollution.[21]

In a study of 42 of the world's major rivers, Jonathan J. Cole and his colleagues from the Institute of Ecosystem

Table 3–2. Sources of Marine Pollution

Source	Share of Total
	(percent)
Runoff and Discharges from Land	44
Airborne Emissions from Land	33
Shipping and Accidental Spills	12
Ocean Dumping	10
Offshore Mining, Oil and Gas Drilling	1
All Sources	100

SOURCE: Joint Group of Experts on the Scientific Aspects of the Marine Environment, *The State of the Marine Environment*, UNEP Regional Seas Reports and Studies No. 115 (Nairobi: U.N. Environment Programme, 1990).

Table 3–3. Primary Causes and Effects of Marine Pollution

Type	Primary Source/Cause	Effect
Nutrients	Runoff approximately half sewage, half from upland forestry, farming, other land uses; also nitrogen oxides from power plants, cars, and so on.	Feed algal blooms in coastal waters. Decomposing algae depletes water of oxygen, killing other marine life. Can spur toxic algal blooms (red tides) that release toxicants into the water that can kill fish and poison people.
Sediments	Runoff from mining, forestry, farming, other land uses; coastal mining and dredging.	Cloud water. Impede photosynthesis below surface waters. Clog gills of fish. Smother and bury coastal ecosystems. Carry toxicants and excess nutrients.
Pathogens	Sewage; livestock.	Contaminate coastal swimming areas and seafood, spreading cholera, typhoid, and other diseases.
Persistent Toxicants (PCBs, DDT, heavy metals, and so on)	Industrial discharge; wastewater from cities; pesticides from farms, forests, home use, and so on; seepage from landfills.	Poison or cause disease in coastal marine life. Contaminate seafood. Fat-soluble toxicants that bioaccumulate in predators.
Oil	46 percent runoff from cars, heavy machinery, industry, other land-based sources; 32 percent, oil tanker operations and other shipping; 13 percent, accidents at sea; also offshore oil drilling and natural seepage.	Low-level contamination can kill larvae and cause disease in marine life. Oil slicks kill marine life, especially in coastal habitats. Tar balls from coagulated oil litter beaches and coastal habitat.
Introduced Species	Several thousand species in transit every day in ballast water; also from canals linking bodies of water and fishery enhancement projects.	Outcompete native species and reduce marine biological diversity. Introduce new marine diseases. Associated with increased incidence of red tides and other algal blooms.
Plastics	Fishing nets; cargo and cruise ships; beach litter; wastes from plastics industry and landfills.	Discarded fishing gear continue to catch fish. Other plastic debris entangles marine life or is mistaken for food. Litters beaches and coasts. May persist for 200–400 years.

SOURCE: Worldwatch Institute, based on sources documented in endnote 18.

Studies at the New York Botanical Garden showed that the level of pollution correlates uncannily with the level of human activity in the watershed. The Rhine, for example, has 10 times the population density of the Mississippi and dumps 10 times more nutrients into the sea, even though the Mississippi drains an area 14 times larger.[22]

About a third of the pollutants entering the marine environment come from air emissions, a large portion of which settle into coastal waters. For many heavy metals and volatile organic chemicals, air is the primary route to the ocean. In the North Sea, about a quarter of the pollution—including most of the polychlorinated biphenyls (PCBs) and other chlorinated organic chemicals—comes from the air. The 7 million barrels of oil that the Iraqi army deliberately spilled during the 1991 Gulf War turned out to be only part of what was estimated to have entered the Persian Gulf as a result of the war. Another 4–5 million barrels is thought to have been carried by oil-laden smoke. Worldwide, about 10 percent of the oil that reaches oceans is airborne.[23]

Another form of pollution—in this case, contamination of the gene pool—comes from introducing species into new habitats where they are not part of the established ecosystem. When the new arrivals outcompete native species, they have a homogenizing effect that reduces marine biological diversity. Alien species have dramatically altered coastal ecosystems around the world, particularly through transport in ocean-going ships' ballast water. Ships entering South African ports discharge some 20 million tons of ballast water every year, and those in the United States discharge 56 million tons, an estimated 6,400 tons every hour. James T. Carlton of the Maritime Studies Program at Williams College in Massachusetts estimates that with a world fleet of 35,000 ships, a minimum of several thousand different ballast-borne species may be on their way across the oceans on any given day.[24]

Coastal pollution and habitat destruction go hand in hand. To build cities along a coast, for instance, developers drain wetlands or pave over other habitats. The effects of pollution from construction, city streets, sewage plants, and industrial facilities are exacerbated by the destruction of wetlands that previously served to trap nutrients, sediments, and toxicants. Commercially burgeoning Singapore, for example, has removed almost all its mangroves and degraded the majority of its seagrass beds and all but 5 percent of its coral reefs. San Francisco Bay, the largest estuary in the western United States, has lost 60 percent of its water area to land reclamation in the last 140 years, is overrun by introduced species, and can no longer support commercial fishing.[25]

Loss of coastal habitat is a global problem, affecting some of the most productive and diverse ocean environments. About half the world's salt marshes and mangrove swamps have been cleared, drained, diked, or filled. Five to ten percent of the world's coral reefs have essentially been eliminated by pollution and direct destruction, and another 60 percent could be lost in the next 20–40 years. Even beaches (which are not highly productive but are essential to many marine species, including sea turtles) are endangered, with 70 percent eroding worldwide.[26]

A large portion of the destruction occurs because of the high population density near coasts. At least half the people in the world are estimated to live within 100 kilometers of a coast. In Southeast Asia, where marine biodiversity is particularly high, more than two thirds of the population lives within the coastal zone. The number of people living near a coast is also particularly high in eastern and southern Asia, Europe, southeastern Africa, and portions of North and South America. And these populations appear to be growing more rapidly than total world population. Coastal cities—which already account for 9 of the 10 largest cities and more than two thirds of the top 50—are expected to grow with increasing urbanization.[27]

According to the United Nations, 20–30 million of the world's poorest people annually migrate from rural to urban areas, especially Third World megacities, drawn by the promise of employment. Coastal cities have the economic benefit of access to oceans for trade. Urban developers seek out estuaries (natural bays and river mouths) because they make excellent harbors. Ships can freely enter from the ocean, and they are sheltered from waves. These urban areas particularly threaten the marine environment because a host of pollutants flow from city streets, industrial installations, sewage systems, and docked ships, while the demand for land gives people an incentive to clear and fill in coastal habitat.[28]

Rural coastal populations may also be increasing. In the Philippines, this group is growing faster than the rest of the country, in part because some people who give up on farming move to the coast to try fishing. Although land is scarce, open access to fishing grounds gives poor people some hope of making a living. Coastal cities may be notorious for degrading and destroying marine habitats, but the most extensive source of direct habitat destruction along coasts actually occurs in rural areas. Shrimp farmers in the Asian and South American tropics, for instance, have cleared extensive tracts of mangroves for holding ponds. Responding to international demand, these farmers meet 20 percent of world shrimp demand, and constitute one of the primary causes of mangrove decimation.[29]

In similar pursuit of coastal farmland, the Netherlands has done more diking, draining, and filling of coastal wetlands in proportion to its size than any other country in the world. The Dutch have increased their land area by more than a third during their thousand-year struggle against the sea. In the United States, extensive flood control and channeling projects at the mouth of the Mississippi have cut the flow of sediments and fresh water into the Louisiana coastal wetlands; with their natural hydrology severely altered, these areas are now eroding at a rate of 150 square kilometers per year.[30]

If the current trends of unsustainable development practices persist, the health of the marine environment will continue to deteriorate under the attack of pollution, development, habitat destruction, and our own increasing numbers. Our war against oceans may be an undeclared one, but so far the coastal attack seems to be a "winning" strategy.

An Ocean of Problems

Though apparently less extensive than in coastal areas, pollution and habitat degradation also reach into the open ocean and deep sea. An estimated 80–90 percent of the material dumped at sea comes from coastal dredging. At least 10 percent of it is contaminated with toxic materials from cities, industry, and shipping. DDT, PCBs, and other persistent synthetic chemicals disperse into oceans from coastal waters and the atmosphere, and garbage and oil slicks line the world's major shipping lanes. Countries have also used the deep ocean to dispose of military wastes and nuclear-powered submarines. (See Chapter 8.) Although dumping nuclear and other highly toxic wastes at sea is prohibited by international treaty, governments continue to consider the deep ocean for the disposal of hazardous wastes.[31]

Because of a lack of ecological studies of the open ocean, the effect of this pollution is unknown. But there is some reason to believe the contaminants may have an effect disproportionate to their concentrations. Chemical pollutants tend to amass in surface waters, which are also where larvae, eggs, and microorganisms concentrate. Heavy metals can be 10 to 100 or more times more concentrated near the surface than in the waters below, and pesticide residues can be millions of times stronger. These chemicals also tend to work their way up through the food chain and accumulate in the fat of marine mammals and other top predators.[32]

Among the threats to oceans on the foreseeable horizon, global atmospheric changes loom large but uncertain. With the stratospheric ozone layer thinning due to the release of chlorofluorocarbons and other ozone-depleting chemicals into the atmosphere, greater quantities of tissue-damaging ultraviolet light are reaching oceans. The increase is already reducing the productivity of phytoplankton in the Southern Ocean. Annually, the ozone layer over the South Pole begins deteriorating in September, opening up a "hole" some 50 percent thinner than normal at the same time that longer days trigger extensive phytoplankton blooms. University of California researchers found that the increased levels of ultraviolet light cut the phytoplankton output at least 6–12 percent in areas under the hole, thereby undermining the Antarctic food chain and its contribution to the biological pump. Other marine life, such as larvae in the surface waters and corals, may also be suffering from the higher levels of ultraviolet light, and the damage could multiply if ozone depletion progresses.[33]

The potential effects of global warm-

ing on oceans are less certain and more complex. The buildup of carbon dioxide and other greenhouse gases in the atmosphere is expected to raise temperatures and probably to alter other climatic phenomena such as patterns of wind, rain, and severe storms. Rapid warming could disrupt temperature-sensitive ecosystems such as coral reefs. Already, reefs have suffered extensive die-offs of corals associated with higher water temperatures. Sea level rise would accelerate with global warming, and could inundate coastal habitats. Changes in oceanic currents could alter local climates and the biological pump.[34]

Devastating as these global changes may be in theory, if they come on the heels of continued, unchecked degradation of coastal waters, they may pale in comparison with the damage already done. The die-off of corals in recent years, for instance, has been associated with high local temperatures, but scientists have been hard-pressed to prove it is the heat that is stressing the corals, let alone whether global warming is the cause of the heat. Scientists meeting at a workshop on coral reefs in 1991 concluded that the die-offs could simply be the product of pollution, and that regardless of global warming, coral reefs are already severely threatened by pollution and direct destruction.[35]

LIMITS OF THE SEA

Fishers are the first to encounter the limits of the sea. Pollution and habitat destruction can certainly harm marine organisms, but it is the pursuit of food and other marine products that has prompted people to actually remove them in mass quantities, and to alter marine ecosystems in the process.

The marine species that succumb

most readily to overexploitation are the slow-growing, long-lived, low-fertility marine mammals. The most dramatic example of a marine extinction was Steller's sea cow, a marine mammal weighing 4–10 tons that lived in the North Pacific. In 1741, a Russian ship became stranded on Bering Island, and the sailors discovered the mammoth sea cows grazing the seagrasses offshore. The gentle behemoths were unafraid, making them easy prey for the hungry sailors. The men found the sea cow's meat and fat delectable, and lived off it until they reached safety and reported their good fortune. Other ships soon sought out the region to stock up on food—until the last Steller's sea cow was killed in 1768, a mere 27 years after the animal was discovered.[36]

Although the sea cow's extinction was exceptionally precipitous, other marine mammals that have also disappeared include the Caribbean monk seal and the Atlantic gray whale, and hunters have driven many more to the brink of extinction. Conservation agreements and laws now protect most of these endangered species; some are on the rebound, but others are still threatened by hunting, fishing, pollution, and habitat destruction. (See Table 3–4.)

Fishers and collectors are also jeopardizing coral reef species such as turtles, sea cucumbers, mother of pearl, and other coveted exotic organisms.

Table 3–4. Changes in Marine Mammal Populations

Species	Past Population[1]	Recent Population[2]
Declines		
Blue Whale	200,000	2,000
Right Whale	200,000	3,000
Bowhead Whale	120,000	6,000
Humpback Whale	125,000	10,000
Sei Whale	200,000	25,000
Fin Whale	470,000	110,000
Northern Sea Lion	154,000	66,000
Juan Fernandez Fur Seal	4,000,000	600
Hawaiian Monk Seal	2,500	1,000
Recoveries		
Pacific Gray Whale	10,000	21,000
Dugong	30,000	55,000
Walrus	50,000	280,000
Galapagos Fur Seal	near extinction	30,000
Antarctic Fur Seal	near extinction	1,530,000
Extinctions		
Atlantic Gray Whale	extinct, c.1730	
Steller's Sea Cow	extinct, c.1768	
Sea Mink	extinct, c.1880	
Caribbean Monk Seal	200	extinct, c.1952

[1]Mid-nineteenth to mid-twentieth century. [2]Late eighties to present.
SOURCES: Trends from Ed Ayres, "Many Marine Mammal Populations Declining," in Lester R. Brown, Hal Kane, and Ed Ayres, *Vital Signs 1993* (New York: W.W. Norton & Company, 1993); extinctions from David Day, *The Doomsday Book of Animals: A Natural History of Vanished Species* (New York: Viking Press, 1981).

They decimate populations of these relatively rare species to meet the demand for specialty products. Collectors have eliminated giant clams from reef after reef in Southeast Asia because the mollusk's meat is a high-priced delicacy in the region. Reef fish also are vulnerable to overfishing because they are long-lived and have low fertility.[37]

The proliferation of fishers and advances in their equipment have recently put more fertile and numerous species at risk as well. Sonar and aircraft enable fishers to locate schools of fish in the open ocean, and giant nets literally strain fish from the sea. The opening of a recently designed Icelandic trawling net is so large that it could trap 12 Boeing 747 airplanes; according to Greenpeace, even larger trawlers are under construction.[38]

As a result, the fish catch from oceans grew rapidly in this century but has now begun to falter. Starting from under 5 million tons at the turn of the century, the annual catch topped 80 million tons in recent years. Between 1950 and 1970, the catch rose 6 percent a year, three times the rate of population growth. Then the annual Peruvian anchovy catch, the largest in the world, collapsed from 12 million to 2 million tons in the course of three years. This event, apparently due to the combined effects of overfishing and natural fluctuations, defined the coming era. For the next two decades the marine catch (including aquaculture) grew by only 2.3 percent a year; after peaking at 86 million tons in 1989, it fell to 80 million tons in 1992.[39]

Like the crash of the Peruvian anchovy catch before it, the recent three-year decline may mark a new era in marine fishing. Fishers have managed to keep the total catch climbing in past decades by abandoning fished-out stocks and pursuing new species. These are typically lower-value species, however, that were previously undesirable and unwanted

because they were deemed too small, bony, unappetizing, or otherwise not good for eating. The five species that accounted for most of the production increases in the eighties, and 29 percent of the world fish catch by weight in 1989, were only 6 percent of the total value. Furthermore, FAO scientists believe that these lower-value species will not yield significant increases in the future.[40]

Without new stocks to exploit, overfishing has become a global problem. FAO now estimates that all 17 of the world's major fishing areas have either reached or exceeded their natural limits, and that 9 are in serious decline. In 1971, a study sponsored by FAO estimated that the marine environment unaided could sustainably yield about 100 million tons of fish per year, 20 million tons more than the 1992 catch. Although such estimates are inherently fraught with uncertainty, the recent faltering of the world catch and the state of the major fishing grounds indicate that this projection could be close to the mark, though optimistic. Today, FAO scientists believe that the world catch is unlikely to reach and maintain the projected 100 million tons unless stocks are better managed. At best, future gains in the marine catch will not come as easily as in the past, if they come at all.[41]

Overfishing has broader implications for the marine environment as well. One of the most pervasive problems is when fishers catch and kill unwanted species, known as bycatch. The most infamous style of fishing that results in a high rate of bycatch is high-seas driftnetting. Data from the U.S. National Oceanic and Atmospheric Administration indicate that in 1990, driftnetters ensnared some 42 million seabirds, marine mammals, and other nontarget species in pursuit of tuna and squid. Shrimp trawlers, however, may have a higher rate of bycatch, pulling in between 80 and 90 percent "trash fish" with each haul—an estimated 10–15 million tons a year. In a growing practice known as "biomass fishing," some fishers are taking all they can catch with fine-mesh trawling equipment. Much of this clean-sweep catch goes to meet the growing demand for feed for fish farming.[42]

As fishers remove an ever greater proportion of the biomass from the marine environment, entire ecosystems begin to suffer. In the Shetland Islands, for example, Arctic terns, puffins, and other nesting birds failed to breed in the mid and late eighties, apparently as a result of overfishing of sand eels, a small shoaling fish caught for fish meal and oil. The birds normally fed young sand eels to their chicks, but sand eel populations declined with the commercial catch, which peaked at 56,000 tons in 1982 and then slid to 4,800 tons in 1988. In the North Pacific, Steller's sea lion, dolphin, and bird populations apparently have declined in recent years due to heavy fishing of Alaskan pollack. And researchers in Kenya found that heavy fishing of triggerfish on coral reefs allowed the proliferation of rock-boring sea urchins that are endangering the entire ecosystem.[43]

Overfishing also has considerable impact on fishers and industry employees, who inevitably suffer when the catch begins to slump. Worldwide, the fishing industry directly employs some 200 million people. Some 50,000 people were put out of work in Canada alone when the country shut down the cod fishery to allow stocks to recover. French fishers fearing for their livelihoods have protested vigorously against the import of low-priced fish from Russia and other countries that are not members of the European Community. Peaceful demonstrations have turned violent when protestors set off small explosives and broke windows, and fishers have fought street battles with the police all along the French coast. Access to fish stocks has also become the source of conflict: in

Indonesia, small-scale fishers have attacked and burned trawling vessels that encroach on their fishing grounds.[44]

With limited political power and equipment, local fishers who use traditional or small-scale equipment inevitably suffer from depleted stocks. In the Indian state of Kerala, the government promoted and subsidized commercial fishing for export, which put poor fishers who could not afford the boats and equipment at a disadvantage. The new fishing techniques then led to overfishing of the coastal waters, further undermining traditional livelihoods. Similarly, uncontrolled fishing by foreign fleets off the coast of Sierra Leone in West Africa led to a decline in the catch of the traditional fishers who supply 75 percent of the animal protein consumed in the small coastal country. The foreign fleets primarily export their catch.[45]

Industrial nations now import nearly seven times as much fish as developing countries do.

Increased international demand and rising prices have put fishers and consumers in developing countries in a tight bind. These nations are exporting an increasing percentage of their fish catch to gain much-needed foreign exchange to pay off foreign debts. Exports from developing countries have increased twice as fast as those from industrial nations, which now import nearly seven times as much fish as developing countries do. On average, people in the industrial world eat three times as much fish as people in developing countries do, despite the high dependence of Third World consumers on this source of animal protein.[46]

The catch of marine life is a telling indicator not only of the effect that overfishing has on nearby communities but also of the health of oceans themselves. As pollution, habitat destruction, and overfishing progress, the ability of oceans to help meet the global demand for food is increasingly limited. The measure of coastal degradation is often the decline of usable stocks, as has happened with the Chesapeake Bay oyster. Indeed, the traditional advice to the lovelorn that "there's plenty more fish in the sea" begins to sound quaintly and sadly dated now that we are seeing just how finite oceans' biological systems are.

GOVERNING THE SEA

During the last few decades, international negotiators have hammered out treaties and management procedures on oil spills, ocean dumping, and whaling and sealing. These have significantly reduced some types of marine pollution and exploitation of marine mammals. Yet the major global treaties have largely overlooked the pressing issues of land-based sources of pollution, habitat destruction, and overfishing, even in terms of setting standards.

Shipping has attracted the greatest amount of global attention and regulations. The International Maritime Organization (IMO) was established 30 years ago to regulate shipping internationally. Disasters at sea raised cleanup and liability issues that have prompted international cooperation, leading to a series of negotiated treaties that cover pollution and dumping from ships and the transport of hazardous materials. Under these IMO-administered agreements, signatory countries have adopted international standards and enforced them under domestic law with some success. Between 1981 and 1989, oil pollution

from ships dropped by 60 percent, according to a study by the U.S. National Academy of Sciences. Under the London Dumping Convention of 1972, signatory countries banned ocean dumping of highly toxic pollutants and high-level radioactive waste, and since 1983 they have had a moratorium on dumping low-level radioactive wastes. The 70 members of the London Dumping Convention are in the process of making this moratorium a permanent ban. The effectiveness of these agreements would increase if more countries participated and implemented them.[47]

In contrast with shipping, fishing agreements are still in the formative stage. Countries cooperate on data gathering and share other information, but they have been reluctant to enter into binding international agreements. Recent international conflicts over dwindling fish stocks, however, have drawn scores of governments to the bargaining table. In July 1993, 150 diplomats convened at U.N. headquarters to follow up on the fishery provisions of Agenda 21, the core agreement from the 1992 Earth Summit. The talks focused on fish stocks that cross lines of national jurisdictions and bring countries into direct conflict. The meeting resulted in a preliminary text to be followed up in 1994. Two camps have formed: countries with major fishing grounds who want a binding international treaty, and countries that have long-range fishing fleets and therefore want only a guideline. The talks will not, however, address overfishing of undisputed coastal waters.[48]

Marine mammals have been the subject of more successful international treaties. The first international agreement on the take of marine life was the 1911 Convention for the Preservation and Protection of Fur Seals. Seal populations were plummeting in the face of uncontrolled hunting. The four signatory countries (Russia, Japan, the United

States, and the United Kingdom on behalf of Canada) agreed to hunt the North Pacific fur seal only on specific breeding islands, and the countries that gave up the right to hunt seals at sea received compensation. The number of seals soared from 125,000 in 1911 to 2.3 million in 1941.[49]

The International Whaling Commission (IWC), established in 1947 by whaling nations to coordinate their activities, did not begin to orient its efforts toward conservation until the seventies, when nonwhaling nations started joining the commission. With a majority of conservation-oriented members, the IWC enacted a moratorium on whaling in 1985. In protest, Iceland withdrew from the commission. Though Japan has continued to kill approximately 300 minke whales a year for "scientific" purposes, much of the whale meat ends up in high-priced restaurants and shops. At the 1993 meeting of the IWC, the majority of the members voted to uphold the whaling ban, drawing bitter protests from Norway and Japan. They argued that IWC research shows that minke whales, with a population of 87,000 in the Barents Sea north of Norway and of 760,000 around Antarctica, can be sustainably "harvested." Although this may be possible, the IWC does not have detailed information on reproduction, nor has it established a working plan for enforcing whaling quotas. Following the meeting, Norway announced that it would resume whaling, and its whalers killed 157 minke whales in the 1993 season.[50]

These existing international agreements are far from perfect, but their achievements are in stark contrast with the lack of any substantive treaties for the protection of coastal waters. In Agenda 21, governments acknowledged the growing crisis in coastal areas, but the international community was reluctant to call for specific global agreements or standards that would cross the traditional line of national sovereignty over coastal waters. The Earth Summit, however, will lead to international meetings and conferences to address pollution from land-based sources and coastal zone management, which could in the future lead to global agreements and standards. The U.N. Environment Programme (UNEP), for instance, is supposed to convene an intergovernmental meeting on the protection of the marine environment from land-based activities. One possibility would be to upgrade UNEP's 1985 Montreal Guidelines on Land-Based Pollution, which is currently just a checklist for interested countries. Coastal habitat protection fell lower on the international agenda, but the World Coast Conference held in The Hague in November 1993 could likewise lead to global standards on habitat protection.[51]

Fishing agreements are still in the formative stage.

Although this follow-up on Agenda 21 is promising, for it to come to any substantive ends countries will have to relinquish some traditional notions of sovereignty over coastal waters. International law divides oceans between nationally controlled coastal waters and globally managed open oceans. From 1973 through 1982, international negotiations were held on the Law of the Sea; countries agreed to create a 200-nautical-mile zone (370.3 kilometers) within which coastal countries have exclusive rights to the natural resources. By 1976, 60 countries had claimed these Exclusive Economic Zones (EEZs), and the concept quickly became an accepted part of customary oceans law. EEZs effectively take the most valuable portion of oceans out of the realm of the global commons and place it within the jurisdiction of coastal states.[52]

Under this regime, coastal nations are on the front lines of marine protection. These governments are arguably in the best position to protect oceans. Unfortunately, at the moment they are not following through sufficiently. The health of oceans depends on the actions of all countries. Global standards would prevent one country from nullifying the environmental gains made by another.

SHORING UP THE SEA

Given the direct influence of coastal countries on oceans, along with the weaknesses of current international law, it will be largely up to individual nations and local communities to take the specific actions needed to turn the tide of marine degradation. The three areas of highest priority for more protective management are fishing, coastal development, and inland sources of pollution. These are the largest causes of degradation, and represent the greatest opportunities for reversal.

The first step is to halt the depletion of fish stocks. Although decision makers have a wide variety of management tools to pick from to reduce overfishing, the broader problem they need to confront is the proverbial "too many fishers chasing too few fish." The undeniable fact is that national fishing fleets have grown too big for existing stocks. FAO conservatively estimates that $124 billion is spent worldwide each year in order to catch just $70 billion worth of fish. Governments apparently make up most of the $54 billion difference with low-interest loans, access fees for foreign fishing grounds, and direct subsidies for boats and operations. These government subsidies keep more people fishing than the oceans can support.[53]

Open access to fishing grounds contributes to the bloated size of fishing fleets. Without restrictions on access, people continue to take up fishing well after the maximum sustainable catch has been surpassed in their areas. Once invested, fishers will only pull out of an area if they can find new fishing grounds where they can use their equipment; otherwise, they stick with the overfished grounds until forced out of business. Government subsidies exacerbate this problem, creating a self-perpetuating cycle that leads to the collapse of the fish stocks.

Rather than carrying the industry as a net budgetary burden, countries could collect rents for the use of fishing grounds as a part of a larger management strategy to limit access. As in the management of grazing, logging, or mining on public lands, fees are an integral part of limiting exploitation and compensating the public for the use of commonly held resources. In Australia, for example, rents for the use of fishing grounds have ranged from 11 to 60 percent of the gross value of the catch, with a weighted average of 30 percent. Rents could be adjusted according to the status of the fish stocks, with fees increasing as stocks become more depleted. They would also serve to streamline national fishing fleets.[54]

Worldwide, the fiscal and economic benefits of improved management would be on the order of tens of billions of dollars per year. Governments could potentially save some $54 billion a year by eliminating subsidies, and earn another $25 billion in rents, with a net budgetary benefit higher than the current gross value of the entire marine catch. Meanwhile, if stocks are allowed to recover, FAO estimates that fishers could increase their annual catch by as much as 20 million tons, worth about $16 billion at today's prices. Although this theoretical exercise does not take into account the broader adjustments that societies will have to undergo to redirect former fishers into new professions, it conveys the magnitude of economic mismanagement that has contributed to the ecological mismanagement of oceans.[55]

Restrictions on commercial fishing not only directly bolster stocks, they can benefit traditional fishers, thereby reducing the pressure on them to use destructive practices such as biomass fishing. In Sierra Leone, for instance, traditional fishers found their catch declining as that of commercial fishers from Europe increased. Because commercial fishers export, whereas traditional fishers feed local people, the government needed to protect traditional fishers' stocks. Sierra Leone established an eight-kilometer fishing zone along the coast where only traditional fishers can fish, and sought to limit overfishing by commercial fishers outside that area.[56]

Fishery management also needs to take into account the broader effects of fishing on the marine environment. An apparently sustainable yield of one species can still harm other species or the entire ecosystem. In an attempt to avoid this problem, the Commission for the Conservation of Antarctic Marine Living Resources (CCAMLR), which regulates the take of marine life in the Southern Ocean (except that of whales and seals, which are covered by other treaties), established an ecosystem approach to the management of the Antarctic fishery. In 1991, CCAMLR set a limit on the catch of krill, the small zooplankton that form a vital link in the Antarctic food chain.

Some environmentalists have questioned the methodology by which the limit (1.5 million tons a year in the southern Atlantic Ocean) was established. Indeed, setting reasonable quotas may prove difficult for krill, cod, or any other marine life. Researchers from the University of Washington and

the University of British Columbia say that the notion of "sustainable yield" is an elusive goal because natural fluctuations in fish stocks and illegal fishing are part of the system but would be hard to account for. Nonetheless, the CCAMLR limit sets an important precedent by approaching the problem of depletion proactively—implementing a solution before the problem has become a crisis.[57]

On land, where the main causes of ocean degradation are pollution and habitat destruction, the highest priority of oceans management is to control coastal development. A first step would be to eliminate subsidies such as government-sponsored insurance and funding for ocean-altering roads, dikes, and dams. The Netherlands, for instance, spends $400 million a year to pump water and repair inland dikes, despite the fact that the Dutch are producing more food than they can use or sell abroad, burdening the country with high payments to farmers to cover their excess production. To save money and begin rehabilitating the coastal ecosystem, the government has made plans to return 150,000 hectares of farmland (15 percent of the total converted area) to the sea over the next 25 years. Although the country plans to continue to dike and develop the coastal zone, this reversal reflects its growing awareness of the long-range importance of managing the coasts for ecological as well as economic purposes.[58]

On land, the highest priority of oceans management is to control coastal development.

Natural buffer zones can protect coastal habitat from nearby development. Wetlands, for instance, trap toxicants, pathogens, and excess nutrients and sediments as they move seaward, while also protecting coastal communities from coastal storms and sea surges. Governments may eventually need to consider restricting or even prohibiting further coastal development altogether, in light of the predicted sea level rise of 0.6 meters during the next 100 years and the increased likelihood of stronger storms from sea.[59]

The third priority of oceans management is to reduce the flow of pollution from land.

Where rural communities use coastal habitat, management efforts can moderate the effects on the natural environment. Ecuador, for instance, which in the past 23 years has lost 80,000 hectares of mangrove forests and salt flats to shrimp ponds, has begun a national program for the management of its coastal resources. This stemmed from a U.S. Agency for International Development pilot project to slow the rapid degradation of Ecuador's coastal resources while still benefiting from them. Since the shrimp industry is a sizable portion of Ecuador's exports and economy—nearly 80,000 tons of shrimp, worth almost $500 million in 1991—the project emphasized training to help shrimp farmers protect the coastal environment while maintaining their livelihoods.[60]

The third major priority of oceans management is to reduce the flow of pollution from land. Forty-four percent of the pollutants entering oceans worldwide are carried from their sources by water, and another 33 percent are transported through the air. These diffuse sources pose the stiffest of all ocean-protection challenges, but because they also contribute to the deterioration of the immediate human environment, we have strong motivation to control them. Efforts to clean up these sources of pollution will more likely succeed if—instead of being treated as separate marine-pollution projects—they are combined with overarching efforts to improve the quality and safety of drinking water, food, and air.[61]

Among the waterborne pollutants reaching oceans, sewage is a matter of primary concern not only for the sake of the marine environment but also for human health. Some 1.7 billion people in the developing world do not have sanitary ways to dispose of their sewage. Successful treatment can vary from sanitary pit latrines to advanced treatment plants. Water recycling efforts, such as those pioneered by Israel, can further reduce the input of excess nutrients into the aquatic environment, while conserving scarce water supplies.[62]

Clean water legislation, while not normally thought of as a response to ocean degradation, is helpful in mitigating it. In industrial countries such as Germany, Japan, and the United States, manufacturers have cut the output of pollutants in the wake of such laws. U.S. farmers have reduced the erosion of soil, which carry fertilizers and pesticides, following farm legislation. These efforts to control water pollution help protect the health of rivers, the people who draw drinking water from them downstream, and the estuaries and coastal waters into which they flow. Similar benefits accrue from clean air and pesticides laws.[63]

For pollution control efforts that span regions to succeed, they need broader coordination. Among the few efforts made specifically to protect the marine environment from pollution, one of the most advanced programs covers the Chesapeake Bay, the largest bay estuary in the United States. It is fed by more than 150 tributary rivers and streams coming from an area that spreads over six states and the District of Columbia. Under the Chesapeake Bay Agreement of 1987, the District of Columbia and the states of Maryland, Pennsylvania, and Virginia agreed to cut nutrients by 40 percent by the end of this decade, control the discharge of toxicants, and increase wetland area. To date, the signatories have reduced some forms of pollution, but runoff from agriculture has increased, the population in the region continues to grow rapidly, development adjacent to the bay continues, and, as a result, the load of nitrogen nutrients entering the bay is still growing.[64]

The limited success of the Chesapeake Bay project demonstrates the difficulty of implementing such programs even in a single country. In many other instances, cooperation between neighboring nations is necessary, creating an even greater challenge. UNEP's Regional Seas Programme, with more than 120 participating countries in 10 regions, has been the leading forum for cooperation in the past decade, but it has foundered in recent years because of the lack of money for implementation of agreements.[65]

In Agenda 21, the delegates to the Earth Summit called for additional funds for the protection of coastal waters and oceans at large. One potential mechanism is the Global Environment Facility (see Chapter 9), which is currently funding the Black Sea regional program and a number of smaller coastal management efforts. Part of its mission is to protect international waters, including the marine environment, and its funds can help stimulate local and regional programs. Nonetheless, international lenders such as the World Bank continue to exert greater influence over coastal waters through their general development lending than through targeted environmental money. Thus their agriculture, water, urban planning, energy, and other development projects merit consideration not only for their direct human benefits, but also in light of the ecological needs of oceans.[66]

Ultimately, reversing the decline of oceans will take action percolating from the grassroots to the international level and filtering back down again in the form of international agreements to be given teeth by national laws and local action. The international moratorium on the use of driftnets, for instance, grew out of activism by such groups as Greenpeace, the Bering Sea Fishermen's Association, the American Oceans Campaign, and the Defenders of Wildlife. The South Pacific Forum advanced the issue by banning the use, possession, and transit of driftnets longer than 2.5 kilometers in the waters and territory of these Pacific island nations—a sizable portion of the Pacific Ocean—and then requesting a U.N. moratorium on driftnetting. The U.N. General Assembly passed its first resolution against driftnetting in 1989, and then renewed it in 1990 and 1991, leading to an international moratorium that went into effect on December 31, 1992. Although a few nations are defying the ban, on the whole driftnetting has fallen off sharply.[67]

Grassroots organizations are replicating that kind of effort around the world to halt a wide range of environmental offenses, not only specifically for the sake of oceans, but also for related purposes on land. To date, their activities have been too few and too small to reverse marine degradation. Yet without their efforts, oceans will continue to deteriorate.

We can no longer afford to act as if the oceans are limitless or unalterable. The marine environment is integrally connected with the human environment and the biosphere, and there are few industries or activities that do not ultimately affect oceans in one way or another. Poverty, population growth, industrial expansion, and overconsumption intensify those effects. To restore the health of oceans, we need to integrate the actions we take expressly to protect the marine environment with those being undertaken to achieve sustainable development worldwide.

The complex links between land and sea may make the task of protecting oceans seem daunting, if not impossible. But it is precisely because of these links—because oceans touch the lives of all of us—that we cannot ignore the health of oceans if we are to protect our own place on the planet.

4

Reshaping the Power Industry

Christopher Flavin and Nicholas Lenssen

When Thomas Edison started the world's first electric power company in New York in 1880, it looked like a typical underfinanced start-up venture, not much different from hundreds of other small businesses. In a Wall Street warehouse, Edison connected a coal-fired boiler to a steam engine and dynamo, then linked the plant by underground wire to a block of nearby office buildings. When the switches were finally flipped at the Pearl Street Station on September 6, 1882, 158 light bulbs (also designed by Edison) flashed on, and the Edison Electric Illuminating Company made converts of its carefully chosen first customers—J.P. Morgan and the *New York Times*.[1]

Electric power was an immediate hit—turning its pioneer into a millionaire and causing the stock of competing gas companies to plummet. Edison viewed electricity as a dynamic, competitive service business, even offering initially to sell lighting to his customers by the bulb. Without government regulation or other controls, electric power companies quickly proliferated, offering both direct and alternating current at various voltages, and often running competing electric lines down opposite sides of the same street.

A century later, Edison would hardly recognize the electric power industry—nor its ubiquitous effects on societies around the globe. With all the world's cities and many of its villages now wired, electric current flows from power plants thousands of times larger than Edison's into millions of homes, providing power for "necessities" such as refrigerators, televisions, and computers. In most countries, the industry has been organized into large, vertically integrated monopolies, with annual revenues estimated at more than $800 billion—roughly twice the size of the world auto industry.[2]

Yet during the past two decades, the utility industry often has been plagued by rising costs, angry consumers, and a series of environmental problems. In many nations, fossil-fuel-burning power plants are a leading cause of air pollution, and at the global level they are one of the largest contributors to the rising atmospheric concentrations of carbon dioxide that are threatening the stability of the earth's climate. None of these problems can be seriously addressed without major changes in the power industry.

For many electric utilities, reforms are already under way, usually under pressure from government agencies. The changes take different shapes in different countries, and frequently divide utilities, consumer groups, and an emerging industry of unregulated power producers. While consensus has not yet been reached about where the industry is headed, many experts agree that it is on the verge of an unprecedented restructuring—comparable in magnitude to the one now under way in telecommunications. If guided by wise policymaking, the world may one day have a power industry that is closer to Edison's original vision: decentralized, service-oriented, and market-driven—and, with a little extra effort, environmentally sustainable as well.

END OF THE LINE

When the twentieth century began, gas lights were still the dominant means of illumination, and steam engines ruled most factory floors. But electric power was on the move, driven by the vision and self-confidence of men like Edison, Samuel Insull, and George Westinghouse. Electricity soon came to be seen as not only an essential tool of development but also a symbol of modernity. Although electric power cost far more than other forms of energy, its ability to run a variety of new industrial equipment and household appliances left it with no real competitors.

Some of the industry's early leaders envisioned a system of stand-alone, mass-produced generators, but they were opposed by a competing vision: large central generators selling power to hundreds of separate customers. The latter concept eventually prevailed, driven in part by the advent of alternating current and the transformer, which made it possible to raise the voltage of electric current and thereby send it over long distances. In addition, the rotary steam turbine, developed by Charles Parsons shortly after Edison's first plant opened, generated power more efficiently. (Water-driven turbines used in hydropower projects provided the other large source of electricity.)[3]

Although Chicago alone was served by four dozen power companies 100 years ago, in just a few decades single utilities were serving whole cities, then regions, and finally entire nations. The industry's growth quickly transformed it, for with monopoly control came an implied public responsibility. Beginning in 1907, state regulatory commissions were formed in the United States to determine—in the absence of an open market—a fair price for electricity and to provide financial stability for utilities. In other parts of the country and around the world, electric utilities were taken over by city or provincial governments, leading eventually to national utilities in the United Kingdom, France, and elsewhere. Often, the resulting monopoly structures bore closer resemblance to the economic visions of Lenin than to the vigorous capitalism of Edison's late-nineteenth-century United States.[4]

As the industry's structure changed, the price of electricity plummeted—from $4 per kilowatt-hour for U.S. consumers in 1892 to 60¢ in 1930 and just 7¢ in 1970 (in 1992 dollars). Demand soared, in some countries doubling every decade, and the industry adopted a "grow-and-build" model in which ever-higher levels of consumer demand were counted on to justify scaling up the technology, which in turn would bring down the price and attract more customers. The impressive improvements in power technology during this period stemmed, however, from a surprisingly narrow frontier of advances in turbine materials and design (allowing them to operate at greater temperature and pressure), the move to larger turbines and boilers, and the development of new techniques for cooling the generators.[5]

By the sixties, this bag of tricks was nearly empty, and average plant efficiencies were levelling off at about 35 percent (meaning that two thirds of the energy in the fuel was still dissipated as waste heat rather than converted to electricity). (See Figure 4–1.) Efforts to get just a bit more out of the technology led to a breakthrough, but not the one expected: for the first time, new power plants were more expensive and less reliable than their predecessors. Yet utility engineers, accustomed to an age of endless progress, resisted the notion that this was anything but a temporary setback, and continued to argue for ever-larger plants.[6]

These relatively minor technical prob-lems were joined by more serious ones when governments began to push the utility industry into nuclear power in the sixties. The plants appeared similar enough to a coal burner (the heat generated by splitting atoms was substituted for the fossil fuels used to boil water), encouraging utilities to order scores of nuclear plants far larger than any that had even been tested. By the seventies, the unique hazards of atomic energy were adding dramatically to the complexity and costs of the new plants—a problem vastly complicated by the nuclear accident at Three Mile Island in 1979. Soon nuclear power was boosting electricity prices in many countries, nuclear orders began to collapse, and many people developed a deep distrust of their local power supplier.[7]

The timing could not have been worse. Electricity demand growth in industrial countries slowed from nearly 8 percent per year in the sixties to an average of 3 percent since the mid-seventies—driven by higher fuel prices and saturation in the use of some appliances. This resulted in a levelling off of the electricity intensity of industrial-country economies. (See Figure 4–2.) Many utility executives saw the trends as a tempo-

Percent

Figure 4-1. Highest Electrical Efficiency of Installed Steam Units, United States, 1882–1992

Sources: Hirsh, Electric Light & Power

Kilowatt-hours Per Dollar of GDP

(in 1985 dollars)

Source: Worldwatch Institute

Figure 4-2. Electricity Intensity in Industrial Countries, 1950–92

rary confluence of aberrant economic conditions, perverse government decisions, and an irrational public, and they waited expectantly for conditions to return to "normal." When that failed to happen, scores of utilities were stuck with multibillion-dollar plants they did not need—creating a $35-billion debt for the state-owned national utility in France and leaving utilities such as the Washington Public Power Supply System and the Public Service Company of New Hampshire in bankruptcy. By the early eighties, electricity forecasting had become a guessing game, and utility regulation was transformed from a dull rubber-stamping dominated by the industry into a series of confrontations with consumer advocates and government lawyers.[8]

Further complicating the electricity business was the growing evidence that power plants—particularly the coal-fired models that provide nearly 40 percent of the world's electricity (see Table 4–1)—cause major environmental problems. Increasingly strict pollution laws forced utilities to control everything from coal ash to elusive gases such as nitrogen oxides. Among the costly pollution controls required in most new power plants

in the early nineties are flue gas desulfurization units to remove the sulfur dioxide that causes acid rain. In some cases, as much as 45 percent of the cost of a coal-fired power plant stems from environmental compliance. Public concern has also blocked the construction of many plants entirely, including hydro dams opposed by environmentalists and indigenous peoples concerned about the vast land areas to be inundated.[9]

Electric power systems of developing countries—most of them government-owned—were caught in the same tidal wave of problems, aggravated by the fact that many were still in the early stages of electrification. Soaring oil prices and mushrooming debt burdens threw numerous Third World utilities into a period of disarray they have not yet recovered from. Pushed by political leaders to expand supply (at rates as high as 10 percent annually) while cutting prices, managers of many Third World utilities saw their financial condition and the reliability of their service deteriorate. On average, rates of return on investment fell from 9 percent in the early seventies to 5 percent in the eighties.[10]

The World Bank acknowledged these problems in a 1993 report: "Opaque

Table 4–1. World Electricity Production, 1971 and 1990

Power Source	1971		1990	
	(terawatt-hours)	(percent)	(terawatt-hours)	(percent)
Coal	2,142	40.3	4,645	39.3
Hydroelectric	1,209	22.8	2,142	18.1
Nuclear	111	2.1	2,011	17.0
Natural Gas	714	13.5	1,578	13.3
Oil	1,102	20.8	1,385	11.7
Others	32	0.6	67	0.6
World[1]	5,311		11,828	

[1]Columns may not add to totals due to rounding.
SOURCE: International Energy Agency, *World Energy Outlook* (Paris: Organisation for Economic Co-operation and Development, 1993).

command and control management of the sector, poorly defined objectives, government interference in daily affairs, and a lack of financial autonomy have affected productive efficiency and institutional performance." In many cases, political manipulation and corruption have made the problem even worse. And given their financial condition, most of these utilities have been unable to add the most basic environmental controls to their power plants.[11]

Since the mid-eighties, many observers have concluded that the traditional model is less and less suited to today's technologies or economic conditions. Environmentalists, consumer advocates, and utility executives are among those calling for new ways of organizing and managing the power industry. Pushed by government regulators, the industry in many countries has begun to experiment with increased competition, made major investments in improving energy efficiency on the customer's side of the electricity meter, and adopted a new planning strategy known as integrated resource planning (IRP).

The early nineties are also marked by efforts to better integrate environmental goals into the power industry. The old approach, whereby utilities respond piecemeal to each new pollution law, often leads to a costly series of end-of-the-pipe devices. The new strategy, as pursued in the United States in various forms by 26 state governments, looks at environmental costs as part of the planning process. Meanwhile, the threat to the earth's climate stability posed by rising concentrations of carbon dioxide has lent an even greater urgency to environmental concerns. With the power sector accounting for 29 percent of the world's carbon dioxide emissions from fossil fuels, reducing the risk of global warming will require fundamental changes in utilities. During the next few years, countries will prepare national climate plans in response to the global treaty signed in Rio de Janeiro in 1992. Their efforts to improve the efficiency of electricity use and to substitute renewable energy sources for coal may accelerate the process of change.[12]

Although there is no simple way to characterize the sometimes contradictory currents in the power industry, a period of unprecedented restructuring appears to lie ahead. Among the contentious issues being debated is the ageless one of public versus private ownership, as well as questions of how vertically integrated the industry should be, how its financial rewards should be established, and how responsive it should be to public concerns. The answers to these questions will have profound impacts not only on how much consumers pay for electricity, but on how successful the world is in addressing such environmental threats as acid rain and global warming.

THE NEW GENERATORS

One of the most far-reaching recent developments is the emergence of a competitive breed of "independent power producers" who build new plants and sell electricity under contract to utilities. The new era has its roots in the U.S. Public Utility Regulatory Policies Act (PURPA) of 1978, which opened a nearly untapped segment of the power market to unregulated companies—construction of generating plants that rely on renewable fuels or that cogenerate heat for industrial facilities. PURPA had its greatest impact in California and a few other states, where thousands of megawatts of renewable-energy-based and cogeneration projects were installed in the eighties.[13]

By the late eighties, companies ranging from small entrepreneurial firms to multinational corporations such as ABB and Texaco were putting their own capital on the line, assuming the risk of cost overruns, and delivering power to U.S. utilities that was often less expensive and more reliable than the average utility-owned plant. The boom in independent power projects coincided with a dramatic fall-off in utility plant building, so that by the early nineties, independent producers were adding about as much capacity as utilities were. (See Figure 4–3.) Although many utility "experts" had predicted this would never work, the success of independent power probably would not surprise Thomas Edison—or Adam Smith, for that matter.[14]

Other countries have begun to open their power grids as well. In Denmark, Germany, the Netherlands, and Switzerland, small-scale generators have been authorized to put wind turbines or biomass plants on their farms or solar cells on their rooftops. And in the United Kingdom, the government-owned power monopoly was broken in 1989 and divided into 12 distribution companies, an open-access national transmission system, and a quasicompetitive generation business. This has created a booming

business in natural-gas-fired power plants and a smaller boom in wind power, resulting from a requirement that the distribution utilities purchase minimum amounts of "nonfossil" electricity. Also, many developing countries burdened by severe financial constraints and power shortages, including China, India, Indonesia, Mexico, and Pakistan, have turned to private companies to build and operate new power plants.[15]

Although large private power plants have been built in some countries, the industry has also helped foster an innovative array of relatively small power projects. In fact, even among utilities there has been a dramatic reversal in the trend to ever-larger generators—from more than 600 megawatts per plant in the United States in the mid-eighties to an average of about 100 megawatts in 1992. Power plants owned by independent producers averaged just 20 megawatts in the late eighties and rose to 24 megawatts in 1991. The new generators coming on-line range from gas turbines to wind turbines and from geothermal power plants to solar cells. Only nuclear power, which has its roots in centralized government and utility control, has been left out of this renaissance of entrepreneurialism in the power industry, though coal has recently begun to lose favor as well.[16]

The outpouring of innovative technology that has accompanied the rise of the independent power industry has surprised many experts. One of the first barriers to fall is the one that confounded utility engineers in the sixties: the inability to build reliable thermal power plants with efficiencies much higher than 40 percent. That limit has been obliterated by a surprisingly familiar device—the jet engine—which burns a pressurized mixture of fuel and air to spin a turbine that generates thrust and propels the plane forward. The same basic device can readily be converted to

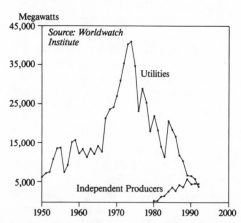

Figure 4-3. Gross Additions to U.S. Installed Generating Capacity by Utilities and Independent Power Producers, 1950–92

run an electricity generator. After a decade-long halt in construction because of unfounded fears of gas shortages, utilities turned their attention to gas turbines in the late eighties, as gas prices fell and the nuclear industry fizzled.[17]

Today's gas turbine renaissance is focused on the "combined-cycle plant"—an arrangement in which the excess heat from the turbine is used to power a steam turbine, boosting efficiency. Combined-cycle plants reached efficiencies of more than 40 percent in the late eighties, with the figure climbing to 50 percent for a General Electric (GE) plant opened in South Korea in 1993. Later that year, ABB announced it was offering a new plant that was 53-percent efficient. These plants are inexpensive to build (roughly $700 per kilowatt, or a little more than half as much as a conventional coal plant) and can be built rapidly—two-and-a-half years for the huge 1,875-megawatt Teeside station in the United Kingdom.[18]

More versatile turbines are also on the way. Using the advanced metals, new blade designs, and high compression ratios of jet engines, engineers are producing smaller "aeroderivative" turbines. By applying a host of modest innovations such as steam injection, the efficiency of these one-cycle devices has recently reached 39 percent and is expected to top 50 percent in the future. Because aero turbines are factory-built, costs are as low as $350 per kilowatt, and they can be installed in just a few months. Moreover, these devices are small—48 megawatts for an adapted 747 aircraft engine and 1 megawatt or less for some smaller models—and therefore have a wide range of applications (as a cogenerator in a large building, for example).[19]

These technologies have major environmental advantages over conventional oil or coal plants, including no emissions of sulfur and negligible emissions of particulates. Nitrogen oxides can be cut by 90 percent and carbon dioxide by 60 percent. (See Table 4–2.) Indeed, the combination of low cost and low emissions could spur utilities to convert hundreds of aging coal plants into gas-burning combined-cycle plants—for as little as $350 per kilowatt. Worldwide, some 400,000 megawatts of gas turbine plants could be built by 2005, according to a GE forecast; units are already up and running in countries as diverse as Austria, Egypt, Japan, and Nigeria. A secondary result of this boom is the emergence of natural gas as the dominant fuel for new power plants in some countries.[20]

Gas turbine power plants can also run on gasified coal—though it is not as clean as natural gas—or, in the near future, on gasified agricultural or forestry residues. These biomass "wastes" are estimated to be so abundant that they alone could supply 30 percent of the world's current electricity. Among the additional power options available are a modest expansion in reliance on hydro dams, which now supply 18 percent of the world's electricity, and increased reliance on the earth's geothermal heat, which already provides significant power in several countries, such as the Philippines and Kenya.[21]

Even more revolutionary generating options are on the way, and they, like biomass, rely on the most abundant resource of all—the world's constant flux of sunlight. Solar energy (and the wind that flows from it) is a nearly unlimited resource that can substitute for the fossil fuels that now threaten the stability of the climate. Although renewable energy sources were not competitive with fossil fuels in the past, their costs have fallen and are expected to decline further when the technologies to harness them are mass-produced—likely within the next decade.

Wind power is among the most mar-

Table 4–2. Conversion Efficiencies and Air Pollutants, Various Electricity-Generating Technologies[1]

Technology[2]	Conversion Efficiency[3]	Emissions		
		NO$_x$	SO$_2$	CO$_2$
	(percent)	(grams per kilowatt-hour)		
Pulverized Coal-Fired Steam Plant (without scrubbers)	36	1.29	17.2	884
Pulverized Coal-Fired Steam Plant (with scrubbers)	36	1.29	0.86	884
Fluidized Bed Coal-Fired Steam Plant	37	0.42	0.84	861
Integrated Gasification Combined-Cycle Plant (coal gasification)	42	0.11	0.30	758
Aeroderivative Gas Turbine	39	0.23	0.00	470
Combined-Cycle Gas Turbine	53	0.10	0.00	345

[1]Data are for particular plants that are representative of ones in operation or under development.   [2]Coal plants are burning coal with 2.2 percent sulfur content.   [3]For natural gas-fired plants, the higher heating value, which gives lower efficiency levels, is used.
SOURCES: Bob Bjorge, General Electric, Schenectady, N.Y., private communication and printouts, August 26, 1993; M.W. Horner, "GE Aeroderivative Gas Turbines—Design and Operating Features," GE Aircraft Engines, GE Power Generation, Evendale, Ohio, 1993; David S. Bazel, ABB, North Brunswick, N.J., private communication and printout, November 2, 1993.

ket-ready of the renewables. Nearly 20,-000 turbines have already been installed, mainly in California and northern Europe, and wind power generation is projected to at least triple in the next decade. By relying on advanced blades, electronic controls, and the economics of mass production, wind power could contend with gas turbines as the least expensive major power source by the end of this decade. Only a few years later, large, cost-competitive solar thermal and photovoltaic power plants may begin to proliferate in the world's sunbelts.[22]

Resource surveys show that solar, wind, and geothermal energy are sufficiently abundant to supply all the world's electricity scores of times over. For example, all U.S. power needs could be met with solar plants spread over 59,-000 square kilometers, less than a third as much land as now occupied by U.S. military facilities. Alternatively, those same needs could be met by fully exploiting the wind power potential of just three states—North Dakota, South Dakota, and Texas. Recent studies show that wind, solar, and geothermal energy each have the potential to meet 10–30 percent of many nations' power needs. Tapping that potential will require continuing advances in renewable technologies, and programs to gradually build markets for them.[23]

Utility engineers have argued for years that wind and solar energy are too intermittent and would require expensive backup storage, but the experience with grid-connected projects—most of them built by independent producers—suggests otherwise. These "intermittent" sources are quite predictable and, with accurate data, can be readily incorporated into utility plans. The winds of the northern Great Plains, for example, coincide with utilities' winter peak load, and the sunniest period in Los Angeles matches the summer afternoon crest in power demand. California's experience with wind farms has shown that intermittent power can meet one third of a utility's load with only minor, inexpensive changes such as building a few extra gas turbines.[24]

Although the independent power industry has shown that it is at least as adept as regulated utilities at seeking out cost-effective and environmentally sustainable power sources, in many parts of the world it is still outlawed. Overcoming these constraints and strengthening the relationship between utilities and independent producers will be essential if this new wave of innovation is to continue. In the United States, a growing number of states have set up bidding systems for acquiring new power supplies, ensuring that the most cost-effective projects are selected. Some have also established special set-asides for the more capital-intensive renewables—to promote sufficient diversity and innovation in the future resource mix.

A NEGAWATT REVOLUTION

In the late seventies, a maverick group of energy analysts reached a startling conclusion: electric utilities and their customers both might be better off if they invested in ways to reduce power use. Studies showed that improving the efficiency with which electricity is used is often less expensive than building and operating new plants. Lawyers for the Environmental Defense Fund and other groups brought this argument to rate hearings in the United States—fiercely resisted by utilities who were accustomed to promoting power use, often by offering lower prices to those who use more electricity.[25]

Although the environmentalists lost some early battles, several regulatory commissions eventually took their side, and ordered the utilities to adopt efficiency programs. Early programs were modest—eliminating discounts for big power users, adding "bill-stuffers" that urged a lowering of thermostats, and offering free energy audits to customers. But they gradually expanded to include cash rebates for purchases of low-energy appliances or compact fluorescent lamps, loans at low interest rates for home weatherization or industrial retrofits, and even rebates for the purchase of solar water heaters. The new approach was known as demand-side management (DSM), or more colloquially as "negawatts."[26]

At the heart of the DSM revolution was a challenge to the utility axiom that more electricity is always better than less. According to the new thinking, electric power is an expensive and highly directed form of energy, and using it to provide low-grade heat is inherently wasteful. Physicist Amory Lovins, for example, compares heating water with electricity to "cutting butter with a chain saw." He and other analysts point out that electricity now provides just 18 percent of the end-use energy of industrial countries, a figure that need not rise much further—despite increasing use of electronic equipment—if power is used more efficiently.[27]

Although the notion that it is less expensive to save electricity than to produce it is straightforward, the idea that utilities themselves should discourage the use of their product is counterintuitive. But utilities do not operate by the normal market rules: they are regulated and protected by governments, face minimal financial risks, and have access to capital at low interest rates. If all those advantages are applied to building central power stations while capital- and information-short consumers have the full responsibility for efficiency investments, the result is clear. Customers end up paying for unnecessary power plants, the output of which is used in outdated, inefficient appliances.

In some cases, companies are now allowed to earn returns on efficiency investments at a higher rate than for building power plants.

The initial approach to remedying this imbalance was to penalize utilities that did not invest in conservation. This worked for a while in several states, but as the eighties drew to a close, investments in efficiency had stalled when executives saw that they were losing money on DSM. The reason: U.S. utilities have traditionally been regulated so that their profits are linked to electricity sales; anything that lowers power use will reduce the return to investors, even if, as in many cases, the efficiency investment is added to the capital base on which utility profits are earned. In other words, the economic interests of electricity consumers are at odds with the interests of the shareholders to whom utility executives are responsible.[28]

The solution to this problem was discovered by pioneering state utility regulators and advocates who realized, in the words of New England Electric System president John Rowe, that "the rat must smell the cheese." In 1989, the National Association of Regulatory Utility Commissioners proposed that regulators offer "cheese" in the form of opportunities to earn equal or greater profits on saved power, compensating

utilities in a variety of ways for profits that would be lost from reduced sales. In some cases, companies are now allowed to earn returns on efficiency investments at a higher rate than for building power plants; in others, utilities share directly in the money saved. Such approaches are spreading rapidly in the United States, and are being experimented with in the United Kingdom.[29]

Beyond adjusting their incentives, 30 states have ordered utilities to adopt the revolutionary new approach of integrated resource planning. Under IRP, planners assess the benefits, risks, and costs—sometimes including environmental costs—of all practical electricity generating and savings options. Often the winning option is determined by seeking competitive bids from energy-saving companies as well as power suppliers. Sometimes, even an efficiency program that raises power prices may be advantageous, so long as it cuts average consumption and thereby lowers customers' monthly bills. For many utilities, IRP has spurred a reassessment of the very nature of their business, changing from commodity suppliers to true energy service companies—much as Edison envisioned 11 decades ago.[30]

In response to all these policies, U.S. utility spending on efficiency grew from less than $900 million in 1989 to an estimated $2.3 billion in 1992. Most of it has been concentrated in California, the Northwest, and the Northeast, where state regulators have been most supportive. Some publicly owned utilities have also moved aggressively to cut power use. An evaluation of 37 of the best North American utility programs by the Results Center of Aspen, Colorado, found that in 31 cases, average efficiency costs were less than 4¢ a kilowatt-hour; in 14, costs were below 2¢. Other studies indicate that poorly managed DSM programs can sometimes cost several times this much. Careful design and implementation of DSM programs is needed, including rigorous evaluations that allow redirection of programs that are not operating as well as they might.[31]

Utilities throughout Canada and Western Europe are also adopting demand-side management. Two of Canada's provincial utilities, Ontario Hydro and BC Hydro, for example, have large programs. More than 50 West European utility-sponsored lighting efficiency programs were launched between 1987 and 1992, and are now spread across 11 nations. Exceptionally strong efforts are found in municipally owned power companies in Denmark, Sweden, and the Netherlands, with Dutch utilities spending around $30 million each year. Data from 40 of these efforts indicate that even with administrative expenses included, improved lighting efficiency costs on average just 2¢ a kilowatt-hour, far less than producing power.[32]

While their programs are continuing to grow, European utilities generally lag behind their U.S. counterparts by about a decade in terms of cultural acceptance of DSM, according to Evan Mills, a scientist at Lawrence Berkeley Laboratory. One reason is that the power companies typically run DSM on the sidelines rather than as an integral part of their business. In the Dutch case, the cost of the lighting programs is derived from a tax on electricity rather than from the utilities' own funds. Most European programs are still the result of simple government mandates, and are not set up to be profitable. The giant German utility, RWE, for example, agreed to spend 100 million deutsche marks ($60 million) on DSM over the next three years as part of a bargain with the government in order to pursue its first priority—a new low-grade coal mine to fuel the utility's power plants.[33]

Developing countries, too, are beginning to pursue improved efficiency. In Thailand, where double-digit power growth is nearly bursting the seams of the energy infrastructure, the national utility will soon begin a $190-million five-year program that includes the purchase of efficient lights, appliances, and motors. Brazil, China, and Mexico are among the other nations developing DSM programs. The Lawrence Berkeley Laboratory in California estimates that efficiency could cut the growth of power use in developing countries by 25 percent over the next 30 years, freeing up billions of dollars otherwise needed to build power plants. Brazil alone could reduce the projected growth in electricity use in 2010 by 42 percent, estimates Howard Geller of the American Council for an Energy-Efficient Economy. And the transitional economies of Eastern Europe and the former Soviet Union could probably meet all growth in electric needs through 2010 with today's generating capacity just by improving their dismally low levels of electricity productivity.[34]

That utility efficiency programs can have major effects is no longer in question. Despite the formative stages of many of their programs, U.S. utilities already anticipate electricity sales being 4 percent less in 2000 than previously projected, and 6 percent less in 2010. The Netherlands expects to cut power use by 2.5 percent by the end of the decade through its lighting programs alone. The most aggressive U.S. utilities, though, are planning to reduce sales by more than 6 percent by 2000, with DSM satisfying half their projected growth in power demand. And the largest privately owned U.S. power company, Pacific Gas & Electric (PG&E), aims to meet 75 percent of its "growth" via efficiency. As a result of DSM and other programs, California has held per capita power use to the 1979 level in 1992—while it rose 19 percent in the rest of the United States. (See Figure 4–4.) If all utilities achieved

Thousand Kilowatt-hours

Figure 4-4. Per Capita Electricity Use, California and Rest of United States, 1960–92

just half their growth through efficiency, projected U.S. electricity use in 2010 could be cut 19 percent, according to Eric Hirst of Oak Ridge National Laboratory.[35]

Although most are cost-effective in their own right, demand-side management programs also have multiplier effects. Since DSM has created a multibillion-dollar market in more efficient technologies, it has encouraged manufacturers to invest in more-efficient light bulbs and super-insulating windows while also creating a whole new industry of "energy service companies." Some utilities have gone even further, banding together to provide incentives for manufacturers to produce more-efficient electricity-consuming products. In one such innovative effort, 24 U.S. utilities established a $30-million prize for an efficient refrigerator competition. The winning entry—manufactured by Whirlpool—slashes electricity use by more than 30 percent compared with commercial models of an equivalent size.[36]

DSM programs are off to a strong start in some areas (mainly in North America), but they have a long way to go to realize their potential. Perhaps the most important challenge is to persuade more governments to do what some already are doing: require utilities to adopt full integrated resource planning that considers environmental costs as well as direct investments, and provide strong financial incentives for utilities to invest in efficiency. In developing countries, a top priority is to change the practices of the World Bank and the regional development banks, which have traditionally been hostile to efficiency. (See Chapter 9.) Until recently, their lending for new power plants outstripped end-use efficiency investments by about 100 to 1. Several loans now in the banks' pipelines do include funding for efficiency, however.[37]

THE DISTRIBUTED UTILITY

The traditional utility model—and the structure of today's industry—is based on the assumption that large central stations are the most economical way to provide power to customers. The advent of more decentralized power plants, along with the option of investing in improved energy efficiency, has already turned this conventional wisdom into myth. The old model may be obliterated entirely in the decade ahead by even smaller, more modular generating technologies, such as fuel cells mounted in basements and rooftop solar systems that allow residential customers to generate their own power and sell excess supplies to other users through the grid.

The move to a "distributed" power system that relies on a broad mix of large and small generating plants could dramatically improve efficiency and lower the environmental burden of today's electric power systems. It would also reduce the need to build and upgrade transmission and distribution lines, avoiding some of the electromagnetic radiation that some scientists believe may be threatening human health. A typical company with 50 power plants connected to its system today could see the figure reach 5,000 or even 50,000 by 2010. The change would be similar to that of a corporation that went from three mainframe computers in 1980 to 30,000 personal computers in 1994, requiring major changes in the way the system is operated.[38]

One of the most revolutionary new technologies is the fuel cell, which produces electricity without the electromagnetic generators that produce virtually all power today. First identified by scientists in the early nineteenth century, fuel cells are electrochemical devices that consist of an electrolyte and two electrodes that generate power by combining hydrogen and oxygen ions. The technology's big boost came in the sixties, when space scientists began looking for a small, self-contained power system and wound up investing billions of dollars in the development of fuel cells that were successfully used on spacecraft.[39]

The fuel cell has three major advantages over conventional power generators: It is relatively efficient, converting between 40 and 70 percent of the energy potential of a fuel such as methane or hydrogen into electricity. It produces less air pollution than a conventional generator due to its lack of combustion and greater efficiency, and virtually no noise. And it is highly modular, with limited economies of scale.[40]

Already, Tokyo Electric Power and Southern California Gas have built fuel cells that are between 200 kilowatts and 11,000 kilowatts (11 megawatts) in capacity that provide power and heat in hospitals, hotels, office buildings, and other commercial facilities. Although these systems are at least 500 times smaller than conventional power stations, the eventual market for fuel cells is likely to demand even tinier ones—perhaps as small as 5–10 kilowatts. A decade or two from now, most new buildings could have natural-gas-powered fuel cells that would not only generate electricity but also replace today's furnace, water heater, and central air conditioner.[41]

Another new generating technology—the photovoltaic (PV) solar cell—shows equally strong potential for decentralization. As a solid-state, mass-produced panel made out of common elements and with no moving parts, a photovoltaic system can be deployed on almost any scale. One of the most exciting applications is to install solar cells on individual rooftops. This has already become popular in remote areas that do not have access to grid electricity—from poor countries like the Dominican Republic to rich nations such as Norway, which already has 50,000 PV-powered country homes. Meanwhile, over the past decade, several dozen grid-integrated photovoltaic buildings have been built, demonstrating the potential of this technology.[42]

A "distributed" power system relies on a broad mix of large and small generating plants.

Government efforts to bring solar-electric buildings into the home market have accelerated in the early nineties. Germany's Thousand Roofs program was recently upgraded to 2,500 roofs, while Switzerland has focused on integrating PVs into the facades of commercial buildings. Also, a Japanese manufacturer has designed an experimental "solar tile" that might become a common roofing material, and a Swiss company has undertaken a similar project. In Germany, a major producer of architectural glass is developing a semitransparent "curtain wall" that will provide filtered light as well as electricity to buildings. With the world market growing at a rate of 15 percent annually, and with more than 30 companies now manufacturing solar cells worldwide, these systems are expected to become cost-effective shortly after 2000.[43]

Utilities are also thinking about strategically integrating solar cells at points in the transmission system where the company cannot handle additional electricity demand without expensive new equipment. In 1993, PG&E of California installed a 500-kilowatt PV plant at its Kerman substation in the San Joaquin Valley. The system avoids the expensive upgrades for the substation and transmission lines that would otherwise be needed, while increasing the reliability of PG&E's system. Indeed, PG&E engineers have estimated the value of electricity at the Kerman station at two to three times the value of centrally generated electricity. In the United States, a coalition of more than 60 utilities plans to install 50 megawatts of solar cells during the next six years—much of it "distributed."[44]

A utility that builds small power plants in a customer's own facility avoids at least some of the distribution cost.

It may be possible to rely on "distributed" storage as well, addressing one of the weakest features of today's power systems—the high cost of storing electricity. Scientists are working on a device called a flywheel; the centrifugal motion of this spinning object contains energy that can be extracted by attaching it to a generator (in effect, a mechanical battery). Although the concept has been around since the nineteenth century, the flywheel only became practical with the development of strong, light-weight composite materials that can be spun in a vacuum at up to 200,000 revolutions per minute, with the potential to store and release energy at an efficiency of more than 90 percent. Scientists at the Lawrence Livermore Laboratory are working to develop, within the next decade, a mass-produced device half the size of a clothes washer that would sit in the basement of a single-family home, storing cheap electricity at night (or solar energy during the day) and releasing it to the grid when demand—and prices—are high.[45]

Such technologies will ultimately require modifying the economic conventions used by utilities. When a utility sells power to residential consumers, roughly a third of the cost stems from transmitting and distributing the power—including occasional upgrades. Most utilities recognize only one "avoided-cost" price and do not consider the location of generators or customers. Yet a utility that builds small power plants in a customer's own facility avoids at least some of the distribution cost. In other words, a utility that purchases power for 5¢ per kilowatt-hour from a remote coal-fired power plant should in theory be willing to buy it from a customer's rooftop solar system for up to 8¢ if that power is used locally. The German government in effect recognized this principle in a 1991 law that requires utilities to buy power from household-scale systems at 90 percent of the retail price.[46]

The same principle should apply to demand-side management, since it allows a utility to defer investments not only in power plants but in transmission and distribution as well. U.S. utilities alone are spending some $11 billion each year on building and upgrading transmission and distribution—one third more than they spend on new power generation. (See Figure 4–5.) Assessing and allocating these costs more

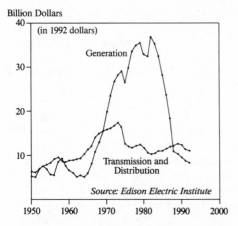

Billion Dollars

(in 1992 dollars)

Generation

Transmission and Distribution

Source: Edison Electric Institute

1950　1960　1970　1980　1990　2000

Figure 4-5. U.S. Investor-owned Utility Expenditures for Generation and for Transmission and Distribution, 1950–92

accurately could yield large savings—not only in building power plants but in upgrading the transformers, switches, and wires that make up the transmission system.[47]

Engineers are accustomed to a mix of baseload plants that operate nearly all the time, with intermediate and peaking plants that are turned on and off to match changes in demand. But the output of solar systems varies according to the weather and time of day, while fuel cells turn on and off with the customer's use of hot water, requiring new modes of operation. Distributed, intermittent generators, backed by "peaking" turbines or hydroelectric plants to adjust for minor load swings, can supply up to 30 percent of a typical utility's demand for less than the cost of new centralized generating and transmission equipment. Increasing the "distributed" share to 50 percent would raise costs by only 10 percent.[48]

Distributed generating sources, some of them intermittent, nonetheless will require changes in the way utility systems are operated. Fortunately, the technology is being developed to put an electronic chip into every fuel cell, flywheel, refrigerator, and air conditioner, allow-

ing the grid to operate as a single "smart" system. Such controls can avoid overloading lines and can be used to turn off distributed generators when crews are repairing wires. Moreover, new electronic metering systems that allow "real time" electricity pricing will be available soon. Using a computer chip that is connected to each home's television cable, the Entergy Corporation is able to "manage" power demand in one Little Rock, Arkansas, neighborhood by controlling the use of major appliances—and dramatically cutting peak demand.[49]

Carl Weinberg, the former research director for PG&E who helped develop the concept of distributed generation, observes: "Operating modes for utility systems are likely to evolve along a path similar to that taken by computer networks, telephone switching, and many other large systems. . . . The networks of future utilities will manage many sources, many consumers, and continuous re-evaluation of delivery priorities. All customers and producers will be able to communicate freely through this system to signal changed priorities and costs." If deployed properly, distributed generation and storage may increase power reliability as well as reducing costs. They offer particular opportunities for developing countries that are plagued by unreliable or incomplete central grids.[50]

COMMODITY OR SERVICE?

Today's utility industry, shaped by economies of scale and efforts to make electricity widely available, has become an anachronism, incapable of taking full advantage of the potential to provide power efficiently and in a more environmentally sound manner. Slowly but unmistakably, the old model is beginning to crack. From its ruin, a broad array of potentially far-reaching experiments are emerging.

Although it is too early to develop a complete strategy for restructuring the power industry, some principles are becoming clear. The keys: a competitive market for power generation; an open-access transmission system; incentives for reliance on a diverse array of power supplies, taking into account the environmental differences between various sources; and development of a service-rather than commodity-oriented local distribution system that is committed to demand-side management. If these principles are followed, a low-cost, ecologically sustainable power system can begin to take shape.

The transition will not be easy. Utilities have long provided comfortable prosperity for those who control them, and are often used to achieve "social" goals. German utilities, for example, are compelled by law to purchase German coal at several times the world price—and even greater environmental cost—to protect the jobs of coal miners, a deal broadly supported by politicians despite the heavy cost to consumers. In Quebec, a costly series of hydro dams is subsidized through the provincial utility, while in France, a massive nuclear industry was created virtually from scratch through government subsidy in the seventies and eighties. Once such industries are in place—and support thousands of jobs—pulling the plug on them is no easy political feat. The stakes are high, and the existing structure well entrenched—supported by government agencies and powerful economic interests. And yet, in order to meet today's economic and environmental imperatives, a restructuring of the industry cannot be avoided.[51]

Much of the early discussion of utility reform has revolved around ways to make the power generation side of the industry more competitive. Over the past decade, independent power production has gone from being viewed as a risky and unreliable experiment to being broadly accepted as a more rational way to organize the industry. Experiences in California, Denmark, and elsewhere have demonstrated the potential of independent companies to provide cost-effective electricity that is derived from relatively innovative and environmentally benign technologies. Recently, the transformation has accelerated in the United States with the passage of a 1992 law that allows a broader range of companies to enter the independent power market, and that ends utilities' monopoly of interstate transmission lines, permitting wholesale buyers and sellers to use an intervening utility's lines.[52]

As the independent power market in the United States and the United Kingdom mushrooms, the big question is how far the commodity approach should be allowed to go. At the extreme, some large industrial users of electricity are clamoring for permission to purchase power directly from independents, using the local utility's lines for transmission, a concept known as "retail wheeling." Although this is not permitted by most governments at the moment, the current spread between the 10–15¢ per kilowatt-hour cost of power from some utility-owned nuclear plants and the roughly 4¢ per kilowatt-hour cost of wholesale power from new combined-cycle plants owned by independents is putting enormous strains on U.S. power systems. Utilities are threatened with the loss of some of their biggest customers, which would raise prices for others, creating a potential "death spiral." In Great Britain, where retail wheeling is being introduced, most of the benefits have gone to large industrial users of electricity.[53]

Such trends have led many U.S. utilities to increasingly desperate cost-cutting in order to bring their electricity prices down. While there is undoubtedly a lot of fat to be trimmed in most companies, these efforts could easily go too far. The possible adverse consequences include slashed investments in demand-side management, distributed generation, and other "energy service" programs that could greatly benefit electricity consumers. Furthermore, a focus on low-cost bulk electricity at the retail level would mainly help large customers with the most bargaining power—at the expense of small customers, including not only rich and poor residential consumers but even the small industries that provide most new jobs. And for utilities themselves, this could be a risky course. With their cumbersome bureaucracies and expensive portfolios of coal and nuclear power plants—many of which will cost huge sums to decommission—few utilities will be able to compete with independents anytime soon.[54]

Fortunately for the utilities, an alternative vision of their future is beginning to emerge: that of diversified electricity service company, committed to providing a growing array of cost-effective energy services for their customers. Here, the focus would be not on achieving the lowest electricity prices but rather on providing services at the least cost. (Greater efficiency, even at the expense of slightly higher prices, can mean lower bills.) A strong and well-managed distribution utility would meet the needs of large and small consumers by bargaining for wholesale power and providing investment capital for demand-side management and the construction of distributed generation and storage devices.

Slowly but surely, a number of utilities are coming around to this new model. In the United States, many have stopped building new plants, and at least one—Pacific Gas & Electric—says that it plans to build no more. Meanwhile, some of the most ambitious transformations have come from small, municipally owned utilities—generally located in forward-looking cities such as Ashland, Oregon; Saarbrucken, Germany; and Sacramento, California. Because they are not governed by a separate regulatory system, these utilities have been able to respond quickly to customers' demands for change.[55]

California's Sacramento Municipal Utility District (SMUD), which serves a population of less than a million, has attracted worldwide attention since 1989 when the concerns of local citizens led to the closing of its only large power plant—the 900-megawatt Rancho Seco nuclear reactor—and to the subsequent hiring of a new general manager, S. David Freeman, the maverick former director of the Tennessee Valley Authority. While temporarily relying on wholesale power from distant suppliers, SMUD is becoming a service-oriented distribution utility. Among its innovations: aggressive DSM programs that include replacing 42,000 refrigerators and planting 500,000 shade trees, purchasing power from four industrial cogeneration plants, investing in a 50-megawatt wind farm, installing solar-electric systems on customers' rooftops, and developing electric cars.[56]

Some large industrial users of electricity are clamoring for permission to purchase power directly from independents.

The SMUD experience demonstrates the potential synergies between a creative, customer-focused local distribution utility and an open, competitive wholesale power market. SMUD does not have to confront the conflicts of being a vertically integrated utility company. Nor, since it is publicly owned, does it have to deal with the legalistic, adversarial relationships between most U.S. utilities and their regulators. And because it serves a single urban area, it is better positioned to respond to the needs of customers. In addition, SMUD has taken advantage of the lower distribution costs inherent in modular technologies, and has considered the environmental benefits of renewable resources that do not depend on the burning of fossil fuels.

Similar innovations are being tried by a few investor-owned utilities, though the process is more complex, requiring an overhaul in the way electric utilities are regulated. In the United States, for example, electricity prices are generally determined on a cost-of-service basis, and "profits" are earned as a percentage of capital investment, which is traditionally concentrated in power plant construction. This system builds in a bias toward selling more electricity—regardless of whether it is being effectively used—and provides little incentive for utilities to improve the efficiency of their own operations, let alone their customers' equipment. Most regulators even allow fuel price increases to be automatically passed to customers. Although these formulas have been in place a long time, many regulators, utility executives, and environmental advocates believe that they need to be revised.[57]

To create a service-focused utility industry, current regulatory formulas will need to be scrapped in favor of a system that rewards utilities based not on how much capital they spend but on their ability to provide cost-effective and environmentally clean energy services to their customers—similar to the way U.S. phone companies are regulated. The government will have to set the rules for this new system, but once regulations are in place, there will be less need for intervention, and a less adversarial relationship between utilities and regulators.[58]

Under this model, distribution utilities would retain a critical "gatekeeping" role, periodically producing integrated resource plans that identify the right mix of investments, including those in demand-side efficiency and a range of distributed generation, storage, and distribution projects, while purchasing their wholesale power from independent suppliers. To ensure that environmental values are included in such a system, utilities and their regulators will need to agree on mechanisms to encourage a diverse array of generating technologies while accounting for the environmental differences among them. If this is not done, some parts of the world could be headed for an unbalanced electricity future based almost entirely on natural gas, while neglecting renewable energy sources that have higher capital costs but much lower fuel and environmental costs. It is therefore essential that regulators establish a system that counts not just initial investment costs but future environmental ones as well, along with other risk factors.[59]

Three mechanisms have been proposed to address these issues: environmental costing, set-asides, and "green pricing." Massachusetts, Nevada, and New York are among the states experimenting with environmental costing. When new generating options are being evaluated there, the cost of pollution is counted against particular projects, which gives renewables a boost. Meanwhile, California and the United Kingdom have adopted simple set-asides for renewables, in which a minimum share (10–20 percent) of the market for new power is reserved for "nonfossil" generating technologies. A third approach being tested by a few utilities, including SMUD, is to sell renewably generated electricity at a slightly higher "green" price to consumers who volunteer, allowing them to subsidize development of technologies such as solar cells. All three show promise for their ability to encourage a diverse and environmentally sustainable mix of generating sources.[60]

Given the advantages of a competitive commodity market in wholesale power, coupled to an efficient energy services market at the retail level, the argument for an end to vertically integrated utility monopolies has become overwhelming. These two sides of the power business are already evolving in opposite directions, and efforts to hold them together or even to reconcile the diverging incentives of the two markets would be costly for everyone—particularly for small consumers and the environment.

The telecommunications industry may provide a model for restructuring the power industry. Though most countries relied until recently on single telephone monopolies, those are now being broken up, and local phone systems are being connected to a growing array of long-distance carriers, satellite networks, and cellular systems. In the near future, computer networks and cable television systems will be integrated into this mix, creating a vibrant, competitive industry and melding the once-separate businesses of phone and television into one giant telecommunications market. While electric power systems will never be as versatile as telecommunications—electricity cannot safely be piped through the air—the power industry's transformation is likely to have broad similarities, driven in part by the same digital technologies.

If it follows the telecommunications model, the electric power industry will be vertically separated—with a competitive commodity market in wholesale electricity connected to service-focused distribution utilities through a "common carrier" transmission system. Most existing power plants would at some point be sold to independent power producers, while many high-cost nuclear plants would be written off as tax losses, with regulators deciding how their excessive costs—now estimated at $25–30 billion a year in the United States—are to be shared between the utility and its consumers. Disposing of those "stranded assets" will keep many lawyers and bankers busy for years.[61]

One of the intriguing aspects of this model is that it might open up new opportunities for utilities, including entering the telecommunications business itself. Some have suggested that power companies could find it cost-effective to wire their customers with fiber optic cable that would provide everything from electricity load management to 1,000-channel cable television and computer services. It is also likely that some creative partnerships will be forged between electric utilities and various phone and cable companies. Although much of the recent excitement has revolved around the wholesale end of the power business—in particular the rapid improvements in combined-cycle plants—the biggest growth markets in the next decade may turn out to be within the distribution system itself.[62]

The service model might open up new opportunities for utilities, including entering the telecommunications business.

Of course, no single model is likely to work equally well everywhere, and new approaches will have to be adapted to local economic and social conditions. (Outside the United States, the old systems are more firmly entrenched, and monopolies more closely guarded.) Developing countries face particular challenges in trying to provide electricity services for rapidly growing economies while maintaining the reliability and financial health of their power systems. This will require extensive infrastructure investment; even so, the newer models, if adapted properly, may be more effective than the central utility approach—providing incentives for efficiency in power supply as well as in energy services. Moreover, distributed utilities may provide more-reliable service in areas now plagued by frequent power outages. So far, developing countries have made promising strides in purchasing power from private generators, yet no country or foreign aid institution has seriously addressed the critical need to develop an institutional framework for improving energy efficiency and decentralizing the power system.

For the world as a whole, the shift to a competitive market for wholesale power, linked to a service-oriented distribution system, offers many advantages. The long-run results are likely to include less-expensive and more-reliable electricity, much more efficient use of energy, and a dramatic reduction in the environmental problems caused by today's utilities. As David Freeman says, "We're at a point in our history where the electric utility industry can start wearing a white hat. We can be the organization that brings cleaner air to our children and economic vitality to our cities."[63]

5

Reinventing Transport

Marcia D. Lowe

Progress in transport has been marked through the ages by inventions, and nothing has had greater impact than the automobile. After the more modest improvements made possible by horse-drawn wagons, trains, and bicycles, cars represented an unprecedented leap in human mobility. As driving enabled people to log more and more kilometers, steady increases in travel became the benchmark of progress.

In the past several decades, however, relentless growth in car travel has begun to challenge traditional notions of what constitutes an advance in transport. In industrial countries, it is worth asking whether the steadily increasing mobility conferred by cars is still improving people's access to destinations. Or is it merely that people have to travel farther and farther to get to markets, job sites, and other vital places? In developing countries, auto travel directly benefits only a small elite, while the bulk of the population is no better off.

The fixation on mobility—and the associated seemingly endless increase in kilometers of travel—also exacts a heavy toll. National economies stagger under the burden of acquiring oil to fuel their growing fleets of cars. Billions of hours are wasted each year in highway gridlock, and hundreds of thousands of lives are lost in road accidents. Environmental damage from driving plagues the farthest reaches of the globe—polluting the air in cities, squandering valuable land, and even altering the earth's climate.[1]

In the search for solutions to these mounting transport problems, societies focus on designing new technologies. Engineers seek to slash oil dependence and smog with electric cars. Commuters are promised that traffic congestion will be eliminated by "smart" cars. For all their twenty-first century dazzle, however, these technologies are not innovative enough. They fail to address the fundamental cause of today's problems: our deepening dependence on automobiles. No car, no matter how smart or fuel-efficient, can eliminate land-gobbling sprawl—one of the most devastating consequences of ever-increasing reliance on motor vehicles, and one of its strongest reinforcing factors. For most of humanity, these new technologies are no more affordable (and very likely much less affordable) than conventional cars. Moreover, if the "greening" of car travel merely perpetuates the traditional pursuit of mobility, even car owners will not have better access to the places and things they need.

The greatest challenge for innovations in transport is not just to redesign vehicles. It is to reinvent the very notion of what transport is for. After decades of seeking to travel ever faster and farther, future progress will require a more sophisticated approach: one that aims to give people access to the places and things they need in the least destructive manner possible. With this change in priorities, societies would have less extraneous travel, would place a higher value on less destructive modes—walking, bicycling, car pools, buses, and trains—and, perhaps more important, would rethink urban land use patterns to break our dependence on automobiles.

Going Nowhere Fast

It is no wonder cars are so popular; speed is almost universally irresistible to human beings. After decades of explosive growth, new roads in congested urban areas often fill to capacity as soon as they open. Even in countries where car fleets are no longer growing quickly, car travel continues to increase. Just how long can this continue? In light of a seemingly limitless increase in kilometers of travel, it seems fitting to ask where all this mobility is taking us.

In 1950 there was one car for every 46 people worldwide. The global car fleet grew rapidly as people in industrial countries acquired cars during the fifties and sixties, quadrupling the total number of automobiles by the early seventies. Once this vast rich-country market began to near saturation, world growth slowed, despite high growth rates in developing countries and Eastern Europe. Auto ownership expanded from one automobile for every 18 people in 1970 to the current level of one car for every 12.[2]

Although the growth in number of automobiles slowed in industrial countries, the increase in kilometers driven did not.

Between 1970 and 1990, kilometers of auto travel in Japan increased 10 percent faster than car registrations did. In the United States, the most car-saturated country in the world (and with a land mass much greater than Japan's), car registrations rose 60 percent in the past two decades while passenger-kilometers nearly tripled.[3]

Governments and individuals seem to have shared a nearly universal willingness to give up rail and other travel options in favor of unprecedented mobility in a car. But was the exchange really as beneficial as generally presumed? After decades of increased movement, the distinction between mobility and access is becoming difficult to ignore. In many cases, greater mobility has failed to give people better access to their destinations.

Experience in the United States shows how as the automobile evolved from a luxury to a virtual necessity, it contributed less and less to improvements in access. In the early decades of this century, U.S. car owners doubtless could meet their basic travel needs more quickly and easily than before they acquired motor vehicles. But as early as 1950 the automobile was no longer a luxury in the United States; the country already had about as many cars per capita as the United Kingdom would have in 1980. Relentless expansion of U.S. car travel, despite approaching saturation in car ownership, raised the number of kilometers the average person drove from some 3,800 in 1950 to more than 9,700 in 1990.[4]

U.S. household travel data disprove common assumptions about the extent to which people choose to drive more. Especially during the seventies and eighties, Americans drove ever farther to accomplish the same everyday tasks. U.S. households drove on average 16 percent more kilometers to get to work in 1990 than they did in 1969, 88 percent more kilometers to do shopping, and 137 percent more kilometers for other personal matters (business travel, trips to school and church, doctor visits, and other such errands). Social and recreational trips, the only category in which car travel did not increase, declined by 1 percent. (See Table 5–1).[5]

Steady growth in driving reflects not only longer trips but also a greater number of them: the annual number of car trips each household took rose from fewer than 1,400 in 1969 to more than 1,700 in 1990. Some of this increase reflects changes in household status—such as a growing number of trips to jobs by women working outside the home. But much of it reflects a vicious cycle in which auto dependence leads to inefficient land use, which results in increased driving.[6]

Overwhelmingly, urban and suburban growth in recent decades has turned away from the compact, diverse communities of the pre-automobile past and toward low-density sprawl. Today's land use patterns are increasingly inconvenient with regard to transport, requiring not only longer journeys—often exclusively by car—but also a separate trip for each errand. The impact of sprawled

land use can be seen in the number of trips people take. For the United States, the current average is 4.6 automobile trips per household each day. Households in sprawled single-family tracts in Orlando, Florida, by contrast, reportedly take 13 car trips a day.[7]

Car-oriented sprawl is costly in more ways than one. The toll includes loss of valuable farmland and the disappearance of plants and animals as forests and other natural areas shrink. Providing sewerage and other services to far-flung subdivisions costs local governments much more per household. And cities' economic health declines as people and jobs move to outer suburbs, taking much-needed investment and large chunks of the tax base with them. This drain places the severest hardship on city dwellers who cannot afford to live in the suburbs and, lacking cars, cannot reach suburban workplaces.

Perhaps the most pervasive costs of sprawl are also the least quantifiable. Homogeneous, low-density development has been linked to worsening social isolation and a loss of neighborliness. In many areas, children grow up unable to play with friends unless an adult drives them somewhere. In the

Table 5–1. United States: Annual Kilometers of Car Travel for Selected Purposes, 1969 and 1990

Purpose	1969	1990	Change 1969–90
	(vehicle-kilometers per household)		(percent)
Home to work	6,730	7,808	16
Shopping	1,495	2,804	88
Personal business	2,043	4,850	137
Social and recreation	6,587	6,533	−1
All purposes[1]	19,989	24,296	22

[1]Includes other purposes not listed here.
SOURCE: United States Federal Highway Administration, *1990 Nationwide Personal Transportation Survey: Summary of Travel Trends* (Washington, D.C.: 1992).

United States, one observer notes that the necessity of owning a car at age 16 forces suburban teenagers to work at minimum-wage jobs to make car payments—instead of studying, meeting friends, and, in essence, growing up.[8]

The disintegration of community and civic life figures high in the price society has paid for its dogged pursuit of mobility. John Whitelegg, Head of the Department of Geography at Lancaster University in England, notes that "making contact with places and people [is] the central organizing feature of human activity." But, he notes, our approach to transport has achieved "the opposite of well-being: a privatised, socially inert world where neighborhood counts for little and status depends on the frequency and speed of movement over longer distances."[9]

In many cases, daily tasks that a suburban family once could accomplish with a single car now require a fleet. During the past two decades, the percentage of households with three or more vehicles quadrupled, to 20 percent. The *Washington Post* recently reported that in the suburbs around the U.S. capital, a fourth of all households now own three or more cars. One resident told of having to buy one car per family member: "Once I would have said having four cars is a luxury. But this is just bread-and-butter transportation for us."[10]

International comparisons suggest that mobility by car saves less time than is generally assumed. Whitelegg cites evidence that people spend roughly the same amount of time on travel regardless of how far they go. "The significance of this empirical work," he says, "is that if we save time we use it to consume more distance." A comparison of travel data in the former Soviet Union and the United States bears this out. In the late eighties, average U.S. work commuting times were about the same as in what was then the Soviet Union—although most

Soviet citizens walked and took public transit, while Americans zoomed in their cars to more distant places outside their own communities.[11]

Time savings made possible by the speed of car travel seem particularly illusory in light of the traffic jams that paralyze the world's largest cities. People in the largest U.S. urban areas annually waste 1–2 billion hours stuck in traffic. The average speed driving into Paris during the morning rush is less than 10 kilometers per hour. In Jakarta, a bank official recently complained that he might as well stay at the office until 7:00 p.m., since he would not reach home any sooner if he left at 5:30.[12]

In addition to the stress and inconvenience of traffic jams, highway congestion now costs countries billions of dollars yearly in delayed delivery of goods and lost employee time. The U.S. General Accounting Office reports that productivity losses from highway congestion cost the country an estimated $100 billion a year. A study by the Bangkok Metropolitan Administration estimated that Thailand's work force loses on average 44 working days in traffic each year, costing several percentage points in the growth of the gross national product.[13]

Perhaps most important, to the extent that cars have improved access or saved time, the benefits are not equally allocated among or within societies. In 1990, there were more than 150 people for every car in Nigeria and more than 360 per car in India. That same year the United States had nearly one automobile for every two people.[14]

In fact, increased mobility for some has actively worsened access for others. The private automobiles of a privileged few hinder and endanger the vast majority of people in Third World cities, who walk, ride bicycles, and squeeze into crowded buses. In North America and Australia, streets are so geared to cars that it is often prohibitively dangerous to walk, ride a bicycle, or wait for a bus or trolley. Literally adding insult to injury, societies scorn people who must live without a car, or who choose to. John Pucher, an associate professor of urban planning at Rutgers University, writes that carless people in the United States not only suffer inferior access, but also are viewed by some Americans as "outright deviants."[15]

Perhaps cars have not taken us as far as we thought. Contributing less and less to improvements in access, the extraordinary levels of travel made possible through driving at best have reached a point of diminishing returns—and for the many who cannot afford an automobile, decidedly negative returns. In many ways, mobility has not delivered on its promise.

TECHNOLOGY TO THE RESCUE?

A number of automotive technologies now under development could help mitigate some of the negative consequences of passenger transport. Largely because of recent regulatory clampdowns on auto-related air pollution in several countries, some engineers and entrepreneurs are embarking on a completely different avenue of vehicle design that may virtually eliminate oil use and air emissions. Others are trying to reduce traffic congestion with electronic communications they hope will make vehicles and the highways they travel on "smarter."

The latest vehicle prototypes go much further than the past two decades' worth of breakthroughs in fuel economy and pollution controls. They also move beyond the many shortcomings of so-called alternative fuels. Blends of methanol or ethanol with gasoline, for in-

stance, have only a marginal effect on air quality since they reduce some pollutants while increasing others. And many of these fuels—even vegetable-based ones such as ethanol derived from corn—do not compare well if evaluated over the entire fuel cycle, including how they are extracted (or grown), refined, distributed, and stored. Even natural gas, which has some clear pollution benefits and is used increasingly in vehicles in several countries, offers only minor reductions in greenhouse gas emissions.[16]

Some auto makers have begun to focus on electric vehicles, which have unquestionable advantages. Using an electric motor instead of an internal combustion engine—substituting electricity for gasoline—eliminates tailpipe emissions. Although recharging the battery with electricity generated from coal entails some emissions (including a greater amount of sulfur dioxide, which contributes to acid rain), large power plants tend to be more efficient and less polluting than small internal combustion engines. In addition, wherever electric vehicles can draw electricity generated by wind, hydro, or solar power, they generate no emissions at all.

Although the benefit of eliminating tail-pipe emissions has long been recognized, several major problems held back electric vehicles. Researchers have yet to come up with a battery without materials that are either toxic, nonrecyclable, or potentially flammable. The main roadblock to wide use of electric vehicles, however, has been that each kilogram of a conventional battery has only one one-hundredth the stored energy of a kilogram of gasoline—which means that keeping the battery to a practical size limits the range an electric vehicle can go before recharging. One way to overcome this is to make the vehicle extremely efficient with what little energy the battery can store.[17]

Several new designs from Switzerland employ ultra lightweight materials and improved aerodynamics to achieve the needed boost in efficiency. Called light electric vehicles, these include small, two-passenger city cars that weigh less than half as much as steel-bodied cars. With top speeds of 50–100 kilometers (30–60 miles) per hour, most designs have a range of 50–80 kilometers, although one prototype can go up to 400 kilometers. The composite plastic bodies consist of a polymer resin poured over glass or stiff carbon fibers—creating a material stronger than steel but only one fourth as dense. The composites are exceptionally able to absorb or deflect the shock of a collision. If meticulously designed, the lightweight vehicles may be safer than much heavier steel-bodied cars.[18]

Ultra-light vehicles may expand the scope of hydrogen, the "ultimate" clean combustible fuel.

Engineers have also devised a hybrid vehicle that combines the advantages of an electric motor with the superior energy density of chemical fuel. This expands the electric vehicle's range. It also overcomes one of the internal combustion engine's major disadvantages: a good portion of the energy is wasted by constant changes in engine speed. By using the gasoline engine not to drive the wheels directly but rather to generate electricity for a small motor that powers the wheels, the hybrid maximizes the gasoline engine's efficiency by allowing it to operate at a steady speed even when the car speeds up or slows down. A regular-sized four-passenger hybrid can go as far as a normal car without stopping to refuel.[19]

In 1993, Volvo announced the devel-opment of an aluminum-bodied hybrid that can do city driving while running only on the battery, or, travelling longer distances at higher speeds, use 5.2 litres of fuel per 100 kilometers (a fuel economy of 45 miles per gallon). According to Amory Lovins of the Rocky Mountain Institute, hybrids can be made still more efficient if built with the same lightweight composites used in light electric vehicles. Lovins has designed and computer-tested an ultralight hybrid that could be built mostly with off-the-shelf technologies. Designed with superior aerodynamics and highly efficient tires, it would weigh less than half as much as a conventional car and could have a fuel economy of roughly 1.6 liters per 100 kilometers (150 miles per gallon). In a more advanced hybrid, a fuel cell would generate the needed electricity directly through a chemical reaction, a conversion process that is twice as efficient as that of an internal combustion engine. Fuel cells could potentially increase fuel economy to 1 liter per 100 kilometers (250 miles per gallon).[20]

Even emission-free cars may emerge soon. Today, electric cars in Switzerland and in Sacramento, California, can be recharged at solar-powered charging stations. And ultra-light vehicles may expand the scope of hydrogen, the "ultimate" clean combustible fuel. Hydrogen requires relatively large, heavy storage tanks—and the more energy-efficient the car, the fewer tanks it needs. Hydrogen combustion emits only water vapor and small quantities of nitrogen oxides, and electric vehicles powered by hydrogen fuel cells would emit just water vapor. In Germany, Japan, and the United States, engineers are working to improve technologies that produce hydrogen from water (using electric current provided by photovoltaic cells). Solar hydrogen probably will not be commercialized soon, but some experts say the cost several years from now may drop to $2–3.50

for the equivalent of a gallon of gasoline, less than many drivers in Europe now pay.[21]

Unfortunately, even if this new generation of "green" cars were successfully mass-marketed (overcoming the daunting task of radically restructuring the auto manufacturing process), the total effect on transport would still only be "greenish." Left unaddressed are many other severe liabilities of automobile-centered transport, including traffic congestion and sprawl. Higher fuel economy may even encourage people to use their cars more, since driving will then be less expensive—a phenomenon witnessed in the surging gasoline sales that consistently follow dips in oil prices. In addition, most experts agree that the first lightweight composites will be more expensive than today's automobiles, although prices are expected eventually to come down to current levels. Even if prices do drop, the new vehicles will merely leave intact the inherent inequity of automobile-based transport systems—since the majority of the world's people cannot afford even a conventional car.[22]

Another set of automotive innovations, computerized "smart" vehicles and highways, aims specifically to reduce traffic congestion. Intelligent Vehicle/ Highway Systems (IVHS), the term used in the United States (in Europe, called Road Transport Telematics), consists of a broad array of electronic communications technologies designed to do several things: smoothly regulate the flow of traffic; give drivers up-to-the-moment information on road conditions; take over some actual driving tasks, such as steering or braking to avoid collisions; assess road tolls without hindering traffic; help track and guide commercial fleets (including freight trucks) and emergency vehicles; and make buses and car pools more efficient and convenient to use.[23]

IVHS research and development has emphasized making traffic flow more smoothly by establishing direct, simultaneous communication between drivers, traffic control centers, and the roads themselves. In one scenario, drivers punch in their destination on a dashboard control panel while sensors along the road detect vehicles' locations and speeds. All this information is then processed by a central station where computers rebroadcast signals to drivers, advising them which route to take.

According to plans for later stages of IVHS, fully automated cars would drive themselves along the highway, guided by wires embedded in the road. Once drivers keyed in their destination, they could just sit back and enjoy the ride. Eventually, convoys of smart cars would travel bumper to bumper at high speeds. By eliminating the distance between vehicles, proponents claim, these caravans would free up extra space on the highway. The explicit goal of IVHS is an effective doubling of infrastructure capacity, although some experts have suggested that the systems, if fully implemented, could yield a three- to seven-fold expansion.[24]

IVHS has been promoted as an advance over the traditional anticongestion approach of building more roads. Acknowledging the proven futility of trying to provide enough additional road space to keep up with steady increases in traffic, IVHS seeks to accommodate projected traffic growth by using existing highway capacity as efficiently as possible. Proponents claim not only that IVHS will prevent traffic jams, but that by making vehicles flow more smoothly, it will reduce fuel use, smog, and accidents.[25]

Critics have challenged the assumptions behind each of these claims. Principally, the emphasis on expanding capacity just repeats the faulty logic behind the discredited roadbuilding strategies of the past—by failing to address the underlying problem of relentless growth in driving. One of the hard-learned lessons from previous roadbuilding experience is that as roads become freer of congestion, more drivers switch over to them to take advantage of the improved conditions—including some who would otherwise take public transport. Unless IVHS specifically emphasizes alternatives to ever greater car use, even the "smartest" technologies will not be able to keep up with expanding traffic volume.[26]

Moreover, even if IVHS technologies had limitless potential to keep highway traffic flowing, what would happen when all those cars reached their exits? Electronic traffic management is designed to include some urban streets, but smart technologies certainly will not blanket any road network. A severalfold increase in traffic would quickly inundate any urban area, jamming roads of merely average intelligence. A ride on a smart highway may well be only a brief spurt in a trip that starts and ends mired in gridlock.[27]

The additional driving that IVHS seeks to accommodate would naturally require expanded parking capacity—yet cities have neither the funds nor the physical space to meet even a doubling of demand. In downtown Washington, D.C., for example, providing twice the parking area currently in lots and garages would take nearly 9 million square meters of extra space, at a cost of up to $6 billion.[28]

As for fuel use and emissions, any benefit gained through reducing start-and-stop driving could easily be wiped out by a combination of a net increase in driving and higher traffic speeds. Washington-based IVHS America, an official federal advisory committee to the U.S. Department of Transportation and the main organization promoting the technologies in the United States, acknowledges in a 1992 report, "there is some

concern that any congestion relief may merely encourage more travel, thus negating most if not all gains in reduced energy consumption and pollution." And according to U.S. Federal Highway Administration studies, fuel efficiency peaks at speeds of 56–64 kilometers per hour. Travelling at 113 kilometers per hour reduces a car's fuel economy by more than a third compared with 64 kilometers.[29]

At any rate, IVHS claims of fuel efficiency pale in comparison to the potential of other transport modes. For example, simulation models and field tests of the "smart" traffic management and driver information systems report fuel savings of 3–13 percent. Much greater savings could be achieved by replacing a share of car travel with existing public transport: Measured in kilojoules per passenger-kilometer under average U.S. commuting conditions, private cars use three to seven times the energy of various bus and rail options. Bicycling and walking are even more energy-efficient —requiring only food calories as fuel— and are completely nonpolluting.[30]

Even the claim of enhanced highway safety—one of the chief selling points of IVHS—is far from a guarantee. In fact, smart cars and highways could actually pose added safety risks. For example, drivers could be distracted by all the messages flashing at them. A more ominous prospect for the more advanced, automated systems (in which a single computer network could be "driving" all the smart cars on a given road) is that a system-wide computer "crash" could lead to literal collisions of an unprecedented scale. Rather than trying to pack additional cars onto highways, it may well be safer to encourage more people to ride public transport: accident rates for buses and trains are already many times lower than the most ambitious IVHS goals for private automobiles. While experts estimate that smart cars and highways could save 1,000 lives by the year 2000, the same target could be met at far lower cost if less than 1 percent of annual passenger car travel were switched to buses.[31]

Despite uncertainty that the new technologies can deliver on their many promises, the industrial world is hotly pursuing IVHS. The European Community's $450-million DRIVE program (Dedicated Road Infrastructure for Vehicle Safety in Europe) and the $800-million PROMETHEUS (Programme for European Traffic with Highest Efficiency and Safety) are developing driver navigation systems, cellular broadcasting beacons, communications centers, and other basic IVHS infrastructure. In Japan, 74 cities have electronic traffic management systems that gather data through road-based sensors, and car makers have on the market some 200,-000 vehicles equipped with onboard navigation equipment.[32]

With the help of rapidly escalating government funding, the IVHS industry in the United States hopes to overtake its more advanced counterparts in Japan and Europe. Federal support for IVHS projects has ballooned from $4 million in fiscal year 1990 to $218 million in 1993. Over the next two decades, U.S. federal, state, and local governments are expected to spend some $40 billion on IVHS.[33]

Although the current focus of IVHS on expanding highway capacity threatens to exacerbate dependence on automobiles, a change in priorities could make a world of difference in the systems' overall impact. Many IVHS programs include new technologies for public transport and ride-sharing—but these efforts may be largely wasted since the vast bulk of IVHS is aimed at accommodating more single-occupant car traffic. Ensuring that the new systems' net impact is positive would require reorienting current schemes that merely include alternatives to solo driving, and actually giving these other modes priority over private cars.

For example, IVHS traffic management technology includes lights at intersections that change in response to the volume of passing vehicles. If programmed to give priority to buses, car pools, and van pools, the signals would provide these alternatives with an important time-saving advantage over cars with solo drivers. In the Netherlands, the ability to preempt traffic signals has helped buses stay on schedule, and the resulting gains in efficiency have reduced operating costs. Officials report that having priority in traffic has led to impressive increases in ridership.[34]

IVHS claims of fuel efficiency pale in comparison to the potential of other transport modes.

Several other IVHS technologies can increase the appeal of public transport and ride-sharing. For example, a credit card–sized "smart" fare card makes bus trips more convenient; the card automatically records all fares, and the passenger receives a periodic billing statement in the mail. User-friendly, electronic information systems can help people sort out confusing bus routes and schedules, and computerized bus services can even allow passengers to "order" a flexible bus route to supplement regular, fixed schedules. Up-to-the-moment information services can match car and van pools with potential riders.[35]

IVHS technology could also be used to turn simple road tolls into automatic "congestion pricing" schemes—charging a higher fee in congested areas and peak periods to reflect each driver's contribution to congestion. Smart technologies could "read" a car's electronic identification tag without even requiring it to slow down, and a central computer system would process and store the information from each car. Drivers' privacy could be protected by recording tolls the way an electronic metro card system registers fares—showing only how far a car has travelled, not where it has been.[36]

Clifford Winston, a senior fellow at the Brookings Institution in Washington, D.C., believes that congestion pricing would help push U.S. drivers out of their cars. He cites a 1983 study in San Francisco that found that congestion tolls would cause a 10- to 20-percent rise in the share of downtown commuters using public transit. A successful congestion pricing scheme has been used in Singapore since 1975, and officials are either planning or considering such systems in Chile, France, Norway, the United Kingdom, the United States, and several other countries.[37]

Although congestion pricing is widely considered an efficient way to discourage discretionary driving, some researchers warn that it may only briefly reduce traffic volume—until latent demand for car travel fills the roads again. And when U.K. researchers recently developed a computer model to evaluate the potential impacts of road pricing on car travel, they found mixed results: while some drivers shifted to public transport, others merely drove longer distances to avoid tolls. John Whitelegg of Lancaster University has noted that in the long run, road pricing schemes could encourage car-dependent sprawl, as people shift their activities away from congested areas (where public transport is most available) to new locations where it is more difficult to provide alternatives to driving.[38]

Like the latest innovations in electric vehicles, IVHS could, if applied sensibly, address some of today's most pressing transport problems. But using any of these promising technologies merely to allow continued, out-of-control growth in driving would be an extremely costly mistake. As Deborah Gordon, Transportation Program Director of the Cambridge, Massachusetts–based Union of Concerned Scientists, notes, "The primary reason for [transportation and environmental problems] is that there are too many cars on the road with only one person in them driving too many miles." No strategy can be fully effective unless it makes driving not only less destructive but less necessary in the first place.[39]

GREENER TRAVEL, BETTER ACCESS

Fortunately, people can have better access to the places and things they need in daily life without perpetuating excessive car travel. Although improvements to car technology grab all the public attention, innovations in bicycles and public transport technologies are important too, because they help attract people to travel modes that are already more environmentally sound than driving—addressing additional problems that the "greenest" or "smartest" car cannot solve. In the end, though, we have to reform land use. Adopting more-benign travel modes will both require and reinforce fundamental changes in the way activities are laid across the landscape; the shorter the distance, the likelier a person can accomplish something without having to get in a car.

With little official recognition, human-powered two- and three-wheelers move many more people worldwide than automobiles do. Bicycles have changed little since they were invented more than a century ago, yet they far outperform motor vehicles in the efficient use of resources, including land. The advantages of recent, relatively minor improvements are mainly to enhance the appeal of bicycling for people who would otherwise drive, and to make life easier and safer for those who already depend on bicycles as their primary means of transport.

All-terrain or "mountain" bikes, and several variations on them, are quickly gaining popularity. In less than two decades, they have come to account for nearly two thirds of U.S. bicycle sales and more than half the sales in Europe. Despite their name, these sturdy bicycles are most often used as road vehicles. With upright handlebars, a comfortable seat, and fat, stable tires, mountain bikes and hybrid "city" bikes have proved to be more practical for everyday travel than the lightweight touring bicycles that were popular in industrial countries in the seventies and eighties. The number of people in the United States who commute to work regularly by bicycle has roughly tripled over the past 10 years, to an estimated 3 million. In more than 300 bike patrols nationwide, mountain bikes have even become an effective tool for police.[40]

In large cities in much of Asia, needed improvements on the traditional cycle rickshaw have great potential to improve transport by making a well-used option more efficient and easier on the operator. Cycle rickshaws account for up to 20 percent of urban passenger trips in India and Pakistan and 43 percent of total passenger-kilometers in Bangladesh. The vehicles are universally found to be poorly designed, however. Among other problems, they are difficult to steer and brake, and they have inadequate gears for carrying heavy loads.[41]

Despite disappointing results from several efforts to improve cycle rickshaws since the early seventies, Robert Gallagher, formerly of the Bangladesh University of Engineering and Technology, is optimistic: "Rickshaw improvement is perfectly possible, and undoubtedly there will be more attempts in the future." He notes that previous foreign-led failures underscore the need to operate within local rickshaw industries, ensuring that all necessary parts can be produced locally. In addition, if foreign support is involved, it should continue until the new technology has been adequately disseminated.[42]

Another important category of technological progress is public transport. Companies in California will soon be able to lease a 14-passenger electric van for employee van pools. Made of lightweight composites, the van has a solar roof to power its air conditioner. A New York firm is developing a hybrid bus that generates electricity from compressed natural gas, and the Santa Barbara Metropolitan Transit District in California recently began operating service with a converted electric bus. Changing diesel buses over to electricity could improve urban air quality considerably, especially in developing countries, where buses are less efficient and operate on highly polluting fuel. A Vancouver company has even developed a hydrogen fuel cell bus, which is currently being demonstrated in several cities.[43]

Companies in California will soon be able to lease a 14-passenger electric van for employee van pools.

Outside the developing world, the greater challenge is to make public transit more popular rather than cleaner. Rail is making something of a comeback after a steady decline, thanks largely to new innovations. One of these is light rail—not a high-tech breakthrough but rather a sleek reincarnation of the popular trolleys of the past. Since light rail can run along regular streets, highway medians, utility corridors, or even back alleys, it can be built without expensive tunneling and elevated structures. Building a light rail system can cost as little as one fifth as much as a surface metro and one tenth as much as an underground subway—but, as with these other rail technologies, sufficient ridership is necessary to contain operating costs.[44]

Light rail helps avoid many of the space problems associated with auto dependence. Assuming vehicle occupancies typical of commuting hours, a four-car light rail train in U.S. conditions would carry as many people at 40 kilometers per hour as a line of cars taking up 20 city blocks. Because of light rail's versatility, construction of new lines can be made compatible with existing streets and structures; road projects, by contrast, are notorious for obliterating whole residential neighborhoods and commercial districts.[45]

Another distinct advantage is light rail's ability to lure people out of their cars. According to a recent survey in Sacramento, 77 percent of light rail riders had the option to drive instead. In San Diego, light rail service is further credited with helping boost ridership on buses in the same corridors by showing die-hard drivers how pleasant and convenient public transport can be. Lines that run on an exclusive right-of-way separate from other vehicles offer an especially strong incentive: riders can go 22 kilometers in 15 minutes on Manila's light rail line, for instance, while the same segment by highway can take two hours.[46]

Train travel also owes its recent resurgence in popularity to high-speed rail. There are two types of high-speed rail technology. Magnetic levitation trains, which "fly" on a magnetic cushion a few centimeters above a guideway, are still under development. The world's first commercial maglev service, planned for 23 kilometers in Florida, is not expected to open until 1996. Wide application of maglev technology in the foreseeable future seems unlikely because of high cost, unresolved safety concerns, and the possibility of electromagnetic fields threatening the health of passengers.[47]

Conventional high-speed rail, by contrast, has been in successful operation since Japan introduced its bullet trains in 1964. Using steel wheels on steel tracks, just like normal trains, conventional high-speed trains gain speed through aerodynamic rail cars, smoother tracks, and more powerful electric motors. Steel-wheel high-speed rail lines link several large cities in Europe and Japan, and new systems are planned in Australia, Canada, the United States, and several developing countries, including Brazil, China, and Pakistan.[48]

High-speed rail is considered ideal for distances of 200–1,000 kilometers, providing an attractive alternative to driving or flying for such trips. Since the overwhelming majority of car travel consists of much shorter trips, however, high-speed rail does not have the potential to displace driving that intercity rail, commuter rail, light rail, and subways have. High-speed rail should therefore be seen as a complement to urban and intercity rail systems rather than as a showpiece that deflects government investment from such services.[49]

All these innovations in transport technology will be for naught unless they are combined with strategies to reduce the need for travel. The most direct way to decrease travel demand is to minimize the distance between activities. More practical urban and suburban land use patterns can help shorten many car trips and eliminate others by making public transit, cycling, and walking viable alternatives to driving. Land development that reinforces automobile dependence occurs every day—yet this same growth, if carefully directed, could help reduce reliance on cars. Although significant land use change is a slow process, several revisions to zoning ordinances and other regulations could facilitate immediate changes. And, contrary to popular belief, there is much potential to improve land use in already built-up areas.

A vast amount of unnecessary movement can be attributed to zoning laws that segregate different activities. The worst example of separating homes from businesses and other sites is undoubtedly found in the United States. But other countries, including those in much of the developing world, have also adopted this approach as they acquired an automobile orientation. Homogeneous zoning creates distances too long for walking and bicycling, an especially inappropriate result in Asia, Latin America, and Africa, where most people do not own cars. Additional excess travel results from the tendency to spread people and activities over a large space instead of encouraging compact development.[50]

A rich diversity of activities combined with medium- and high-density land use not only reduces the need for travel, it also helps make extensive public transport feasible. The powerful impact of land use on transport is demonstrated by a study in the San Francisco Bay area that compared five sections with varying characteristics. At one end of the scale was a community with 293 households per residential hectare (where most blocks have at least one market, restaurant, or laundry) and close access to buses, trolleys, cable cars, ferries, the metro, and commuter trains. At the other end was a typical suburban bedroom community with 10 households per residential hectare, businesses mainly confined to a commercial strip, and a single feeder bus route to a metro station and nearby counties. Each house-

hold in the latter community logged on average some 50,350 kilometers of car travel annually—more than four times as much as their counterparts in the other community.[51]

This reinforces the conclusions of studies of other major cities in Canada, the United Kingdom, and the United States: doubling residential or population density corresponds with a 20–30 percent reduction in annual kilometers of auto travel per person. Moreover, the San Francisco study calculated that the combination of increased density and extensive public transport service had a surprising "leverage" effect on travel reductions. Because of shorter distances and increased convenience, each kilometer that city residents travelled on public transport in effect substituted for more than 8 kilometers of driving by residents of the suburban community.[52]

Doubling residential or population density corresponds with a 20–30 percent reduction in annual kilometers of auto travel per person.

Obviously, it is easiest to integrate activities and achieve adequate density in an area of new growth. But it is not too late to incorporate these features into already-developed areas. Both cases require reforms of local land use controls. Properties frequently change ownership, for example, but opportunities for conversion are lost because conventional zoning codes lock sites into the same uses again and again. If zoning and other land use regulations are modified to encourge rather than prohibit diversity, communities are more likely to evolve with the natural mingling of activities that comes from neighborhood stores, home-based businesses, and apartments above storefronts.[53]

Mixing like this can be promoted in numerous ways. Several U.K. cities are encouraging the conversion of vacant space in commercial buildings into apartments under the slogan "living over the shop." In the United States, most municipalities prohibit apartments or group dwellings in single-family zones, so removing such restrictions can increase density in residential neighborhoods. Existing houses could be converted to accommodate at least one if not more extra units; "empty-nesters" and others living in large homes could benefit from rental income, and there would be more housing available. According to a 1985 estimate, 12–18 million U.S. homes had surplus space that could have been converted to such use.[54]

Both higher density and a greater variety of activities can be achieved by filling in the vacant and underused space in an existing urban area. Many cities have surprisingly large amounts of land idled or with abandoned structures—space that could be used for buildings or green space. Local governments themselves hold old school buildings, tax-foreclosed properties, and other parcels not currently in use. Often it takes major changes to tax laws and other regulations to encourage full use of such sites.[55]

Changes in zoning also can encourage more effective use of land wasted on parking lots. In the United States, minimum parking quotas frequently require developers to devote more land to parking than to a building's actual floor area. Cities in much of the world have adopted U.S.-style lavish parking requirements, even if the lots lie empty most of the time; the result is vast spaces that discourage pedestrians and unnecessarily lengthen distances between buildings.[56]

A formidable obstacle to reforming current regulations is public opposition—although many popular objections are based on misconceptions about what constitutes compact, mixed land use. In their 1984 book *Beyond the Neighborhood Unit*, Tridib Banerjee and William C. Baer describe a study done in Los Angeles among upper-, middle-, and low-income families that found that people want more diversity in their residential neighborhoods than zoning codes allow. All groups showed a strong desire to have markets, drugstores, libraries, and post offices near their homes. When asked to rank desirable characteristics in a neighborhood, the respondents rated sociability first and friendliness second. Convenience was placed above property safety, and quiet was ranked last.[57]

In the United States, economic factors and shrinking household size have recently spurred greater demand for higher-density living arrangements. Still, the vehemence of public reaction against high urban density inspired numerous studies during the seventies and eighties. Two conclusions from this research challenge the popular myths. First, density itself does not yield crowded conditions. An important distinction must be made between density (number of people per hectare) and crowding (number per household or room). This is reinforced by researchers' findings that overcrowding often is higher in rural settings than in metropolitan areas.[58]

Second, density itself is not a determining factor in many of the ominous conditions people relate to it (crime, squalor, or harsh physical surroundings). These things are instead determined by sociological and socioeconomic forces—which are much stronger and more difficult to define. In a study of the world's 100 largest cities, Hong Kong—the world's densest—had a lower crime rate than all but 11 others. Paris, with 235 people per hectare in the central city, had a much lower rate of crime than Detroit (with only 11 people per hectare in the central city) or Los Angeles (with 29). Comparisons within individual countries also failed to show clear links between crime and urban density.[59]

Also contrary to popular belief, high density does not create a hostile physical environment. Design rather than degree of density determines whether a given space contains the elements people naturally find appealing, such as trees, peace and quiet, comfortable places for walking or sitting, interesting views, and—perhaps most important—other people. A distinct advantage of compact urban neighborhoods is the relatively little space devoted to cars. Low-density development, by contrast, requires such vast expanses of road and parking space that creating a pleasant, convivial atmosphere is all but impossible.

WHAT PRICE MOBILITY?

Underlying many of the world's transport problems is a defining paradox: while societies have greatly overvalued mobility, they have underestimated its true costs. Excessive auto travel has taken an enormous toll on economies, the environment, social equity, and even human relationships. Today the damage is nearly impossible to ignore. Yet transport policies that disregard the full costs of driving continue to skew important decisions—from a government's spending priorities to a commuter's choice of where to live. In fact, the single most important goal for policy reform may be to ensure that a more accurate tally is used to guide all public and private decisions in the future.

The first task is to expose the many hidden costs of the current fixation on mobility. A number of recent studies have focused on driving, attempting to separate "internal" costs (those incor-porated in the price the driver pays) from "external" ones—those paid for by others, or even whole societies. Even though many people cannot afford cars, the hidden costs of driving render it extremely underpriced. Drivers in the United States are surprised to learn that gasoline taxes, road tolls, and other user fees typically cover less than two thirds of the cost of road construction and maintenance; the rest comes from local property taxes and other general sources. Additional expenses not covered by U.S. drivers include highway patrols, traffic management, and police and fire services—totalling an estimated $68 billion annually—and the real cost of "free" parking, which may be more than $85 billion per year.[60]

Much more difficult to quantify are the costs that drivers impose on society as a result of traffic congestion, road accidents, air and water pollution, dependence on imported oil, solid waste, loss of cropland and natural habitat, and climate change. Numerous studies suggest that these external social costs amount to roughly 2.5 percent of the gross domestic product for several countries in Europe. According to a recent study by the Brussels-based European Federation for Transport and Environment (T&E), the unpaid social costs per passenger-kilometer of driving far exceed those not only for train travel but for air travel as well. Car travel in Germany involved nearly twice the external costs of air travel and seven times that of trains; results were roughly similar in 10 other countries. (See Table 5-2.)[61]

Obviously, if these social costs and the external market costs of infrastructure and services are considered, drivers pay only a fraction of the total expense of driving. Although most analysts agree that making drivers fully pay their way would be politically difficult, to say the least, many maintain that the price of car

Table 5–2. Germany: Estimated External Costs of Passenger Transport, 1993

Category	Train	Aircraft	Automobile
	(ECUs per thousand passenger kilometers)[1]		
Air pollution	0.9	7.3	14.6
Carbon dioxide	2.2	9.2	4.5
Noise	0.3	1.6	1.2
Accidents	1.4	0.2	13.7
Total[2]	4.7	18.3	34.0

[1]European Currency Units: as of October 15, 1993, 1 ECU equalled $1.17.   [2]Columns may not add to totals due to rounding.
SOURCE: Per Kågeson, *Getting The Prices Right: A European Scheme for Making Transport Pay its True Costs* (Stockholm: European Federation for Transport and Environment, 1993).

travel should more closely reflect the consequences.

The most common and probably most effective way to achieve this is by increasing taxes on fuel; since filling the gas tank is the expense motorists feel most directly, a gas tax is a strong determinant of how much people drive. And since fuel is relatively inexpensive compared with the fixed costs of owning an automobile (including insurance, registration fees, and financing), low gas taxes contribute to the illusion that using a car is virtually free at the margin. The T&E report found that gas taxes in the countries studied varied from 0.24–0.55 ECUs per liter (roughly $1–2.50 per gallon, compared with the current U.S. federal gas tax of 18¢ a gallon), and concluded that setting a more realistic price for driving during the next 10 years would require gas taxes at least double Europe's current levels.[62]

Another priority is to internalize the costs of parking. Free parking at the workplace, for instance, seems an almost irrestible lure for solo commuting. One effective policy cure is to require employers who provide free parking to offer the alternative of a travel allowance worth the value of the parking space. People who choose the less expensive options of walking, riding bicycles, or using public transport can pocket most of the allotted amount. The County of Los Angeles has successfully used this strategy to reduce its employees' incentive to drive. In 1990, when the county substituted travel allowances for free parking, so many employees chose not to drive to work that demand for parking dropped 40 percent.[63]

As mentioned earlier, congestion pricing is one way to shift some of the costs of traffic jams to the drivers responsible for them. At the very least, the charges would need to reflect the costs of traffic delays. According to a 1990 estimate, each driver in peak traffic in central London cost all the others on the road some 36 pence (about 50¢) per kilometer in wasted time—about four times the actual expense of driving. Ideally, congestion tolls would be set high enough to reflect the society-wide effects of excessive fuel use and emissions. It is also important to implement congestion pricing in the context of broader policies to reduce demand for driving. Otherwise drivers may merely divert to other roads. And, as with gas taxes and other fees, those who can afford the tolls will simply pay more, without driving any less.[64]

The idea of increasing the price of driving raises concerns that the higher fees would disproportionately hurt the poor and the middle class. Although it is important to offset any unfair effects on individual drivers—for example, through refunds for low-income drivers or cuts in income taxes—it is unclear whether higher driving fees actually would be regressive. Recent research suggests that the external costs of driving currently amount to a huge regressive subsidy, accruing disproportionately to wealthy households and paid in part by people who can afford relatively little driving, or none at all.[65]

A crucial determinant of whether gas taxes, parking fees, congestion tolls, and other charges are fair—and effective—is how the revenues are invested. Typically, funds raised through road user fees are put back into maintaining and expanding road facilities, a cycle that reinforces the dominant role of private cars. Since the point is to reduce demand for driving, raising the price of car travel without providing adequate alternatives is self-defeating. It is often important, therefore, to invest a substantial portion of the revenues in public transport, ride-sharing, and ways to facilitate cycling and walking—which would not only give drivers other choices, but also benefit lower-income people by providing more affordable options. And in countries where nondriving modes are already well developed, offering a portion of the revenues as a general tax cut may help make higher fuel taxes more politically palatable.

In addition to changing people's individual transport decisions, recognizing the full costs of driving would dramatically alter governments' regulatory goals and transport research priorities. Public policy would be much more aggressive in requiring vehicles to be as "green" as possible. Increased fuel taxes would encourage car manufacturers to improve fuel economy, but it is also necessary to hold the industry to strongly enforced standards of energy efficiency. Tax breaks and other positive financial incentives, along with funding support for research and development, would reduce the companies' risk in pursuing innovative technologies. Governments could also help new vehicles, such as electric cars, compete in the automobile market by waiving the sales tax or offering generous rebates.

A more accurate accounting of costs

would logically shift the emphasis toward reducing demand for driving and improving the alternatives. Accordingly, government funds for major technology undertakings such as IVHS would channel support to projects on public transport, ride-sharing, congestion pricing, emissions monitoring, and information services to save trips. Applications that foster more private vehicle use, including driver navigation systems and the eventual automation of highways, would not receive government funding.[66]

Raising the price of car travel without providing adequate alternatives is self-defeating.

Local policymakers' infrastructure decisions would also change if the hidden costs of new highways were weighed against other options. A model for moving beyond the traditional capacity-expanding approach to transport planning already exists in the U.S. electric utility industry. An analytical tool called integrated resource planning enables utilities to minimize future costs by evaluating not just capacity-increasing strategies (new power plants) but a full range of options (including ways to reduce power demand) in order to satisfy their customers' needs. (See Chapter 4.) Some 30 states now require utilities to use integrated resource planning. If applied with careful attention to otherwise hidden factors such as the external costs of air pollution, this approach can help identify how to meet the need for power at the least societal cost.[67]

In a recent study for the Washington-based International Institute for Energy Conservation, Mia Layne Birk and P. Christopher Zegras propose that governments adopt integrated transport planning patterned after the utilities' approach. Obviously, considerable refining would be required to handle the greater complexity of transport decisions, but if done carefully, the approach could greatly improve governments' decision making. Birk and Zegras suggest that this would help developing countries avoid the industrial world's costly mistakes. All nations, however, would benefit from an evaluation process that no longer prizes mobility above all.[68]

Given this much-needed change in priorities, improved access could replace mobility as the benchmark of future progress in transport. Such a transformation will not happen quickly. But it may be hastened by people's growing sense that the long-standing preoccupation with automobiles has degraded our communities to such a degree—physically and otherwise—that our destinations are no longer places worth reaching. Eventually, societies may come to welcome a transport system in which access, not excess, is the predominant feature.[69]

6

Using Computers for the Environment

John E. Young

Computers were born and raised by the armed forces, and popularized by the consumer economy. But their greatest value may prove to be neither military nor commercial. With the cold war receding, we are confronted by two daunting challenges: a faltering world economy that despite its huge reach and productivity we only poorly understand, and a deteriorating global environment whose vast workings we understand even less. Coming to grips with the great task of the twenty-first century—reconciling hopes for global prosperity with the need for a healthy environment—will require a far more detailed comprehension of both. Given how rapidly ecosystems are now declining, that understanding will have to be pursued far faster than it has been. It is in this pursuit that the computer may find its greatest application.

The machines were first applied to massive mathematical problems for

An expanded version of this chapter appeared as Worldwatch Paper 115, *Global Network: Computers in a Sustainable Society*.

which the military wanted answers, such as explaining the turbulence created by atomic explosions or predicting the flight of artillery shells. They were later put to work on exhaustive civilian tasks involving the management of unwieldy amounts of information: computing the payrolls of large companies or tabulating responses to census questionnaires. For a quarter-century, computers were regarded as exotic machines that could be understood and operated only by geniuses.[1]

But computers have changed, and so have their roles. No longer the exclusive province of a technical priesthood, they are just beginning to fulfill their destined purpose as organizers in an age of information glut. Their value lies in their ability to sort an overwhelming mass of raw industrial, economic, demographic, and scientific data into forms that can be used to solve problems—in other words, to turn information into knowledge. And nowhere is the need for knowledge greater than in the drive to create a sustainable global economy.

The measure of any new technology extends beyond the benefits of applying it, however. The environmental and human costs of producing and using it must also be considered—and the costs of computerizing the globe are substantial. These machines have become a major electricity consumer in industrial countries. And instead of creating "paperless offices," computers have stimulated an ever-growing demand for paper. In addition, computer manufacturing, which has quickly grown into one of the world's largest, most powerful industries, has environmental impacts that have largely gone unrecognized until recently. If these miracle machines are to help us build a sustainable society, each of these problems must be addressed.

A New Technology, A New Industry

One reason the impacts of computers and their production have been little considered is that both the technology and the industry have evolved at an astonishing rate. The first electronic digital computer—the ENIAC, built in 1945—contained more than 17,000 vacuum tubes in a cabinet 3 meters high, 1 meter deep, and 30 meters long. It weighed 27 tons. By today's standards, it was laughably low-powered. Tubes have disappeared, and computers are now built of microprocessors, thumbnail-sized chips of silicon onto which are etched thousands of microscopic transistors. Microchips have allowed computers to evolve from room-sized to note-book- and even palm-sized devices.[2]

Since the early eighties, when personal computers (PCs) began to catch on, rapidly increasing capabilities and plummeting prices have caused an ex-

plosive rise in the number of machines used. The amount of computing power available for a given price has been doubling every two years or less for three decades, making the computer easily available to many individuals and most institutions. There were probably fewer than 2 million computers in the world in 1980, most of them mainframes or somewhat smaller multiuser minicomputers. Now the total is an estimated 148 million, with 135 million of them PCs. Because new machines are orders of magnitude more powerful than old ones, growth in global processing power is even more rapid. Measured in MIPS— million instructions per second, the standard measure of a computer's ability to perform certain basic operations—the total power of the world's computers has risen elevenfold in the last six years. (See Figure 6–1.)[3]

Computers are heavily concentrated in industrial nations. There are 265 machines per 1,000 people in the United States, 57 per 1,000 in Italy, and only 1 per 1,000 in China and India. (See Table 6–1.) The United States—where the microchip and the PC were invented—has almost half the world's computers but only a twentieth of the world's people.

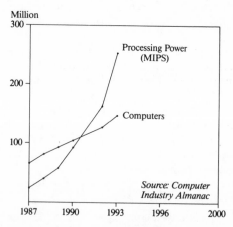

Figure 6-1. **World Computers and Total Processing Power,** 1987–93

Table 6–1. Computers and Computing Power, Selected Countries, 1993

Country	Computers	MIPS[1]
	(per thousand population)	
United States	265	516
Australia	175	278
Canada	162	264
Norway	153	256
United Kingdom	134	217
Switzerland	133	220
Ireland	126	208
Singapore	116	178
France	111	180
Germany	104	141
Japan	84	139
Italy	57	98
Greece	47	71
South Korea	33	49
Hungary	24	34
Mexico	13	19
South Africa	9	13
Brazil	6	10
Former Soviet Union	4	6
Indonesia	2	2
India	1	1
China	1	1
World Average	27	47

[1]Million instructions per second.
SOURCE: Karen Petska Juliussen and Egil Juliussen, *6th Annual Computer Industry Almanac* (Lake Tahoe, Nev.: Computer Industry Almanac, Inc., 1993); population figures from Population Reference Bureau, *1993 World Population Data Sheet* (Washington, D.C.: 1993).

The computer industry—including software—is now worth $360 billion per year worldwide. The greatest profits are earned by software producers and the makers of the most sophisticated microprocessors, whose value lies largely in the basic programs etched within them. Once the realm of fat profit margins, computer manufacturing has become highly competitive. Many companies are finding it difficult to stay in business and are scrambling for opportunities to cut costs. In search of cheap labor, the industry has expanded into developing countries from its original centers in the United States, Japan, and a few other wealthy nations. Several newly industrialized countries of the Pacific Rim—including Malaysia, Singapore, South Korea, and Taiwan—have become major producers of parts and equipment. A few other developing countries, such as Brazil and India, have substantial, carefully protected computer industries that produce primarily for domestic markets.[4]

The computer sector is distinctively different from traditional heavy industries because small size and high value make its products cheap to ship long distances, and because widespread use of computers for international communications has given manufacturers the flexibility to locate production and assembly operations far from design and management teams. In the structure of its labor force, however, the computer business resembles many older industries. Indeed, the divisions between production workers and the supervisors and designers are probably greater in the computer industry. Small numbers of well-paid executives and technicians oversee much larger numbers of manual laborers, who do the repetitive, less-skilled work of making and assembling components. In the United States, 70 percent of the managers and 60 percent of the professionals are white males. In contrast, only 17 percent of the semiskilled production workers are white males, while 63 percent are women, half of them non-white.[5]

Electronics industry workers are also rarely unionized. In the United States, union members account for more than 50 percent of steel and automobile workers, 32 percent of those in aircraft manufacturing, 21 percent in petrochemicals, and 17 percent of the country's workers overall but less than 3 percent of electronics workers. Although lack of a union is probably not a problem for the industry's well-paid professional workers—the best of whom often benefit from bidding wars for their services—it leaves production workers without an organized voice. This situation, combined with widespread international subcontracting, sometimes to illegal sweatshops or to unregulated, household-based pieceworkers, makes it difficult to be sure that any computer was produced under decent labor conditions.[6]

The highly competitive, mobile nature of the computer industry has given it enormous power over national governments, communities, and its own workers. This leverage, and a reputation as the industry of the future, has led some communities and countries to bid for facilities with generous tax breaks and concessions on environmental standards. New Mexico, for example, has offered Intel $2 billion in industrial revenue bond financing, $300 million in tax abatement, the right to pump 6 million gallons a day of scarce desert water, and permits for 350 tons per year of volatile air pollution as incentives for siting a new chip-production facility within the state.[7]

In its overall impacts on the world, the computer is a technological loose cannon—a device with huge capacity to change ecological and economic health for better or worse, built by an industry that does not yet have its own house in order. Above all, it epitomizes the speed with which the conditions of human activity are changing: even as the computer industry begins to come to grips with its own social and environmental failures, it is already having profound impacts on the way many other human activities are conducted.

MONITORING AND MODELING

We understand remarkably little about the planet's ecosystems or the millions of species that make them up. All too often, species vanish forever before they are even identified and named, let alone studied; Harvard biologist Edward O. Wilson has estimated that some 50,000 species are condemned to extinction each year in the tropical rain forests alone, mostly as a result of human activity. Our understanding of the full impacts of this activity—whether in mining, farming, ranching, or manufacturing—is also minimal.[8]

Computers offer enormous power for collecting, storing, and organizing information that can help us understand the global environment and our effect on it. Systems for performing these tasks fall into two main categories: monitoring and modeling. Monitoring systems are used to study and keep track of industrial and natural processes—such as the release of carbon dioxide or the rise in atmospheric temperature. Modeling systems are used to test theories about complex processes, such as the causal relationship between carbon dioxide and atmospheric temperature—thereby allowing the simulation of experiments too dangerous or time-consuming to conduct in the "real world."

One form of industrial monitoring the United States has made rapid progress in is pollution tracking—the identification of what toxic substances are being released where, in what quantities, and by whom. In 1986, U.S. environmentalists fought for and saw enacted the Emergency Planning and Right-to-Know Act, which created the world's most comprehensive national pollution data base—the Toxics Release Inventory (TRI). This includes data on toxic chemicals released to land, air, and water from about 24,000 U.S. industrial facilities each year. When first proposed, the TRI was assailed by the Reagan administration and many industry groups as a paperwork nightmare. Indeed, with traditional methods of recordkeeping, the system would likely have become just that. Using computers, however, the U.S. Environmental Protection Agency (EPA) and the state pollution agencies, which collect the original forms, have been able to manage efficiently the large amount of data—82,000 reporting forms for 1991, the most recent year for which data are available—and to issue national and state reports on a timely basis.[9]

Public release of TRI data has proved to be a powerful stimulus for industrial cleanup. Grassroots groups around the country have used TRI figures to produce more than 150 reports on local, regional, and national toxic pollution problems. Such studies have repeatedly exposed chronic polluters, putting pressure on them to reform. Their preparation has been made easier by the fact that the inventory is not only compiled in computerized form but can be—and often is—retrieved by outside groups using their own PCs. The Toxics Release Inventory was the first federal data base that Congress said must be released to the public in a computer-readable format.[10]

The TRI is a limited system that does not cover some important industries and toxic chemicals. Nonetheless, the concept has attracted attention beyond U.S. borders. Agenda 21, the blueprint on sustainable development agreed to at the 1992 Earth Summit in Rio de Janeiro, recognized the concept of community right-to-know and recommended that all nations establish TRI-style pollution tracking systems. Canada's National Pollutant Release Inventory system—largely modeled on the TRI—was expected to begin collecting data in late 1993. And the European Community is considering a toxics reporting system for its 12 member nations.[11]

In addition to providing effective means of storing and retrieving data, computers can speed and simplify their collection. Somewhat surprisingly at a time when satellites systematically scan every inch of the globe, a wide variety of environmentally important data are in short supply. A 1992 World Resources Institute study stated "there is no global monitoring of . . . transboundary [air] pollution flows . . . ultraviolet radiation, acid precipitation . . . desertification or land degradation, land conversion, deforestation . . . ocean productivity, biodiversity, [or] species destruction." New computerized monitoring techniques provide a means of quickly closing some of these data gaps. Technicians can now make rapid assessments of air quality at industrial facilities or hazardous-waste cleanup sites by using handheld sampling devices that store readings directly on disks. Computers connected to networks of fixed sampling devices can continuously monitor ambient concentrations of pollutants, automatically delivering reports at regular intervals or when an irregularity is detected.[12]

Monitoring technology can also be used to study biological systems. David Mech of the U.S. Fish and Wildlife Service and his team of field researchers, for example, use computerized animal collars equipped with miniature radio transmitters and sedative darts to study wolf behavior in northern Minnesota, one of the last places in the lower 48 states where this species runs wild. Handheld radio sets allow researchers to track wolf movements and activity states (motion sensors reveal whether an animal's head is up or down) and to control the collars. A researcher who wishes to examine, inoculate, or relocate an animal simply sends a coded radio signal that ejects a sedative dart from the collar into the animal, immobilizing it.[13]

Biologists—and others interested in such findings—can review data on animal populations, migrations, breeding sites, and hunting areas in conjunction with land use information and other data by using geographic information systems (GIS), which both store and organize geographic information and allow it to be quickly displayed in the form of maps. In British Columbia, the Sierra Club of Western Canada is using a GIS to create detailed maps of forest cover on Vancouver Island. The project has revealed that 23 percent of the island's original low-elevation temperate rain forests—an increasingly endangered ecosystem—remains uncut, and that 82 percent of the island's land is currently allocated to logging. The GIS has provided vital information in the fight to extend government protection for old-growth forests on the island beyond the current 3 percent.[14]

The Sierra Club of Western Canada is using a GIS to create detailed maps of forest cover on Vancouver Island.

Beyond monitoring, computer systems serve a far more ambitious and potentially critical function: to model natural and industrial systems. The capacity of the computer to help us bridge the critical gap between information and knowledge is illustrated by the recent history of climate science. Scientists have theorized since 1896 that emissions of carbon from the burning of fossil fuels could warm the global atmosphere. It was not until the early eighties, however—when computers powerful enough to model the complex behavior of the atmosphere became available— that they were able to test their theories. Supercomputers at such centers as the

Geophysical Fluid Dynamics Laboratory in Princeton, New Jersey, and the Goddard Institute of Space Studies in New York have been programmed to simulate the effects of increased greenhouse gas concentrations. In minutes, they perform calculations that would take an unaided scientist a lifetime.[15]

This computer-based modeling of the atmosphere has produced a remarkable consensus among climatologists about the likelihood and potential scope of global warming. Climatologists are also using computers to try to determine from local temperature measurements whether such warming has already begun. The task would be difficult or impossible without computers, since it involves a complex calculation based on thousands of daily readings from around the world that must be adjusted for a variety of complicating factors, including the uneven geographical distribution of monitoring stations and the tendency for urban areas—with their relative lack of trees and abundance of pavement—to yield higher readings.[16]

Computers can also be used to shape responses to the problems they help foresee. For example, a computer model developed for the U.S. Agency for International Development has been used by government planners in Madagascar and the Philippines to predict and graphically present the economic and resource consequences, including levels of carbon dioxide emissions, of various population growth scenarios. Other models have helped environmentalists sketch out realistic plans for reducing carbon emissions through greater energy efficiency and the use of alternatives to fossil fuels, such as wind and solar power. Computers are also helping to design a wide variety of products for reduced environmental impacts; modeling of automobile aerodynamics, for instance, has helped raise the fuel economy of new cars.[17]

On a smaller scale, the computer revolution is changing patterns of personal learning as well as institutional research. Popular programs like SimEarth allow users to simulate the growth and impacts of entire civilizations. EnviroAccount lets people assess their environmental impacts—and track how changes in lifestyle can reduce them. And the Global Lab, an international project of the Boston-based Technical Education Research Center, has helped schoolchildren learn about environmental problems by monitoring them themselves. Students use computers to collect data and examine their results, and to share those results—through computer networks—with children in other countries.[18]

Networking for Sustainable Development

In August 1993, a note typed into a computer at Worldwatch Institute in Washington was sent by electronic mail to a colleague based in Zambia. As it happened, the intended recipient had left Zambia for a visit to England. But instead of awaiting his return, like a conventional letter, the message was automatically relayed to a computer in England. When the recipient replied, he apologized for his "delayed" response. The entire process had taken 44 hours— less than two days—and the cost was negligible.

Experiences like this are common in the world of computer networks. Electronic mail (e-mail) is so fast—a lengthy document can go from London to Sydney in a few hours, or even a few seconds, depending on the system used— that enthusiasts refer to conventional postal service as "snail-mail." E-mail is

cheaper than international phone calls, facsimile machines, or express package services, and allows users to bypass busy signals, unpredictable postal service, and schedule conflicts created by different time zones.

Electronic mail has become a vital tool for those who work on environmental and social issues. Thousands of activists and organizations around the world are now using computer networks to coordinate campaigns and exchange news. Commercial systems, such as CompuServe and America Online, offer environmental information sources and online discussions of such issues. The Internet—the world's largest collection of computer networks—has extensive resources for environmentalists. And specialized systems, such as Poptel/GeoNet and those of the Association for Progressive Communications (APC)—a group of 11 computer networks—make peace, human rights, labor issues, world development, and the environment their primary focus.[19]

Computer networks are still in their adolescence. Many remain difficult to use, reflecting their origins as communications tools for computer scientists. And, like local phone systems at the dawn of the telephone age, many networks today are unable to communicate with each other, either because they are not physically connected or because they are built to different standards. This is changing rapidly, however. The Internet is a fast-growing collection of computer networks that can talk to one another, and it is beginning to resemble the global phone system in its scope. With nearly 1.5 million host systems—large computers on which many users, who may connect to them by telephone, have accounts—it now serves an estimated 11 million people. Thousands of systems, large and small, are adopting Internet standards every month, bringing a multitude of users into the global web. Both the number of host computers and the volume of information flowing through the system are estimated to be doubling every five months.[20]

Greenpeace campaigners use their network to monitor international traffic in hazardous waste.

The Internet was developed in 1969 to connect U.S. computer centers doing defense-related research. By the late eighties it had become an important link for other academic researchers, from English professors to physicists, and gone beyond academia and U.S. borders. Internet connections now reach into more than 50 countries. The resources available—which include the catalogs of the Library of Congress and many U.S. university libraries and specialized data bases on thousands of subjects—are expanding as rapidly as the system itself. At last count, 135 different journals were being published electronically, and Internet users were discussing everything from Shakespeare to population growth through thousands of computer conferences. This new and unique form of communication functions like an electronic bulletin board: participants "post" items, which are then available for others to read when they log in, allowing conversations that are lively, global, and immediate. Dozens of conferences on the Internet deal with environment and development topics.[21]

Internet users can also connect through it to the APC networks, the largest assembly of on-line environmental information and activists. Organized on the model of Econet/Peacenet (its partner network in the United States and the source of the system's common software), APC also includes networks based in Australia, Brazil, Canada, Ecuador, Germany, Nicaragua, Russia, Sweden, the United Kingdom, and Uruguay. The system connects 17,000 activists in 94 countries. And users pay just $3–20 per hour to be a part of the system.[22]

People who use the APC networks can exchange e-mail, and can read and participate in nearly a thousand of the system's own conferences on virtually every topic related to the environment, sustainable development, and peace issues, as well as in thousands more from the Internet and other systems. Though the quality and level of participation in the individual conferences varies greatly, the information can be detailed, global, and breathtakingly up-to-date. On a recent day, for example, a conference on rain forests included a news bulletin from Brazil about the murder, discovered three days earlier, of Yanomami Indians in a remote corner of the Amazon Basin—a story reported two to three days later by U.S. newspapers—and several recent news reports on the struggle of indigenous tribes in Sarawak, Malaysia, for land rights.[23]

APC networks played an important role in enabling citizen participation in the June 1992 U.N. conference in Rio. Preparatory and draft conference documents entered the system starting in late 1990, and final versions were made available at the end of the conference. APC's Brazilian member network, Alternex, set up computer facilities in Rio for users attending the U.N. meeting and the '92 Global Forum, the parallel gathering of nongovernmental organizations (NGOs). This made it easy for NGO representatives to tell their offices about the progress of the meeting, work out lobbying positions, and communicate with the press back home.[24]

The electronic mail service provided by computer networks can help international organizations share information and keep track of their own activities.

Greenpeace campaigners, for instance, use their network to monitor international traffic in hazardous waste, staying in virtually hourly contact about movements of waste by ship, train, and truck. They used the system in 1988 to spread the word about a large toxic waste dump found in the Nigerian village of Koko, and about the waste's effects on the health of local citizens.[25]

By itself, a computer is a valuable device. But there are limits to the amount of information and the variety of programs that can be assembled on even the largest individual machine. Networks put enormous resources and reliable, inexpensive global communications at the fingertips of ordinary citizens. They allow people to sift through large collections of environmental data for the information they need. Econet/Peacenet, APC's U.S. affiliate, makes available a variety of useful data bases, including EPA and other library catalogs, a data base of environmental funding sources, and an extensive collection of information on energy-efficient technologies and policies.

The Right-to-Know Computer Network (RTK Net), operated jointly by two Washington, D.C., nonprofit groups, offers more than 800 users on-line access to the U.S. government's TRI data base on industrial releases of toxic chemicals. Information can be combined with other government environmental data bases—such as Superfund hazardous-waste cleanup sites and pending environmental litigation—and a variety of census data, including the ethnic and economic characteristics of the local population. RTK Net users have produced some particularly compelling studies. For example, Florence Robinson of the North Baton Rouge Environmental Association, a community group, has been using the TRI data and census information to demonstrate that Louisiana's minority communities live with disproportionately high levels of toxic pollution. She has reported her findings in a series of papers and testified on the subject at a U.S. Civil Rights Commission hearing on environmental racism.[26]

RTK Net was created because the federal government was not making TRI data available on-line at low or no cost. The same data are available on a federal system—Toxnet, administered by the National Library of Medicine in Bethesda, Maryland—but for $18–20 per hour, which few community-based activists can afford. The federal system also lacks RTK Net's on-line community of activists, who share tips on how to conduct searches and spiritedly debate a variety of topics, including environmental racism and the health effects of toxics.[27]

For those without access to networks, data bases and other environmental information are available on computer disks. The World Bank, the World Resources Institute, and Worldwatch Institute all now provide some of their data on floppy disks. GreenDisk, a Washington-based "paperless environmental journal," provides on floppy disk the full text of dozens of environmental reports and articles in its six issues per year. And census, transportation, and other data are increasingly available on CD-ROMs—laser disks identical to audio compact disks that can store thousands of pages of text or large amounts of other data.[28]

COMPUTERS AND DEVELOPING COUNTRIES

At first glance, computer technology might seem of little consequence for the more than 3 billion people who live in developing countries. These nations produce few computers themselves, and usually suffer from chronic shortages of foreign exchange for imports. They generally lack computer-literate office workers, programmers, service technicians, and spare parts. Their antiquated, overburdened, sometimes nonexistent telephone and electric power systems can pose substantial obstacles to operating computers and linking them into networks.

Nevertheless, when these problems can be surmounted, the potential benefits of computer use in developing countries are enormous. The machines can be an extraordinary tool for the fight against the two great interconnected problems of Third World development—poverty and environmental degradation. Without computers, residents of developing countries risk becoming even more marginalized within the rapidly evolving world economy. With them, they can communicate with each other and gain broad access to essential information from around the world. Networks can relay the information—protocols for medical treatment, weather reports and crop market figures, potential sources of funding—that health professionals, farmers, development workers, and others need to do their jobs better. They can link those in even the remotest areas to the global information system. Word-processing, spreadsheet, and data-base programs can help people manipulate, manage, and understand the wide variety of information that computers and networks make accessible.

Computers can also be a powerful force for democracy. Boston University professor Sheldon Annis observes that networks are now bringing information and new channels of communication to Latin America's poor. While the poor do not own computers and modems themselves, says Annis, they increasingly belong to organizations that do. And with these and other communications tools, the organizations are helping the poor

participate actively in policy decisions that affect their lives—whereas before they were often ignored by governments and wealthy elites.[29]

Although computers are far less numerous there than in industrial countries, networks already reach into the Third World, Eastern Europe, and the former Soviet Union. A few academic institutions in such countries have Internet connections. In Latin America and the Caribbean, the Organization of American States launched a Hemisphere-Wide Networking Initiative in 1991 to connect academic computer systems throughout the region. Such systems are technically complicated, however, and require costly, high-quality telecommunications lines. As a result, they are not available in most of the Third World. In particular, they are almost nonexistent in sub-Saharan Africa, with the exception of South Africa.[30]

Luckily, alternatives exist. APC networks, for example, reach into dozens of developing countries. The RIO Network—a project of ORSTOM, a French public research institute—has 800 users in France and a dozen tropical developing countries in Africa, the South Pacific, and the Caribbean, with connections to six more countries made in 1993. Third World computers can also gain access to the worldwide web of electronic networks through a grassroots networking program called FidoNet, developed by U.S. computer hobbyists. This is a low-cost method of linking computer bulletin board systems through ordinary phone lines. Its virtue—and its usefulness in developing countries—lies in its ability to overcome the limitations of inadequate phone systems. FidoNet systems automatically contact each other at night, when phone rates are low, to exchange conference postings and electronic mail messages. Regular connections between FidoNet computers and other systems allow users to communicate with virtually anyone with an electronic mail address, with most messages reaching their destination within 24 hours.[31]

FidoNet computers can even operate where no telephone system exists through packet radio sets, small devices with simple antennas. These are attached to a computer much like a modem, and can be used to exchange electronic mail and other data automatically. In areas where the computers are separated by long distances, packet radio sets can transmit messages through low-orbit satellites, which—as they pass overhead—relay the information to other computers. Motorola is developing a system of 77 such satellites that will provide continuous coverage everywhere on earth.[32]

Such technology is being used to get valuable information into the hands of people in remote areas who need it. SatelLife, a Boston-based nonprofit organization, uses low-orbit satellites and electronic mail to distribute medical information in sub-Saharan Africa. The Boston office uses Peacenet to communicate with its African staff and clients who have FidoNet connections. The system's primary users are doctors at African universities, who can receive *New England Journal of Medicine* articles free of charge, as well as other medical information.[33]

As mentioned earlier, however, programs such as these face a variety of obstacles—including a lack of computers in the developing world and the expense of importing new machines. Some manufacturers have created donation programs to get new machines to deserving organizations, but the recipients have usually been educational institutions or NGOs in industrial countries. Another solution is for users in industrial countries, where computers are quickly outmoded, to pass them on to Third World users. While Internet and other high-technology computer networks require powerful machines, some old, outmoded personal computers can run FidoNet programs, providing a communications link that is as fast as a telex at a fraction of the cost.[34]

One of the greatest assets of computers in the Third World is their ability to function without reliable infrastructure—not only telephones, but even reliable electricity. In developing countries, power is often not available—and when it is, it may go on and off unpredictably or vary substantially in frequency or voltage, posing major problems for computers and other sophisticated electronic devices. Such difficulties can be avoided, however, by using battery-powered portable computers or an "uninterruptible power supply," a widely available device that isolates a machine from the outlet power and provides hours—or days, if necessary—of battery power if the main power fails.

Software is often a problem for Third World users. Legitimate copies of basic programs are frequently difficult to obtain, and, if they can be found, are usually very expensive. As a result, most software used in developing countries is pirated—illegally copied—rather than purchased from the firm that produced it. Instruction manuals are rarely available, and even if the software maker offers local support services (rare in developing countries), they are not usually available to those who cannot prove they acquired the software legitimately. Additional problems stem from the fact that most software is written in the United States for the U.S. market—and the rest is created mainly in other wealthy, industrial countries for local use. The lack of software in local languages can reinforce existing inequities, limiting the pool of computer users to those fluent in the country's colonial language or another foreign language.[35]

If planners or funders of Third World

computer systems fail to take software needs into account, their investments can be rendered useless. Expensive, sophisticated computers donated by aid organizations or development institutions often sit idle because of inappropriate, undocumented, or improperly installed software—or because no one in the local organization or area has the expertise to solve even basic problems.[36]

A variety of programs can help give people in developing countries access to the growing web of computerized information. Particularly important are efforts to funnel both new and used computers, properly equipped for local conditions, into the Third World. Programs also need to provide sufficient access to repairs, spare parts, and technical advice—and assistance with the development of networks. Donations of software, in which the license of old software is actually transferred from the original user to the new group, would be a great help. And there is a pressing need to develop basic computer education programs in Third World schools and universities to build pools of programmers versed in both software and local languages and customs. These individuals could then modify and adapt foreign programs for local needs—and develop their own.

ENVIRONMENTAL AND HEALTH CONSEQUENCES

Computers have always been viewed as "clean." Film, television, and press images from the industry's early years portray computers in spotless laboratories operated by clean-cut technicians in white coats. The machine's basic components—first the tube, then the transistor and the microchip—were seen as funda-

mentally different and more sophisticated than the technologies that made earlier, "dirty" industries possible. Microprocessors were made in "clean rooms," where even the smallest particles of dust were continuously filtered from the air so they would not contaminate the tiny chips.[37]

In reality, computer production is not as clean as the industry's verdant office parks would seem to suggest. The electronics industry uses a large number of toxic or environmentally hazardous substances, many of which escape into work spaces and the environment. While the air in "clean rooms" may be dust-free, it is still often contaminated with hazardous chemical vapors. And the bucolic lawns surrounding semiconductor manufacturers often conceal seriously contaminated land and groundwater.

The most startling contradiction of the notion that computer manufacturing is a "clean" industry is to be found in Santa Clara County, California. Once known mainly for its extensive orchards, the county underwent a transformation in the seventies, becoming the birthplace and center of the booming computer industry, now known as the famous Silicon Valley. Not so well known is that this valley contains the largest concentration of hazardous-waste cleanup sites in the United States. Much of its groundwater is contaminated with trichloroethylene (TCE) and 1,1,1-trichloroethane—two chemicals linked to serious health problems—and with a variety of other chemicals used to manufacture and clean electronic components. At least 150 different sites in the area are now being examined or monitored by state, federal, or local authorities; 23 of them are on the EPA's Superfund list of the nation's most hazardous toxic dumps.[38]

The electronics industry long benefited from a presumption that its activities were environmentally benign. In Silicon Valley, little attention was paid to environmental conditions until 1982, when a leak of toxic solvents from an underground tank at a Fairchild Semiconductor plant was shown to be contaminating the local groundwater and a public water-supply well. The ensuing publicity led to the discovery of similar problems at scores of other locations in the area. Since then, millions of dollars have been spent in attempts to clean up sites, but with only limited success. Some of the chemicals, such as TCE, are virtually impossible to remove completely once they have settled into an aquifer. At some sites, contamination is still uncontrolled and spreading.[39]

At least since 1979, government and public interest groups have suspected that glycol ethers—solvents commonly used in chip-making—could cause reproductive health problems. (See Chapter 7.) Indeed, a high incidence of such problems among some computer-industry workers has been clearly linked to their exposure to toxic substances. In late 1992, studies by IBM and by the Semiconductor Industry Association identified glycol ethers as the cause of high rates of worker miscarriages. And although conclusive data are lacking, epidemiological studies and a variety of informal reports suggest that water pollution from electronics firms may be causing more widespread health problems. A 1985 California Department of Health Services study, for example, found that communities exposed to water contaminated by the Fairchild leak experience two to three times as many miscarriages and birth defects as the general population.[40]

Environmental problems have been identified in most electronics-industry manufacturing areas that researchers have looked at. In Phoenix, Arizona—a desert community where drinking water is at a premium—a large plume of TCE spread through the city's primary aquifer, apparently from a Motorola chip-production facility. In Japan, where nearly half the world's semiconductors are made, the industry is believed to be causing extensive groundwater pollution. In South Korea, a toxic form of phenol leaked in April 1991 from an electronics plant storage tank into a public water supply serving 1.7 million people. It is likely that such problems also exist in other newly industrializing areas where the electronics industry operates.[41]

Silicon Valley contains the largest concentration of hazardous-waste cleanup sites in the United States.

In the United States, the electronics industry has taken steps to reduce the risk of environmental contamination and worker exposures to hazardous substances. Digital, for example, eliminated ethylene glycol ethers from its semiconductor manufacturing processes by early 1990. Some other companies, however, have moved much more slowly, prompting bitter complaints from labor and environmental activists. Only since the two 1992 studies have most firms—including IBM and many other members of the Semiconductor Industry Association— formally warned their workers of hazards from the chemicals, although some had already taken actions to significantly reduce their use.[42]

It is unlikely that much attention would have been devoted to the environmental impacts of electronics-industry pollution without crusades by public interest groups. In the industry's heartland, a local activist group—the Silicon Valley Toxics Coalition (SVTC)—has played a crucial role in the debate over the impacts of electronics production since the early eighties. When it was formed, SVTC was a somewhat unusual (for the United States) combination of community, environmental, and labor activists. Its membership is ethnically diverse, since minorities and lower-income citizens are disproportionately represented among both the work force and the neighbors of Silicon Valley's electronics facilities. SVTC has fought for proper environmental safeguards and reduced use of toxics in electronics facilities, and was principally responsible for the passage of tough local ordinances regulating the industry.[43]

When the U.S. government required electronics firms to cut their CFC use, the industry rapidly came up with substitutes.

Building on that example, groups in other U.S. communities with major electronics facilities are now actively campaigning on the same issues. They include, among others, the Southwest Organizing Project based in Albuquerque, New Mexico, and the Austin, Texas–based People Organized in Defense of Earth and its Resources. Such groups have joined together with SVTC in a coalition, the Campaign for Responsible Technology (CRT), to raise such issues at a national level. The coalition scored a major victory in 1992, when it persuaded Congress to allocate a tenth of the federal contribution to SEMATECH—a government/industry consortium that develops U.S. chip-making technology—for the development of environmentally sound microprocessor production processes.[44]

The potential for success of electronics-industry cleanup efforts is illustrated by companies' experience with reducing the use of chlorofluorocarbons (CFCs), the ubiquitous chemicals primarily responsible for the depletion of the stratospheric ozone layer. When it was first suggested that the industry—one of the largest users of CFCs—might have to dramatically reduce or eliminate CFC use, many companies protested that the chemicals were irreplaceable. But when the U.S. government, in accord with international agreements on ozone depletion, required electronics firms to cut their CFC use, the industry rapidly came up with substitutes. In one well-known case, IBM found a particularly easy substitute for CFCs in one of its manufacturing operations—soap and water—that was also cheaper. The U.S. electronics industry expects to have eliminated most CFCs from its operations by early 1994.[45]

Cleaning up the electronics industry will require better environmental regulations wherever companies operate, as well as enlightened trade rules, given the industry's global nature. The inclusion of labor and community groups in efforts to reduce environmental and health problems could also help. CRT and other groups met recently with SEMATECH officials to recommend priorities for research. And beyond SEMATECH, electronics firms and professional associations have already initiated a number of cooperative projects aimed at cleaner production. The Institute of Electrical and Electronics Engineers devoted a large conference to environmental issues in mid-1993.[46]

The Microelectronics and Computer Technology Corporation (MCC)—a research consortium supported by about 80 firms—assembled seven industry-wide task forces in 1992 to examine a variety of computer-related environmental issues. A recent 350-page report of their findings included a recommendation that the industry move toward "green design": crafting their products—and the processes by which they are made—for minimal environmental impact. MCC is now working with the industry to establish a national initiative to address environmental issues. If the industry takes its own recommendations seriously, the prospects for improving its environmental performance should be very good. Few sectors are as accustomed to rapid technical change as the computer industry, where products often become outmoded within months of their debut.[47]

Computers have not always reduced the environmental impacts of those who use them, either. Far from creating a "paperless office," for example—as some early, breathless descriptions of a computerized future forecast—computers and high-speed printers have enabled office workers to routinely use more paper than before. One very conservative estimate puts the current annual paper consumption by the world's personal computers at 230 million reams, or 115 billion individual sheets.[48]

A few small changes in equipment and behavior could sharply cut computer-related paper use. For instance, most word-processing programs now allow people with laser printers to fit more words on a page by printing in smaller, but still readable, type and by using narrower margins. Laser-printer manufacturers are also beginning to offer two-sided printing, long a common feature in copiers using virtually the same technology. A combination of these measures could cut certain types of paper use by three fourths.

In the long run, however, paper use will be most dramatically reduced when people routinely choose not to print documents. In certain applications, paper documents are already being phased out. For instance, more than 18,-000 U.S. organizations already save paper and postage, as well as speed their transactions, by exchanging purchase orders, invoices, and other business information in a standard electronic format called EDI (Electronic Data Interchange). Much more paper could be saved if most of the documents now prepared or recalled on computer screens—from letters to books and articles—were not printed out by those wishing to read them. Such restraint is not likely until viewing computerized documents is as easy as picking up a book or a magazine, which will be accomplished through the use of lightweight, book-sized reading devices that display high-resolution, full-color text and graphics. Recent rapid progress in monitor technology and miniature computers suggests that such devices may soon be possible—and affordable.[49]

Taken together, computers also use substantial quantities of energy. In the United States, they now account for an estimated 5 percent of the commercial electricity load and constitute its fastest-growing segment. According to EPA, computers' share could reach 10 percent by the end of this decade. A typical machine uses 80–160 watts of power, about as much as an incandescent light bulb. Worldwide, computers consume an estimated 240 billion kilowatt-hours of electricity each year—about as much as Brazil uses overall annually.[50]

Only a small fraction of this electricity now runs machines in active use. Most computers are left on all day, even while their users take phone calls, meet, file papers, or go to lunch, and 30–40 percent of them are left running at night and on weekends. Most current machines do not turn on quickly, so many users prefer to keep them always at the ready. The answer to this problem is to develop machines that automatically drop into a low power-consumption state—in effect, go to sleep—when not in use, yet wake up immediately when needed. Computer makers have already developed low-power computer technology for another segment of their market: notebook-sized portable machines. Limited by the low power-storage capacity of existing batteries, designers of portable machines have made them highly energy-efficient. Virtually all such machines now feature an automatic sleep mode.[51]

To encourage computer makers to design such features into all their equipment, in June 1992 EPA launched the Energy Star Computers program, a cooperative venture between the agency and leading computer and monitor makers. Participating companies agree to make their products meet Energy Star's power-saving standards—which require computers or monitors to be able to drop into a sleep mode of 30 watts or less—in exchange for the right to use a special logo on their products and in advertising. The first Energy Star products were released in June 1993; by August that year 89 computer companies, 19 printer producers, and 39 component and software makers had signed up for the program.[52]

EPA is working with other federal agencies and private firms to encourage the purchase of Energy Star products. The U.S. government, which spends $4 billion a year on computer equipment, is the industry's largest customer. EPA estimates that if Energy Star products capture two thirds of the market by the end of the nineties, 20 million fewer tons of carbon will pour out of electric power plants each year—an amount equal to the output of 5 million automobiles. Also kept out of the air will be thousands of tons of nitrogen and sulfur oxides, the principal causes of acid rain.[53]

Other aspects of computer design are also important in determining the machines' lifetime impacts on the environment. The MCC study assessed the overall life-cycle impacts of a model computer workstation. It identified such important design features as the use of recycled materials, ease of disassembly and reuse, use of low-toxicity materials,

and reduced product packaging. In Europe, the long-term fate of computers has become a major issue. Germany is developing an ordinance requiring manufacturers of all electronic consumer goods—including radios, televisions, and computers—to take back their products at the end of their useful lives. This is likely to compel manufacturers to design computer components for upgradability or reuse whenever possible. The ordinance was scheduled to take effect in early 1994, with its most restrictive provisions likely to be phased in over several years.[54]

Somewhat surprisingly, it now seems clear that there should be very little need to actually dispose of computers. They rarely wear out; they are usually discarded because the users regard them as obsolete. But old machines can still be valuable to those who cannot afford new ones. Schools and community groups are often overjoyed to receive donated equipment, and many local programs now facilitate such exchanges. Even machines that seem completely outdated can be highly prized in countries where computers are rare. Since 1990, the East-West Educational Development Foundation in Boston, Massachusetts, has funneled thousands of donated personal computers to universities, NGOs, and journalists in Eastern Europe and the former Soviet Union. The group tests donated machines, repairs them when necessary, and identifies potential recipients. In 1992, it identified 200 times as much need for computers as it could satisfy.[55]

The environmental effects of computers can be accompanied by physical effects on their users. Thousands of people now suffer from carpal tunnel syndrome—a painful wrist inflammation—and other injuries linked to long hours working at computer keyboards. Staring at a computer screen for long hours can cause vision problems, and magnetic fields from video display terminals are also a suspected cause of reproductive problems. Variations in work tasks for those who use computer terminals could help alleviate or avoid some such problems. Technological change is the ultimate solution, however: voice recognition programs and equipment could eventually eliminate the need to type, and newer types of display terminals, such as the liquid crystal screens now common on portable computers, do not put out strong magnetic fields.[56]

COMPUTERS AND GLOBAL THINKING

From the beginning, humans have been toolmakers. And since we first sharpened sticks and stones into spears and knives, technological development has been driven almost completely by the desire to expand our dominion over nature and each other. The significance of any tool lies not in its technological wizardry but in how we use it. While our tools have become enormously sophisticated, our use of them often has not—and the consequences lie all around us, in devastated ecosystems and impoverished people.

Are computers any different from the technologies that preceded them? It is certainly possible to view them in the same light. Indeed, their principal uses in the early decades of their existence were military, bureaucratic, and commercial. The first program run on the first computer was used to help design the hydrogen bomb, and computer guidance systems have made intercontinental ballistic missiles and the possibility of global thermonuclear war a reality. Computers are widely used by governments and corporations to track our credit records, our tastes in music, food,

and sex, and our political opinions—and to target them for the next election or advertising campaign. There is ample possibility that the use of these machines will simply prime the pump of consumer economies, accelerating the relentless assault of modern industry on the planet's resources and peoples while exacerbating existing social inequities.[57]

But computers also have the potential to serve a fundamentally different purpose: extending human understanding of the environment and our own effect on it. Computers will not provide us with all the answers to our global problems. They are simply machines—extremely precise and lightning fast, but not very bright—that do what we tell them to do. They can, however, give us global eyes and ears in an age when our actions often have worldwide impacts.

Computers have the potential to extend human understanding of the environment and our own effect on it.

Global thinking is a tall order: human beings are not naturally adept at it. To achieve it, we need tools that extend our senses and enhance our ability to comprehend the information they collect. Computers can compensate for the natural limits to our view of the world by helping us convert unintelligible masses of data into forms we understand. Sifting through pages of raw data on even the most fascinating subject can be a stultifying experience, but seeing the same data as graphs, charts, or enhanced photographs can grab our attention by allowing us to use the same visual skills that make it possible—miraculously—to pick out a familiar face in a crowded room.

Computers have become useful, personal devices because a few visionaries among the early developers dared to believe that machines could be something more than inscrutable, centralized tools operated by experts for large institutions. Computers are continuing to evolve toward forms that will allow us to communicate with them—and get back answers—in forms that appeal to all our senses, making the most of our powerful human ability to recognize patterns by sight, sound, and touch. The metal boxes with keyboards and screens that we now think of as computers may well disappear as the microprocessors at their heart are integrated with other devices. No longer will people have to learn to think like computers; computers will instead be programmed to communicate like people. Working with a computer may become more like talking to a television that talks back—and that can quickly search the world for the information a person needs.

The same kind of vision is needed as we develop the extensive computer networks, the "information highways" of popular discussion, that will soon link much of the world. Those networks have the potential to bring all of us—rich and poor, rural and urban—the information we need to make the difficult choices required for the creation of a sustainable society. But without careful attention to the public policies that govern their evolution and application, they are unlikely to be a force for reducing the environmental impacts of industrial civilization, ending poverty, and strengthening participatory democracy. Particularly important is that they become easy to use and accessible to all, and that governments take steps to make a wide range of public information—from industrial pollution data to health and census information—easily and cheaply available through them.

Whether they are used to rebuild the world's economy or simply to drive it mindlessly faster, the most intriguing fact about computers is that they vastly increase our ability to control. In this, they have so far followed the pattern of all human history, as each new technology has been turned by its users to the control of nature or other people rather than their own increasingly unsustainable behavior. It would be an all-too-predictable mistake to use the computer as simply a new, more effective way for us to dominate our world. We have another choice: computers can help us learn to live with nature. Rather than our machines controlling us, we can begin to control them—and ourselves.

7

Assessing Environmental Health Risks

Ann Misch

Throughout the second half of this century, chemical companies have trumpeted the miraculous powers of chemicals on billboards, in magazine ads, and on television: "Better Things for Better Living Through Chemicals," appealed a long-running Du Pont ad. "Without chemicals, life itself would be impossible," claimed Monsanto. And they did bring us miracles—antibiotics, penicillin, and a vast selection of creature comforts far beyond anything our forebears could have imagined. Synthetic fibers, dry cleaning, spoil-proof food, crop-saving pesticides, contraceptives, contact lenses . . . the list is endless. All in all, chemical manufacturers have heaped tens of thousands of compounds on the bandwagon of progress, creating every possible convenience—and chasing every imagined ache or emptiness from our lives.[1]

But along with all their benefits, these new creations have generated a long list of problems, including serious health consequences. Our enthusiasm for new chemicals and the products and services they allow has outstripped our attention to their long-term effects. While billions of dollars have been lavished on product development, marketing, promotion, and advertising, little has been spent on observing chemicals' interactions with living things and the environment. And these effects can never be thoroughly tested; the combinations of chemicals now in our food, water, clothing, and homes defy measurement.

Historically, research on chemicals' effects has led environmental health experts to one conclusion: there is an indisputable link between exposure to certain industrial substances and specific serious diseases, particularly cancer. Leukemia has been linked to benzene, an ingredient in gasoline, for example, and mesothelioma, a form of cancer, is considered a signature of asbestos exposure. The share of total chronic disease due to environmental pollution is still vigorously debated, however.[2]

But some scientists are also beginning to look beyond the obvious—cancer and other easily diagnosable problems—to other health consequences of the chemical age. What they are finding puts a different face on claims of harmlessness accepted by consumers in a less questioning era. In the summer of 1991, for example, 21 scientists gathered at the Wingspread Conference Center in Wisconsin presented fresh evidence that a wide assortment of environmental pollutants had the potential to undermine biological functioning and so affect the overall competence of animals studied both in the lab and in the wild. Many of the substances they investigated had caused broad yet subtle damage by disrupting vital physiological systems, including the nervous system, the endocrine system (responsible for regulating hormones), and the immune system (which defends the body against infectious disease and cancer).[3]

What the industrial chemicals discussed at Wingspread have in common—beyond, in some cases, their cancer-causing potential—is the ability to wreak silent havoc at much lower levels of exposure than those typically associated with cancer. Because most of the damage observed by the scientists reporting at Wingspread was so insidious, the group determined that similar effects in people exposed to the same contaminants might go unnoticed unless researchers specifically hunted for them. They called for a major investigation to better assess the extent of subtle chemical damage to human health.[4]

Although the suspicion that chemicals can cause toxic effects more subtle than cancer, acute poisoning, or birth defects is not new, toxicologists and other scientists until recently lacked the tools to investigate many less obvious health effects. U.S. regulatory agencies have emphasized avoiding cancer; in the process, they presumed that a public protected against cancer was also a public protected against other toxic outcomes of chemical exposure. But environmen-

tal health research is proving that assumption false with each revelation that environmental pollutants can impair functioning and overall biological competence—in the absence of overt signs of disease.

The findings of scientists like those gathered at Wingspread do not mean that our previous focus on avoiding cancer was wrong. Yet the recent research on noncancer health effects certainly implies that our view of chemical risks is incomplete. The discovery that a whole universe of other health effects may be associated with the products of our industrial age has profound implications for public health and regulatory policy. The continuous appearance of toxic effects at lower and lower levels of exposure is especially troubling, since low-level exposure to some chemicals is practically universal.

The growing repertoire of toxic effects that scientists are beginning to document begs for a much more conservative approach to chemical regulation. To include these fresh findings in chemical risk assessment, regulatory agencies must look beyond cancer to assess the effect of chemicals on overall biological competence. This task involves, at a minimum, careful consideration of potential toxic effects on the nervous system, the endocrine and reproductive systems, and the immune system.

THE CHEMICAL LOAD

Society has understood for centuries the dangers posed by many natural and synthetic substances, often through casual observation of diseases that have beset workers in various "dirty" industries. Both Hippocrates in late fourth century B.C. and Charles Dickens in the mid-nineteenth century noted cases of lead poisoning among workers, for example. But with the Industrial Revolution came a new era of broad population exposure to natural and synthetic substances, as large-scale chemical production began and naturally occurring chemical substances were refined and altered.[5]

By the twenties, industry began to produce synthetic chemicals, some of which began to escape into the environment. Polychlorinated biphenyls (PCBs), for instance, were introduced in the United States in 1930 but banned there and in Canada beginning in the late seventies; they were used for decades in electrical transformers, plastics, paints, varnishes, and waxes. PCB residues have been found in the tissues of people and animals in disparate parts of the globe—even in the fat of polar bears in the Arctic.[6]

By the fifties, industry had invented thousands of important industrial compounds, some of which were as-yet-unrecognized toxicants. Among them were a number that contained chlorine, an important element in the production of many synthetic chemicals. Chlorine proved useful to the chemical industry, since it bonds readily with carbon compounds. Between 1920 and 1990, U.S. production of chlorine rose hundredfold, and now stands at roughly 10 million tons a year—roughly a third of the world total.[7]

Unfortunately, thanks to their chlorine-carbon bonds, many industrial compounds are quite stable, and only break down slowly. Many organochlorine substances (compounds containing carbon and chlorine) are not water-soluble, but do dissolve in fat. Like filings drawn to a magnet, these substances migrate to the reserves of fat stored in the tissues of fish, birds, mammals, and people. DDT, an organochlorine pesticide, caused eggshell thinning among American bald eagles, leading to the death of unhatched eaglets and to broad population declines among these birds. Two recent studies in the United States have linked tissue concentrations of DDT with an increased risk of breast cancer in women.[8]

In addition to creating brand-new hazards, twentieth-century industry has coaxed many other naturally toxic substances from rock and soil to use in manufacturing, and thereby released them into the environment. Industry's reliance on these metals has pushed more than 300 times the amount of lead, 20 times as much cadmium, and four times as much arsenic into the atmosphere than is naturally present. Gold mining in the Amazon Basin pollutes the region with some 90–120 tons of mercury annually as miners collect gold from the riverbeds of the region. Elevated levels of mercury have been found in fish, river waters, and people, suggesting that the pursuit of gold has caused a vast public health problem in the basin. Global emissions of mercury to the atmosphere are estimated at 4,500 tons a year. Minute quantities of cadmium, lead, and mercury have proved poisonous to the central nervous system.[9]

The world's understanding of how all these substances affect human beings is still elementary. A few years ago, the National Research Council (NRC) looked into just how much is actually known: it found no information at all on the possible toxic effects of more than 80 percent of the 50,000 or so industrial chemicals (a category that excludes pesticides, food additives, cosmetics, and drugs) used in the United States. And there are still many important unanswered questions about the remaining 20 percent. Occupational exposure limits have been set for fewer than 700 of these 50,000 chemicals. For those produced in amounts exceeding 1 million pounds a year, for example, the NRC found that virtually no testing had been done on the potential for neurobehavioral damage, birth defects, or toxic effects that might span several generations by passing from parents to offspring.[10]

The NRC report is not really so surprising, since even the U.S. Environmental Protection Agency (EPA) in the vast majority of cases does not require manufacturers of industrial chemicals to run specific tests to determine whether their products have adverse effects before putting them on the market. Most chemicals, says Erik Olson, an attorney at the Natural Resources Defense Council, "are innocent until proven guilty."[11]

Pesticides' toxic effects are slightly better understood than those of industrial chemicals. The U.S. government began to make some progress with a 1988 law requiring that manufacturers submit health data on 620 active ingredients in older pesticides, although it turns out that much of the information EPA wants simply does not exist. Unfortunately, there still is not enough information to determine the health effects of more than 60 percent of the pesticides currently used in the United States.[12]

Chemical manufacturers usually do not submit full reports on their products' potential toxic effects, but independent researchers have documented some of these. Based on current scientific literature, the NRC estimates that a third of the 197 substances to which a million or more American workers are exposed have the potential to be neurotoxic or to damage the central nervous system and the brain. A partial list of these products includes many solvents, pesticides, and several metals.[13]

Many common industrial substances—including benzene, dioxin, certain pesticides, and some metals—also have the ability to interfere with the immune system. Many organochlorines (including dioxins, furans, and PCBs), as well as the pesticides chlordane, DDT, heptachlor, and hexachlorobenzene, disrupt the endocrine system and impair reproductive abilities. Some toxic organochlorine substances have been banned in the United States and other countries, but they can remain in the environment for decades. And many, like DDT, are still used in other parts of the world.[14]

Although workers often have the highest exposures to these toxic compounds, other people are exposed through consumer products, through drinking water and indoor air, or by virtue of living next to a factory or hazardous waste site. Some 53 million Americans apply herbicides to their lawns, for instance, and millions use commercial bug sprays inside the home. Shoe polish, glues, household cleaners, varnishes, and other everyday consumer products stored in the home contain neurotoxic chemicals. Some hazardous waste sites harbor neurotoxic chemicals that threaten to contaminate the drinking-water supplies of nearby communities. Outside the workplace, however, little is known about the precise extent to which people are exposed to single toxic chemicals, let alone this dangerous mix of hazardous substances.[15]

CANCER AND THE ENVIRONMENT

One of the most feared and most investigated consequences of exposure to environmental pollutants is cancer. Like industry, cancer and chronic diseases are prominent features of the twentieth century. In industrial countries, cancer causes 20 percent of all deaths. By contrast, infectious and parasitic diseases account for less than 5 percent of all deaths in these nations. The reverse holds true in developing countries, where infectious and parasitic diseases cause far more deaths.[16]

Explanations for the higher rates of cancer in industrial countries often invoke the vast differences in diet, smoking habits, and methods of preserving food. Compared with these factors, pollution may play a smaller part. Nonetheless, the role of industrial pollutants in cancer is not negligible. Indeed, for some cancers, toxic substances may make an important contribution. But it is difficult to quantify the role of toxicants in human cancer for three reasons: little is known about the toxicity of most chemicals, most exposures occur at very low levels, and people are exposed to countless substances. As a result, estimates of the share of cancers attributable to toxic exposure range from 7 percent to more than 20.[17]

Until recently, a heated dispute among cancer experts and epidemiologists surrounded the question of whether the already high rates of cancer in industrial countries were increasing. The debate was compounded when cancer related to the use of tobacco, a risk factor that experts hold responsible for roughly 30 percent of all tumors, was included. Smoking's overwhelming impact on the prevalence of cancer means that increases in smoking-related cancers can drive overall cancer trends upward.[18]

But recent data show that one of the most important cancers related to smoking, lung cancer, has levelled off in some industrial countries. The rates of death from lung cancer among men from Finland and the United Kingdom, for example, peaked in the seventies and are now falling. In other industrial countries, including Canada, Germany, Sweden, Switzerland, and the United States, deaths from lung cancer are not increasing as fast as previously. (They are falling, for example, for American men under the age of 45.) This suggests that if cancer is increasing overall, then lung cancer is not the explanation.[19]

In recent studies, a number of researchers have found increases in the incidence and mortality rate of cancers with no known links to smoking, as well as increases in overall cancer. Many of these increases have occurred in older people. A 1990 study of trends in countries reporting mortality data to the World Health Organization found that between 1968 and 1987, death rates from cancer of the central nervous system (including brain cancer), breast cancer, kidney cancer, multiple myeloma, non-Hodgkin's lymphoma, and skin cancer had increased in people over age 54 in six different countries. (Roughly two thirds of all deaths from cancer occur after the age of 60.) Cancers of the brain and central nervous system more than doubled in people between the ages of 75 and 84 and almost doubled among those aged 65 to 74. Total cancer among people 55 or older in all six countries also increased when lung and stomach cancer (both of which account for a large share of cancer and are linked to well-known risk factors) were excluded.[20]

Researchers have found increases in the incidence and mortality rate of cancers with no known links to smoking, as well as in overall cancer.

But the increases are not confined to older people. For example, the incidence of brain cancer and cancer of the central nervous system in American boys under age 20 rose 16 percent between 1973–77 and 1983–87, while the incidence of lymphoma rose 15 percent. Leukemia also rose during this period.[21]

Studies in Europe and the United States have also revealed two- to fourfold increases in the incidence of testicular cancer during the last 50 years. One investigation in the United States found an "apparent epidemic increase over time in the risk of testicular cancer for young men aged 15 to 44." The authors based their observation on rates of testicular cancer recorded in the Connecticut Tumor Registry between 1935 and 1979, during which the incidence of testicular cancer among men aged 25 to 44 rose more than two and a half times. Although they offered no specific explanations for the increase, the authors commented that "the greater rate of increases seen for the recent [generations] suggests either the introduction of new carcinogens during the 1950s or increased exposure to already present carcinogens."[22]

Cancer statistics are far from straightforward. One of the first questions experts often ask is whether the increases measured are "real." Many factors could cause deceptive increases in the spread of cancer. One of these is the reliability of national registries in which cancer deaths are recorded. If cancer deaths are incompletely reported to the registry, for example, better reporting causes an apparent increase. Artificial peaks in cancer incidence can also follow new techniques for diagnosis, new programs for cancer screening, and gains in access to health care. A portion of the increase in the incidence of breast cancer in American women, for example, is probably due to the increased use of mammography.[23]

A number of cancer researchers speculate that much if not all of the rise in cancer stems from improvements in diagnosis. But researchers Devra Davis, currently a senior scientific advisor in the U.S. Department of Health and Human Services, and David Hoel of the Medical University of South Carolina, in Charleston, contend that for improved accuracy to explain the increase, there should be a corresponding decline in recorded cases of poorly diagnosed cancer. Traditionally, undiagnosed cancers are recorded as deaths due to unknown cancer or other unknown causes. As diagnoses sharpened, reason Davis and Hoel, then some of the cancers in these categories should shift into ones for which the specific causes of death are identified.[24]

But what a number of researchers found when they looked closely at the mortality statistics in different countries was not a shift in the distribution of deaths (those attributed to nonspecific causes versus a specific cancer), but a rise in both well-diagnosed and poorly diagnosed cases. This means that cancer itself must be on the increase. Further, they argue that for better diagnosis to explain the consistent increase in cancer in many different industrial countries, advances in diagnosis would need to be spread evenly across the industrial world. Such uniform improvements in detection both among different countries and among men and women are unlikely.[25]

If cancer truly is increasing in many industrial countries, as these recent studies suggest, then improvements in treatment may not be enough to deflect the impact of the disease. Researchers thus will need to pay renewed attention to the origins of cancer in order to better prevent it.

Despite being the focus of intense medical research in industrial countries, cancer is still a complex and elusive disease. It is startling that the specific causes of most cancers still evade medical understanding. But researchers do know that many factors, including alcohol, diet, genes, and environmental pollution, can all play a role.

Certain genes, for example, confer a unique susceptibility to cancer. Recently, a section of DNA containing a gene that predisposes individuals to develop colon cancer was discovered by researchers at Johns Hopkins University.

The malfunctioning of genes that normally suppress tumors may account for the appearance of some cases of cancer. Researchers have also identified around 50 so-called oncogenes. Proto-oncogenes are genes that are normally involved in cell growth and specialization. When mutated, they transform into oncogenes and orchestrate the appearance and growth of tumors.[26]

Yet the apparent rises in cancer incidence in the United States and other industrial countries happened too suddenly to make broader genetic susceptibility a plausible explanation. This means that an answer must be sought in the environment.[27]

Experts estimate that environmental factors—which include diet, smoking, drinking alcohol, viruses, occupation, and geographical location—account for at least 60 percent of all cancer. Preserving food through salting, smoking, or pickling raises the risk of oral and stomach cancer, for example. Eating a diverse variety of vegetables may actually block certain kinds of cancer; the disappearance of these ingredients from modern diets may, in turn, lead to higher rates of these cancers in industrial countries.[28]

Environmental cues clearly interact with genes. Dietary fat, for instance, may act as a cancer promoter, fanning the spread of malignant tissue. The fat-laden diet of typical Americans, who derive more than 40 percent of their calories from fat, has been tied to colon cancer and implicated by some researchers in breast cancer.[29]

Chemical substances, too, can spur the development of cancer. But very few substances have been tested for their cancer-causing potential. Most of those known to cause cancer in mice or rats are not regulated by U.S. agencies. The International Agency for Research on Cancer has identified 60 environmental agents that can cause cancer in people. These include chemicals, groups of re-lated chemicals, mixtures of different chemicals, radiation, drugs, and industrial processes or occupational exposures linked to cancer.[30]

Exposure to toxic substances can begin a cascade of events that ultimately leads to cancer. This can happen in a number of ways. One mechanism is by directly damaging the DNA and causing mutations. Other toxicants may cause cancer by suppressing immunity. There is no direct evidence linking chemically lowered immunity to cancer, but a number of substances that are known carcinogens also appear capable of suppressing the immune system. Benzo(a)-pyrene, a chemical found in automobile exhaust and coal smoke, and asbestos, a natural mineral fiber, are two examples.[31]

A third way exposure can lead to cancer is by having the toxic substance act like a hormone. Diethylstilbesterol (DES), a drug prescribed to American women in the fifties and sixties to prevent miscarriages, is a synthetic version of estrogen, a female sex hormone. Like estrogen, DES promotes tumors in laboratory animals. It has also been associated with vaginal cancer in the daughters of women who took the drug. A number of other environmental pollutants appear to have the potential to perturb the endocrine system, which is responsible for the regulation of hormones (as discussed later in this chapter).[32]

Other toxic substances disable the enzymes that normally break down toxicants, or interfere with the body's ability to mend flaws in the DNA. Under normal circumstances, these flaws constantly arise but are promptly repaired by processes in the cell.[33]

Epidemiological studies in a broad sample of industrial countries have found higher rates of certain cancers among farmers and other agricultural workers who are exposed to a wide array of natural toxins and synthetic hazards. (See Table 7–1.) In most countries, farmers are on the whole healthier than other people. They smoke less and get more exercise than the average person, so their rates for overall cancers and heart disease are lower. But despite their better health status, farmers across the industrial world appear to be at greater risk for developing some forms of cancer. Most of these have been associated with exposure to one or more industrial toxicants.[34]

Many of the cancers that are rising in farmers and in industrial countries have also been observed in patients that have suppressed immune systems. Evidence from laboratory animals confirms that some environmental pollutants, such as

Table 7–1. Increased Risk of Cancer Among Farmers in Industrial Countries

Cancer/Site	Range of Increased Risk[1]	Number of Studies	Known or Suspected Risk Factors
Brain Cancer	0.7–6.5 times	18	solvents; lubricating oil; phenolic compounds; polycyclic aromatic hydrocarbons; electromagnetic radiation; organochlorines; insecticides
Melanoma	0.5–6.3 times	11	sunlight; various chemicals
Multiple Myeloma	0.4–2.5 times	12	pesticides; diesel exhaust; processed grains
Non-Hodgkin's Lymphoma	0.6–1.4 times	14	herbicides (phenoxyacetic acid herbicides, such as 2,4-D and triazine); organophosphate insecticides; fungicides; fuel use; pentachlorophenol (a wood preservative); AIDS
Leukemia	0.3–2.4 times	23	animal viruses; pesticides (DDT); animal insecticides
Prostate	0.9–2.7 times	22	no identified risk factors; age, body weight, and diet have been suggested by some researchers; others have proposed fetal exposure to estrogen
Stomach	0.6–2.0 times	24	nitrates (in drinking water); pesticides
Connective Tissue	0.9–1.5 times	7	pesticides (for soft-tissue sarcoma)
Testis	0.6–1.4 times	10	fertilizers; pesticides; estrogens

[1]A risk of 1 is equal to the average risk in the general population; a figure of less than 1 indicates reduced risk compared with the general population.
SOURCE: Adapted from Aaron Blair et al., "Clues to Cancer Etiology from Studies of Farmers," *Scandinavian Journal of Work, Environment and Health*, Vol. 18, 1992, pp. 209-15.

pesticides, can suppress the immune system (as discussed in a later section), which leads researchers to speculate that environmental pollutants may also promote cancer by dampening immunity. Aaron Blair and Sheila Hoar Zahm reviewed various studies linking farming and cancer risks and suggested that farmers might be the vanguard of a population at risk for cancers linked to environmental pollutants. Though it is undoubtedly not a role they wanted, farmers may be the "canaries" of environmental health—providing a signal that all is not well, much as the canaries kept in cages in mines did by dying when there was not enough oxygen to breathe.[35]

ENDANGERED NERVOUS SYSTEMS

The human nervous system may be the most sensitive target of environmental pollutants. A number of pollutants that are ubiquitous in the environment, home, or workplace—including lead, solvents, and pesticides—have the potential to injure the nervous system.

The central nervous system's sensitivity is due in part to the fact that nerve cells do not replenish themselves when they die, unlike most other cells in the body. This fixed endowment of nerve cells can only shrink, not expand: as people age, they lose neurons. Healthy 90-year-olds, for example, have about 75 percent of their original set of neurons. Fortunately, since these nerve cells number in the billions, the brain has a large "reserve capacity" of them. Because of this, old people occasionally retain much of the intellectual crispness they had in their twenties. But exposure to certain toxicants increases the rate at which

nerve cells are lost. So people who lose an additional one tenth of a percent a year might in their sixties have the same number of neurons as healthy nonagenarians.[36]

Very few industrial chemicals have been tested for their neurotoxic potential, as already mentioned. Tests of 197 chemicals that at least a million American workers are exposed to found that 65 of them could cause neurological damage. Roughly 20 million U.S. workers are exposed to neurotoxic chemicals, many of which are solvents. (See Table 7–2.)[37]

The most infamous example of a substance poisonous to the nervous system—albeit not a synthetic one—is lead, recognized for its far-reaching toxicity in workers since ancient Greece. Modern standards for occupational exposure to lead still fall short of protecting workers in the United States and other countries, in the eyes of a number of experts. Lead is now ubiquitous in the environment. In the late sixties, it was found in the snow of Greenland at 200 times ancient levels. The metal is considered a major environmental health threat in Eastern Europe, the United States, and many other countries.[38]

Lead is one of the best studied neurotoxins. The more closely researchers have looked at the metal's toxicity, the more concerned they have grown about its effects at very low levels. Between 1972 and 1991, the amount of lead concentration in blood that U.S. federal agencies deemed "safe" dropped by 75 percent. In 1991, the Centers for Disease Control announced that subtle effects on the central nervous system of children began at blood-lead concentrations above 10 micrograms per deciliter. The previous guideline had established blood-lead levels over 25 micrograms per deciliter of blood as cause for concern.[39]

The burning of leaded automobile

Table 7–2. United States: Number of Workers Exposed to Selected Neurotoxic Chemicals

Chemical	Selected Activities, Industries, and Products	Number of Workers
		(million)
Carbon Disulfide	rayon manufacturing, soil and grain fumigant, oils, waxes, rubber manufacture	1.0
Carbon Monoxide	unintended product of incomplete burning, metallurgy, manufacture of petroleum products and metal carbonyls	10
Formaldehyde	fungicide, germicides, preservation, synthetic fibers, composite wood products, dyes	1.7
Lead	batteries, ammunition, oxides and pigments, solder, construction, shielding from diagnostic x-rays, cable covering, pipes	1.4
Mercury	lab equipment manufacture, dental fillings, batteries, fungicide, latex paint, chloralkali industry, municipal and solid waste incineration, emissions from coal-fired utilities	0.6
Perchloroethylene	dry cleaning, degreasing, chemical intermediate	2.0
Trichloroethylene	degreasing	3.6
Toluene (exposure by inhalation only)	solvents, dyes, explosives, polyurethanes	4.8
Xylene (exposure by inhalation only)	petrochemicals, solvents	4.3

SOURCE: Worldwatch Institute, based on sources documented in endnote 37.

fuel is an important source of children's exposure to lead in many countries. A second source is leaded paint, which still lines millions of American homes as well as those elsewhere. When the United States began removing lead from gasoline (which is scheduled to be finished by 1996), concentrations of lead in blood also dropped. Many countries in Europe, Latin America, and Asia still rely heavily on leaded automobile fuel, however. (See Table 7–3.)[40]

U.S. researchers are beginning to appreciate the hazards of some other neurotoxins, one group of which is solvents. These can cause short-term memory problems, dizziness, fatigue, irritability, and an inability to concentrate, as well as structural changes in the brain and nervous system. Some 10 million

Table 7–3. Use of Leaded Gasoline, Selected Countries, 1991

Country	Leaded Gasoline Market Share
	(percent)
Australia	64
France	74
Hong Kong	62
Italy	93
Malaysia	96
New Zealand	68
Norway	53
Singapore	56
Thailand	93
United Kingdom	59

SOURCE: CONCAWE, *Motor Vehicle Emission Regulations and Fuel Specifications—1992 Update* (Brussels: 1992).

American workers and 1–2 million German workers are exposed to solvents.[41]

Many ordinary items that can be bought at any hardware store or drugstore contain solvents. Shoe polish, rubber cement, nail polish remover, furniture polish, bathroom tile cleaners, disinfectants, paints, and paint thinner all contain varying amounts of solvents. Clothes brought back from the neighborhood dry cleaners release percholorethylene, a chlorinated solvent, as they hang in the closet.

In the eighties a series of studies, mostly Scandinavian, tied neurological damage to chronic solvent exposure among painters, woodworkers, and other workers. In some studies, investigators found lower performance among workers who were exposed at levels within the legal limits set by the government. For example, a Swedish study of car and industrial spray painters found a statistically significant rise in psychiatric symptoms such as irritability and difficulties concentrating. The investigators also found slower reaction and perception times, reduced manual dexterity, and poorer short-term memory. Workers with solvent-related symptoms accounted for the majority of patients in Sweden's occupational medicine clinics in the mid-eighties. Psychiatric problems that can be traced to occupational solvent exposure are compensated in Sweden by the Swedish National Social Insurance Board.[42]

A New York State Department of Health study of apartment buildings that also housed dry cleaning shops found that the indoor levels of solvents sometimes exceeded workplace standards by a wide margin. Since few, if any, studies of nonoccupational exposure to solvents other than for glue sniffers have been done, it is hard to know what these exposures mean. Judith Schreiber, a toxicologist with the New York Department of Health, points out that health effects of using solvents outside the workplace may in some cases be more serious than those associated with some exposures on the job since evaluations of the risks posed by workplace exposures are based on studies of healthy middle-aged white workers. Workers are exposed only during the working day, but people living in solvent-contaminated apartments may spend most of their time at home.[43]

Solvents can cause short-term memory problems, dizziness, fatigue, irritability, and an inability to concentrate.

In addition, infants and children are probably more susceptible than the typical worker to the neurotoxic effects of solvents. Infants lack the fully developed "blood-brain barrier" that protects adults from some toxicants and, because of their high metabolism, both infants and young children assimilate more of an airborne toxicant than adults do.[44]

Kaye Kilburn, a cardiologist with training in neurology, has investigated subtle changes in certain nervous system functions among communities exposed to trichloroethylene in their drinking water. "Balance is very sensitive to solvents," says Kilburn. He also found that people with solvent exposure had diminished or absent blink reflexes and were slower to react on perception and coordination tests. Kilburn thinks that such tests of nervous system performance are the "future of neurotoxicity because all normal people test the same on them. It doesn't matter whether or not they were dull or brilliant."[45]

Another possible consequence of exposure to neurotoxic substances is neurodegenerative disease. Parkinson's disease, for example, is caused by the deterioration of nerve cells in regions of the brain governing movement. Telltale signs of the disease include a shuffling walk, tremor, and rigidity. But because the brain has so much extra capacity, the disease can progress quite far before any warning signs occur. The hallmark symptoms of Parkinson's appear only after the level of a brain chemical called dopamine drops 70–80 percent. Dopamine, one of a handful of neurotransmitters that shuttle messages between nerve cells, is produced by a specific group of motor neurons.[46]

Some evidence suggests that dopamine-producing neurons can be assailed by various environmental agents. In the early eighties, researchers stumbled across cases of a syndrome very similar to Parkinson's among California drug addicts who had manufactured batches of a heroin-like drug in their own basements. The drug contained a chemical known as MPTP. When metabolized, MPTP converted into a toxic chemical, MPP+, that turned out to be responsible for the mysterious cases like Parkinson's found among these young adults.[47]

MPP+ bears a close resemblance to the herbicide paraquat, which has been banned in many industrial countries but which is still allowed in many developing nations. A number of epidemiological studies have detected higher levels of Parkinson's disease in farmers and other workers exposed to herbicides. One study reported in *Neurology* in 1992 found a threefold higher risk among people with herbicide exposure compared with controls. Conditions resembling Parkinson's disease have also appeared in workers exposed to carbon disulfide, carbon monoxide, and manganese.[48]

The case for an environmental cause of neurodegenerative illnesses is complicated by the contribution of genes to some forms of these diseases. It may turn out that genes create an underlying susceptibility to nerve loss, in effect setting the stage for a disease's later appearance when prompted by environmental cues.[49]

Gender, Reproduction, and Development

Recent research has stirred intense interest in the potential effects of pollutants on fertility and the normal development of the fetus. In the United States, a fifth of all pregnancies end in spontaneous abortion before the fifth month. Fifteen percent of all babies are born prematurely or with low birth weight. And close to 14 percent of all married couples in their childbearing years (aged 18–54) have trouble conceiving. The origin of an estimated 60 percent of reproductive and developmental disorders is unknown, leaving ample room for environmental pollutants to play a contributing role.[50]

Epidemiological studies have recently

detected adverse reproductive effects associated with a group of chemicals known as glycol ether solvents. These are used in a wide variety of products and industrial processes, including the manufacture of paints, varnishes, primers, film, and electrical wire insulation, and as printing inks, cleaners, and deicers on aircraft. A series of studies among semiconductor workers has revealed higher rates of spontaneous abortions and delayed conception among women who worked closely with these chemicals. Two of the studies came up with remarkably similar estimates of raised risk among women in a process called photolithography and among those with the greatest exposure to short-chain glycol ethers.[51]

The U.S. Occupational Health and Safety Administration (OSHA) recently proposed lowering the maximum airborne concentrations of four of the glycol ethers to a fraction of their current legal levels. If OSHA adopts this rule, it will be the first time a substance or group of substances has been regulated by the agency because of its reproductive toxicity.[52]

While glycol ethers pose a hazard in the workplace, a number of researchers are pursuing the theory that a whole menu of environmental pollutants have a broad influence on reproductive behavior and function by modulating the effects of hormones. Independently, many scientists have observed these effects in laboratory animals and in wildlife populations that live in polluted environments.[53]

By enhancing or dulling the effects of hormones, these pollutants have a far-reaching effect on fertility, gender, and sex-linked behavior. Traits that seem fixed or inherent are surprisingly malleable when changes in the internal hormonal environment occur. A group of Canadian scientists, for example, studied the offspring of gerbils; they discovered that the litter's sex ratio, a trait thought to be under the master control of genes, was strongly influenced by the hormonal environment of the mother at an early age. Developing females that shared the womb with male siblings got exposed to male hormones produced by their brothers. Unerringly, female gerbils with such exposure gave birth to more males when they themselves bore litters. Conversely, female fetuses that had been sandwiched between two fetal sisters produced more female offspring.[54]

Recently, attention has focused on chemicals that duplicate or interfere with the effects of estrogen, the female sex hormone. Tampering with estrogen levels can have profound effects on the normal development of sexual organs of the fetus, and on later sexual function. In male laboratory rats, estrogen reduces the number of sperm and also inhibits the descent of the testes from the abdomen. (Male rat pups, like male human infants, are born with undescended testes.)[55]

These effects are mirrored in studies of the only estrogen inadvertently tested in people—diethylstilbesterol. A higher than average number of men exposed to DES while in their mother's womb have testes that failed to descend. They also have a higher incidence of abnormal urethral tubes and reduced sperm counts and semen. Undescended testes are a major risk factor for testicular cancer. Two small studies also found that DES-exposed women (daughters of women who took DES during their pregnancies) were three to five times as likely to have a homosexual or bisexual orientation as women who were not exposed to the hormone through their mothers.[56]

Exposure to other environmental estrogens is constant. Natural estrogens, known as phytoestrogens, exist in plants and fungi. Oral contraceptives, taken by millions of women, contain synthetic estrogens. High-fat diets also appear to increase circulating levels of estrogen in women, while increasing dietary fiber may have the opposite impact. Finally, a whole array of chemicals are estrogenic in their effects: PCBs, DBCP (a nematicide), and kepone and methoxychlor (both organochlorine pesticides), as well as some components of plastics, all have effects that resemble estrogen.[57]

Recent evidence suggests that this load of environmental estrogens could have a pervasive influence on human reproduction. A 1992 study in the *British Medical Journal* by a group of Danish researchers reported a 50-percent decline in the quantity of sperm in human semen in 20 different countries. In an article several months later in *The Lancet*, Niels Skakkebaek, the lead author of the study and an endocrinologist at the University of Copenhagen, hypothesized that this dramatic spread of subfertility might be due to the "sea of estrogens" bathing the twentieth-century environment. The increase in subfertility that Skakkebaek and his colleagues discovered coincides with documented increases around the world in other reproductive defects, such as testicular cancer, failed testicular descent, and abnormalities of the urethra.[58]

One mystery is how potent the different environmental estrogens are. For the most part, we do not know. Many environmental estrogens seem only weakly estrogenic. In theory, however, continuous exposure to weak estrogens or exposure at a critical point during development could lead to reproductive abnormalities and changes in sex-linked behavior.[59]

A number of scientists believe that the natural estrogens found in plants are not the most likely explanation for widespread reproductive problems seen by scientists in wildlife populations in North America and in marine mammals around Scandinavian countries. Theo-

dora Colborn, a zoologist at the World Wildlife Fund, claims that chemicals that interfere with hormones are responsible for the widespread reproductive dysfunction many wildlife biologists have observed among populations of birds and mammals around the Great Lakes in the United States and Canada. A list of the hormonally active chemicals in the Great Lakes includes PCBs, dioxin, and an assortment of pesticides.[60]

A second mystery is how such a diverse group of structurally unrelated chemicals have practically identical biological effects. "It's been an enigma for years. We still don't know what makes an estrogen an estrogen from a chemical standpoint," says John McLachlan, scientific director of the U.S. National Institute of Environmental Health Sciences and an expert on environmental estrogens. McLachlan, for one, expects to find more and more substances that interfere with natural estrogen levels.[61]

THE IMMUNE SYSTEM

AIDS has made clear the role of a healthy immune system in fending off disease by showing what happens when immunity is weakened or abolished. AIDS patients die of bacterial and viral infections, such as pneumonia and cytomegalovirus, that surmount lowered immune barriers. Similarly, people who received organ transplants and take immunosuppressive drugs in order to lull their immune system into accepting alien tissue run a greater risk of developing cancer.

Researchers are still feeling their way around the main contours of the immune system, however. Basic questions, such as how large the immune system's reserve forces are and whether a well-functioning component can compensate for a disabled one, remain unresolved. Immunotoxicology is such a recent off-shoot of toxicology that few chemicals have been banned or regulated because of their adverse effects on the immune system. "Not until the mid-eighties were there enough people on board to fully assess immunotoxicity of a variety of chemicals," says Loren Koller, dean of the Oregon State University School of Veterinary Medicine in Corvallis.[62]

Many industrial chemicals and pollutants have an effect on one or more parts of the immune system when they are tested in animals. Benzene, dioxin, lead, mercury, ozone, nitrogen dioxide, PCBs, pesticides, and chemical mixtures like those found in contaminated groundwater all perturb the immune system. But it is difficult to say what these perturbations mean. Some epidemiological studies, for example, have found that people exposed to polybrominated biphenyls (used as fire retardants), asbestos, and certain metals experience changes in the populations of certain cells of the immune system (such as B cells and T cells). But scientists still have not determined the significance of these changes to overall immune functioning and health.[63]

The best evidence for a link between broad environmental pollution and immune dysfunction may be the effect of air pollution on asthma and respiratory illnesses. Deaths as a result of asthma are rising in a number of industrial countries, including Australia, Canada, Denmark, New Zealand, Sweden, the United Kingdom, and the United States. In the last two, the prevalence of asthma also seems to be increasing, especially among children. Between 1982 and 1991, for example, the prevalence of asthma rose 56 percent in Americans under the age of 18, compared with 36 percent in the general population. Between 1979 and 1987, Americans under the age of four

were the fastest growing group of people entering the hospital because of asthma attacks.[64]

Many cases of asthma are due to an abnormal immune response known as allergic hypersensitivity. This lies at the opposite end of the spectrum from immune suppression. A suppressed immune system is less capable of mounting a response to invading bacteria and viruses. A hypersensitive immune system, on the other hand, is extra-vigilant, overreacting to the slightest provocation. Asthmatic attacks may be a manifestation of this underlying vigilance.[65]

The best evidence for a link between broad environmental pollution and immune dysfunction may be the effect of air pollution on asthma.

Certain kinds of air pollution common in industrial countries, such as acidic aerosols, nitrogen dioxide (NO_2), ozone, and sulfur dioxide (SO_2), worsen asthma. Acidic aerosols are formed from SO_2 and NO_2 by a chemical reaction that recruits ground-level ozone. (A different reaction, involving sunlight and the volatile organic chemicals present in automobile exhaust, produces ground-level ozone.) Studies of the effects of acidic aerosols and sulfur dioxides on asthma patients show that both pollutants increase spasms in the airways. Acidic aerosols are currently not included as one of the six "criteria" air pollutants (carbon monoxide, lead, nitrogen dioxide, ozone, particulates, and sulfur oxides) regulated under EPA's national air quality standards.[66]

Particles are another pollutant whose role in triggering asthma may be substantial. They are made up of a variety of substances and come in many different sizes, which complicates the task of regulating them. Some particles, for example, incorporate acidic aerosols; others do not. Studies of the health effects of fine particles in Canada and in U.S. cities have found a connection between concentrations of particles in the air and hospital visits for asthma. A recent study in Seattle found an increased risk of asthma attacks (measured by emergency admissions) even when particulate concentrations in the air met federal air quality standards.[67]

Scientists do not fully understand the causes of asthma and propose diverse explanations for its increase. Some of the theories include lack of physician training, indoor air pollution (especially cigarette smoke and house mites), and poorly regulated acidic and nonacidic particles. Whatever role these other factors play in asthma, there is little question that air pollution increases both the incidence and severity of asthma and that air pollutants linked to asthma exist at health-threatening levels in many urban areas.[68]

PROOF AND THE LIMITS OF SCIENCE

Establishing an industrial pollutant or pollutants as the cause of a specific health outcome in people is no easy job. The task requires a mix of toxicological and epidemiological evidence. Data showing that a substance causes cancer in laboratory animals, for example, are generally not regarded as sufficient to prove carcinogenicity in people. EPA and the International Agency for Research on Cancer require both experimental and epidemiological data before listing substances as known human carcinogens.[69]

Epidemiological evidence is considered more reliable than toxicological data, since it provides direct information on human health effects. But the very terms used by epidemiologists betray the limitations of their science: they speak of "associations" instead of "causes."

As a general rule, epidemiology is a blunt tool. Epidemiological studies often miss the small contribution of a pollutant among all the competing explanations for higher disease rates. Investigations of cancer clusters in communities in the United States, for example, have mostly failed to pinpoint a specific cause for the unusual outcroppings of the disease.[70]

This is partly due to the fact that cancer is a broad outcome influenced by many factors, including alcohol, diet, and genes. But it is also the result of another weakness of many epidemiological studies—the lack of "statistical power." Rarer toxic effects that would occur only in a very large study population often fail to appear in small communities. Detecting small increases in risk, such as a one-in-a-million increase in the incidence of cancer, is practically impossible in most cases, since epidemiologists would have to study a very large population for a long period of time. (Cancer latency is often 20 years or more.) The chances that all the members of such a large population would stay in place long enough to let investigators count any excess cases of cancer are very slight. Epidemiologists also find it difficult to assess the health effects of slight exposures to toxicants, since the outcome of such exposures can be subtle and since it is difficult to reconstruct exposures that happened many years ago.[71]

In general, the minimum increased risk that epidemiological studies can detect is somewhere between 10 and 20 percent. Yet U.S. regulations generally allow no more than a one-in-a-million risk of cancer from lifetime exposure to any chemical carcinogen. As a result, even risks that are many times above those that laws supposedly allow might exist but remain undetected by epidemiological studies, and unassigned to any environmental cause.[72]

But the biggest disadvantage of epidemiological studies is that they only measure ill effects once they have occurred, and so furnish no predictions for future effects given present exposures. This limitation can be offset by toxicological studies, which can provide some warning of risk to humans before exposure occurs. But there are many gaps in toxicological evaluations of chemicals as well. Toxicologists are often forced to test at high doses, meaning that they also collect little direct information on health effects at low levels of exposure. High doses are used to ensure that any toxic effects that might exist are evoked in small populations of laboratory animals. Health outcomes at high levels of exposure are then extrapolated to effects at lower levels, using mathematical models. Finally, scientists make educated guesses as to the human health effects that might parallel theoretical low-level effects in laboratory animals.

Low-level exposures could be extremely important in terms of subtle and persistent toxicity. Human epidemiological studies of populations exposed to low levels of PCBs and lead have suggested that levels of exposures entirely within the range experienced by the general population can be detrimental to the central nervous system—slowing growth, delaying development, and creating IQ deficits.[73]

Toxicology falls short of reflecting reality in another way. While most substances are tested individually, in isolation, people rarely encounter chemicals one at a time. Most exposure to solvents, for example, is to mixtures rather than single chemicals. Researchers have garnered little information on the health effects of various combinations of chemicals, but what little there is suggests that chemical interactions may affect toxicity profoundly. Adding chemicals together can produce synergistic, additive, or antagonistic effects. Alcohol, for example, enhances the toxicity of carbon disulfide and other solvents.[74]

Epidemiological studies only measure ill effects once they have occurred, and so furnish no predictions for future effects given present exposures.

Pesticides, too, interact synergistically. Malathion and a pesticide known as EPN enhance each other's effects. EPA permitted both pesticides to be applied to 33 different crops. (The permit to use EPN was cancelled by EPA in 1987.) According to the National Research Council's latest report on the health effects of pesticides in children, "the existence of synergism at low levels of exposure cannot be assessed directly. It is conceivable that two compounds, innocuous by themselves, might interact chemically even at low doses to form a new substance that is toxic."[75]

There is also some evidence suggesting that part of the population is more sensitive than the average person to the effects of a whole range of chemicals. For these people, who suffer from a syndrome known as multiple chemical sensitivity (MCS), the risks posed by even very slight exposure to chemicals might be much greater than currently is appreciated. MCS is an extreme example of the general problem of how to tie chemical causes to real or apparent health outcomes. There is little evidence to suggest so far that chemically sensitive people actually have been injured. No adverse effects are generally believed to exist at such low concentrations, making MCS extremely controversial within the medical community. Nonetheless, people who have chemical sensitivity often claim their memory and other intellectual abilities have been damaged.[76]

However the debate on MCS is resolved, the condition adds to the evidence that people differ remarkably in their susceptibility to the toxic effects of individual chemicals, for a variety of reasons. Genetic defects, poor nutrition, and lowered immunity can exacerbate certain toxic effects. Low-income children who lack iron and calcium in their diet, for example, tend to be more severely affected by lead exposure than better-nourished children exposed to similar lead levels.[77]

The wide range in individual sensitivity to chemicals and scientific uncertainties about the potency of many substances mean that no neat formulas for the health risks posed by environmental pollutants exist. Even the most painstakingly performed "risk assessments" are plagued by genuine scientific controversy.[78]

Yet in most countries where chemical emissions and pollution levels are controlled, regulations are based on the assumption that people are fairly similar in their susceptibility to toxicants and that numbers can be plugged into risk formulas. Regulatory agencies charged with evaluating the hazards posed by pollutants use a factor of 10 to account for individual differences that might make some people more vulnerable to toxic effects than others. This estimate of individual differences may not be appropriate. Risk assessments of suspected toxicants also generally fail to consider the extra danger many chemicals pose to the fetus during critical stages of development and children's weaker defenses against toxic hazards.[79]

Just as worrisome is the fact that some portions of the population are exposed to more pollutants than others. Many workers, for example, are routinely exposed to health-threatening levels of toxic substances. U.S. laws often permit workers to be exposed to health risks from chemicals that are 100 times greater than those allowed for the general population—such as a one-in-a-thousand risk of cancer instead of one-in-a-million. In many developing countries, protections for workers are nonexistent or not enforced.[80]

In the United States, environmental health risks are widely acknowledged to be more severe in low-income and minority communities. Traditional civil rights groups, such as the National Association for the Advancement of Colored People, have begun to turn their attention to "environmental justice." Studies by public interest groups have documented that three out of five African Americans and Hispanic Americans live in communities with toxic waste sites. Some 55 percent of poor black children have blood-lead levels associated with adverse effects on the nervous system. One quarter of poor white children run this risk, compared with 7 percent of affluent white children.[81]

Studies in the United States and in other industrial countries have shown higher rates of cancer in farmworkers and other groups who work with pesticides, as mentioned earlier. Pesticides are also well-known neurotoxins. But little is known about rates of cancer or neurological illness among certain groups of farmworkers, such as migrants in the United States, and farm laborers in developing countries, who have high exposure to pesticides. (Only 1–2 percent of pesticide-related illnesses that occur in the United States are thought to be reported.)[82]

The poor are at higher risk from chemical exposure for a number of reasons: they are more likely to work in dirty professions, to live close to polluted sites, to suffer from inadequate nutrition (which can exacerbate toxic effects), and to have less access to health care. A recent study found measurable impacts of low levels of lead on children's cognitive performance. The authors note that had they studied poor children in place of middle-class children, such effects might have been difficult to distinguish from other variables affecting development, despite the fact that the effects in poor children may loom even larger than those among affluent children.[83]

Unfortunately, most risk assessments ignore the fact that exposure to toxic chemicals is unequal and rely instead on estimates of "average" exposure levels. But just as hunger can exist as a problem of serious proportions even while average food consumption is adequate, levels of toxic exposure may be a problem in many local regions without being a problem on a national level.

In order to really assess the risks posed by chemicals, regulators must act not only as toxicologists but as sociologists. "Who has poor access to health care, who lives in dirty neighborhoods, and who suffers from bad nutrition? From a public health perspective, these are all relevant answers to the question, Who is at risk from toxic exposure?" comments Robert Ginsburg, an environmental health consultant in Chicago. He notes that one-part-per-million benzene exposure in Winnetka, Illinois, represents an entirely different risk than in a southeast Chicago neighborhood where 80 percent of the residents are poor and live close to a major highway, a steel plant, a landfill, and a sewage treatment plant.[84]

Translating such realities into policies that better safeguard public health is not exactly straightforward. The most desirable, long-term solution is preventing exposure in the first place. This is best accomplished by lowering our reliance on synthetic chemicals, perhaps through a combination of pushes and prompts, such as tax incentives and federally mandated phaseouts. Farmers can be weaned off pesticides, for example, if they move toward integrated pest management, which combines nonchemical methods of pest control, such as rotating crops and introducing pests' natural enemies, with selective use of chemicals. In fact, the Clinton administration recently proposed just such an approach.[85]

Most risk assessments ignore the fact that exposure to toxic chemicals is unequal and rely instead on estimates of "average" exposure.

Implementing similar measures in industry is far more complicated, but many substitute chemicals or new processes may remove the need for a number of toxic chemicals currently in use. The semiconductor industry, for example, originally dependent on such toxic solvents as methylene acid and hydrochloric acid for its manufacturing processes, during the last few years has substituted more-benign water-based processes in a number of instances. Other substances, such as lead and mercury, could be removed from many products. Until recently, for example, mercury was allowed in interior latex paints in the United States. The death of a toddler in Michigan due to evaporation of mercury fumes from fresh paint belatedly led to an EPA ban.[86]

Unfortunately, more modest, interim measures will probably govern the exposure to toxic substances that communities and workers endure for the next few generations. But some intermediate steps nonetheless have the potential to make a significant contribution to protecting the public. The first one is education: both workers and the general public need much more information about the chemical hazards they routinely face. A second step involves more research into groups likely to live in hot spots of contamination, such as around the Great Lakes region in North America, in the Amazon Basin, and in inner cities everywhere.

Caution also clearly calls for the thorough evaluation of suspect substances for their ability to cause a wide range of health effects in different groups of people. Safeguarding public health is presumably the ultimate goal of regulatory agencies. Adopting one of the central principles of the public health field—prevention of disease—would amount to a revolution in the way most governments now regulate chemicals. Government, industry, and the public have implicitly regarded synthetic chemicals as benign until epidemiological studies provide evidence to the contrary. By definition, action at this stage comes too late.

Questions no doubt remain about the precise contribution of industrial pollutants to human disease and dysfunction. But there is ample evidence that cumulatively they are causing significant harm to humans. Given the shadow this casts over these "conveniences" of modern life, overturning the presumption of innocence about chemicals is long overdue.

8

Cleaning Up After the Arms Race

Michael Renner

The method was crude, the language blunt: when the U.S. military sank entire ships filled with chemical weapons during the sixties, the program's code name was "Operation CHASE"—Cut Holes and Sink 'Em. Operation CHASE was far from exceptional. From the end of World War II to the late sixties (and in some cases until today), governments jettisoned hundreds of thousands of tons of obsolete chemical warfare agents, nuclear weapons wastes, and conventional ammunition through ocean dumping, land burial, or open-air burning—with little thought of the environmental consequences.[1]

As a series of pathbreaking disarmament treaties comes into effect in the aftermath of the cold war, a volume of military equipment that far surpasses any routine scrapping of obsolete stocks now awaits disposal. Compared with the sixties, the language today is more guarded and the methods less crass. But there is still no well-developed, environmentally acceptable way to dispose of unwanted weapons. Governments and

their contractors have long honed their expertise in building ever more sophisticated weapons, but they have devoted comparatively little effort to devising ways to dismantle them safely.

Faced with deadlines for arms reductions mandated by international agreements, with growing pressure to respect environmental laws, and with greater public scrutiny, governments are belatedly scrambling to improve disposal methods. Some proposals border on the absurd. The Chetek Corporation, for example, a spinoff of the former Soviet nuclear weapons complex, proposed in 1991 to destroy chemical weapons in underground nuclear explosions—an idea that the U.S. Defense Nuclear Agency also briefly flirted with in 1982. Others have proposed shooting chemical weapons into the sun or dumping them in an active volcano.[2]

An array of weapons and materials need to be destroyed or dismantled in an environmentally acceptable manner, including nuclear and chemical warheads, conventional explosives and propellants, solid and liquid rocket fuel, and reactor cores from nuclear-powered submarines. These challenges of disarmament come on top of another cold war legacy: the production and maintenance of nuclear, chemical, and conventional weapons generated enormous quantities of toxic and radioactive substances that led to massive contamination problems at virtually every military base and arms factory.[3]

Luckily, the cold war did not turn into a hot one. But the bitter irony is that in the name of deterring attack, each protagonist effectively poisoned itself. The threat of annihilation has vanished, but the threat at home persists.

The massive arms buildup of the past half-century rested on a political consensus that elevated "national security" to a virtually unquestioned goal. But the sense of mission and destiny that sustained the cold war effort has largely dissipated. It will be much harder to marshal the political support and the resources needed to meet the disarmament challenge.

ARMED TO THE TEETH: NOW WHAT?

During 40 years of East-West confrontation, government planners seemed prepared for every possible scenario and braced for every contingency save one: the end of the cold war. Military strategists, procurement officials, and weapons designers all pursued the overriding goals of devising more sophisticated weapons and producing and deploying as many of them as their nations' economies could possibly sustain. Hundreds of billions of R&D dollars spent since World War II "have revolutionized the reach, accuracy, speed of delivery, and lethality of modern armaments. Increases of 200 to 600 times in the 'quality' of weapons are not uncommon," concluded Ruth Sivard in her 1989 *World Military and Social Expenditures* report. By contrast, finding ways to get rid of the arsenals, and doing so safely, was unlikely to further the careers of government scientists or to win a badge of national honor. Dismantling weapons is only belatedly attracting more serious funding, even as huge amounts of money continue to be thrown into military R&D.[4]

The world's governments have acquired a collective destructive arsenal that defies comprehension. By the early nineties, they had either deployed or stockpiled more than 50,000 nuclear warheads (containing the explosive equivalent of an estimated 13 billion tons of TNT); more than 70,000 tons of poison gas; millions of tons of conventional ammunition and explosives; some 45,000 combat aircraft; 172,000 main battle tanks; 155,000 artillery pieces; and close to 2,000 major surface warships and submarines. The destructive force contained in these weapons was so great that years ago a new term had to be coined to describe it: overkill.[5]

The thawing of the cold war broke the seemingly unrestrained momentum of the arms race. A series of treaties since 1988 mandate the reduction of nuclear, chemical, and conventional arsenals, and recent political transformations have permitted additional, unilateral cuts. With the exception of chemical weapons, which are to be eliminated altogether, the overkill arsenals are in effect being weeded out, leaving still very substantial stockpiles. Almost all these treaties are between industrial nations that own the bulk of armaments worldwide, so they do not bind Third World governments, some of which are building considerable military machines of their own. Thus although recent years have brought some welcome disarmament breakthroughs, large quantities of arms will remain unless additional treaties are signed.[6]

What happens with surplus weapons and military equipment? To date, international arms agreements have been narrowly focused on the numbers and kinds of weapons that may be deployed by the armed forces; they have largely given insufficient or no attention to the fate of weapons withdrawn from deployment. Surplus weapons and equipment could therefore simply be put in storage or be exported to countries not subject to treaty limits. Storage is undesirable, however, because it can easily be reversed, and export is objectionable because it merely redistributes weapons across the globe and could fuel regional arms races. The best path is to dismantle or destroy these items or, where feasible, convert them to civilian use. To achieve true and irreversible disarmament, future arms agreements—or amendments to existing treaties—will need to specify in precise terms the ultimate disposition of weapons and equipment.

Can armaments be converted to peaceful uses rather than demolished? In an age of disarmament, does military equipment become waste material to be discarded? Or is it a resource, an asset that can yield civilian benefits or at least pay for the costs of disarmament?

Three basic conversion options exist. First, military hardware might be reconfigured for civilian tasks: tanks could become fire-fighting equipment, helicopters and trucks be put to nonmilitary use, and missiles be used in civilian space exploration. Second, military materials might be processed to make them usable for civilian purposes: chemical warfare agents transformed into feedstocks for the chemical industry, fissile materials diluted for consumption in nuclear power reactors, or conventional explosives recycled for use in mining or construction. Third, in place of reusing entire pieces of equipment, scrap materials from dismantled weapons and equipment might be salvaged: tanks, missiles, warplanes, and submarines contain substantial amounts of such valuable metals as copper, aluminum, chromium, titanium, and special high-strength steels.

International arms agreements have given insufficient or no attention to the fate of weapons withdrawn from deployment.

Facing both a massive disarmament task and a difficult economic transformation, the Russians are particularly eager to derive some financial benefit from dismantling their vast weapons stocks. But there are clear limits to such a strategy. Civilian reuse of entire pieces of equipment is likely to be difficult technically and marginal economically; most of the military hardware has little intrinsic civilian value. Even such "dual-use" items as army trucks are problematic, given their comparatively high fuel consumption. The second and third options also have some potential drawbacks. If large amounts of materials are released from military stocks, civilian markets could be flooded and prices depressed, causing severe problems for civilian industries. And from an environmental perspective, the desirability of making supplies available to chemical and nuclear industries deserves careful scrutiny. Out of the three options above, it appears that the third is the most practicable, while the second may be applicable in some cases.

Whichever disposal route is chosen, it must be verifiable by inspectors or monitoring equipment, make renewed military use difficult or impossible, prevent the theft or diversion of military materials (of particular concern in the former Soviet Union where, given bleak economic prospects, scientists and technicians might be tempted to sell weapons materials or know-how on the black market), meet the deadlines for completing weapons destruction stipulated in arms treaties, and be affordable.

Arms treaties have by and large skirted another criterion—compliance with safety and environmental standards—but pressure from citizens groups to develop adequate technologies and provide for greater public involvement is growing. There is at least some potential for conflicts between disarmament and ecological priorities, as a dispute over chemical weapons destruction indicates: Arms control groups prefer that weapons be eliminated as quickly as possible. Environmentalists agree, but are concerned that quick disposal could come at a substantial safety and environmental price. But weapons and equipment can be "demilitarized"—rendered inoperable—in a manner that both meets the disarmament requirements of international agreements and provides breathing room to figure out environmentally acceptable ways of disposing of these items.[7]

Although most governments have only begun to consider technologies for dismantling weapons and institutional frameworks to master the challenge, myriad political and financial obstacles may yet impede a swift completion of current disarmament plans. There are, for instance, lingering fears about whether the turbulent politics within and among the Soviet successor states will derail nuclear disarmament. Ukraine, for one, locked in a series of disputes with neighboring Russia (the principal heir to the Soviet arsenal), is having second thoughts about its pledge to become a non-nuclear state. All the Soviet successor states are in dire economic straits that may force them to give weapons dis-

mantlement—a costly endeavor—low priority. And growing public mistrust of government agencies that deceived their own people about the health and environmental consequences of the arms race is likely to slow down or even halt projects to destroy weapons in East and West alike.[8]

NUCLEAR MATERIALS

Through much of the eighties, when East-West antagonism reached new heights, peace campaigners' demands were quite simple, and quite appropriate to their time: they called for a freeze on new deployments of nuclear arms and for the withdrawal of those already in place. As the demand for disarmament has found its way from banners and leaflets into government documents, the way to do this deserves much greater scrutiny. Missiles are being scrapped, submarines decommissioned, and bombers mothballed, but the ultimate fate of fissile materials contained in nuclear warheads—plutonium and highly enriched uranium (HEU)—remains to be decided. In fact, none of the treaties between the United States and the former Soviet Union even addresses the issue.

At its peak in 1988, the global nuclear arsenal is believed to have numbered some 25,000 strategic warheads and close to 35,000 tactical warheads, of which the two superpowers controlled more than 95 percent. The Strategic Arms Reductions Treaties (START I and II) will shrink the number of warheads deployed worldwide to perhaps 12,000 over the next decade, although another 10,000 or so may remain in storage.[9]

Though precise numbers remain government secrets, rough estimates of fissile materials are available. The amounts are clearly staggering: there are an estimated 257 tons of weapons-grade plutonium and at least 1,300 tons (though possibly more than 1,800) of HEU, either assembled in warheads or held in storage. (See Table 8–1.) By way of comparison, about 150 kilograms of plutonium, appropriately distributed, would be sufficient to cause lung cancer in the entire human population. Assuming that the United States and the Soviet successor states reduce their arsenals to a total of 10,000 warheads, some 140 tons of weapons-grade plutonium and 640 tons of HEU will be released. Adding the

Table 8–1. Estimates of Global Plutonium and Highly Enriched Uranium (HEU) Inventories, 1990/1991[1]

Country	Plutonium[2]	HEU[3]
	(tons)	(tons)
Former Soviet Union	125	720[4]
United States	112	550
Britain	11	10
France	6	15
China	2.5	15
Israel	0.33	—
India	0.29	—
South Africa	—	0.2–0.5
Pakistan	—	0.13–0.22
World	257	1,310

[1]The figures represent rough estimates (due to the lack of more accurate, publicly available information), with error margins of plus or minus 15 percent for plutonium, and plus or minus 30 percent for HEU. [2]There are also 654 tons of plutonium held by nonmilitary sources, more than 80 percent of which is unseparated (that is, contained in spent reactor fuel); in contrast, virtually the entire stock of military plutonium exists in separated form. [3]Almost all HEU is used for military purposes; there are only about 20 tons in civilian stockpiles. [4]Possibly as high as 1,200 tons.
SOURCE: Compiled from David Albright, Frans Berkhout, and William Walker, *World Inventory of Plutonium and Highly Enriched Uranium 1992* (Oxford: SIPRI and Oxford University Press, 1993).

stocks of weapons-grade material held in storage, the totals would rise to around 200 and 1,180 tons, respectively. (In addition to the fissile materials, non-nuclear yet often hazardous components such as casings and fuses need to be disposed of as well: in the United States, some 1,000 tons worth).[10]

Exactly what portion of these materials will actually be "demilitarized"—irrevocably removed from any possible renewed military use—is unclear, however. Existing arms treaties provide no guidance and impose no constraints on the disposition of warheads withdrawn from deployment or on the fissile materials contained in them. Both the United States and Russia have apparently decided to disassemble most of the withdrawn warheads, even though they are not required to do so, and to put the remainder in storage. But the fate of the fissile materials has not been decided.

Dismantling warheads is a difficult undertaking, generating a variety of radioactive and toxic wastes and posing potential health hazards for workers. The poor record of the nuclear weapons industrial complex makes outside scrutiny imperative to ensure that this takes place in a safe manner. Many of the older Soviet nuclear weapons are in an unreliable, dangerous condition; apparently, numerous weapons design specialists faced with unemployment are leaving to find work elsewhere, raising the specter that much of the know-how needed for safe dismantling may not be available.[11]

Once the warheads are dismantled, the weapons-grade materials could theoretically be reused in new warheads. The United States used to do this quite a bit during the cold war years, though the Soviet Union did much less so. In unilateral promises to the United States and the other nuclear successor states to the Soviet Union, Russia has agreed not to "recycle" fissile materials recovered from dismantled warheads into new weapons. Although U.S. warhead production has come to a halt, Washington has made no reciprocal pledge.[12]

Once a decision is made to remove a given quantity of plutonium and HEU from future military use, the fundamental outstanding question is how to "dispose" of these dangerous, long-lived substances. A recent report by the U.S. Office of Technology Assessment (OTA) concluded that these materials will need to be put in storage, perhaps for decades, regardless of their ultimate fate because other options will not be available for many years. Existing facilities are not designed for long-term storage, and there are limits to how long fissile materials can be safely stored without additional processing. Furthermore, storage does not erect much of a barrier to military reuse if the government owning the materials decides it needs weapons. To prevent the diversion, theft, or loss of any materials, it is preferable to place them under international safeguards.[13]

The long-term options are more straightforward for HEU than for plutonium. Many observers have proposed blending HEU with depleted or natural uranium, in effect diluting it from weapons-grade enrichments of 90–95 percent to below 5 percent, and thus making it usable as commercial nuclear reactor fuel. Princeton University's Center for Energy and Environmental Studies (CEES) estimates that enough HEU exists to fuel the world's nuclear power reactors for about two years. (Although the HEU would no longer be directly available for military purposes, burning uranium in reactors does of course generate long-lived waste products, including plutonium.) Environmentalists may balk at prolonging the operation of nuclear reactors, but military uranium alone will not make or break that industry. If the choice is between using diluted HEU in an existing nuclear reactor and

mining and processing more virgin uranium, the former is environmentally preferable.[14]

Desperate to earn hard currency, the Russian government is exploring ways to export diluted HEU. In February 1993, the U.S. government agreed to buy some 500 tons of HEU from Russia during the next 20 years—10 tons annually during the first five years, and 30 tons a year thereafter. Diluted to 15,000 tons of low-enriched uranium, the fuel would be able to run existing U.S. power reactors for at least a decade, and would earn Russia some $12 billion in foreign exchange. By contrast, the U.S. government has so far been reluctant to make its own HEU available for commercial purposes.[15]

Weapons-grade plutonium poses a greater challenge. It can be stored in three different forms: as undismantled warhead "pits" (the term for the shaped core of a nuclear weapon) or, if further dismantled, as either a metal ingot or an oxide powder. Pits can be made useless for weapons in a manner that would require extensive refabrication for any new military use. Plutonium in metal form is pyrophoric (spontaneously combustible in air), although some steps can be taken to prevent that. Converting plutonium from a metal into oxide form entails some environmental risks, but plutonium oxide is safer and easier to handle. And it is largely unsuitable for weapons use; it would require expensive and difficult chemical reprocessing to convert the oxide back to metal.[16]

For the longer term, a variety of options are being discussed for plutonium, though none appears entirely satisfactory. Extensive research, development, and testing is needed to evaluate whether these are acceptable solutions. For technical, environmental, financial, or political reasons, however, "getting rid" of plutonium by exploding it underground, blasting it into the sun or into solar orbit, burying it below the seabed, dumping it in the ocean, using it to fuel advanced thermal reactors, or transmutating it in accelerators are all either impractical or unacceptable solutions. Most discussed are proposals to fuel commercial light-water or breeder reactors with plutonium—that is, treat it as a resource—or to vitrify it for burial in so-called geological repositories, and regard it therefore as waste.[17]

Companies or government agencies in Russia, Japan, and the United States continue to push for the use of breeder reactors as a way to "consume" plutonium from warheads. The Japanese government has proposed a "plutonium furnace" that, unlike traditional designs, would burn more plutonium than it breeds. Although the spent plutonium would not be directly useful for weapons, it would still be highly toxic. Two 1,300-megawatt reactors could apparently consume all Soviet weapons-grade plutonium within about 30 years. In April 1993, General Atomics, a U.S. company, and the Russian Ministry for Atomic Energy signed an agreement to build a $1.5-billion high-temperature, gas-cooled fission reactor in Russia, fueled at least partly by weapons plutonium. The reactor would apparently destroy up to 95 percent of the fuel and leave a residue unattractive for weapons purposes.[18]

Yet even under optimistic assumptions, it would take at least 10 years before either of these two reactor designs would be operating. It appears that these proposals are not so much dedicated to resolving the challenge of what to do with weapons-grade materials as they are a last-ditch effort to resurrect a moribund, expensive, unproven technology. Rather than surreptitiously creating a plutonium economy, with global trafficking in these dangerous materials and the possibility of their theft,

the world community would be well advised to place them under strict international controls.[19]

Another proposal is to blend plutonium oxide at concentrations of 3.5–5 percent with uranium into so-called mixed oxide (MOX) fuel, so that it can be used in commercial nuclear reactors. (Current designs would allow reactors to be run with a one-third MOX, two-thirds uranium mixture, but it is possible to design a reactor that burns exclusively MOX fuel). Yet there are numerous technical and economic difficulties. Existing capacities to produce MOX fuel are limited. In 1990, MOX fabrication plants worldwide consumed about 4 tons of (civilian) plutonium per year, a figure expected to grow to at most 18–19 tons annually by 2000. Given the availability of low-priced uranium, the appeal of plutonium fuels has been eroded even on economic grounds, which has curtailed investment in MOX fabrication facilities. Construction and licensing of any new plants would likely experience substantial delays.[20]

A variety of options are being discussed for plutonium, though none appears entirely satisfactory.

Given high economic, regulatory, and political hurdles, U.S. utilities rejected the option of MOX fuel as long as a decade ago, and their counterparts in Western Europe and Japan are growing increasingly reluctant to use plutonium fuel. Russia's Ministry for Atomic Energy has expressed interest, but appears ill equipped technically and economically to move ahead decisively. CEES at Princeton University concluded that "it appears highly unlikely that more than 60–70 tons of plutonium could be used as fuel through 2000''—roughly half of the weapons-grade plutonium that may be released and only a fraction of combined military and civilian stocks. MOX fabrication plants are controversial on safety and environmental grounds. Like any nuclear fuel, using MOX in nuclear reactors generates some long-lived fission products. And plutonium can be extracted again by reprocessing the spent fuel.[21]

A preferable approach is called vitrification: plutonium oxide could either be mixed with liquid high-level radioactive waste and then converted into borosilicate glass blocks for disposal in a geological repository, or the plutonium could be incorporated in pure silica glass without the waste. The advantage of doing so is that it makes plutonium retrieval for weapons use very difficult, though not entirely impossible. The second vitrification option has a number of advantages over the first: it makes it more difficult to extract the plutonium again, it could be designed to be more leach-resistant, and it would make the resulting material easier to handle because it would be less radioactive.[22]

Planned U.S. facilities to vitrify military high-level wastes are sizable enough to accommodate all U.S. weapons plutonium (although no decision has been made to pursue this option), while insufficient capacities in Russia make vitrification there only a partial solution for now. Yet U.S. plans to construct and operate two vitrification facilities—one at the Hanford Reservation in Washington state and the other at Savannah River in South Carolina—have experienced considerable delays, technical difficulties, and cost overruns.[23]

Regardless of what is done with the plutonium, eventually it will have to be placed in some kind of repository—whether in pure form, vitrified, or embedded in spent fuel. In that sense, vitrification offers the most direct disposal

route. Still, long-term underground burial of nuclear materials and wastes remains an unresolved and highly controversial endeavor in both the civilian and the military realm. For example, the U.S. Department of Energy's plans to open a repository near Carlsbad, New Mexico, experienced yet another setback in February 1992 when a federal judge ruled that the agency needed prior approval from Congress and the state. And the projected opening date for the Yucca Mountain, Nevada, repository has slipped to 2010, although it is unclear whether it will ever open.[24]

Besides the fissile materials contained in warheads, nuclear disarmament also concerns the equipment used to launch them—the arsenal of ballistic missiles, submarines, and intercontinental bombers that the United States and the former Soviet Union have deployed. By and large, the START treaties do not directly require the destruction of missiles. Instead, strategic arms reductions are primarily carried out by destroying the launch systems (that is, the missile silos, submarine launch tubes, and long-range bombers). Under START II, Russia agreed to eliminate all its "heavy" SS-18 missiles by cutting them apart. In principle, other surplus missiles may be retained, even though they could not be deployed. All in all, the START treaties reduce the number of deployed ballistic missiles by 850 in the United States and by 1,450 in the former Soviet Union.[25]

The way they—or, more specifically, the fuels that propel them—are discarded is critical. Missiles that either government decides to eliminate could be destroyed on the ground or discarded by being launched untargeted. Alternatively, they could be used in civilian space programs, although any missile launch, whether military or civilian, releases toxic compounds and contributes to acid rain and ozone depletion. Most Soviet-made missiles are liquid-fueled, whereas U.S. missiles are primarily solid-fueled. Both contain highly hazardous materials, and each presents distinct disposal problems. Alternatives to established practice—open-air burning—are just now being developed.[26]

The START treaties also do not directly limit the number of nuclear-powered submarines. But they do impose an indirect cap by constraining the number of nuclear warheads that the United States and Russia may deploy at sea. In addition, as older submarines become obsolete—their useful life is about 25–30 years—they need to be decommissioned independent of any requirements of arms treaties. Some 300 nuclear-fueled submarines worldwide will need to be taken out of service by the turn of the century, a process that involves removing the nuclear fuel, cutting out the reactor compartment, and scrapping the remains of the submarine. Russia faces by far the greatest decommissioning task, but appears least able to master it.[27]

CHEMICAL WARFARE AGENTS

Chemical weapons share some unpleasant attributes with nuclear arms. They are, as Lenny Siegel of the Military Toxics Network in the United States puts it plainly, "dangerous to produce, dangerous to use, and . . . dangerous to destroy." The first two characteristics have long been recognized, but the world is only now beginning to come to terms with the need to develop safer ways of disposing of chemical weapons.[28]

From the end of World War II until at least the late sixties, captured and old chemical weapons were disposed of in the crudest manner imaginable—open-air burning, detonation, land burial, or ocean dumping. The United States, the Soviet Union, the United Kingdom,

France, and others sank hundreds of thousands of tons of chemical agents off the coasts of Alaska, California, and Florida, in the Baltic and North Seas and the Skagerrak (which connects these two bodies of water), in the Mediterranean, in the Barents and White Seas, and in the Sea of Japan. Large amounts of chemical munitions were also dumped on land in China, the Soviet Union, East and West Germany, Austria, and presumably elsewhere, typically with inadequate or no recordkeeping. The long-range dangers, including the possible threat to fisheries, are still largely unknown.[29]

Much of this was done without public knowledge and at a time when environmental awareness was limited. Now, however, as a major new round of chemical weapons disposal is about to begin, public scrutiny and international rules are setting new parameters for how the job should be done.

Only the United States and Russia have acknowledged they possess chemical weapons, but 18 other countries may secretly be in this club.

The Chemical Weapons Convention (CWC) was completed in late 1992 and is expected to come into effect in 1995. It requires the destruction of chemical warfare agents beginning no later than one year and finishing no later than 10 years after it takes effect (although countries can request a one-time five-year extension under exceptional circumstances). Individual states decide what destruction method they will use, although the treaty outlaws dumping in any body of water, land burial, and open-pit burning. Only the United States and Russia have acknowledged that they possess chemical weapons, but as many as

18 other countries may secretly be in this club. The U.S. arsenal contains some 31,400 tons of chemical warfare agents. The Russian Federation (the sole Soviet successor state that possesses chemical weapons) has a stockpile estimated at 40,000 tons, one quarter of which is of prewar vintage. Combined, these are more than enough to kill every living creature on the planet.[30]

It appears that neither the United States nor Russia is fully prepared for the requirements of the treaty. Technical difficulties and growing public opposition remain powerful obstacles to the successful destruction of chemical weapons within the time constraints imposed by the CWC. The United States has by far the most experience in the field but still lacks an environmentally sound disposal technology. Designing, constructing, and testing a destruction facility takes at least five years, and perhaps up to 12 years before full-scale operations can be undertaken.[31]

Anatoliy Kuntsevich, chairman of the Russian Committee on Chemical Weapons Disposal, faces three major problems: the possibility that chemical weapons specialists, whose expertise is needed in the dismantling process, may emigrate to escape economic hardship in Russia; inadequate funding for R&D to develop safe destruction methods; and deep-rooted opposition among local authorities and the public to planned destruction facilities. Public protests forced the Soviet government in September 1989 to abandon its only, nearly completed, destruction plant, near Chapayevsk on the Volga River in Saratov Oblast. Construction had begun in 1987, but local residents were neither consulted nor informed about the project.[32]

A new weapons destruction plan for the Russian Federation has been drawn up. It envisions three facilities that are to begin operating in mid-1997—one for-mer production plant, in Novochebok-sary in the Chuvash Republic, and two to be built (in Saratov Oblast and in Kambarka in the Udmurt Republic). These plants will be able to eliminate only about 43 percent of existing stocks by 2004, but growing public resistance raises questions about whether even this goal can be accomplished. So strong is the opposition that, according to the *Wall Street Journal*, "while Moscow has disclosed to the U.S. all seven of its storage sites, only four have been made known to Russians because officials fear public demonstrations." Deputies in the Supreme Soviet objected to plans to transport chemical weapons by train from storage locations to the designated destruction sites. And the Chuvash legislature opposes having a destruction facility in its territory. Kuntsevich is trying to win over the local populations—bribing may be a proper description—by promising them amenities such as new housing, hospitals, and laboratories.[33]

Russian officials are eager not just to destroy their chemical arsenal but to derive valuable materials to offset at least some of the high costs of disarmament. One widely reported proposal is to extract arsenic from lewisite weapon stocks and to transform it into gallium arsenide used to make semiconductors. Up to 2,000 tons of arsenic could be extracted and sold for perhaps $9 billion. Another suggestion is to turn phosphorus derived from nerve gas into phosphate fertilizer. Other plans would convert mustard gas into compounds that accelerate the vulcanization of rubber, and transform nerve gas into antiseptics and fire retardants. But numerous uncertainties plague such schemes, including practicality, cost (which could absorb a large part of any profits gained), and environmental implications. For example, the process of extracting arsenic could cause soil and water pollution.[34]

Besides the chemicals, other materials

incorporated in chemical weapons—assuming they are not contaminated—might be sold off for civilian purposes. The U.S. chemical weapons stockpile, for instance, contains an estimated 71,-000 tons of ferrous metal and 5,300 tons of aluminum.[35]

After the more indiscriminate disposal methods of ocean dumping and land burial were abandoned, a number of governments began to experiment with alternative methods, mostly incineration and chemical neutralization. But these efforts have involved relatively small quantities compared with the huge amounts that now need to be disposed of. For example, the former Soviet Union destroyed only some 438 tons of chemical agents between 1970 and 1990. And the destruction of Iraq's arsenal under United Nations auspices during 1992–93 involved roughly 500 tons.[36]

Only the United States has experience with destroying larger amounts of chemical warfare agents. Between 1969 and 1976, the U.S. Army used alkaline hydrolysis (a chemical neutralization process) and incineration to dispose of more than 7,000 tons of nerve and mustard gas at Rocky Mountain Arsenal, Colorado, and at Tooele Army Depot, Utah. In 1984 the Army formally adopted high-temperature incineration as the sole destruction method. It has operated two test facilities—in Tooele and on Johnston Island in the Pacific Ocean (the Johnston Atoll Chemical Agent Disposal System, or JACADS). In addition, the Army is constructing or planning to build incinerators in seven other states where chemical weapons are stockpiled. (See Table 8–2.)[37]

The decision to incinerate was endorsed at the time by the National Research Council (NRC), but that support, as the Office of Technology Assessment explains, was based "on a review of existing data supplied almost entirely by

Table 8–2. United States: Chemical Weapons Incinerators, 1992

Name, Location	Share of Stockpile
	(percent)
Tooele Army Depot, Utah	42.3
Pine Bluff Arsenal, Arizona	12.0
Umatilla Depot, Oregon	11.6
Pueblo Depot, Colorado	9.9
Anniston Army Depot, Alabama	7.1
Johnston Island, South Pacific	6.6
Aberdeen Proving Ground, Maryland	5.0
Newport Army Ammunition Plant, Indiana	3.9
Lexington-Blue Grass Army Depot, Kentucky	1.6
Total	100.0

SOURCE: U.S. Congress, Office of Technology Assessment, *Disposal of Chemical Weapons: Alternative Technologies—Background Paper* (Washington, D.C.: U.S. Government Printing Office, 1992).

Army research." OTA argues that "it is not clear that the same endorsement would be made today." Lenny Siegel of the Military Toxics Network argues that the real reason for embracing incineration was the Pentagon's eagerness to have Congress approve renewed chemical weapons production. In a quid pro quo, Congress gave the go-ahead, but required that old stocks be destroyed by 1994. Incineration was seen as the quickest way to meet the congressional deadline.[38]

The incineration program has come under growing criticism. Incinerators certainly make disarmament irreversible by destroying the compounds in question, but they have significant environmental and safety problems. As an open-ended system, they cannot completely prevent the emission of heavy metals, unburned chemical agents, and newly formed chemicals. And there could be accidental releases. The products of incomplete combustion include such highly toxic substances as polychlorinated dioxins and furans. These chemicals are very resistant to degradation by natural processes and therefore persist in the environment for long stretches of time, accumulating in the tissues of living creatures and building up to higher concentrations as they move up the food chain. Even at extremely low levels, they can lead to birth defects, liver and kidney damage, immune suppression, and neurological, developmental, and reproductive problems. (See Chapter 7.) The incinerator waste stream also includes toxic ash and brine, which need to be disposed of in a hazardous waste landfill.[39]

It is possible to render chemical munitions inoperable or make the materials unusable for military purposes while deferring on their final disposition.

Greenpeace has criticized the Army for being less than forthcoming about the precise volume of ash and brine that its Johnston Atoll test facility is generating. And, as OTA has pointed out, because the Clean Air Act does not apply to JACADS, "the Army is not collecting data to demonstrate compliance with this act, [even though] the continental sites are covered by the Clean Air Act." Thus in terms of public discussion, JACADS turns out not to be a true test facility in the sense of providing answers to all relevant issues.[40]

The experience at the two U.S. proto-type facilities has seriously undermined the Army's case that safety, efficiency, and cost considerations make incineration the technology of choice. They have experienced persistent mishaps in operating the plants, and the target date for completing the destruction of the stockpile has slipped from September 1994 to December 2004. A further delay cannot be ruled out. Meanwhile, projected costs have more than quintupled.[41]

Opposition to the planned incinerators has been particularly strong in Kentucky, Maryland, Indiana, and Utah. In part, local opposition is driven by fears that in addition to chemical weapons, the incinerators might later also be used to get rid of vast quantities of obsolete conventional munitions or military-generated hazardous waste. Congress initially prohibited such add-on usage, but in 1989 reversed itself and asked the military to explore the issue. Spurred by public protests, the state legislatures of Utah, Kentucky, and Indiana have imposed strict conditions and performance requirements on the incineration program in order to enhance safety. Kentucky also requires the Army to certify that alternatives safer than incineration do not now exist and will not be available before it can commence the burning of any chemical stocks. As opposition to incineration continues to build, many observers predict that the Army will never be able to proceed with its plans in Maryland or Kentucky.[42]

Public opposition also prompted another review of alternative disposal methods. Congress requested the Army to submit a report by December 1993 on alternatives to incineration, and to refrain from initiating any new plant construction until then. Furthermore, if the Army determined that the use of alternative technologies could meet the 2004 deadline at a cost equal to or less than incineration, Congress requires it to use the alternatives at the Kentucky, Indiana, and Maryland sites (which together account for about 10 percent of the total stockpile).[43]

Greenpeace and the Military Toxics Network have demanded a halt to all incineration and a vigorous effort to develop sound alternatives. Some arms control groups have taken issue with this position, fearing that environmental considerations could derail disarmament. And they are worried that no alternative will be ready in time to meet the 10-year deadline imposed by the Chemical Weapons Convention. Yet it is possible to render chemical munitions inoperable or make the materials unusable for military purposes in a manner consistent with the treaty's requirements, while deferring on their final disposition. This could be done by disassembling the weapons (separating the chemical agents from the explosives and propellants) and detoxifying the chemicals through partial oxidation. It would also eliminate the risk of leaks or catastrophic releases of chemical agents inherent in continued storage. Although it would take several years to develop any alternative technology, the U.S. Army's continuing technical problems and stiff public opposition to incineration are likely to delay the destruction process, at least at some sites.[44]

A broad range of possible alternative destruction technologies exist, including a variety of chemical, photochemical, electrochemical, and biodegradation processes. A recent National Research Council report categorizes them by the temperatures and pressures they use. Although "all possible alternative technologies will produce some set of wastes," as the NRC study points out, there are important differences among various methods. For instance, leaks are less likely to occur from low-pressure systems than from high-pressure equipment. And low-temperature chemical and biological processes are generally

not expected to lead to the formation of chlorinated dioxins. Similarly, nitrogen oxides are only generated in high-temperature oxidation processes.[45]

The major advantage of low-temperature processes, the NRC explains, is that they "permit highly controlled, closed environments"—that is, they involve no or minimal uncontrolled emissions of gaseous wastes. Within this category, hydrolysis and neutralization techniques (collectively referred to as detoxification processes) have been studied much more closely than low-temperature oxidation and biological methods. Detoxification processes must be carefully designed to meet the differing destruction requirements of mustard and nerve gas compounds. They are generally not applicable to the propellants and explosives contained in chemical munitions.[46]

Moderate-temperature, high-pressure processes can be used to treat chemical warfare agents, propellants, and explosives. Process temperatures are low enough to avoid the formation of nitrogen oxides, dioxins, and particulates. And these technologies can also be operated as a closed system, so that potential products of incomplete combustion can be treated rather than emitted through the smokestack. By contrast, high-temperature processes appear more problematic due to the formation of various hazardous waste products, large energy requirements, or technical complexity.[47]

Unlike some other destruction methods, the U.S. Army's incineration approach can handle not only all the different types of chemical agents but also the explosives and propellants and the munitions casings and containers. In contrast to this "one-size-fits-all" approach, Greenpeace argues it is better to tailor a demilitarization program to the diverging destruction requirements of the different components of the stockpile. To be most effective, individual processes are best combined in sequence. For instance, detoxification by chemical hydrolysis might be followed by a biological process or by a moderate-temperature process to further destroy organic materials. The resulting effluents might then undergo additional treatment in a catalytic oxidizer.[48]

Unfortunately, the U.S. Army's narrow focus on incineration means that so far, little thought has been devoted to developing alternatives or to the most effective combinations of individual processes. With the Chemical Weapons Convention's deadline on the horizon, time is running out.

CONVENTIONAL AMMUNITION AND EQUIPMENT

The end of the cold war and German unification set in motion a thinning-out of the massive conventional arsenals deployed in Europe. Some cuts were made unilaterally; others are mandated by the Conventional Forces in Europe (CFE) Treaty between members of the North Atlantic Treaty Organization (NATO) and the now-dissolved Warsaw Pact. To comply with the treaty, European arsenals have to be slashed by almost 15,000 tanks, more than 10,000 armored vehicles, and about 5,000 artillery pieces. As much as 90 percent of these cuts are to be made by the members of the former Warsaw Pact. The treaty gives considerable leeway, however, as to how the reductions may be carried out. A good portion of the surplus equipment will not be destroyed, but will be relocated outside the geographical area covered by the treaty, exported, converted to civilian use, or recategorized.[49]

Given the range of options, it is not clear what share of excess military material will actually be destroyed. It appears, however, that one of the largest arsenals to be dismantled is that of the defunct Nationale Volksarmee (NVA), the armed forces of the former East Germany. As part of the unification bargain, the new Germany pledged it would not be militarily stronger than West Germany alone would have been under the CFE Treaty limits; thus, some 80 percent of the NVA arsenal will be eliminated. Indeed, the armed forces of unified Germany will be one quarter smaller than the old Bundeswehr (West German army) alone. An estimated 30 percent of existing Bundeswehr material and equipment will also become surplus. All in all, close to 11,000 large weapons systems (mostly tanks and armored vehicles) will be eliminated by 1995, and as many as 25,000 during the next 15 years.[50]

One of the largest arsenals to be dismantled is that of the defunct armed forces of the former East Germany.

The options laid down in the CFE Treaty for scrapping tanks and other weapons—cutting, blasting, deforming them, or using them as ground targets—may be effective in preventing future military use but are rather unrefined with regard to potential environmental hazards. Tanks and armored vehicles are usually composed of alloy metals that produce toxic fumes when vaporized. Large-scale cutting operations can therefore result in substantial amounts of air pollution. The outer and inner surfaces of Soviet-made tanks are covered with paints that, when heated, emit nitrous gases and vapors of hydrochloric acid.[51]

Of concern are also various hazardous components and materials. In a typical battle tank, these include used oil (about

150 liters), lubricants (about 30 kilograms), hydrogen mixtures (about 100 kilograms), asbestos, radioactive materials, fiber-reinforced materials, and heavy metals. No matter what destruction method is used, the fluids contained in the equipment to be discarded—anywhere from 350 to 700 liters for a typical tank—must first be drained. As Stephen Ledogar, U.S. representative to the Conference on Disarmament in Geneva, has pointed out: "If these fluids are mixed when drained, they have to be treated as toxic waste in many countries. In addition, if these fluids are not drained and the explosive demolition method of destruction is used, it is possible that the equipment will be set on fire and will produce large volumes of hazardous smoke."[52]

As with nuclear and chemical weapons, certain materials can be extracted from conventional armaments for civilian reuse. For instance, Hans-Joachim Giessmann of the University of Hamburg points out that a typical main battle tank incorporates about 18 tons of high-alloy steel, 8 tons of low-alloy steel, 4.5 tons of nonferrous steel, 1 ton of aluminum, 145 kilograms of brass and bronze, 80 kilograms of copper, and 52 kilograms of lead.[53]

Data on existing ammunition stockpiles worldwide are not easy to come by, but it appears that by far the largest amounts are held by governments in the former Soviet Union. Russia apparently has some 35 million tons of ammunition, some of it dating back to the early parts of the century and entirely obsolete; Belarus has 1 million tons, and Ukraine, 550,000 tons. In addition, the Soviet Army had an estimated 1 million tons (some estimates speak of 2.5 million tons) stored in East Germany, much of it old and fragile. The East German armed forces controlled about 295,000 tons of ammunition, of which 54 percent is to be destroyed, 41 percent sold, and the re-

mainder retained by the German armed forces. (See Table 8–3.)[54]

What to do with the surplus ammunition? In the past, dumping at sea was the preferred option, typically without any monitoring of environmental effects. In fact, the U.K. government continued this practice until the beginning of 1993, when new international restrictions under the Convention for the Protection of the Marine Environment of the North East Atlantic came into force. The United Kingdom jettisoned an estimated 16,000 tons between 1987 and 1992 in this manner. Currently, no country is known to be dumping munitions at sea.[55]

Experience with destroying ammunition—other than dumping—is limited compared with the size of the task at hand. Complicating the endeavor is the bewildering variety of ammunition types, each of which requires different procedures to ensure safe disposal. The East German armed forces, for example, had 532 different types of ammunition.[56]

Currently, open-air burning and deto-

Table 8–3. Former East Germany: Disposition of Armed Forces' Conventional Ammunition Stocks, Early 1993

Disposition	Ammunition
	(tons)
Retained by Armed Forces of Unified Germany	16,000
Already Sold or Exported	50,000
To Be Sold or Exported	70,000
Already Destroyed	70,000
To Be Destroyed	89,000
Total	295,000

SOURCE: Artur Volmerig, "Die Materielle Hinterlassenschaft der NVA," *Wehrtechnik Spezial*, May 1993.

nation appear to be the most common methods, releasing a variety of hazardous substances. For each kilogram of explosives detonated, one cubic meter of toxic gaseous products is discharged into the atmosphere. Alternative methods under consideration stretch across a spectrum similar to that for chemical weapons. The characteristics and particularly the environmental implications of most of these processes still require considerable scrutiny. Few technologies have progressed beyond the research or pilot program stage. As millions of tons of ammunition are to be discarded, the need for developing sound methods is urgent.[57]

The U.S. Defense Department currently has some 400,000 tons of surplus ammunition, an amount expected to grow considerably during the next few years. The armed forces routinely dispose of conventional munitions through open-air burning, which the Defense Department considers the "fastest, safest, most reliable, and least expensive" method. The German government has placed a premium on the fast elimination of surplus and obsolete stocks. Capacities for processing ammunition were quadrupled. But the tight timelines also mean that open-pit burning is by far the predominant method used. One contractor in Torgau, Sachsen, is burning propellants in an area important as a drinking-water reservoir for the city of Leipzig. As in the case of chemical weapons, incineration is touted as the major alternative to conventional approaches, but most planned facilities failed to pass the permitting process because the technologies were found wanting. With the startup of a large incinerator in Sachsen, however, open-air burning was expected to stop in early 1994.[58]

An alternative to ammunition destruction is being pursued by Ukraine in a joint venture with a U.S. company, which is helping to discard more than 200,000 tons of surplus ammunition. After the munitions are taken apart, the propellants and explosives are removed and put to commercial use in mining and construction or converted into fertilizers. Scrap metal from munitions casings is to be sold on the commercial market. Sales of scrap copper, steel, brass, and aluminium are expected to generate more than $100 million in revenue in the next five years. Russia is likely to pursue a similar strategy.[59]

Destruction of surplus weapons covered by the CFE Treaty will have to be finished by 1995, but there are no international agreements imposing similar deadlines on the elimination of ammunition stocks (or, for that matter, even requiring reductions per se). Thus explosives and propellants could be rendered militarily unusable as an international confidence-building measure while time is taken to develop more acceptable disposal methods. Since substantial quantities of ammunition remain in national arsenals, doing the job correctly now will provide invaluable lessons for the future as well.

ARM NOW, PAY LATER

The full costs of meeting the dismantlement challenge can only be guessed at, but it is abundantly clear now that early assessments were much too optimistic. Estimates for destroying the U.S. chemical weapons stockpile, for example, have surged from $1.7 billion in 1985 to $9 billion. Putting a figure on the likely cost of destroying Russia's chemical arsenal is even more difficult, but estimates in the $10–20 billion range are common. Generally speaking, it will cost at least 10 times as much to destroy chemical weapons as to produce them. The cost of dismantling nuclear warheads in the United

States alone could approach $1 billion a year, and decommissioning U.S. submarines through the end of this decade carries a price tag of $2.7 billion. Disposing of surplus conventional ammunition worldwide could run to as much as $5 billion annually over several years, and destroying tanks and other equipment is likely to add several billions more. Combining these costs with the trillions of dollars spent to build the weapons in the first place and the hundreds of billions required for cleanup operations yields a truly staggering bill for the arms race.[60]

Russia faces the most formidable challenge: it needs to discard far more warheads, missiles, submarines, tanks, and ammunition rounds than any other nation, but it is broke. The United States, Japan, and several West European governments have pledged hundreds of millions of dollars of technical assistance to Russia (and to other Soviet successor states). But only a small portion has actually been made available so far, and much more may be needed. For instance, the U.S. Congress earmarked $25 million to help destroy Russia's chemical weapons, but Moscow is looking for as much as $650 million in western aid. More important, these pledges appear to be piecemeal—geared more toward storage and transport than toward dismantlement—at a time when a coordinated and strategic effort is needed.[61]

Although other countries face a less monumental task, their problems are basically similar. Thus a cooperative international program to investigate, develop, and share promising technologies to safely dispose of military equipment and materials is vitally important. Such an undertaking could easily be financed out of the still tremendous budgets now devoted to developing new weapons systems. Future arms agreements will need to be written in a manner that mandates measures to render equipment militarily

unusable while allowing flexibility regarding the ultimate, safe disposition of these items.

As military budgets shrink in many countries, arms contractors are transforming themselves into disarmament experts, expecting lucrative opportunities to dismantle the very weapons they themselves produced (and profited from) in the first place and to clean up the massive wastes they generated in the process. It could be argued that these companies bring special expertise to bear. But their usual enormous cost overruns and poor health and environmental records do not inspire much confidence that their performance will improve sufficiently.[62]

By default, it is the military bureaucracies that are in charge of disarmament. Infused with a philosophy that regards military preparedness as the paramount task, they have long put arms production ahead of environmental and safety considerations. This institutional mindset runs counter to the task now at hand. To pursue the dismantling with dedication and sincerity, it may be necessary to establish new agencies—disarmament ministries—and to transfer the requisite resources from the defense ministries.

The issues at hand—how best to dismantle and eliminate surplus arms—may seem to be best "left up to the experts." But there is in fact a need for much greater public involvement. It is important that contractors are held to high standards and their operations scrutinized. It is equally imperative that the military bureaucracies, historically given to secrecy and an aversion of public regulation, become more accountable and respectful of health and environmental laws.

Public pressure was instrumental in earlier years in persuading the armed forces to abandon such questionable practices as ocean dumping, and it has been the impetus for rethinking the open-air burning and incineration approaches currently in fashion with military-industrial decision makers. To be meaningful, public involvement will need to extend not just to oversight of dismantlement operations but also to the very process by which a particular technology is chosen and a facility site selected, to guard against an outcome that burdens politically or economically weak communities with the most hazardous facilities. Accountability can be strengthened by taking measures to ensure that civilian government agencies are in a position to enforce all applicable environmental and public health laws. At present, there is very little scope for public scrutiny. In 1992, the U.S. Congress took a small but important step in the right direction when it required the U.S. Army to establish Citizens Advisory Commissions at three sites chosen for chemical weapons incineration.[63]

Public involvement will need to extend to the very process by which a particular technology is chosen and a facility site selected.

The arms that are now awaiting disposal constitute but a part of the enormous arsenals that were built up during the cold war. Daunting as the task of safe elimination is, additional challenges already wait in the wings—be it as a result of new treaties that mandate further arms reductions, or simply as a consequence of the fact that weapons systems, like other human artifacts, become obsolete and must eventually be decommissioned.

As the difficulties of disposing of arms become clearer, logic would dictate greater apprehension toward new arms production, which inevitably imposes additional environmental and other

costs. By and large, however, the issue of future production has been sidestepped in almost all existing arms agreements. With the exception of the Chemical Weapons Convention, they indirectly put a cap on production by specifying how many weapons a government may deploy, but they do not as such limit or outlaw production.[64]

Military procurement spending has declined in most countries since the mid-eighties. Yet numerous arms production programs continue despite the end of the cold war. For example, some 13 major U.S. procurement programs for a variety of jet fighters, warships, submarines, and other items—all initiated during the cold war—will cost a total of $652 billion by the time they are completed. A similar picture emerges in other countries as well: although some arms programs have been cancelled or curtailed, many unneeded projects are kept alive. NATO procurement expenditures have declined by about a third from their 1987 peak, but are just barely below the level of the early eighties. And in East Asia, rising prosperity and unresolved conflicts have triggered a military spending boom.[65]

Particularly with regard to nuclear arsenals, the overkill is so tremendous that treaty limits have rendered some production programs moot. The United States, for example, is awash in weapons-grade fissile materials and has therefore stopped producing them; similarly, Russia will soon terminate its military fissile materials production, and France has stopped manufacturing plutonium and will end HEU production. Also, facing a difficult economic transition, Russia simply cannot afford to keep turning out as many weapons as the Soviet Union used to. Its production of intercontinental missiles has all but ceased and that of heavy bombers been cut back substantially; the construction of nuclear-powered submarines is to stop in 1994 or 1995. In 1992, Russian output of tanks fell by 33 percent and that of jet fighters by 57 percent compared with 1991, before the Soviet breakup. But no international treaty requires that the U.S., Russian, or any other government maintain such unilateral restraint, and changes in the political and economic outlook could cause any one of them to reverse course.[66]

Arms production ad infinitum flies in the face of one of the key lessons emerging from the cold war period: the production, maintenance, and disposal of huge quantities of arms incur significant environmental damage and immense financial costs. Governments and their arms contractors have hardly begun to come to grips with the legacy of 50 years of "peace through strength." Enormous amounts of military-generated hazardous waste need to be detoxified and disposed of, countless sites with heavy contamination of soil and water await cleanup and rehabilitation, and mountains of obsolete and surplus weapons need to be dismantled in an acceptable manner. By any account, these are daunting challenges that will require our careful attention—and considerable money—for many decades.

9

Rebuilding the World Bank

Hilary F. French

In July 1944, some 700 delegates from around the world convened at the Mount Washington Hotel in Bretton Woods, New Hampshire, to create a brave new international order in the wake of World War II. According to their vision, the institutions they were establishing—the International Bank for Reconstruction and Development (the World Bank) and the International Monetary Fund—would help ensure that international economic cooperation paved the way for improved living standards and peace worldwide.[1]

U.S. Treasury Secretary Henry Morgenthau captured the spirit of the moment in his opening address to the delegates. He foresaw the "creation of a dynamic world economy in which the peoples of every nation will be able to realize their potentialities in peace . . . and enjoy, increasingly, the fruits of material progress on an earth infinitely blessed with natural riches. . . . The opportunity before us has been bought with blood," he told the delegates. "Let us meet it with faith in one another, with faith in our common future, which these men fought to make free."[2]

Fifty years later, the optimism present at Bretton Woods has faded. The institutions created there have contributed in no small measure to the fivefold growth in world economic output and the twelvefold increase in international trade since 1950. But rather than being lauded as agents of material well-being and peace, the Bretton Woods institutions find themselves increasingly under fire as promoters of an economic development model that has failed to significantly dent the growth in poverty around the world. In addition, Morgenthau's faith that the earth is infinitely blessed with natural riches has run up against the sobering realities of global ecological decline. All too often, these institutions have acted as agents of environmental destruction rather than as instruments to combat it.[3]

In recent years, putting the world on the path toward sustainable development has become widely recognized as a pressing international priority. But our understanding of what this really entails lags behind the rhetoric. At its root, sustainable development is a form of development that satisfies current human needs without jeopardizing the resource base on which future generations depend. It is premised on the belief that protecting the environment and combating poverty are interlinked challenges—one cannot be accomplished in isolation from the other. Among other things, creating a sustainable society will require stabilizing and ultimately reversing the buildup of carbon dioxide in the atmosphere; preserving the earth's forest cover, soils, and biological diversity; reducing overconsumption of resources in rich countries and population growth rates in developing countries; decreasing income inequalities between and within nations; and improving the status of women.

At the Earth Summit in Rio in 1992, more than 150 governments pledged themselves to the goal of sustainable development, and charged international institutions with promoting it. The fiftieth anniversary of the Bretton Woods conference is an opportune time to begin putting in place the reforms that would enable the World Bank to accomplish this. If the Bank and the international community do not rise to the challenge, then any one-hundredth anniversary "celebration" will take place in a world of almost unimaginable biological and human impoverishment.[4]

THE LENDING LANDSCAPE

The impact of the World Bank extends far beyond the size of its lending program. (Four regional development banks have also been created in the postwar period that together lend almost as much money as the World Bank itself,

and have many of the same goals and problems. The discussion here is confined to the World Bank due to space constraints, but the rebuilding that is needed applies equally to these other institutions.) The Bank's involvement in a project or country often provides a "seal of approval" that opens the spigot for additional bilateral and multilateral funds, as well as for private bank loans. Projects supported are typically two to three times bigger than the size of the Bank's own contribution, with cofinancing from other sources making up the difference. More fundamentally, the Bank influences the type of development paths pursued by borrower nations through the economic and other policy advice it provides and the conditions attached to loans.[5]

World Bank lending has increased sharply since the institution was founded. (See Figure 9–1.) In 1993, the institution committed a total of $23.7 billion (see Table 9–1), making it the world's single largest lender. It was created to lend to governments rather than the private sector. Of the total in 1993, $17 billion was in regular International Bank for Reconstruction and Development loans, which are made to middle-income countries at near-market rates

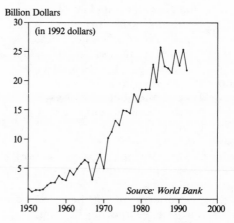

Billion Dollars

(in 1992 dollars)

Source: World Bank

Figure 9-1. World Bank Lending, 1950–92

State of the World 1994

Table 9–1. World Bank Lending by Sector, Fiscal Year 1993

Sector	Amount	Share
	(billion dollars)	(percent)
Energy[1]	3.6	15
Nonproject[2]	3.6	15
Agriculture and Rural Development	3.3	14
Transportation	3.2	13
Education	2.0	9
Urban Development	2.0	8
Population, Health, and Nutrition	1.8	8
Water Supply and Sewerage	1.2	5
Industry	1.1	5
Public-sector Management	0.6	3
Development Finance Companies	0.6	2
Technical Assistance	0.5	2
Telecommunications	0.4	2
Total[3]	23.7	100

[1]Includes $2.6 billion for the electric power sector and $1 billion for oil, gas, and coal projects.   [2]Mainly structural adjustment lending. Various sectors also include some funds for sectoral adjustment, making the total figure for adjustment lending $4 billion.   [3]Columns do not add up to totals due to rounding. SOURCE: World Bank, *Annual Report 1993* (Washington, D.C.: 1993).

over 15–20 year payback periods. This money is raised primarily in world capital markets with the backing of member governments. The remaining $7 billion was in International Development Association (IDA) "credits." A program initiated in 1960, IDA makes interest-free, "soft" loans (with a small annual service charge) to the world's poorest countries—those with per capita annual incomes of $805 or less—with payback periods spanning 35–40 years. It is funded almost entirely by direct contributions from member countries.[6]

A relatively new development for the World Bank is adjustment lending—cash assistance designed to ease balance-of-payments problems while policy reforms are undertaken. In exchange for access to these funds, governments agree to work on setting their domestic economic houses in order through such reforms as reducing government spend-ing, cutting subsidies, lowering inflated exchange rates, and lowering trade barriers. The International Monetary Fund is the primary practitioner of such policy-based lending. But the World Bank also began to devote substantial resources to this in the eighties as pressure mounted to respond to the debt crisis. Though the Bank originally planned to devote no more than 10 percent of its funds to this purpose, adjustment lending reached a peak of 29 percent of total lending by 1989. It has declined somewhat since then, but is still sizable—$4 billion in 1993, 17 percent of total lending.[7]

Another source of funds is the Global Environment Facility (GEF), a partnership between the World Bank, the U.N. Development Programme (UNDP), and the U.N. Environment Programme. The facility was created in 1991 to provide grants to cover the additional costs of investing in efforts to protect the global environment. In theory, it is a distinct entity from the Bank itself, operating under its own governing structure and by its own rules. Yet the Bank provides the physical location for the GEF secretariat and acts as the administrator. Projects accounting for more than 60 percent of GEF funds are implemented by the Bank; of these, more than half are attached to larger Bank undertakings. In practice, this means that the Bank's regular staff, management, and operating procedures exert a strong influence on GEF endeavors.[8]

Initially, governments committed $1.2 billion over three years for GEF projects that would protect biological diversity, combat global warming and ozone depletion, and protect international waters. In April 1992, projects to stem land degradation became eligible to the extent that they related to the four focal areas—though no project has received funds yet in this new category. Governments are now considering replenishing GEF with an additional $2.8–4.2 billion for the next three to four years.[9]

The process by which loans come to fruition within the World Bank—and by which overall lending priorities are set—is complicated and somewhat difficult to discern. In part, this is because the Bank is an unusual combination of commercial bank and development institution. As such, its operations represent a delicate dance between the interests of borrowing nations, the political priorities of funding nations, and the inclinations and bureaucratic inertia of the institution itself.

Officially, the Bank is answerable to a board of directors composed of donor nations. Voting power is related to the level of a country's financial contributions: for the IBRD, the United States holds 17 percent of the voting shares; Japan is the next largest, with 7 percent of the votes; and Germany has 5 percent.

Twenty-four executive directors representing the Bank's donor and borrower members meet regularly to consider policies. Major contributors have executive directors of their own; others share representation. Technically speaking, the directors approve all projects, as well as any major new policy direction.[10]

In practice, however, international civil servants may have more real power than the directors. The staff, after all, identifies and prepares the loans, and thus plays a central role in influencing lending directions. Members of the board sometimes have difficulty obtaining the documents used in the project preparation process, meaning they are all too often presented with a project to either approve or reject when it is too late to materially influence its course. Indeed, to date not a single project has been rejected by the World Bank's board, though several have been opposed by individual directors on environmental grounds.[11]

In practice, international civil servants may have more real power than World Bank directors.

Although it includes many dedicated people, the staff as a whole is not particularly well equipped for the task of promoting sustainable development. For one, they tend to work at the headquarters, far removed from on-the-ground realities. Some 6,800 staff members are based in Washington, D.C., with only 314 professional staff assigned to 69 field offices. In addition, the heavy concentration of economists and engineers on the staff has meant that other ways of viewing the world—be they ecologically or anthropologically inspired—tend to be neglected. This bias is compounded by the fact that their official counterparts in borrower nations are often their mirror image: finance and planning ministry officials with degrees in similar fields and from the same northern universities.[12]

The missing voice in this equation has typically been people whose lives will directly be affected by Bank decisions. Time and again, projects are approved with little or no consultation with local people. With the relevant documents secret and until recently no channel for their complaints, ordinary citizens in developing countries have often been left with little opportunity to influence projects that might relocate them, pollute their environment, change property rights, or otherwise greatly alter their lives.[13]

MOUNTING PRESSURE

In the early eighties, environmental nongovernmental organizations (NGOs) began to uncover and publicize numerous examples of World Bank projects that created environmental degradation and social dislocation on a massive scale. Bank support for the Polonoroeste regional development scheme of road-building and agricultural settlement in the Brazilian state of Rondônia, for instance, contributed to rapid deforestation of the area during the eighties; by one estimate, the share of the state that had been deforested increased from 1.7 percent in 1978 to 23.7 percent by 1988. World Bank backing was also instrumental to a coal mining and power plant scheme in Singrauli, India, that is one of the largest single sources of carbon emissions on earth. In addition, more than 200,000 people have been displaced from their homes by the project's five large power plants, 12 open pit mines, and eight cement plants. Some of the people have been forcibly resettled

as many as four or five times in the last 25 years without compensation.[14]

The effects of structural adjustment on the environment are also substantial—though complicated. Some proposed policy reforms under these loans, such as the removal of certain governmental subsidies, can be environmentally beneficial. Removing subsidies to the timber industry would benefit the forest and the indigenous peoples who live in it, for example, and cuts in government subsidies to fossil fuels might help encourage the more efficient use of energy. Including recommendations for policies that help internalize environmental costs—such as energy taxes—would also help adjustment loans serve the goal of sustainable development. Yet when currency devaluations lead to more exports of commodities whose production causes environmental harm, the natural resource base suffers, particularly if efforts to see that environmental costs are internalized are not undertaken at the same time. And to the extent that adjustment hurts the poor, studies indicate that it can also harm the environment, as desperate people cut down forests or till marginal land in their struggle to make ends meet.[15]

In response to the growing number of environmental debacles involving the World Bank, the U.S. Congress passed legislation in 1985 making U.S. contributions to it contingent on environmental reforms there. By 1987, this pressure began to yield some results. Newly installed Bank President Barber Conable announced a major environmental reform plan in May. He created a new central environment department and four regional units. In addition, he announced that all loans were to be screened for their environmental impact, and that NGOs would be more actively consulted in both donor and borrowing countries. Conable also committed to a range of new lending programs aimed at achieving environmental goals, including increasing the number of projects aimed specifically at environmental protection, incorporating environmental components in other projects, and increasing lending for ecologically sensitive forestry projects.[16]

Under the IDA replenishment agreement in 1989, a new policy was instituted requiring countries to prepare comprehensive environmental action plans in order to be eligible for IDA assistance. Developed by the countries themselves with the assistance of the World Bank, these plans are intended to identify environmental needs and define a strategy for responding to them, including policy changes, institutional and educational reforms, and investment priorities. Countries receiving IBRD loans are also "encouraged," though not required, to undertake such plans.[17]

In the years since these initiatives were launched, significant progress has been made in implementing them. For one, the amount of money devoted to free-standing environmental loans has indeed increased. By 1993, the Bank committed nearly $2 billion for 23 projects specifically designed to improve environmental quality—$1.3 billion for pollution control, $500 million for projects aimed at protecting natural resources, and $140 million for environmental institution-building. This amounted to a doubling in the funding of such projects over 1992 and a thirtyfold increase from 1989, though at least some of that increase is due to a change in the classification system. Second, the environmental screening process announced by Conable has been in place since 1989; projects are subject to different levels of scrutiny, depending on their expected impacts. Third, environmental action plans have been completed for 22 of a total of 70 IDA-eligible countries. Finally, the World Bank has begun to specifically address environmental issues in

many adjustment loans: between 1988 and 1992, 60 percent of a sample basket of loans explicitly included some environmental objectives or conditions. Though this represents some progress, adjustment loans are not routinely subjected to environmental impact assessments, let alone used as strong vehicles for promoting environmentally helpful policy reforms. Meanwhile, some damaging projects continue to be funded, suggesting that the holes in the World Bank's environmental net remain large.[18]

Damaging projects continue to be funded, suggesting that the holes in the World Bank's environmental net remain large.

In the wake of the Earth Summit, sustainable development is now recognized as an official priority of the World Bank. The 1992 edition of the *World Development Report*, an annual Bank publication, concluded that significant policy changes could be undertaken in developing countries that would encourage both environmental protection and economic development, including removing environmentally harmful subsidies and encouraging the efficient use of resources. The Bank will be working to identify such "win-win" strategies. In January 1993, a new Vice-Presidency for Environmentally Sustainable Development was created to help do this, with responsibility for three departments: environment; agriculture and natural resources; and transportation, water, and urban development. Unfortunately, the new post does not include responsibility for several other critical sectors, such as energy and population.[19]

Efforts to orient World Bank lending more explicitly toward combating poverty—a key component of sustainable development—have a longer, rather different, history. The first push came not from the grassroots but from the very top, when Bank President Robert McNamara made "basic human needs" the watchword of his tenure from 1968 to 1981. Under McNamara, lending to the "poverty sectors" increased dramatically. Loans for agriculture and rural development grew twenty-two-fold between 1968 and 1981. Investments in basic human needs, such as education, food and nutrition, drinking water, family planning, shelter, and health care, picked up speed as well, amounting to 15 percent of the lending portfolio by the end of the seventies. Importantly, Bank research conducted at the time demonstrated that these types of investments paid for themselves at a rate equal to if not higher than traditional infrastructure projects.[20]

In its growing obsession to lend progressively larger amounts of money, the Bank lost sight of the reason it was created.

During the eighties, the debt crisis burst onto the world scene, posing new challenges in the effort to fight poverty. The primary response was to emphasize structural adjustment lending in an effort to inject cash quickly into debt-ridden countries to help them service their obligations to foreign banks, while at the same time requiring domestic policy reforms that would ultimately restore these countries to economic health and creditworthiness. Without more fundamental debt relief, such assistance was badly needed by many countries. Critics charged, however, that the strategy amounted to a bailout of overextended commercial banks.[21]

Meanwhile, the medicine was proving extremely painful for many countries, particularly to the poor. Though the reforms were intended to fall evenly across the board, a number of reports, most notably UNICEF's landmark *Adjustment With a Human Face*, demonstrated that the poor were especially vulnerable to the adjustment process, partially because the politically powerful often manage to use their influence to escape the budget axe. Cuts in governmental budgets can translate into the loss of social security programs, for instance. And removing price ceilings on agricultural products can mean that the urban poor go hungry. As austerity took a bitter toll, protests in developing countries over the conditions attached to adjustment loans began to mount. In response to these developments, the Bank began to target the poor specifically in its lending.[22]

Whether the goal be environmental restoration or fighting poverty or a combination of the two, a precondition of success is ensuring that the people a project is designed to help are included both in defining its scope and in carrying it out. Though this would seem to be beyond question, it is in fact the exception rather than the rule for Bank projects, despite the fact that several evaluations have demonstrated that projects designed and instigated in cooperation with the people they are intended to benefit are far more likely to be successful than those that are not. The World Bank has come under increasing criticism for its failure to involve local people adequately in project design and execution.[23]

In an effort to improve its performance in this area, the Bank has begun a "learning process" on participatory development, in which 20 existing projects will be carefully studied to determine the feasibility of introducing participatory approaches more widely. In addition, it has gradually been increasing the share of its projects that involve NGO collaboration. In 1993, 30 percent of all projects included NGOs. A further challenge is to use Bank leverage within countries to create the policies, regulations, financial systems, and other government structures needed for grassroots organizations to thrive.[24]

Though criticism of the World Bank in the nongovernmental community had been building for some time, the last few years have brought some confessions of failure from other, surprising places. In June 1992, a report from the first independent commission set up to evaluate a controversial World Bank project was published. Dubbed the Morse Commission after its chair, former U.S. Congressman and UNDP head Bradford Morse, the group (established by Bank President Conable) concluded that involvement in the controversial Sardar Sarovar dam and the accompanying Narmada Sagar dam projects in India had been badly bungled from its inception. The Bank's own rules on environmental impact assessment and the resettlement of displaced peoples had been blatantly violated, vindicating the decade-long protests of thousands of local peoples and international NGOs. Though the Bank at first refused to back away from the project, negotiations behind the scenes led to the Indian government's announcement, in March 1993, that it was withdrawing its request for Bank funding for the project. (India confirmed its commitment, however, to move ahead with construction on its own, though it remains unclear if this will happen.)[25]

The second wake-up call came from within the Bank itself—the publication in June 1992 of the Wapenhans report on implementation of bank projects, written by former Bank Vice-President Willi Wapenhans. He concluded that World Bank projects were routinely failing to live up to the Bank's own criteria for success, such as rates of return and other lending conditions. The report cited Operations Evaluation Department data showing that the share of Bank projects deemed "unsatisfactory" in their results increased from 15 percent in 1981 to 38 percent in 1991. In addition, the report found that 78 percent of the financial conditions attached to loans were not being complied with.[26]

If private banks had this kind of failure rate, they would go out of business. But as the World Bank often points out, it has an unusually high loan repayment rate, which enables it to borrow money at favorable rates in the world's financial markets. This unique combination of a strong repayment rate and projects failing to meet expectations can be traced to the fact that—unlike private businesses—governments can and do draw down national treasuries to pay back poorly performing loans. Whether or not a project manages to pay for itself as projected, the loan is repaid because the country's credit rating and future World Bank funding depend on it.[27]

The Wapenhans report called particular attention to what it called the "Bank's pervasive preoccupation with new lending." This fixation has many sources, including the desire to infuse debt-burdened countries with cash and the tendency of many large organizations to confuse quantity with quality. By calling attention to the phenomenon, the report was endorsing a view of outside observers never before given official acknowledgement by the World Bank—that in its growing obsession to lend progressively larger amounts of money, the Bank was losing sight of the reason it was created: to improve the well-being of the billions of poor people living in developing countries.[28]

The GEF is also undergoing a certain amount of introspection of late. As part of the negotiations over its replenishment, member countries commissioned an independent assessment of the effectiveness of its pilot phase. A September 1993 draft of the report pointed to serious shortcomings. One of the more important is the stipulation that projects justified on local environmental and economic benefits alone are technically ineligible for GEF funds—a curious stipulation that can have the perverse result of discouraging cost-effective investments such as energy efficiency projects. Other problems highlighted by the independent assessment include the difficulties GEF has had working with local communities, and a counterproductive rush to lend money in the facility's early months.[29]

The World Bank has begun to respond to the challenges implicit in this damaging string of findings. In July 1993, in response to the Wapenhans report, the board of directors approved an action plan—the "Next Steps"—intended to create incentives for more effective project implementation. Among other recommendations, it calls for evaluating staff based on how well they shepherd projects to successful conclusions instead of on how much money they move. It also points to the need to evaluate implementation country-by-country, and to develop better indicators of the impact of projects. Unfortunately, however, the primary emphasis of the Wapenhans report and its followup has been on improving the financial performance of projects—which is not necessarily the same thing as making sure they contribute measurably to sustainable development.[30]

Indeed, in one important respect the Next Steps initiative may serve to undermine rather than promote the cause of sustainable development. All Bank operational directives are now to be shortened into summary form, in theory to make it easier for people implementing projects to digest and carry them out.

Many observers are concerned, however, that the effect will be to take the teeth out of these important policies—including the new energy, forestry, and water ones—by removing from the summary documents all binding commitments and leaving them as just exhortations to do better.[31]

Two other important initiatives were approved by the board in 1993—a new policy on the release of information, and the creation of an independent appeals mechanism for citizens. NGOs that had lobbied on behalf of the new information policy were disappointed at the extent to which it was watered down: though a new "Project Information Document" will provide a summary of proposed projects early in their development, the critical project appraisal reports will only be available after a loan has been approved—too late to influence its course. The independent appeals mechanism shows greater promise. Roughly modeled on the Morse Commission, it will provide an impartial forum where board members or private citizens can raise complaints about projects that violate the Bank's own policies, rules, and procedures. How well the new information policy and the appeals mechanism work in practice will do much to determine if the Bank can turn its rhetoric about sustainable development into reality.[32]

ENERGIZING DEVELOPMENT

Given their dominance in the total lending package and their profound environmental implications, the energy and transport sectors merit special attention as the World Bank considers how to move toward sustainable development. Smoothly functioning energy and transport systems are key building blocks in that process. But these needs are now being met, often with the complicity of the Bank, in a manner that achieves neither economic nor environmental goals.

Aggressive efforts to use energy more efficiently and reduce the use of fossil fuels would make billions of dollars that developing countries spend on oil imports available for much needed investments in health, education, and other neglected programs. Providing mobility in a cost-effective and environmentally sound manner also is essential to meeting development goals: when people spend half their days fetching water, or walking to work, or caught in traffic, they are not contributing productively to the economy. (See Chapter 5.) And land paved for highways or parking lots is land unavailable for crops. Beyond these "development" rationales for transformations in energy and transport systems, there are also compelling local and global environmental reasons to change course: if developing countries follow the industrial world's energy-intensive path as they refurbish their economies, the chances of combatting air pollution, acid rain, and global warming are slim.[33]

Large energy and transport infrastructure projects have traditionally been among the Bank's mainstays. In the first few decades, such projects accounted for the bulk of Bank lending. Between 1961 and 1965, 77 percent of the lending was devoted to electric power or transportation, with only 6 percent for agriculture and less than 1 percent for social services. The numbers began to shift during Robert McNamara's term as president, as investments in agriculture and social services increased. Still, energy and transport investments remain dominant, between them accounting for 29 percent of total lending in 1993. Energy alone is the World Bank's single largest sector.[34]

To date, the World Bank has emphasized the importance of pricing changes and other policy reforms in the push to improve energy efficiency. Though these are indeed important, the Bank has had only limited success in prevailing on recipient countries to make the needed changes. In addition, specific strategies designed to reduce demand by investing in energy-efficient technologies have been shown time and again to generate high economic returns by lowering the need for costly expenditures on new sources of energy supply. Such end-use energy efficiency initiatives merit Bank support. Yet less than 1 percent of the $45 billion loaned for energy between 1980 and 1990 was devoted to this purpose, according to Michael Philips of the International Institute for Energy Conservation (IIEC) in Washington, D.C. In contrast, demand-side management programs garnered roughly 7 percent of all U.S. utility expenditures in 1992. (See Chapter 4.)[35]

Although it is not surprising that developing countries invest more than the United States does in building up new supply capacity, far higher expenditures on end-use energy efficiency could be justified on economic and environmental grounds. Nevertheless, the Bank projected in 1991 that its efficiency investments will account for less than 1 percent of total energy lending through 1995.[36]

For transportation, the bulk of lending is spent on improving and building roads. Rail and other forms of public transport, as well as the infrastructure and equipment for nonmotorized transport such as bicycles, rickshaws, and pedestrian travel, have been largely neglected. Lending for land transportation at the World Bank in 1992 added up to just over $2 billion. Seventy-four percent of this was spent on roads, with most of the rest allocated to rail projects. A rather small share of the total goes to urban transport projects—roughly $150 million per year since 1980 at the World

Bank. Of the funds allocated during the eighties, more than half financed road construction and maintenance; bus systems accounted for 18 percent, rail for 12 percent, traffic management for 9, and technical assistance and training for the remaining 7. In 1980, lending for urban rail systems ceased altogether, as did lending for urban busways in 1982. As a result, roads accounted for 81 percent of total expenditures for urban transportation by the late eighties.[37]

Under pressure, the World Bank is currently preparing a review of its transport sector lending.

Though lending priorities continue to be badly skewed, some steps in the right direction have been taken in recent years in both the energy and transport sectors. In late 1992, the executive directors approved energy policy papers on efficiency and the electric power sector. These called for a more aggressive Bank role in supporting efficiency, both through the standard approach of encouraging energy pricing and other policies that promote it, such as the removal of subsidies, and through more hands-on policy interventions to encourage efforts to improve end-use efficiency. Under pressure, the World Bank is currently preparing a review of its transport sector lending, which could reveal the economic and environmental opportunities being missed by its failure to promote transport alternatives adequately.[38]

In addition to movements toward better policies, there are also some limited signs of real change. Power sector loans in the pipeline for Colombia, Indonesia, Mexico, and Poland include demand-side management components. In one project that is already up and running,

GEF is contributing $15.5 million in 1993 to a project in Thailand aimed at promoting energy efficiency through measures such as improving household lighting and refrigeration technologies, promoting the use of double-paned windows, and encouraging the use of high-efficiency motors in industry. The World Bank would do well to follow the lead of the Asian Development Bank, which has recently announced that it will include environmental costs in all future assessments of electric power projects.[39]

Some progress has also been made on the supply end. The Bank has increased its financing of natural gas investments, a welcome shift away from the traditional emphasis on more-polluting coal and oil. Support for tapping and building pipelines for domestic sources of natural gas increased from 10 percent of total energy lending in 1990 to almost one third in 1991. Renewable energy sources are also beginning to receive a small amount of support, often with the help of GEF grants. A combination of IBRD and IDA funds was devoted to a noteworthy $175-million loan to India approved in 1993 that will help finance a variety of renewable energy technologies, including minihydro plants on irrigation canals and bagasse-fueled newsprint production. GEF will provide an additional $30 million in grants to support the development of photovoltaic plants and wind farms.[40]

In the transport sector, as well, the Bank has funded some worthy projects, often as a result of dedicated staff members willing to put in extra hours to shepherd relatively small projects to successful conclusions. More are in the pipeline. A planned loan to South Korea aims to encourage a shift from cars toward bus and subway usage through pricing policies and the creation of "suburban transportation nodes" designed to shuttle commuters to the subway on buses. In addition, a $4-million transport loan to Lima, Peru, is being prepared that will finance the construction of 90 kilometers of separated bicycle lanes and provide access to credit to help people purchase bicycles. An additional loan of $100,000 will fund a master transportation plan for the city that is intended to facilitate the use of nonmotorized transport.[41]

Replication of these projects on a far broader scale would yield impressive economic and environmental returns. The Institute for Transportation and Development Policy (ITDP) in Washington, D.C., has looked at two private projects on nonmotorized transport—one provided bicycles to fishers in Mozambique and the other, a "Bikes not Bombs" project in Nicaragua, supplied health care workers and other individuals with bikes. ITDP found the economic rates of return on the projects to equal 213 percent and 400 percent, respectively. In other words, both projects quickly paid for themselves—in the first case by providing access to markets and in the second by replacing costly bus fares. Most road infrastructure projects, by comparison, have rates of return of about 20 percent. If environmental costs such as air pollution and the creation of greenhouse gas emissions were included in the equation, the number would be lower still.[42]

Despite these few promising signs, the general direction of energy and transport lending is largely unchanged. In a replay of Singrauli, the World Bank appears to be moving ahead with a planned series of loans to India totalling $1.2 billion for the construction of nearly 17 gigawatts of new coal-fired electric generating capacity over 10 years. The first $400 million was approved by the board in June 1993, despite the abstentions of the Belgian, German, and U.S. governments. According to the New York-based Environmental Defense Fund (EDF), no serious consideration was

given to energy efficiency as an alternative, nor has a full environmental analysis been completed, local communities adequately consulted, or a resettlement plan formulated. Meanwhile, a U.S. Agency for International Development study finds that an aggressive effort to promote energy efficiency in India could reduce peak power demand by 22–36 gigawatts by 2005, saving 250–400 billion rupees ($8–13 billion) in investments to expand the supply.[43]

RETHINKING LENDING FOR AGRICULTURE

Agriculture and rural development run a close second to the energy sector as a share of total World Bank project lending. In 1993, investments in this sector added up to $3.3 billion, 14 percent of the overall total. Included within the broad category of agriculture and rural development are a variety of types of projects, including fisheries, irrigation, livestock, and forestry. (See Table 9–2.)[44]

The share of lending devoted to the agricultural sector has fluctuated over the years. In the early days, it represented a small proportion of the total. Under McNamara, lending in this sector was viewed as a cornerstone of the basic human needs approach; it climbed dramatically, reaching a peak of 39 percent in 1978. Since then, however, agricultural lending has stabilized while overall lending has continued to grow, so that investment in the sector as a share of total Bank lending has been on a steady downward course. (See Figure 9–2.) The decline is worrisome, given the importance for poverty alleviation of many agricultural investments. In addition, stepped-up investments in agricultural

Table 9–2. World Bank Agricultural Lending, Fiscal Year 1992

Subsector	Lending	Share of Total Agricultural Lending
	(million dollars)	(percent)
Irrigation and Drainage	1,027	26
Rural Finance	671	17
Forestry	458	12
Natural Resource Management and Environment	380	10
Research and Extension	341	9
Area Development[1]	292	7
Agriculture Sector[2]	225	6
Perennial Crops	209	5
Livestock	138	4
Fisheries	95	2
Other	58	1
Total	3,894	100[3]

[1]Projects to improve agricultural production, including micro-loans to rural community groups and loans for restructuring rural agricultural agencies.   [2]Includes agricultural-sector adjustment lending and investments in institution building and public-sector management.   [3]Percentages do not add up to 100 due to rounding.
SOURCE: Agriculture and Natural Resources Department, "Annual Sector Review: Agriculture and Rural Development FY92," World Bank, Washington, D.C., December 1992.

research and production are sorely needed in many parts of the world if food production is to become ecologically sustainable, and if it is to keep pace with rapidly growing populations.[45]

Bank officials have offered a number of justifications for the trend, including claims that agricultural projects perform poorly more often than projects in other sectors and that the shift is logical as many countries industrialize. Robert Paarlberg of Wellesley College and Michael Lipton of Sussex University's Institute for Development Studies have carefully examined these and other explanations, and found them not to be terribly convincing. The most compelling interpretation, they find, is that the move toward adjustment lending during the eighties diverted funds from agricultural investment projects. The emphasis on moving money quickly to replenish depleted national treasuries is at odds

with the labor- and time-intensive nature of successful agricultural projects, which generally require 20–30 percent more staff time and resources to prepare than others do.[46]

In theory, the policy changes encouraged by adjustment loans could be of significant benefit to the agricultural sector, perhaps outweighing the foregone investment programs. For instance, in many countries price ceilings keep the charge for agricultural products artificially low to benefit urban consumers. Removing these ceilings, an element in reforms recommended by many adjustment loans, would help raise the price paid to farmers, encouraging production. Paarlberg and Lipton point out that while the reforms did unfold more or less according to plan in some countries, such as Turkey and Chile, the Bank's own research indicates that many other governments found it difficult to imple-

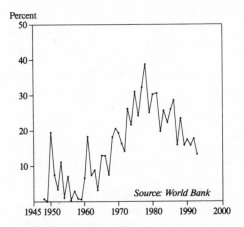

Percent

Figure 9-2. Agriculture and Rural Development Lending as Share of Total World Bank Lending, 1948–93

ment them, given the political clout of urban dwellers and other interests who stood to lose. They argue that where adjustment lending has spurred the needed reforms, it would now be wise to declare success. Where it has not, it may be necessary for the Bank to cut its losses. In both cases, the proper response would be renewed emphasis on lending for investments, not just policy change.[47]

Returning to agricultural project lending does not mean returning to lending as it has been practiced in the past, however. Though McNamara's intentions were good, in retrospect his strategy cannot be said to have been a complete success. For one thing, projects aimed at poor farmers did not benefit the true "poorest of the poor," largely because these people were usually either landless farmers, agricultural laborers, or too poor to obtain credit. As a result, many loans actually exacerbated income inequality. Second, the model of agricultural development that was promoted encouraged farming for national and international markets, and thus disrupted the subsistence forms of agriculture that many of the poor depend on for sustenance and that women rely on to feed

their families. The participation of the supposed beneficiaries was often not encouraged, and many projects fell victim to graft and corruption.[48]

To some degree, the sins of the past could be corrected. Bank evaluations reveal that many of the failures of agriculture projects can be attributed to inadequacies in design, technology, or local institution-building—problems that could in theory be fixed. Indeed, agricultural projects that have been designed specifically to reach the poor have been more successful than the average agricultural project, providing important models.[49]

But the problem projects also stemmed in large measure from a fatal flaw of World Bank operations that continues to plague it today—the pressure to lend money. During McNamara's tenure, total lending expanded more than fivefold in real terms, and the staff increased from 1,574 to 5,201. In addition, McNamara instituted the practice of devising lending targets for countries. Under pressure to make as many loans as possible, staff paid too little attention to following them through to a successful conclusion.[50]

The Bank has approved a number of new policies in the agricultural area during the past few years that, if implemented, would help reorient lending toward ecologically sustainable practices. In July 1992, an operational directive advocated greater use of integrated pest management techniques so that natural systems replace chemical pesticides wherever possible. A year later, the board approved a sector review paper on the reforms needed in agriculture, such as involving local communities in project design and assisting in land reform initiatives, if food crises are to be averted in the decades ahead. And a water policy issued in September 1993 calls for adoption of a "comprehensive approach" to water management in which competing demands for the resource can be assessed—the hope being that the most cost-effective and environmentally benign option will be adopted.[51]

THE FATE OF FORESTS

The most controversial sector within agriculture in terms of its environmental implications is lending for forestry. Since its first policy paper on forests in 1978, the Bank has committed more than $2.2 billion to this sector spread over 73 projects. Lending picked up with Conable's 1987 speech: the institution disbursed $474 million in these loans between 1987 and 1989, when Conable announced a further tripling of lending. It now expects to increase its annual forestry lending to $438 million between 1992 and 1995, double the $217 million it averaged between 1985 and 1990.[52]

The Bank has tended to emphasize forestry lending as part of an effort to "green" its image. Many projects could serve this end. For instance, plantations and the rehabilitation of degraded lands could help meet demand for wood without destroying ecological patrimony. Other areas meriting Bank support are extractive reserves for nontimber forest products, and projects that promote the development of more wood-efficient processing technologies. In addition, the Bank could promote "natural forest management" techniques that mimic natural systems, thereby preserving biological diversity. (See Chapter 2.)

To date, however, the institution has done little to instill confidence in its potential to be an ally rather than an enemy in the effort to staunch the loss of the earth's forest cover. Indeed, it was projects such as Polonoroeste, in which the Bank was implicated in Amazonian deforestation, that first brought widespread attention to its checkered ecological record. In 1985, the World Bank became involved in the Tropical Forestry Action Plan (TFAP), a joint initiative with UNDP, the U.N. Food and Agriculture Organization, and the World Resources Institute that was intended to mobilize $8 billion over five years in bilateral and multilateral investments in tree planting programs and efforts to slow deforestation. Instead, many of the programs developed have financed expanded commercial logging, often with little if any consultation with the people affected. Rather than arresting deforestation, the TFAP threatened to accelerate it. In the face of widespread criticism, the plan fell apart and the Bank distanced itself from it.[53]

Meanwhile, it was forging ahead on its own with preparations for two major forestry loans—one to the West African country of Guinea and the other to neighboring Côte d'Ivoire. Both projects were roundly criticized by NGOs for promoting deforestation, and—in the case of the Côte d'Ivoire loan—for flagrantly violating the stated Bank policy of having a resettlement and relocation plan for people displaced by its projects. When the latter project came before the board in April 1990, the U.S. executive director did not vote for it because of concerns about its environmental impact, but it was approved nonetheless.[54]

These troubled projects did create enough unease among the executive board to prompt a temporary moratorium on forest lending pending the development of a new policy. In an important step forward, the Bank consulted extensively with citizens' groups from around the world in preparing this. The document, completed in July 1991, marked a significant departure from past practices. Most notably, the Bank announced that under no circumstances would it support commercial logging in primary tropical moist forests. It also pledged to fund poverty alleviation projects near threatened forests, to carefully review the environmental impact of all infrastructure projects in tropical forests, and to support the establishment of parks and other wilderness reserves to protect biological diversity.[55]

This new policy was an addition to the already sizable repertoire of World Bank policies relevant to forests. For instance, an indigenous peoples policy established in 1982 and updated in 1991 requires the Bank, before funding activities that affect indigenous peoples, to prepare a plan that addresses a number of critical issues, including land tenure. The policy on the resettlement of displaced peoples, which dates from 1980, states that any projects that cannot avoid resettlement must provide plans to ensure that affected individuals are left no less well off economically than they were prior to the move. The 1986 wildlands policy stipulates that any project that involves the conversion of wildlands should be offset by other investments in conservation. If these policies were adhered to, they would provide a solid basis for protecting forests and forest dwellers. Unfortunately, experience has shown that they often are not.[56]

Some observers do credit the forest policy with reducing the number of troublesome World Bank projects. But it has by no means solved all the problems. In June 1992 the first loan was approved under the new policy: $22.5 million for forest management in the central African country of Gabon. The Environmental Defense Fund and Friends of the Earth-UK charge that the new loan adheres to the letter of the new policy but violates its spirit—its sectoral adjustment component encourages the privatization of the country's forest industry without requiring effective regulation of it, thereby creating conditions that will accelerate deforestation.[57]

GEF is a major new provider of funds for forest preservation under the rubric of its biological diversity preservation role. Unfortunately, a number of its projects have already run into trouble, raising questions as to whether the Bank has the technical expertise and the ability to work with local people that is needed to make these kinds of projects work. One GEF forestry project in Ecuador was recently abandoned when an independent review commissioned by the GEF chairman and conducted by former Costa Rican Minister of Natural Resources Alvaro Umaña concluded that it violated the Bank's indigenous peoples policy and had other flaws.[58]

The Bank has done little to instill confidence in its potential to be an ally rather than an enemy in the effort to staunch the loss of forest cover.

In the worst of cases, GEF projects may inadvertently encourage destructive forestry projects. Small GEF grants for biodiversity preservation are sometimes attached to larger forestry loans. Critics charge that the GEF grant money in some cases improves the attractiveness of the larger project enough to make it viable. The good done by setting aside a small protected area is then overwhelmed by the destruction caused by the broader project. Internal Bank memorandums obtained by EDF suggest that this was in fact the explicit strategy in the case of a troubled natural resources management loan to the Congo. After EDF publicized the situation, the GEF component was separated from the larger loan, which was then cancelled. A proposed Bank/GEF forestry loan for Laos shares many of these same troubling features.[59]

INVESTING IN PEOPLE

The road to economic health through economic adjustment has proved far more arduous than originally anticipated, particularly for the poorest, most heavily indebted countries. According to an internal Bank review in 1992, two thirds of the countries with adjustment programs under way were experiencing declines in both public- and private-sector investment, and poverty was on the rise in many of them. In Côte d'Ivoire, the report found that poverty increased 4.8 percent a year during 1980–85, and that extreme poverty rose by 7.9 percent annually.[60]

During the eighties, increases were registered not only in the absolute number of poor people in sub-Saharan Africa, the Middle East, North Africa, and Latin America, but also in the proportion of the population that is poor. Moreover, in both Latin America and sub-Saharan Africa, poverty deepened during the decade, meaning that the poor fell farther and farther below the poverty line. In addition, the trend in the sixties and seventies toward steadily rising improvement rates on a range of social indicators was reversed. In sub-Saharan Africa, the rate at which life expectancy and infant mortality indicators had been improving dropped, and the percentage of children enrolled in primary schools actually fell.[61]

As pressure grew to stem the tide of rising poverty, the World Bank gradually—and belatedly—introduced some changes. It began to emphasize reforms in its structural adjustment loans that would benefit the poor, such as encouraging investments in primary health care rather than urban hospitals, and creating social safety nets to protect those hurt by the adjustment process. During fiscal years 1984–86, less than 5 percent of all adjustment loans considered social issues at all; by 1990–92, more than 50 percent did. Meanwhile, under pressure from the U.S. Congress, the reauthorization of IDA agreed to in 1989 stipulated that countries that had demonstrated a special commitment to reducing poverty were to be given preferential access to IDA funds, which are already designated for the world's poorest countries.[62]

In 1990, the *World Development Report* was devoted to the theme of poverty reduction. It came to two primary conclusions—that labor-intensive forms of economic growth should be supported and that investments in education, population, health, and nutrition should be stepped up. Following this report, the Bank accelerated its efforts to undertake detailed country poverty assessments that delineate the dimensions of the challenge and propose reforms to address it. By 1993, 20 poverty assessments had been completed for 19 countries, containing two thirds of the developing-world population and most of the world's poor, with 68 more scheduled to be completed by July 1996. The next step is to incorporate their findings into future assistance strategies—a process that needs to move forward more quickly.[63]

The Bank also began to aim its loans more specifically at the poor under the Program of Targeted Interventions. To qualify for this designation, a loan must either contain a specific mechanism designed to reach the poor or it must be aimed at a group that contains a significantly higher proportion of poor people than exists in the country at large. In 1992, 14 percent of lending fell under this rubric—51 projects valued at $3 billion. In addition, the Bank has worked to increase lending for education and for population, health, and nutrition on the grounds that these sectors are of particular benefit to the poor. Lending to them increased from 5 percent of total lending in fiscal years 1981–83 to 14 percent in 1990–92. (See Figure 9–3.) This trend is

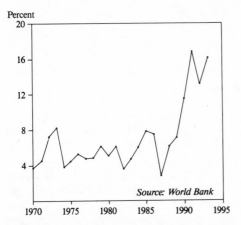

Figure 9-3. Population, Health, Nutrition, and Education Lending as a Share of Total World Bank Lending, 1970–93

The share of agricultural projects that included some provision to reach women increased from 9 percent to 30. For education projects, the share went from 22 to 33 percent, and for population, health, and nutrition programs, it remained constant at 75 percent. The next challenge is to see that this concern is addressed more widely in other types of projects, as well as in adjustment loans—and to ensure that rhetorical references to incorporating women translate into on-the-ground realities.[66]

expected to continue, in part because a growing body of internal research shows that many of these investments are among the most cost-effective available.[64]

The institution has also been working in recent years to address criticisms that its lending has traditionally overlooked the role of women in development. For instance, though women play an active role in harvesting food, fuel, fodder, and other goods from forests, out of 22 social forestry projects appraised from 1984 through 1987, only one specifically mentioned women as a beneficiary. And only 4 of 33 more general rural development programs that involved forestry included women. In large measure, this failure stems from the fact that women in developing countries work mainly outside the formal sector, and thus tend not to be counted in official statistics.[65]

In an effort to improve on this sorry record, a special Women in Development division was created in 1987, and a coordinator placed in each regional office. On paper, this appears to be having some results. In a recent evaluation, 73 projects approved in 1988 and 1989 were compared with a similar batch of projects approved from 1980 to 1987.

BUILDING A NEW WORLD BANK

In this year of the fiftieth anniversary of the Bretton Woods conference, the time is ripe for a fundamental rethinking of how well the World Bank is serving the needs of today's world. Though the idealism that led to its creation was virtuous, in today's context it is hard not to view it as somewhat naive. The belief that large, governmental institutions could be marshalled to solve daunting problems was fundamental to the postwar years. Experience since then, however, suggests that a far different, smaller-scale approach is needed if the World Bank is to effectively mobilize the human and financial resources required in the transition to a sustainable society.

As the Wapenhans report documented, much that is wrong with the World Bank can be traced to the fact that success is measured there primarily in terms of quantity of lending rather than its quality. Rather than continually pleading with donor nations to contribute more funds, the Bank might do well to look within. By reorienting its own lending away from large infrastructure projects toward smaller efforts done in close cooperation with local peoples—whether they be for ecologically sensitive agricultural techniques, solar-powered water pumping, or the rehabilitation of degraded lands—the Bank could cut its costs by millions if not billions of dollars. Though it would be lending less money, every dollar spent would contribute far more to the cause of sustainable development. Some of the savings could then be devoted to providing the extra staff time required to make these smaller projects work.

This is not entirely uncharted waters. Privately, endeavors such as the Foundation for the Philippine Environment and the Grameen Bank have achieved remarkable results by funneling small amounts of money to individuals and NGOs. These initiatives have been replicated by governments through bilateral initiatives, including the U.S.-funded Inter-American and African Development foundations and Appropriate Technology International. These three institutions are designed to provide small grants and loans, typically less than $500,000 each, to local communities, small businesses, farmers, entrepreneurs, NGOs, and cooperatives in the Third World. The annual budget in 1993 for the Inter-American Foundation, by far the largest of the three, was $31 million—less than most individual World Bank projects.[67]

Following a similar approach should not be impossible for the Bank, at least if two innovative programs at a regional development bank are any guide. Since the late seventies, the Inter-American Development Bank (IDB) has had a facility that disburses about $20 million annually to small projects involving NGOs, small enterprises, and cooperatives. More recently, IDB established a global microenterprise credit program in which loans ranging from $10–50 million are made to intermediary financial institutions, in many cases the country's central bank, which then rechannel the funds to thousands of individual entrepreneurs. Together, these two programs lent $65 million in 1992—1 percent of IDB's total lending. The World Bank is studying the feasibility of undertaking similar initiatives.[68]

One primary obstacle to transforming the World Bank along the lines of this more decentralized vision is the place the institution has recently come to occupy at the epicenter of the international financial system. To prevent defaults on its own and private bank loans, the Bank has largely pursued a strategy of lending still more money. This distracts from its central mission as a development institution, where the quality of projects should matter more than the quantity of funds dispersed. And it is also counterproductive, because it only serves to compound future debt burdens, thereby creating a vicious circle in which countries are forced to overexploit natural resources such as timber and fisheries in order to generate the foreign exchange needed to pay the loans back. As long-time Bank critic Bruce Rich of the Environmental Defense Fund writes in a forthcoming book, "The Bank should no longer be used as a money moving machine to address global macro-economic imbalances the real solution to which lies with a new global economic bargain between North and South."[69]

Yet the World Bank could help countries step off the debilitating debt treadmill by devoting a significant share of its funds to reducing total debt burdens. The Debt Reduction Facility is one mechanism it has at its disposal to help do this. Established in 1990 to ease the commercial debt burden of IDA countries, this facility arranges deals in which discounted debt is purchased on the secondary market. So far, five operations totalling some $45 million have been completed, which have together had the effect of cancelling out $623 million in debt. This is a promising initiative that merits expansion. Yet it is of limited value to many poor countries, especially those in Africa, that owe their debt primarily to governments and multilateral institutions like the World Bank itself. One Bank effort, however, does try to address this problem. The Fifth Dimension program lets some debt-burdened countries borrow low-interest IDA funds to pay the interest on IBRD loans. This, too, deserves more support. In addition, the time may have come for the Bank to reconsider its policy against forgiving its own loans.[70]

If the Bank is to become an institution that promotes sustainable development, it will also need to revamp the criteria by which it judges success. Although the Next Steps action plan approved by the Bank's board in July 1993 acknowledged that projects should be measured by their development impact, not just by their financial rate of return, the Bank is not currently well set up to put this into practice. First, indicators of sustainable development need to be developed that take adequate account of social and environmental goals. Attention to these indicators then must figure prominently in the ratings that Bank staff assign to projects to measure success. Finally, the indicators as well as the findings of the environmental action plans and poverty assessments need to be fully integrated into country assistance strategies.[71]

The more widespread use of natural resource accounting is also sorely needed, and both the World Bank and the International Monetary Fund are well placed to pioneer the use of these techniques. When national income accounts and projections of project rates of return fail to take account of the depreciation of natural assets, economic policymaking is based on a false set of books. In a recent review of 23 projects from 1985 to 1993, Bank economists

John Kellenberg and Herman Daly discovered that only in a few cases was any attempt made to account for the drawing down of the natural resource base. As would be expected, projects for which these "user costs" were calculated had lower rates of return than other projects, as the natural resource depletion was subtracted from expected income gains. On paper, projects that did not account for "user costs" thus looked to be better investments than they really were. This type of faulty accounting creates an incentive to invest in projects that damage the natural resource base.[72]

The time may have come for the Bank to reconsider its policy against forgiving its own loans.

More accountability to the public will also be key to reshaping the World Bank. One of the only ways ordinary citizens can currently make their voices heard is through the rather circuitous route of lobbying executive directors, who themselves have limited influence. It was thus unfortunate that several member countries opposed recent initiatives to fully open the flow of information on Bank projects. This secrecy runs exactly opposite to the worldwide trend toward more democracy. Given its fundamental importance to reforming the Bank, making information freely available remains a high priority. In the meantime, the new independent appeals mechanism provides an important opportunity for people to reassert some measure of control over decisions made in Washington, D.C., that may fundamentally alter their lives thousands of miles away.

Though the Bank needs a fundamental overhaul, it does have an important role to play in the transition to a sustainable society. Alone among development agencies, it is powerful enough to redirect the course of national policymaking. It also has acquired a well-deserved reputation for technical competence. Notes Robert Repetto of the World Resources Institute, "The World Bank has the largest and most capable group of development economists and related professionals anywhere in the world. It has the largest financial resources of any development agency. It has the best access to data and information of any development agency. It is in a position to take a leadership role and to make a major contribution to progress."[73]

The problem, of course, is that these impressive powers have all too often been directed toward the wrong ends.

The World Bank is not alone in this. Reorienting economic activity toward sustainable development is a daunting task everywhere. For national governments and international agencies alike, there is a powerful momentum built into maintaining the status quo. The world community is starting to realize, however, that the notions of development and progress that prevailed 50 years ago have little to do with today's sobering realities. If this influential institution is to live up to the high hopes that inspired its founders, it will need to accept that the extraordinary changes of the last several decades must be mirrored by transformations of a similar order at the World Bank itself.

10

Facing Food Insecurity

Lester R. Brown

As the nineties unfold, the world is facing a day of reckoning. Many knew that this time would eventually come, that at some point the cumulative effects of environmental degradation and the limits of the earth's natural systems would start to restrict economic expansion. But no one knew exactly when or how these effects would show up. Now we can see that they are slowing growth in food production—the most basic of economic activities and the one on which all others depend.

After nearly four decades of unprecedented expansion in both land-based and oceanic food supplies, the world is experiencing a massive loss of momentum. Between 1950 and 1984, world grain production expanded 2.6-fold, outstripping population growth by a wide margin and raising the grain harvested per person by 40 percent. Growth in the world fish catch was even more spectacular—a 4.6-fold increase between 1950 and 1989, which doubled the seafood catch per person. Together, these developments reduced hunger and malnutrition throughout the world, offering hope that they would one day be eliminated.[1]

But in recent years these trends in food output per person have been reversed with unanticipated abruptness.

By 1993, the fish catch per person had declined some 7 percent from its historical high in 1989. And after 1984, the growth in grain production slowed abruptly, falling behind that of population. From 1984 until 1993, grain output per person fell 11 percent. Historians may well see 1984 as a watershed year, one marking the transition from an era of rapid growth in food production to one of much slower growth.[2]

In a world of growing food insecurity, grain output per person becomes a proxy for progress, a basic indicator measuring success in accelerating food output and slowing population growth. It readily measures the effect on demand of both population growth and rising affluence, as the latter boosts the amount of grain used to produce livestock products.

Human demands are approaching the limits of oceanic fisheries to supply fish, of rangelands to support livestock, and, in many countries, of the hydrological cycle to produce fresh water. Even as these constraints become more visible, the backlog of unused agricultural technology is shrinking in industrial and developing countries alike, slowing the rise in cropland productivity. At the same time, soil erosion, air pollution, soil compaction, aquifer depletion, the loss of soil organic matter, and the waterlogging and salting of irrigated land are all slowing the rise in food output. At present, there is nothing in sight to reverse the worldwide decline in grain output per person.

The bottom line is that the world's farmers can no longer be counted on to feed the projected additions to our numbers. Achieving a humane balance between food and people now depends more on family planners than on farmers. Against this backdrop, the timing of the International Conference on Population and Development in September 1994 in Cairo could not be better.

Between 1950 and 1990, the world added 2.8 billion people, an average of 70 million a year. But between 1990 and 2030, the world is projected to add 3.6 billion, an annual average of 90 million. Such growth in a finite environment raises questions about the earth's carrying capacity. (See Chapter 1.) Will the earth's natural support systems sustain such growth indefinitely? How many people can the earth support at a given level of consumption?[3]

As food production per person falls, the nature of famine itself is changing. Traditionally it was geographically defined, concentrated where there were crop failures. With today's worldwide food distribution system, malnutrition so severe that it is life-threatening is found mainly among the Third World's landless rural laborers and urban poor. Although the hungry are more dispersed and less visible, they are no less numerous. The latest U.N. assessment puts the number of malnourished at close to 1 billion, nearly one in five persons.[4]

The ideological conflict that dominated the four decades from 1950 to 1990 is being replaced by the conflict between our steadily growing demand for food and the earth's physical capacity to satisfy those demands. In a world of spreading hunger, desperate people

may cross national borders in unprecedented numbers in their search for food. The deteriorating balance between food and people in one way or another will increasingly preoccupy national political leaders, reorder national priorities, and dominate international affairs.[5]

This chapter builds on the assessment in Chapter 1 of how environmental degradation is affecting the food economy, adding to it an analysis of cropland productivity trends, to provide a base for looking ahead at the food-population balance. Looking at trends in the use of land, water, and fertilizer and at cropland productivity during the last 40 years provides some insights into what to expect during the next 40. It would be tempting to use a shorter time frame, but in dealing with basic policy questions—the need to stabilize both population and climate, and to develop and disseminate new farming technologies—such an approach is of limited value.

LOOKING BACK, LOOKING AHEAD

During the last four decades, economic policies dominated the evolution of the global economy. During the next four, environmental limits interacting with population growth will have far more influence. Fully 96 percent of the projected addition of 3.6 billion people between 1990 and 2030 will occur in the Third World. In countries where demands already exceed local carrying capacity, the resulting deforestation, overgrazing, soil erosion, and aquifer depletion will accelerate and spread—creating a highly unstable relationship between people and their natural support systems. The changing relationship is clearly visible at the global level, where population growth is outrunning production of oceanic fisheries, rangelands, and croplands.[6]

Between 1950 and 1989, the world fish harvest—a major source of animal protein—increased from 22 million to 100 million tons, lifting the supply per person from an average of 9 kilograms to 19. (See Figure 10–1.) This phenomenal growth may have ended, however. Marine biologists from the U.N. Food and Agriculture Organization estimate that oceanic fisheries may not be able to sustain a harvest higher than that of recent years. (See Chapter 3.) If they are right, then the rise in the seafood catch per person of the past four decades has come to an end, to be replaced by a steady decline for as long as population grows.[7]

The world's rangelands, another major source of animal protein, are also under growing pressure. Between 1950 and 1990, world output of beef and mutton increased 2.6-fold, raising the per capita supply some 26 percent. With extensive overgrazing on every continent, however, rangelands—like oceanic fisheries—may be at their maximum carrying capacity. If so, rangeland production of beef and mutton may not increase much, if at all, in the future. Here, too,

availability per person will decline indefinitely as population grows.[8]

If the supply of fish, beef, and mutton is to expand in the future, it will have to come from feeding fish in ponds or livestock in feedlots. And this in turn will depend on producing more grain. Yet production of grain—the mainstay of the human diet, accounting for half of human caloric intake consumed directly and part of the remainder consumed indirectly as livestock products—has also slowed. Between 1950 and 1984, the world grain harvest grew at a record 3 percent a year, boosting per capita grain availability by some 40 percent. But from 1984 to 1993, annual growth slowed to less than 1 percent, dropping per capita availability by 11 percent.[9]

These slowdowns in major food-producing sectors of the global economy affect overall economic trends. Growth in the world economy reached its historical high of 5.2 percent a year during the sixties; it slowed some in the seventies and still further in the eighties, dropping to 2.9 percent. (See Table 10–1.) Despite this, the per capita output of goods and services rose as overall economic growth stayed ahead of population. Now that, too, may be changing. From 1990 to 1993, the world economy expanded

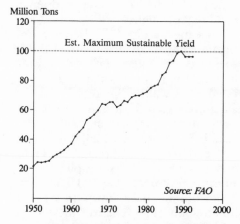

Million Tons

Figure 10-1. World Fish Harvest, 1950-92

Table 10–1. World Economic Growth by Decade, Total and Per Person, 1950–93

Decade	Annual Growth	Annual Growth Per Person
	(percent)	
1950–60	4.9	3.1
1960–70	5.2	3.2
1970–80	3.4	1.6
1980–90	2.9	1.1
1990–93 (prel.)	0.9	−0.8

SOURCE: Worldwatch Institute, based on sources documented in endnote 10.

annually at just 0.9 percent, leading to a per capita decline of 0.8 percent a year. Thus three years into the new decade, income per person is 2 percent lower than it was when the nineties began. Even using an economic accounting system that overstates progress because it omits the depletion of natural capital, living standards are falling.[10]

These economic trends help explain why grain production per person could be falling so much without any rise in grain prices. The worldwide decline in income during the early nineties was preceded by a drop in incomes between 1980 and 1990 in some 42 countries with some 850 million people—including many of the world's poorest, those for whom the link between income and food consumption is strongest. In addition, the collapse in purchasing power in the former Soviet Union following economic reforms has lowered grain use, sharply reducing imports.[11]

The experience of recent decades with overfishing and overgrazing gives a sense of the limits to the carrying capacity of fisheries and rangelands.

Although the first three years of the nineties were recession-ridden and thus should not be taken to represent the new decade, the world economy is not growing as easily as it once did. Economic mismanagement in key industrial countries (particularly the United States, Germany, and Japan) and the disruption associated with economic reform in Eastern Europe are impeding economic growth. But global economic expansion is also now constrained by no growth in the fishing industry, no growth in the production of beef, mutton, and other livestock products from the world's rangelands, and a world grain harvest expanding at less than 1 percent a year.[12]

While farming, ranching, and fishing are not as dominant in the modern industrial world as they once were, a slowdown in these basic sectors affects the entire economy. With constraints emerging in primary food-producing sectors—which the Third World depends on heavily—the world may be moving into an era of slower economic growth overall. (See Table 10–2.)

THE CHANGING FOOD OUTLOOK

New information on the sustainable-yield potential of the three food production systems—fisheries, rangelands, and croplands—makes it easier to project future output. The experience of recent decades with overfishing and overgrazing gives a sense of the limits to the carrying capacity of fisheries and rangelands. And with grain yield per hectare in countries now growing much more slowly and the cropland area essentially fixed, trends can now be predicted with some confidence, assuming no dramatic new breakthroughs.

If oceanic and inland fisheries cannot sustain a catch any greater than the record catch of 1989, and if—for purposes of calculation—it is assumed that additional grain will not be available to sustain future growth in aquaculture, seafood supply per person will decline steadily from now until 2030, reversing the trend of the last 40 years. (See Figure 10–2.) By then, the per capita seafood supply, which peaked at 19 kilograms in 1989, will be back down to 11 kilograms—only slightly above the level in 1950.[13]

Table 10–2. Comparison of Key Global Indicators in the Economic Era and the Environmental Era

Indicator	The Economic Era: 1950–90	The Environmental Era: 1990–2030
World Population	More than doubled from 2.5 to 5.3 billion, adding 2.8 billion or 70 million per year and slowing progress.	Projected to increase from 5.3 to 8.9 billion, adding 3.6 billion or 90 million per year. For much of humanity, this may reverse progress.
Grain Production	Nearly tripled from 631 million tons to 1,780 million tons, or 29 million tons per year.	Expanding by 12 million tons per year (rate of last eight years) may be best that can be expected.
Beef and Mutton Production	Increased 2.6 times, from 24 to 62 million tons.	Little growth expected.
Fish Catch	From 22 to 100 million tons; per capita up from 9 to 19 kilograms.	No growth expected; per capita dropping from 19 kilograms to 11 kilograms.
Economic Growth	Economy expanded 4.9-fold from nearly $4 trillion to $19 trillion, an annual gain of 4.2 percent. Growth is focus of national economic policymaking.	Averaging even half the 1950–90 rate may be difficult. Focus will shift from growth to sustainability and distribution.
Growth in Grain Demand	Two thirds from population growth; one third from rising incomes.	Nearly all expansion will be needed to sustain population growth.
National Security	Largely ideological and military in nature; defined by the cold war.	Food and job security will dominate, often driving hungry and jobless people across national borders.

SOURCE: Worldwatch Institute.

Pressures on rangelands are similar to those on fisheries. With extensive overgrazing on every continent, the rangeland production of beef and mutton is unlikely to increase much if at all, leading to a steady decline in per capita supply. This affects most directly the pastoral economies of Africa, the Middle East, and Central Asia.[14]

Trying to maintain the historical growth in seafood supplies of 2 million tons a year would require an enormous increase in fish farming, which would use vast amounts of land, water, and feed. Even though fish are among the more efficient converters of grain into meat, needing only 2 pounds of feed per pound of weight gain, this would still require 4 million tons of additional grain per year. And if the million-ton-per-year

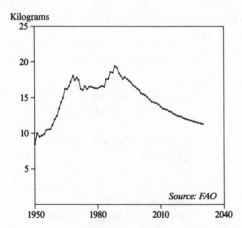

Kilograms

Source: FAO

1950   1980   2010   2040

Figure 10-2. World Fish Harvest Per Person, 1950-92, With Projections to 2030

historical growth in beef and mutton output from rangelands is to rest on expanded feeding in feedlots, it will take an additional 7 million tons of grain each year, since steers in a feedlot typically require 7 pounds of grain for each pound of additional live weight gain. Thus maintaining the historical growth in both fish and beef supply would take 11 million tons of additional grain each year, an amount roughly equal to the annual increase in the world grain harvest in recent years.[15]

This raises the question of how rapidly grain production can be expanded, either by increasing planted area or by raising land productivity. Prospects for a major expansion of cropland that is economically profitable and environmentally sustainable are not good, since there is little fertile land waiting to be plowed. The last effort to expand the world's cultivated area, which followed a doubling of world grain prices in 1972, ended in a massive retrenchment.[16]

Between 1972 and 1981, farmers responded to sustained high prices by expanding the world grain area from 664 million to 735 million hectares, a gain of nearly 11 percent. Much of this expansion came in the Soviet Union and the

United States on land that, unfortunately, was highly erodible and not capable of sustaining cultivation. After peaking at 123 million hectares in 1977, the Soviet Union's grain harvested area has declined each year, dropping to 99 million hectares in 1993 as fast-eroding land was either planted to soil-stabilizing forage crops, fallowed, or abandoned. In the United States, some 14 million hectares of the most erodible cropland were converted to grass or trees between 1985 and 1992 under the Conservation Reserve Program. In an emergency, some of this land could be farmed in rotation with forage crops or by using other appropriate conservation tillage practices.[17]

The United States is holding an additional 8 million hectares of grainland out of production under commodity supply management programs in 1993, and European countries may be holding out up to 3 million hectares. But even bringing all this land back into production would expand the world grain area by only 1.6 percent, not half enough to get it back to the historical high reached in 1981. The combination of the continuing abandonment of severely eroded land and the conversion of cropland to nonfarm uses means that net gains in the world's cropland area will not come easily.[18]

Since mid-century, countries that have not doubled, tripled, or even quadrupled the productivity of their cropland are the exceptions, not the rule. But with many of the world's farmers already using advanced yield-raising technologies, this rapid rise has lost momentum in recent years. A sense of the emerging constraints can be gleaned by analyzing historical trends in yield per hectare for each major cereal in the most agriculturally advanced countries.

Yields of corn, a cereal widely used for feed and food, are highest in the United States, which accounts for more than 40

percent of the world harvest. Data for
U.S. corn yields from 1866 to 1993 divide into three distinct periods. (See Figure 10–3.) For seven decades, corn
yields were essentially unchanged, aver-
aging about 1.6 tons per hectare. The
period from 1940 to 1985 saw an extraordinary growth of more than fourfold in the average yield, pushing it to
7.4 tons per hectare. In the eight years
since then, the rise has slowed to a near
standstill.[19]

A similar situation exists for wheat in
the United Kingdom, which has the
highest yield of any major wheat-pro-
ducing country. From 1884 until 1940,
yields were remarkably stable. From
1940 until 1984, they more than tripled.
But in the following nine years, U.K.
wheat yields fluctuated around 7.5 tons
per hectare, showing little evidence of a
continuing rapid rise.[20]

The rise in wheat yields in other parts
of Europe with similar growing conditions is slowing as the output approaches the U.K. level. Among these
are Germany and France, the latter a
wheat exporter. The rise is also slowing
in the United States and China, the
world's two largest wheat exporters.
(See Figure 10–4.) Since wheat in these
two countries is grown in low-rainfall re-

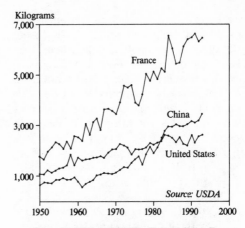

Figure 10-4. Wheat Yield Per Hectare, China, France, and United States, 1950–93

gions, the rise in yields is slowing at yield
levels one third to one half those in
Western Europe. In China, the big jump
in wheat production came after the economic reforms in 1978, as yields climbed
81 percent from 1977 to 1984. During
the nine years since then, they have risen
only 16 percent.[21]

After increasing for nearly a century,
the rise in rice yields in Japan came to a
halt in 1984. Since then they have actually fallen slightly. (See Figure 10–5.)
Yields in China, the world's largest rice

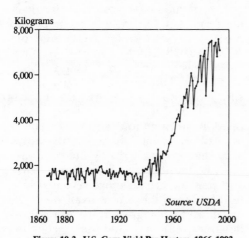

Figure 10-3. U.S. Corn Yield Per Hectare, 1866–1993

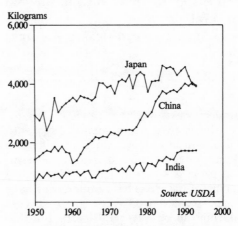

Figure 10-5. Rice Yield Per Hectare, China, India, and Japan, 1950–93

producer, now approach Japan's and have been stable since 1990. In India, the second ranking rice producer, the rise in yields has slowed at a much lower level, however. In Japan and China, 99 and 93 percent, respectively, of the rice is irrigated; in India, the figure is only 44 percent, making it far more difficult to achieve high yields. The yield rise has also slowed in other major rice-producing countries, including Indonesia, Pakistan, and the Philippines.[22]

The overall picture is equally sobering. From 1984 until 1993, world grain yields rose only 9 percent, or 1 percent year—less than half the rate of the preceding 34 years. For those who remember biology class experiments measuring the growth in a petri dish of an algae population with an unlimited food supply, this deceleration will not come as a surprise. With algae, it is the buildup of waste that eventually checks growth, bringing it to a halt. For grain with unlimited fertilizer supplies and abundant soil moisture, the plant's photosynthetic efficiency will ultimately check the rise in yield.[23]

Few countries that have doubled or tripled grain yields during the last several decades can expect to match that record during the next few.

Grain production per hectare is a natural process, one that relies on photosynthesis to convert solar energy into biochemical energy. Albeit modified by human intervention, it is—like all natural processes—subject to the biological limits of nature. These boundaries have been pushed back with great success during the last several decades, but that does not mean this can go on forever.

The engine driving the rise in grain

yields from mid-century onward was the expanding use of fertilizer—specifically, the synergistic interactions of rising fertilizer use with expanding irrigation and the spread of grain varieties that were responsive to ever heavier applications of fertilizer. This formula was phenomenally successful from 1950 to 1984, when fertilizer use climbed from 14 million to 126 million tons. Moving to a new high nearly every year, it was one of the most predictable trends in the world economy. During this time, each additional ton of fertilizer applied boosted grain output 9 tons. (See Table 10–3.)

But 1984 was the last year in which a large increase in fertilizer use led to a comparable gain in world grain output. During the next five years farmers continued to use more fertilizer, but their crops did not respond much. Each additional ton of fertilizer used raised grain output by less than 2 tons. Given such a weak response, applying more fertilizer was clearly not a money-making proposition. Farmers' reaction, both predictable and rational, was to use less. Between 1989 and 1993, they cut fertilizer use some 12 percent. Even excluding the precipitous drop in the former Soviet Union following economic reforms, usage elsewhere dropped by 3 percent.[24]

The phenomenal growth in fertilizer use from 1950 to 1984 was due in part to the record growth in irrigation from 1950 to 1978. Since then, however, irrigation has expanded at scarcely 1 percent a year. And new varieties that would respond strongly to still heavier applications of fertilizer have not been developed. Restoring rapid, sustained growth in fertilizer use and, hence, in the world grain harvest is not likely unless someone can develop varieties of wheat, corn, and rice that are far more responsive to fertilizer than those now available.[25]

Failure to recognize this recent slowdown in yield gains and the reasons for it can generate overly optimistic projec-

Table 10–3. World Grain Production and Fertilizer Use, 1950–93

Year	Grain Production	Increment	Fertilizer Use[1]	Increment	Incremental Grain/Fertilizer Response[1]
	(million tons)				(ratio)
1950	631		14		
1984	1,649	1,018	126	112	9.1
1989	1,685	36	146	20	1.8
1993	1,719	34	130	−16	—[2]

[1]Assumes that all fertilizer is used for grain; although this is obviously not the case, it provides a broad picture of the changing response.   [2]Incremental ratio cannot be calculated because fertilizer use declined. SOURCE: U.N. Food and Agriculture Organization, *Fertilizer Yearbook* (Rome: various years); International Fertilizer Industry Association, *Fertilizer Consumption Report* (Paris: 1992); U.S. Department of Agriculture, *World Grain Database* (unpublished printout) (Washington, D.C.: 1993).

tions. In a forthcoming study entitled *The World Food Outlook: Malthus Must Wait*, World Bank economists Donald O. Mitchell and Merlinda D. Ingco project world food supply and demand to 2010, assuming that the rate of growth in grain yield per hectare between 1960 and 1990 will simply continue until 2010. This makes for a rather hopeful set of projections. Unfortunately, there is no scientific foundation for this assumption, given the dramatic slowdown in the rise of grain yield per hectare during the late eighties and early nineties. Indeed, from 1990 to 1993, the first three years in the 20 years projected, worldwide grain yield per hectare actually declined.[26]

Donald Plucknett of the Consultative Group on International Agricultural Research presented a paper in late 1993 in which he argues there is no evidence of a slowdown in the rise in grain yields. Looking at both longer-term yield trends and those from 1980 to 1990, he notes that yields have increased substantially in almost every country. This is not debatable. But both these analyses miss the abrupt deceleration in the rise in yields that has occurred since 1984—

from a 2.3-percent annual increase in grain yield per hectare between 1950 and 1984 to a mere 1-percent annual increase from 1984 to 1993.[27]

Environmental degradation is also slowing the rise in yields. The earlier rapid rise in fertilizer use may have obscured the negative effects on yields of soil erosion, air pollution, waterlogging and salting, and other forms of degradation. But where fertilizer use is no longer rising, these effects may become more visible.

Few countries that have doubled or tripled grain yields during the last several decades can expect to match that record during the next few with existing technologies. Most have either already achieved the easy dramatic rises or lack the natural conditions needed to do so. In semiarid Africa, for example, where yields have risen little, the prospects for sharply raising output during the next four decades are no better than they were for Australia's farmers, who boosted wheat yields by less than half between 1950 and 1990. Every country that has multiplied its yields has relied heavily on the same basic combination of water (either from relatively generous

rainfall or from irrigation), fertilizer, and
grain varieties that are highly responsive
to fertilizer.[28]

In one sense, it is surprising that the
rise in yields is slowing in so many countries at the same time. An analysis of
these trends in all countries reveals that
the slowdown affects each of the major
cereals—wheat, rice, and corn. And it
affects rainfed and irrigated crops, temperate and tropical regions, industrial
and developing countries. But in another sense, the deceleration is not surprising since farmers everywhere now
draw on the same international pool of
yield-raising technologies.

In Western Europe, the slowdown
came after population had stabilized, but
in many developing countries it has occurred while population is still growing
rapidly. Not surprisingly, slowly rising
grain yields per hectare are a matter of
particular concern for countries where
massive population gains are projected.
These new yield trends help explain why
annual growth in the world harvest
dropped from an average of 30 million
tons from 1950 to 1984 to 12 million
tons from 1984 to 1992. If population
grows as projected and farmers cannot
increase grain output by more than 12
million tons per year, per capita supplies
will continue to diminish, dropping from
the historical high of 346 kilograms in
1984 to 248 kilograms in 2030. In effect,
the next four decades could be a mirror
image of the last four, with grain availability levels in 2030 returning to those of
1950. (See Figure 10–6.)[29]

The contrast between mid-century
and today in terms of the backlog of agricultural technology could not be more
striking. When the fifties began, there
was a great deal of technology waiting to
be used. Justus von Liebig had discovered in 1847 that all the nutrients extracted from the soil by crops could be
replaced in mineral form. Gregor Mendel's work establishing the basic principles of heredity, which laid the ground-

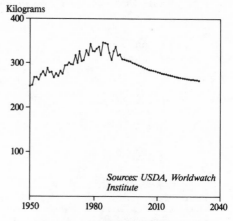

**Figure 10-6. World Grain Output Per Person,
1950-93, With Projections to 2030**

work for future crop breeding advances,
was done in the 1860s. Basic irrigation
technologies had been around for several thousand years. Hybrid corn varieties were commercialized well before
mid-century. And the dwarfing of wheat
and rice plants in Japan to boost fertilizer responsiveness dates back a century.[30]

As these long-standing technologies
have been exploited during the last four
decades, no new technologies that could
lead to quantum leaps in world food output have taken their place. As a result,
the nineties begin with the more progressive farmers looking over the shoul-
ders of agricultural scientists seeking
new yield-raising technologies only to
discover that they have little to offer.
The pipeline of new yield-raising agricultural technologies has not run dry,
but the flow has slowed to a trickle.[31]

Most future growth in grain output
must therefore come from exploiting
technologies not yet fully used. Technological advances that could dramatically
expand food output include a wholesale
reduction in the cost of desalting seawa-
ter or the redesign of the photosynthetic
process to enable it to convert solar energy into biochemical energy more efficiently. Unfortunately, leading scientific

bodies, such as the National Academy of Sciences and the Royal Society of the United Kingdom, do not hold out much hope for such far-reaching break-throughs in the foreseeable future.[32]

Some have high hopes that biotechnology will dramatically improve the food prospect. But this is not a panacea. It permits researchers to reach some goals faster and at less cost. And, uniquely, it permits the transfer of germ-plasm from one species to another. Thus far its contributions have centered more on such things as improving the resistance of crops to insects and diseases. Successes in this area reduce dependence on chemical controls, but they raise production only when the incorporated resistance is more effective than the pesticides previously used. After a small conference involving many of the world's leading agricultural scientists, Vernon Ruttan, an agricultural economist at the University of Minnesota, summarized the group's feeling: "Advances in conventional technology will remain the primary source of growth in crop and animal production over the next quarter century."[33]

During the last decade, the real price of grain has declined somewhat, continuing a long-term trend and leading some to argue that the loss of momentum in food output growth could be reversed by a scarcity-induced price rise. Higher grain prices will undoubtedly stimulate additional investment in agriculture, but whether they will greatly expand output is another question. This will happen only if the higher prices make profitable the expanded use of basic inputs, such as land, water, fertilizer, and more productive varieties. But as noted earlier, the last major effort to expand the world's cropland, in the late seventies, ended in retrenchment. Over the last decade, the world's grain harvested area has actually declined. The reality is that there is simply not much fertile land waiting to be plowed.

Similarly, the global potential for dramatically expanding the irrigated area is constrained by aquifer depletion and the lack of suitable sites for irrigation dams. Expansion of irrigation will continue as new projects are completed, but whether it can expand fast enough to offset the negative effects of waterlogging and salting of existing irrigated area, and make a major net contribution to world food output, is problematic. And with fertilizer, the response curves are such that even if the world's farmers were to double fertilizer use, it would only marginally boost the grain harvest.[34]

Perhaps the best test of the price hypothesis has occurred in Japan, where the government supports rice prices at six times the world market level. Boosting rice yields in Japan is extraordinarily profitable, but try as they might, Japan's farmers—scientifically literate, hard-working, and with access to cheap credit—have not raised rice yields at all over the last decade.[35]

In summary, there are innumerable opportunities for expanding food production, many of them locally unique. But all the identifiable ones are small, adding a little here and a little there. There are no large jumps in output in prospect comparable to those that followed the expanding use of fertilizer or the hybridization of corn. Without such dramatic, broad-based advances, the world's farmers may not be able to restore the rapid steady growth in food output that characterized the period from 1950 to 1984.

NATIONAL CARRYING CAPACITY ASSESSMENTS

With grain yields now plateauing in some countries, with national fish catches unlikely to increase much, if at all, and with rangelands widely over-grazed in most countries, there is an urgent need for national assessments of carrying capacity. Otherwise, there is a real risk that countries will blindly overrun their food carrying capacity, developing massive deficits that will collectively exceed the world's exportable supplies. Recent data showing the level at which the rise in grain yield per hectare is slowing or levelling off in countries with a wide range of growing conditions provide all governments with the refer-

ence points needed to estimate the population carrying capacity of their croplands.

China, which already has one of the slowest population growth rates in the developing world, is projected to add 490 million people over the next four decades, increasing to 1.6 billion in 2030. (See Table 10–4.) Currently it is adding 14 million people per year. Meanwhile, its economy is expanding at 10 percent or more annually, fueling steady rises in consumption of pork,

Table 10–4. Population Growth 1950–90, With Projections to 2030, for the Most Populous Countries[1]

Country	1950	1990	2030	Increase 1950–90	Increase 1990–2030
			(million)		
Slowly Growing Countries					
United States	152	250	345	98	95
Russia	114	148	161	34	13
Japan	84	124	123	40	−1
United Kingdom	50	58	60	8	2
Germany	68	80	81	12	1
Italy	47	58	56	11	−2
France	42	57	62	15	5
Rapidly Growing Countries					
Philippines	21	64	111	43	47
Nigeria	32	87	278	55	191
Ethiopia and Eritrea	21	51	157	30	106
Iran	16	57	183	41	126
Pakistan	40	118	260	78	142
Bangladesh	46	114	243	68	129
Egypt	21	54	111	33	57
Mexico	28	85	150	57	65
Turkey	21	57	104	36	47
Indonesia	83	189	307	106	118
India	369	853	1,443	484	590
Brazil	53	153	252	100	99
China	563	1,134	1,624	571	490

[1]Census Bureau data are used because they are updated more often than the U.N. medium-range projections; the two series are usually similar, but small differences do exist.
SOURCE: U.S. Bureau of the Census, in Francis Urban and Ray Nightingale, *World Population by Country and Region, 1950–90 and Projections to 2050* (Washington, D.C.: U.S. Department of Agriculture, Economic Research Service, 1993).

poultry, eggs, and fish—all produced with grain.[36]

On the supply side, rapid industrialization in China, including the construction of thousands of factories during this decade, is consuming vast amounts of cropland even as the rise in per hectare yield of rice and wheat is slowing. The result, according to a detailed study commissioned by the Australian government, is that China's grain imports could go from 12 million tons in 1993 up to 50-100 million tons by the end of this decade, with the latter amount being above current U.S. exports. If China's economy expands as planned and its population grows as projected, its grain import needs are likely to continue to soar, exceeding by 2015 the world's current exportable grain supplies.[37]

India—already faced with extensive soil erosion and falling water tables—will be adding 590 million people by 2030, even more than China, as its population increases to 1.44 billion. With wheat yields that have already tripled and rice yields that are rising more slowly than in the past, India will find it difficult to support these growing numbers.[38]

The United States, though it is the world's third most populous country, has kept demand for grain well below the sustainable yield of its land, maintaining a large exportable surplus. However, with population projected to expand by 95 million as a result of natural increase and immigration during the next four decades, pushing the total to 345 million in 2030, large areas of farmland will be claimed for housing, schools, and shopping centers. Unless some way can be found to reestablish the rapid rise in yields that prevailed from 1950 to 1984, the exportable grain surplus—which dropped from 100 million tons in the early eighties to 70 million tons in the early nineties as consumption climbed and as highly erodible cropland

was converted to grassland—may well continue to fall.[39]

Ethiopia was unable to expand grain production fast enough to keep pace with the 30 million people added between 1950 and 1990. Now it is projected to add, in the next four decades, 106 million people—which would triple its 1990 population. Few believe this will happen. The only question is whether the projected growth will not materialize because the transition to smaller families accelerates or because starvation checks the growth.

For Nigeria, the situation is scarcely any more comforting. After adding 55 million people from 1950 to 1990, Nigeria is projected to add 191 million by 2030. With soils that are already heavily eroded, it is difficult to see how crop yields can rise enough to accommodate this tripling of population to 278 million.

An environmental assessment for Pakistan noted that the nation's population is projected to reach 400 million.

Mexico, facing severe water scarcity, is projected to add 65 million people during the next four decades, compared with 57 million in the last four. Wheat yields there have already plateaued, showing no increase in the last nine years. Although there is still an unrealized potential for raising corn yields, it is difficult to see how Mexico can stop its annual grain deficit from rising far beyond the 5 million tons of recent years.[40]

Such projections can be invaluable to national governments. An environmental assessment for Pakistan undertaken with the assistance of IUCN–The World Conservation Union noted that the nation's population is projected to reach 400 million. The report pointed out that while Pakistan might accommodate an increase from its current 121 to 200 million, it could not go much beyond that. If it remains on the trajectory of 400 million Pakistanis, it "will become an international charity case—like Haiti, Ethiopia, Sudan, and Bangladesh—dependent on the good will of others, with no realistic opportunity to improve the lot of its people and no expectations other than the continual decline of living standards for the vast bulk of them." This set of projections gives the government the information needed to establish a public dialogue on choices in the trade-off between family size and consumption levels.[41]

Aside from the obvious value to governments of doing such assessments, these studies collectively give a sense of the future relationship between import needs and exportable supplies. During the past decade, world grain exports totalled roughly 200 million tons annually, with close to half coming from the United States. The other half came from Argentina, Australia, Canada, France, South Africa, and Thailand. With world grain exports even more concentrated than those of oil, the risk that a U.S. crop shortfall presents to the more than 100 grain-importing countries is clear. Although exportable supplies could well decline during the next four decades, particularly if farm subsidies are reduced, import needs are expected to soar in countries where the projected population increase of 3.6 billion is concentrated.[42]

Even while national carrying capacity assessments are under way, a global set of projections is needed, one that draws on them and analyzes the human carrying capacity of the planet. Without this global effort, countries with soaring import needs will have no way of knowing whether exportable supplies will be available. This assessment could be used as a basis for international discussion. And, like national studies, it should be updated every two years or so, taking into account the availability of new farming technologies, fresh evidence of the effects of environmental degradation on food production, and the most recent data on population growth.

Carrying capacity projections at the global level give a sense of global options as well. For example, the world grain output projections discussed earlier assumed annual growth of 12 million tons, yielding a harvest in 2030 of 2.2 billion tons. This could satisfy populations of varying sizes, depending on consumption levels. At the U.S. consumption level of 800 kilograms per person a year, such a harvest would sustain 2.75 billion people—half as many as are alive today. At the Italian consumption level of 400 kilograms, it would support 5.5 billion people, the 1993 world population. And at the Indian level of 200 kilograms, it would support 11 billion people. Although much of humanity aspires to the U.S. diet, population growth has foreclosed that option.[43]

At its peak of 346 kilograms in 1984, world grain output per person was well above the 300 kilograms of China and climbing toward the 400 kilograms of Italy. But that trend has been reversed. The harvest for 2030 of 2.2 billion tons would provide an average of 248 kilograms for each of the 8.9 billion people projected for that year—28 percent below the historical high. Stated otherwise, average grain consumption per person in 2030 would be well below that of China today, and falling toward that of India. Coming at a time when U.N. estimates show nearly 1 billion people in developing countries already failing to get enough calories to maintain normal levels of physical activity and when 36 percent of all preschool children in developing countries are below weight for their age, this prospective decline is not a pleasant one.[44]

TREADING MORE LIGHTLY

In low-income countries, where diets are often dominated by a single starchy staple, rises in income quickly translate into consumption of more livestock products. This rise in animal protein intake, which both improves nutrition and adds variety to an otherwise monotonous diet, is widely seen as an early sign of progress. When asked by a *New York Times* reporter if living conditions were improving, a Chinese villager responded, "Overall life has gotten much better. My family eats meat maybe four or five times a week now. Ten years ago we never had meat."[45]

Thus as incomes rise, so does grain use. In low-income countries, grain consumption per person averages some 200 kilograms a year, roughly one pound per day. (See Table 1–2 in Chapter 1.) At this level, diets are high in starch and low in fat and protein, with up to 70 percent or more of caloric intake coming from one staple, such as rice.[46]

By contrast, individuals in affluent societies such as the United States consume some 800 kilograms of grain a year, the bulk of it indirectly in the form of beef, mutton, pork, poultry, milk, cheese, yogurt, ice cream, and eggs. Grain use tracks income upward until it reaches this level, producing a grain-consumption ratio between those living in the world's wealthiest and poorest countries of roughly four to one.[47]

The 800 kilograms of grain consumed per person each year in the United States translates into a diet rich in livestock products: as meat, it includes 42 kilograms of beef, 28 kilograms of pork, and 44 kilograms of poultry. (See Table 10–5.) From dairy cows, it includes 271 kilograms of milk, part of it consumed directly and part as cheese (12 kilograms), yogurt (2 kilograms), and ice cream (8 kilograms). Rounding out this protein-rich fare are more than 200 eggs a year.[48]

This contrasts sharply with the situation in India, where most of the 200 kilo-

Table 10–5. Per Capita Grain Use and Consumption of Livestock Products in Selected Countries, 1990

Country	Grain Use[1]	Consumption						
		Beef	Pork	Poultry	Mutton	Milk[2]	Cheese	Eggs
	(kilograms)				(kilograms)			
United States	800	42	28	44	1	271	12	16
Italy	400	16	20	19	1	182	12	12
China	300	1	21	3	1	4	—	7
India	200	—	0.4	0.4	0.2	31	—	13

[1]Data rounded to nearest 100 kilograms, as the purpose here is to contrast the wide variation in consumption of livestock products associated with different levels of grain use. [2]Total consumption, including that used to produce cheese, yogurt, and ice cream.
SOURCE: U.N. Food and Agriculture Organization, *FAO Production Yearbook 1990* (Rome: 1991).

grams of grain available per person are eaten directly just to meet basic food energy needs. With little grain available to feed livestock and poultry and with a limited cultural acceptance of beef, consumption of livestock products is low. For the average Indian, it totals 31 kilograms of milk; 1 kilogram of pork, poultry, and mutton combined; and about 170 eggs.

In between the United States and India are Italy, using 400 kilograms of grain per person annually, and China, with 300 kilograms. The big difference between the United States and Italy is meat consumption: 115 kilograms per year versus 56. And just as India matches the industrial countries in egg consumption per person, China nearly equals them in consumption of pork, its most popular livestock product. Among these four countries, life expectancy is highest in Italy—perhaps in part because it may have the healthiest all-around diet, one where animal protein intake is high enough that even the poor are adequately nourished but not so rich in animal fats that it damages health.[49]

As the demand for meat rises, growth in supply is shaped in part by how efficiently various species convert grain into meat. For cattle in the feedlot, it takes roughly 7 kilograms of grain to add a kilogram of live weight. For pork, it takes roughly 4 kilograms. Poultry and fish are much more efficient, requiring 2 kilograms for each kilogram of live weight gain. Cheese and eggs are in between, requiring 3.0 and 2.6 kilograms of grain, respectively.[50]

The worldwide use of grain for feed, which includes the by-products of grain milling, such as rice bran, climbed from 289 million tons in 1960 to 650 million tons in 1986, accounting for 40 percent of total grain use, an all-time high. (See Figure 10–7.) Since then, the amount of grain used for feed has actually declined, dropping to 37 percent of world grain use in 1992. This reflects a shift toward

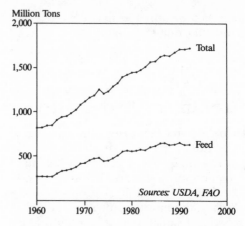

Figure 10-7. World Grain Use, Total and for Feed, 1960–92

the more efficient meats, such as poultry, along with a worldwide fall in incomes since 1990, including a particularly sharp drop in Eastern Europe and the former Soviet Union.[51]

Contrary to popular impressions, a large share of world feedgrain use occurs in the Third World. The two countries that feed the most grain to livestock, poultry, and fish are the United States and China—160 and 140 million tons, respectively.[52]

For health reasons alone, people in the most affluent societies should reduce consumption of fat-rich livestock products. The question is how. If governments in these societies want to lower consumption to improve health and to free up grain for the world's poor, they can do it through public education and exhortation, through taxing consumption of livestock products, or through rationing. Scarcity-induced price rises can also cut the amount of livestock products people eat. Following the doubling of world grain prices between 1972 and 1973, for example, total grain use in the United States dropped from 178 million to 136 million tons. Relying on the market to reduce grain use among the affluent through scarcity-induced price rises, however, could threaten the survival of millions in low-income countries who already spend most of their income on food.[53]

No modern society has voluntarily reduced consumption of livestock products by a meaningful amount. Any such drops have been the result of sharply rising prices, as in the United States during the mid-seventies; wartime rationing, as in the United Kingdom during World War II; or the removal of food subsidies, as in the former Soviet Union during the early nineties.

Once feedgrain use is reduced, whether by rationing, taxing, or another means, a way must be found to finance its purchase and distribution to those who are hungry. No one knows how much food could be redistributed internationally. Since 1980, some 10–11 million tons of grain have been shipped annually as aid from all sources, most of it under the auspices of the U.S. Food for Peace Program and the U.N. World Food Programme. At issue is whether this could be greatly expanded to alleviate hunger if massive shortages emerge.[54]

Would the earth's more affluent be willing to greatly simplify their diets for a one-time gain in consumption elsewhere? And could governments in industrial countries finance a far greater redistribution of food at a time when fiscal stringencies are reducing foreign aid budgets? Could the United Nations respond to massive famine threats in several countries simultaneously? In the absence of some major changes, it would be unwise for countries facing potential food deficits to assume that food aid would automatically be available to cover their shortfalls.

Stabilizing Our Numbers

New information on the carrying capacity of both land and oceanic food systems argues for a basic rethinking of national population policies, for an accelerated international response to unmet family planning needs, and for the recasting of development strategies to address the underlying causes of high fertility. As national demands cross the sustainable-yield thresholds of biological support systems, the resource base itself is being consumed. In this situation, the question may not be what rate of population growth is sustainable but whether growth can continue without reducing living standards. Even now, the food needs of the 90 million added each year can be satisfied only by reducing consumption among those already here.

Perhaps the greatest gap in formulating population policy has been the failure to consider carrying capacity.

In a world where the cropland area is not expanding, grain yield per hectare has to rise as fast as population growth merely to maintain the existing inadequate supply of food. But with the rise in yields slowing so dramatically, reversing the decline in per capita grain production under way since 1984 may now depend on quickly slowing population growth. Otherwise, hunger may continue to spread, claiming more and more lives.

Perhaps the greatest gap in formulating population policy has been the failure to consider carrying capacity. If national governments calculate the food carrying capacity of their countries, they can integrate this analysis into population policy. Few national political leaders even use the term carrying capacity, much less incorporate the concept in policymaking. The national carrying capacity assessments discussed earlier, outlining the potential social costs of carrying capacity overruns, could mobilize public support for quickly moving to smaller families.

If people know that maintaining current family size will reduce cropland area per person by a third or half during the next generation, they can see what that will mean for their children. If they know that large families will almost certainly bring more hunger, and even mass starvation, they may well decide to shift to smaller families. People can understand the central importance of population policy if it is put in terms they can relate to.

People need to know the longer term consequences of having an average of, say, six children, four children, or two children. Couples who have this information may realize that the key question is no longer "How many children should I have for my old age security?" but "How will the number of children I have affect the world in which they live?" Since people everywhere do care about their children, answering this question can spawn an important shift in thinking, one with a potentially profound effect on family size decisions. If population policy is not grounded in public discussion of these options, it is not likely to succeed.

For countries that decide to accelerate the shift to smaller families, the challenge is to provide the needed family planning services. The first, perhaps most obvious step is to fill the family planning gap. The fact that more than 100 million women in the Third World want to limit the number of children they have but lack the means to do so is inexcusable. The restoration of U.S. funding for the U.N. Population Fund announced in early 1993 is a step in the right direction.[55]

The basic ingredients in a strategy to slow population growth are well known to governments and the international community, and will not be repeated at length here. The most successful programs provide a cafeteria approach to services by including the entire range of contraceptives so that individual needs are most fully satisfied. Each country where population has stabilized thus far, all in Europe, has had a wide range of family planning services backed up by abortion in the event of a contraceptive failure.[56]

Even as the family planning gap is being filled, there is an equally urgent need to improve the status of women, particularly in developing countries, where females suffer discrimination from birth. High on the agenda are increasing access to reproductive health care and raising the level of female literacy. In addition, any strategy that reduces poverty sets the stage for a shift to small families.[57]

What is missing in this strategy to reduce human fertility is a broad-based public commitment to do so. There is little recognition that the nature of the population threat has changed in recent years: continuing rapid population growth once slowed the rise in living standards; now it is lowering them for much of humanity.

Given the limits to the earth's carrying capacity, every national government needs a carefully articulated population policy, one that takes into account their carrying capacity at whatever consumption level citizens decide on. As Harvard biologist Edward O. Wilson observes in his landmark book *The Diversity of Life*, "Every nation has an economic policy and a foreign policy. The time has come to speak more openly of a population policy. By this I mean not just the capping of growth when the population hits the wall, as in China and India, but a policy based on a rational solution of this problem; what, in the judgment of its informed citizenry, is the *optimal* population?"[58]

In the end, only national governments

can assume the responsibility of feeding their people, only they can formulate the agricultural and population policies that will ensure an adequate diet for all their people. The international community can support national initiatives, but it cannot replace them.

A TEST OF CIVILIZATION

Humanity faces many challenges as this century nears its end, but none looms larger than that of reversing the fall in grain production per person that has been under way since 1984. If this decline continues indefinitely, it will lead to political instability and social disintegration of the sort seen in Somalia, the Sudan, and Haiti. This trend is a test of our political institutions—indeed, of our humanity and modern civilization.

The drop in grain output per person is not merely an agronomic trend; it is an indicator of the crisis emerging between us, now 5.5 billion in number, and the natural systems and resources that support us. It is a systemic threat that requires a systemic response.

After nearly four decades of rapidly rising cropland productivity, many assumed that this trend would continue indefinitely. Unfortunately, it will not. Environmentalists, long concerned by a potential deterioration in the balance between food and people, are now being joined by the scientific community. Its leaders, observing the shrinking backlog of yield-raising agricultural technologies and the cumulative effects of the environmental degradation on agriculture, have started to speak out. In early 1992, the U.S. National Academy of Sciences and the Royal Society of London warned in an unprecedented joint statement that advances in science and technology no longer could be counted on to avoid either irreversible environmental degradation or continued poverty for much of humanity.[59]

Later in the year, the Union of Concerned Scientists issued a "World Scientists Warning to Humanity" signed by some 1,600 of the world's leading scientists, including 102 Nobel Prize winners. It observes that the continuation of destructive human activities "may so alter the living world that it will be unable to sustain life in the manner that we know." And the scientists warned: "A great change in our stewardship of the earth and the life on it is required, if vast human misery is to be avoided and our global home on this planet is not to be irretrievably mutilated."[60]

A systemic response to the deteriorating food situation depends heavily on slowing population growth, halting the degradation of the natural systems that support agriculture, and boosting investments in agriculture. As noted earlier, the keys to slowing population growth are filling the family planning gap, raising the status of women, and reducing poverty, the latter long an elusive goal of development strategists.

Protecting agriculture's support systems includes reducing soil losses from erosion below the natural rate of soil formation, preserving its biologically diverse germplasm base, and protecting the ozone layer to avoid increases in crop-damaging ultraviolet radiation. Food security also depends on stabilizing climate and reducing crop damage from air pollution. Both of these in turn require the phaseout of fossil fuels.

If there are no quantum jumps in world food output in prospect, such as those that came from the expanding use of fertilizer or the adoption of hybrid corn, it will be far more difficult to expand food output in the future. The era when applying another million tons of fertilizer would boost the world grain harvest by 9 million tons may now be history. Future gains in output have to come from more localized technological advances, a little here and a little there. Such a situation means spending far more on agricultural research. In a water-scarce world, it means investing heavily in irrigation water efficiency as a way of expanding irrigation. And every little gain in output is needed: 82,000 tons of additional grain satisfies growth in world demand for a day, buying one more day to slow population growth.

The new information on the earth's carrying capacity brings with it a responsibility to educate and to act that, until recently, did not exist.

The combination of falling grain output per person and a shrinking seafood catch per person is taking the world into uncharted economic territory. Glimpses of the new future can be seen in the rising prices in fresh-seafood shops, in the spreading hunger in Africa, and in the growing nervousness about the adequacy of future water supplies in the Middle East. At the most fundamental level, we need to recognize that we are approaching a potential crisis and that we need to respond on an appropriate scale. The national carrying capacity studies described earlier, using the most recent population projections and the latest information on sustainable yields of fisheries, grasslands, and croplands, can help fill the gap in our collective understanding. For countries needing help preparing such reports, the logical sources are the World Bank and the bilateral aid agencies.

Seldom has the world faced an unfolding emergency whose dimensions are as clear as the growing imbalance between food and people. The new information on the earth's carrying capacity brings with it a responsibility to educate and to act that, until recently, did not exist. A massive global environmental education effort, one in which the communications media are heavily involved, may be the only way to bring about the needed actions in the time available.

Ensuring future food security is an all-encompassing undertaking that will require far more attention from leaders and a greater commitment of public resources than even the cold war did. Aside from the military sectors of the superpowers, the day-to-day involvement of most people in the cold war was negligible. By contrast, restoring a rise in grain output per person will require the involvement of nearly all of humanity, either in reducing birth rates, expanding food production, or both.

Some of the components required in this effort to stem and reverse the tide of spreading hunger are becoming clear. For example, improved literacy plays an important role not only because among females it correlates closely with reducing fertility, but also because for farmers it is often the key to the adoption of more sophisticated agricultural management practices. At a time when some planners are already worrying about computer literacy in the Third World, hundreds of millions of people still lack the rudimentary skills to take advantage of Gutenberg's printing press, invented some five centuries ago. A U.N.-led effort to achieve universal literacy, patterned after its highly successful effort to promote childhood immunizations, could appeal to the ideals and energy of young people throughout the world.[61]

If the world were to collectively address the population issue on a scale commensurate with the human suffering that is almost inevitable if rapid growth continues, population-related issues would dominate national cabinet meetings and the U.N. General Assembly. World leaders would speak out on the issue, urging couples everywhere to stop at replacement-level fertility, essentially two surviving children per couple. In discussions among world leaders, changes in birth rates would get at least as much attention as changes in interest rates. Gains in female literacy would rank in importance with gains in savings rates. Governments would report monthly changes in birth rates with the same diligence and concern that they now report changes in the unemployment rate.

Although it is hard to overestimate the difficulty of reversing the deteriorating food/population balance, it can be reversed. Abrupt change is possible. Images flashing across television screens in recent years of the Berlin Wall coming down, of Nelson Mandela leaving prison, and of Yasir Arafat and Yitzhak Rabin shaking hands remind us that sudden change can happen, that we can reverse the deteriorating food situation. Other signs of hope include the new administrations in Tokyo and Washington. Leaders in both governments represent a new generation, one that is more globally aware and environmentally conscious than their predecessors were. The newly elected Parliament in Japan, its ranks liberally sprinkled with women and young people in their twenties, includes many environmentalists. With four women now serving in the Japanese cabinet, the perspective of that powerful body has broadened dramatically.[62]

In Washington, President Clinton was quick to sign the biodiversity treaty from the 1992 Earth Summit, reversing the Bush administration's position. His decision to join other countries in committing to limit year-2000 carbon emissions to their 1990 level was also a major step forward. These and other initiatives indicate that the United States is reassuming a global environmental and population leadership role, something essential to an effective global address of the complex set of issues associated with falling food production per person. Perhaps the most logical next step for the United States would be to lead an international effort to fill the family planning gap, to get services to more than 100 million women who want to limit the size of their families but lack the means to do so. Congress, which has already approved an increase in funding for international family planning assistance of $40 million for fiscal year 1994, would almost certainly support such an initiative.[63]

The question at this hinge point in history is a simple one. Can we mobilize to reverse the continuing decline in food production per person that now clouds the future of civilization? If we start thinking seriously about what it will take to do this, then we may also begin to understand how different the future will be from the recent past.

What will future historians write of us? Will they say that we were the generation whose selfish pursuit of materialism and inability to limit family size put civilization at risk? Or will they say that the initiatives that we took in the nineties put the world on an environmentally sustainable path? Only we can provide the answer.

Notes

Chapter 1. Carrying Capacity: Earth's Bottom Line

1. David R. Klein, "The Introduction, Increase, and Crash of Reindeer on St. Matthew Island," *Journal of Wildlife Management*, April 1968.

2. The resource projections for 2010 are not predictions but extrapolations based largely on recent trends—primarily those observed from 1980 to 1990—and current knowledge of the resource base, as discussed and documented later in this chapter.

3. Thomas F. Homer-Dixon et al., "Environmental Change and Violent Conflict," *Scientific American*, February 1993; Norman Myers, *Ultimate Security: The Environmental Basis of Political Security* (New York: W.W. Norton & Company, 1993).

4. These proportions are based on per capita gross national product data that are unadjusted for purchasing power parity (PPP), which measures the relative domestic purchasing powers of national currencies and therefore may convey a more realistic comparison of actual living standards.

5. Alan Thein Durning, *How Much is Enough? The Consumer Society and the Future of the Earth* (New York: W.W. Norton & Company, 1992); Alan Durning, *Poverty and the Environment: Reversing the Downward Spiral*, Worldwatch Paper 92 (Washington, D.C.: Worldwatch Institute, November 1989).

6. Sandra Postel, *Last Oasis: Facing Water Scarcity* (New York: W.W. Norton & Company, 1992); 1.2 billion figure from Joseph Christmas and Carel de Rooy, "The Decade and Beyond: At a Glance," *Water International*, September 1991.

7. Number of people without enough food and percentage of necessary calories consumed by the average African from Kevin Cleaver and Gotz Schreiber, *The Population, Agriculture, and Environment Nexus in Sub-Saharan Africa* (Washington, D.C.: World Bank, 1992); fat-laden diets in rich countries from Alan Durning and Holly Brough, *Taking Stock: Animal Farming and the Environment*, Worldwatch Paper 103 (Washington, D.C.: Worldwatch Institute, July 1991); increase in global harvest is a Worldwatch Institute estimate, based on U.S. Department of Agriculture (USDA), *World Grain Database* (unpublished printout) (Washington, D.C.: 1992), and on Population Reference Bureau (PRB), *1990 World Population Data Sheet* (Washington, D.C.: 1990).

8. Gross world product in 1950 from Herbert R. Block, *The Planetary Product in 1980: A Creative Pause?* (Washington, D.C.: U.S. Department of State, 1981); gross world product in 1990 from International Monetary Fund (IMF), *World Economic Outlook: Interim Assessment* (Washington, D.C.: 1993); increase in value of internationally traded goods from $308 million in 1950 to $3.58 trillion in 1992 (in 1990 dollars) is a Worldwatch Institute estimate, based on IMF, Washington, D.C., unpublished data base; World Bank, Washington, D.C., unpublished data base.

9. Industrial roundwood from United Nations, *Statistical Yearbook, 1953* (New York:

1954), and from U.N. Food and Agriculture Organization (FAO), *1991 Forest Products Yearbook* (Rome: 1993); water from Postel, op. cit. note 6; oil from American Petroleum Institute, *Basic Petroleum Data Book* (Washington, D.C.: 1992).

10. U.S. Bureau of the Census, Department of Commerce, *International Data Base* (unpublished printout) (Washington, D.C., November 2, 1993); population of Mexico from PRB, *1992 World Population Data Sheet* (Washington, D.C.: 1992).

11. Shiro Horiuchi, "Stagnation in the Decline of the World Population Growth Rate During the 1980s," *Science*, August 7, 1992.

12. Figure for 2030 from Larry Heligman, Estimates and Projections Section, Population Division, United Nations, New York, private communication, November 3, 1993; United Nations, Department of Economic and Social Affairs, *Long-Range World Population Projections: Two Centuries of Population Growth 1950-2150* (New York: 1992).

13. IUCN–The World Conservation Union, *The IUCN Sahel Studies 1991* (Gland, Switzerland: 1992).

14. Ibid.

15. Maria Concepcion Cruz et al., *Population Growth, Poverty, and Environmental Stress: Frontier Migration in the Philippines and Costa Rica* (Washington, D.C.: World Resources Institute, 1992).

16. Peter M. Vitousek et al., "Human Appropriation of the Products of Photosynthesis," *BioScience*, June 1986.

17. Ibid.

18. Cropland expansion from FAO, *Production Yearbook 1991* (Rome: 1992); figure of 76 million from "Crops from Pasture Land," *International Agricultural Development*, March/April 1993, and from Richard J. Thomas, Centro Internacional de Agricultura Tropical, Cali, Colombia, private communication, July 21, 1993.

19. Vaclav Smil, "China's Environment in the 1980s: Some Critical Changes," *Ambio*, September 1992; cropland areas of European countries from FAO, op. cit. note 18; number of Chinese people that 35 million hectares could support is Worldwatch Institute estimate, based on USDA, op. cit. note 7.

20. L.R. Oldeman et al., "The Extent of Human-Induced Soil Degradation," in L.R. Oldeman et al., *World Map of the Status of Human-Induced Soil Degradation* (Wageningen, Netherlands: United Nations Environment Programme and International Soil Reference and Information Centre, 1991).

21. FAO, op. cit. note 18.

22. Oldeman et al., op. cit. note 20.

23. Fish catch from FAO, Fisheries Department, "Global Fish and Shellfish Production in 1991," COFI Support Document: Fishery Statistics, Rome, March 1993; percentage of human protein consumption from FAO, *Food Balance Sheets* (Rome: 1991); contribution to coastal diet from FAO, "Marine Fisheries and the Law of the Sea: A Decade of Change," Fisheries Circular No. 853, Rome, 1993.

24. Fivefold increase in world fish catch from FAO, *Yearbook of Fishery Statistics: Catches and Landings* (Rome: various years); other figures from M. Perotti, chief, Statistics Branch, Fisheries Department, FAO, Rome, private communication, November 3, 1993.

25. Advent of fisheries technologies and assessment of all fishing areas from FAO, "Marine Fisheries and the Law of the Sea," op. cit. note 23; FAO, "World Review of High Seas and Highly Migratory Fish Species and Straddling Stocks," Fisheries Circular No. 858 (preliminary version), Rome, 1993.

26. Estimate of potential catch from FAO-sponsored book by J.A. Gulland, ed., *The Fish Resources of the Ocean* (West Byfleet, Surrey, U.K.: Fishing News (Books) Ltd.: 1971); 2010 projection is Worldwatch Institute estimate,

based on data from FAO, "Maine Fisheries and the Law of the Sea," op. cit. note 23.

27. Postel, op. cit. note 6.

28. Ibid.

29. Annual loss of irrigated land to salinization from Dina L. Umali, *Irrigation-Induced Salinity*, World Bank Technical Paper Number 215 (Washington, D.C.: World Bank, 1993).

30. 1700 figure does not include woodlands or shrublands, from R.A. Houghton et al., "Changes in the Carbon Content of Terrestrial Biota and Soils Between 1860 and 1980: A Net Release of CO_2 to the Atmosphere," *Ecological Monographs*, September 1983. FAO and the U.N. Economic Commission for Europe/FAO (UN-ECE/FAO) used somewhat different definitions in their 1990 forest assessments, which precludes a strict comparison of the data between tropical and temperate zones when calculating the change in world forest cover between 1980 and 1990. For both regions, "other wooded areas" have been excluded from all calculations. Because of gaps and discrepancies in the data, FAO does not plan to make any estimate of global deforestation at the conclusion of the 1990 assessment (in progress as of October 1993), according to Klaus Janz, senior forestry officer, Resources Appraisal and Monitoring, Forestry Department, FAO, Rome, private communication, October 29, 1993. The estimated net loss of forests refers to the conversion of forests to an alternative land use, minus the net addition of plantations in tropical regions. As defined by FAO, loss of forests does not include forest that was logged and left to regrow, even if it was clear-cut (unless the forest cover is permanently reduced to less than 10 percent). Thus, the statistics fail to reflect the fragmentation or degradation of forests.

Given these limitations, the 1990 figure is a preliminary and rough Worldwatch Institute estimate, based on: FAO, *1961–1991 . . . 2010: Forestry Statistics Today for Tomorrow* (Rome: 1993); FAO, "Areas of Woody Vegetation at End 1980 for Developing and Developed Countries and Territories by Region," Table 1, in *An Interim Report on The State of Forest Resources in the Developing Countries* (Rome: 1988); all tropical countries from FAO, *Forest Resources Assessment 1990—Tropical Countries*, Forestry Paper No. 112 (Rome: 1993); Australia, Europe, Japan, and New Zealand from UN-ECE/FAO, *The Forest Resources of the Temperate Zones: the UN-ECE/FAO 1990 Forest Resource Assessment, Vol. 1: General Forest Resource Information* (New York: United Nations, 1992); Canada from Canadian Council of Forest Ministers, *Compendium of Canadian Forestry Statistics 1992*, National Forestry Database (Ottawa: 1993); Joe Lowe, Forest Inventory and Analysis Project, Petawawa National Forestry Institute, Canadian Forest Service, Chalk River, Ontario, unpublished printout and private communication, November 4, 1993; United States from USDA, Forest Service, *An Analysis of the Timber Situation in the United States: 1952-2030*, Forest Resource Report No. 23 (Washington, D.C.: 1982); Karen Waddell, Daniel Oswald, and Douglas Powell, Pacific Northwest Experiment Station, Forest Service, *Forest Statistics of the United States 1987*, Research Bulletin 168 (Portland, Oreg.: USDA, 1989); James Bones, branch chief, Forest Inventory Research and Analysis, Forest Service, USDA, Washington D.C., private communication, October 22, 1993; former Soviet Union from Anatoly Shvidenko, International Institute for Applied Systems Analysis (IIASA), Laxenburg, Austria, unpublished printout and private communication, July 18, 1993; China from Smil, op. cit. note 19; Argentina from The Republic of Argentina, National Commission on the Environment, National Report to the United Nations Conference on Environment and Development, July 1991; rough estimates for the other temperate developing countries based on trends and projections in FAO, Forest Resources Division, *An Interim Report on the State of Forest Resources in the Developing Countries* (Rome: 1988), and on J.P. Lanly, *1980 Forest Resources Assessment* (Rome: FAO, 1983); area of tropical plantations from FAO, *Forest Resource Assessment 1990—Tropical Countries,* op, cit. in this note. The estimated loss of 148 million hectares of natural forest was offset by the 18-million-hectare gain in tropical plantations to arrive at the figure of 130-million-hectare net loss between circa 1980 and circa 1990.

31. Tropical natural forest loss and plantation gain from FAO, *Forest Resources Assessment 1990—Tropical Countries,* op. cit. note 30; China from Smil, op. cit. note 19. The former Soviet Union reported a net gain of 22.7 million hectares between 1978 and 1988, from Shvidenko, op. cit. note 30. This figure is the only one available, but it is problematic. It can be assumed that the reported increase has been in low-productive sites with limited growing stocks, while excessive harvesting has taken place in the mature and old-growth forests, according to Sten Nilsson, Forestry and Climate Change Project, IIASA, Laxenburg, Austria, private communication, September 30, 1993. 2010 projection is Worldwatch Institute estimate, based on two decades of loss in forests calculated for 1980–90; 1990 global population from PRB, op. cit. note 7; 2010 population from Bureau of the Census, op. cit. note 10.

32. USDA, op. cit. note 7.

33. 1992 grain production figure from Francis Urban, section leader, Markets and Competition, Economic Research Service, USDA, Washington, D.C., private communication, October 20, 1993; 1984 grain figure from USDA, op. cit. note 7; population figures from U.S. Bureau of the Census, in Francis Urban and Ray Nightingale, *World Population by Country and Region, 1950–1990 and Projections to 2050* (Washington, D.C.: USDA, Economic Research Service, 1993).

34. Genetic yield potential from Lloyd T. Evans, *Crop Evolution, Adaptation and Yield* (Cambridge: Cambridge University Press, 1993); new crop strains from Donald O. Mitchell and Merlinda D. Ingco, International Economics Department, *The World Food Outlook: Malthus Must Wait* (Washington, D.C.: World Bank, July 1993 (draft)).

35. Engineering of maize from Gabrielle J. Persley, *Beyond Mendel's Garden: Biotechnology in the Service of World Agriculture* (Wallingford, U.K.: CAB International, 1990); Gabrielle J. Persley, World Bank, Washington, D.C., private communications, July 1993.

36. R.P.S. Malik and Paul Faeth, "Rice-Wheat Production in Northwest India," in Paul Faeth, ed., *Agricultural Policy and Sustainability: Case Studies from India, Chile, the Philippines, and the United States* (Washington, D.C.: World Resources Institute, 1993).

37. Willem Van Tuijl, *Improving Water Use in Agriculture: Experiences in the Middle East and North Africa* (Washington, D.C.: World Bank, 1993).

38. Postel, op. cit. note 6.

39. For an overview of some traditional methods and their use, see Chris Reij, *Indigenous Soil and Water Conservation in Africa* (London: International Institute for Environment and Development, 1991); Will Critchley, *Looking After Our Land: Soil and Water Conservation in Dryland Africa* (Oxford: Oxfam, 1991).

40. Sandra Postel and John C. Ryan, "Reforming Forestry," in Lester R. Brown et al., *State of the World 1991* (New York: W.W. Norton & Company, 1991).

41. Ed Ayres, "Making Paper Without Trees," *World Watch,* September/October 1993; 9 percent figure from FAO, *Pulp and Paper Capacities 1992–1997* (Rome: 1993).

42. Quotation from Donella H. Meadows, Dennis L. Meadows, and Jørgen Randers, *Beyond the Limits* (Post Mills, Vt.: Chelsea Green Publishing Company, 1992).

43. Population and densities from PRB, *1993 World Population Data Sheet* (Washington, D.C.: 1993); area of cropland from FAO, op. cit. note 18; grain imports are Worldwatch Institute estimates, based on USDA,

op. cit. note 7; wood imports from FAO, op. cit. note 9.

44. Real GDP per capita figures are adjusted for purchasing power parity, from U.N. Development Programme, *Human Development Report 1993* (New York: Oxford University Press, 1993). See note 4 for description of PPP.

45. Figure of 24 million hectares from Mathis Wackernagel et al., "How Big is Our Ecological Footprint?: A Handbook for Estimating A Community's Appropriated Carrying Capacity," discussion draft, Task Force on Planning Healthy and Sustainable Communities, University of British Columbia, Vancouver, B.C., July 1993; area of Dutch croplands, pastures, and forests from FAO, op. cit. note 18.

46. Herman Daly, *Steady-State Economics* (Washington, D.C.: Island Press, 2nd ed., 1991).

47. Worldwatch Institute estimates, based on FAO, AGROSTAT-PC 1993, Forest Products Electronic Data Series (Rome: 1993); Taiwan from Philip Wardle, senior forestry economist, FAO, Rome, unpublished printout from FAO Forestry Products Database, September 21, 1993; broad conversion factors for converting non-roundwood products into green solid wood equivalent, which differs from roundwood raw material equivalent, were supplied by Philip Wardle, unpublished printout and private communication, July 1, 1993.

48. He Bochuan, *China on the Edge: The Crisis of Ecology and Development* (San Francisco: China Books and Periodicals, Inc., 1991); rise in Chinese demand is Worldwatch Institute estimate for 1991, based on sources and methodology cited in footnote 47.

49. Gretchen C. Daily and Paul R. Ehrlich, "Population, Sustainability, and Earth's Carrying Capacity," *BioScience*, November 1992.

50. Postel and Ryan, op. cit. note 40.

51. Net trade in forest products is a Worldwatch Institute estimate, based on sources and methodology from FAO, op. cit. note 47; estimates of sustained yield vary, depending on assumptions of how fast cutover forests grow wood and how much forest is to be opened to logging; timber production in Sarawak, Malaysia's primary timber-exporting region, exceeds sustainable yield by four times, from Kieran Cooke, "Warfare Escalates Over Use of the Tropical Forests," *Financial Times*, August 31, 1993; timber production exceeds sustained yield in Malaysia by 71–228 percent, according to François Nectoux and Yoichi Kuroda, *Timber from the South Seas: An Analysis of Japan's Timber Trade and Its Environmental Impact* (Gland, Switzerland: World Wide Fund for Nature International, 1989).

52. Hilary F. French, *Costly Tradeoffs: Reconciling Trade and the Environment*, Worldwatch Paper 113 (Washington, D.C.: Worldwatch Institute, March 1993).

53. This analogy is borrowed from Herman Daly, senior economist, World Bank; Herman E. Daly, "Allocation, Distribution, and Scale: Towards an Economics That is Efficient, Just, and Sustainable," *Ecological Economics*, December 1992.

54. Union of Concerned Scientists, "World's Leading Scientists Issue Urgent Warning to Humanity," Washington, D.C., press release, November 18, 1992.

55. External debt in developing countries from IMF, *Annual Report of the Executive Board for the Fiscal Year Ended April 30, 1993* (Washington, D.C.: 1993).

56. Wangari Maathai, "The Green Belt Movement for Environment & Development," presented at the International Conference on Environmentally Sustainable Development, World Bank, Washington, D.C., October 1, 1993.

57. United Nations, Statistical Division, *Integrated Environment and Economic Accounting: Handbook of National Accounting*, Studies in

Methods (New York: forthcoming); Peter Bartelmus, Officer in Charge of the Environment and Energy Statistics Branch, Statistical Division of the United Nations, New York, private communication, October 21, 1993.

58. Unmet family planning needs from John Bongaarts, "The KAP-Gap and the Unmet Need for Contraception," *Population and Development Review*, June 1991; efforts needed for women from Jodi L. Jacobson, *Gender Bias: Roadblock to Sustainable Development*, Worldwatch Paper 110 (Washington, D.C.: Worldwatch Institute, September 1992); Jodi L. Jacobson, *Women's Reproductive Health: The Silent Emergency*, Worldwatch Paper 102 (Washington, D.C.: Worldwatch Institute, June 1991).

59. Restoration of international family planning funding from Susan Cohen, Senior Policy Associate, Alan Guttmacher Institute, Washington, D.C., private communication, October 21, 1993; Timothy Wirth, Counselor, U.S. Department of State, Speech at Second Preparatory Committee for the International Conference on Population and Development, New York, May 11, 1993.

Chapter 2. Redesigning the Forest Economy

1. Global forest cover from John F. Richards, "Land Transformation," in B.L. Turner II et al., eds., *The Earth as Transformed by Human Action* (New York: Cambridge University Press, 1990), and from R.A. Houghton et al., "Changes in the Carbon Content of Terrestrial Biota and Soils Between 1860 and 1980: A Net Release of CO_2 to the Atmosphere," *Ecological Monographs*, September 1983; forest history throughout introduction primarily from Alexander S. Mather, *Global Forest Resources* (Portland, Oreg.: Timber Press, 1990).

2. Estimates of tree cover based on calculations and sources documented in endnote 30 of Chapter 1.

3. Intact forest ecosystems from Sandra Postel and John C. Ryan, "Reforming Forestry," in Lester R. Brown et al., *State of the World 1991* (New York: W.W. Norton & Company, 1991).

4. Tropical Forestry Action Plan, "Report of the Independent Review," Kuala Lumpur, Malaysia, May 1990; Marcus Colchester, "The International Tropical Timber Organization: Kill or Cure for the Rainforest?" *The Ecologist*, September/October 1990; for deforestation trends, see Chapter 1.

5. Jagat Mehta, president, Seva Mandir, Udaipur, Rajasthan, India, private communication, July 24, 1991; Seva Mandir's efforts from author's observations during visit, late July 1991.

6. India from Betsy McGean, forestry consultant, Chevy Chase, Md., private communication, October 12, 1993; Philippines from Delfin J. Ganapin, Jr., deputy secretary, Department of Environment and Natural Resources, Quezon City, Philippines, private communication, July 14, 1992.

7. Nationalization of tropical forests from Theodore Panayotou and Peter S. Ashton, *Not by Timber Alone* (Washington, D.C.: Island Press, 1992); Linka Ansulang, Carmen, Philippines, private communication, July 9, 1992.

8. Nancy Lee Peluso, "The Ironwood Problem: (Mis)Management and Development of an Extractive Rainforest Product," *Conservation Biology*, June 1992.

9. Alan Thein Durning, *Guardians of the Land: Indigenous Peoples and the Health of the Earth*, Worldwatch Paper 112 (Washington, D.C.: Worldwatch Institute, December 1992).

10. Area of Yanomami reserves from ibid.; sizes of parks and nature reserves from International Union for Conservation of Nature and Natural Resources, *1990 United Nations List of National Parks and Protected Areas* (Gland, Switzerland, and Cambridge, U.K.: 1990).

11. Kirk Talbott, "Central Africa's Forests: The Second Greatest Forest System on Earth," World Resources Institute, Washington, D.C., January 1993.

12. Mac Chapin, program director, Rights and Resources, Arlington, Va., private communication, June 3, 1993.

13. Randal O'Toole, *Reforming the Forest Service* (Washington, D.C.: Island Press, 1988).

14. Ibid.

15. Scott Zens, research assistant, College of Forest Resources, University of Washington, Seattle, private communication, September 21, 1993.

16. Walter V. Reid et al., *Biodiversity Prospecting* (Washington, D.C.: World Resources Institute, 1993).

17. Hirudin from Edward O. Wilson, *The Diversity of Life* (Cambridge, Mass.: Harvard University Press, 1992).

18. Share of U.S. prescriptions from World Resources Institute, IUCN–The World Conservation Union, and U.N. Environment Programme, *Global Biodiversity Strategy* (Washington, D.C.: 1992); value of world pharmaceuticals industry and share of developing-country residents employing herbal medicine from Reid et al., op. cit. note 16.

19. Wilson, op. cit. note 17; loss of indigenous cultures from Durning, op. cit. note 9.

20. Reid et al., op. cit. note 16.

21. Ibid.

22. Michael J. Balick and Robert Mendelsohn, "Assessing the Economic Value of Traditional Medicines from Tropical Rain Forests," *Conservation Biology*, March 1992.

23. Rattan from Jenne H. De Beer and Melanie J. McDermott, *The Economic Value of Non-timber Forest Products in Southeast Asia* (Amsterdam: Netherlands Committee for IUCN, 1989); *xate* from John C. Ryan, "Goods from the Woods," *World Watch*, July/August 1991.

24. John C. Ryan, *Life Support: Conserving Biological Diversity*, Worldwatch Paper 108 (Washington, D.C.: Worldwatch Institute, April 1992).

25. Galik from Peluso, op. cit. note 8.

26. William Dietrich, *The Final Forest* (New York: Penguin, 1992).

27. B&Q from Alan Knight, "B&Q's Timber Policy Towards 1995," B&Q plc., Eastleigh, U.K., December 1992; local governments from Nels Johnson and Bruce Cabarle, *Surviving the Cut: Natural Forest Management in the Humid Tropics* (Washington, D.C.: World Resources Institute, 1993).

28. Duncan Poore, *No Timber Without Trees: Sustainability in the Tropical Forest* (London: Earthscan Publications, 1989).

29. CITES from Bruce D. Rodan, Adrian C. Newton, and Adalberto Verissimo, "Mahogany Conservation: Status and Policy Initiatives," *Environmental Conservation*, Winter 1992.

30. Micorrhyzal fungi from Wilson, op. cit. note 17.

31. Net present value of salmon from Carolyn Alkire, *Wild Salmon as Natural Capital* (Washington, D.C.: The Wilderness Society, 1993).

32. Babassu from Wilson, op. cit. note 17; value of Malaysian carbon storage from Panayotou and Ashton, op. cit. note 7; Table 2–3 based on the following: export value of commodities that originated in tropical forests from U.N. Food and Agriculture Organization (FAO), *Trade Yearbook, 1991* (Rome: 1993); share of Third World farmers depending on forests for water from World Bank, *Wildlands* (Washington, D.C.: 1987); flood control value from Panayotou and Ashton, op. cit. note 7; cost of siltation from K. Mahmood, *Reservoir Sedimentation: Impact, Extent, and Mitigation* (Washington, D.C.: World Bank, 1987); Manaus fisheries from Michael Goulding, *The Fishes and the Forest* (Berkeley, Calif.: University of California Press, 1980); Northwest fisheries from Jack Ward Thomas

et al., *Viability Assessments and Management Considerations for Species Associated With Late-Successional and Old-Growth Forests of the Pacific Northwest* (Washington, D.C.: Forest Service, U.S. Department of Agriculture, 1993); tropical deforestation's responsibility for climate change from Richard A. Houghton, "The Role of the World's Forests in Global Warming," in Kilaparti Ramakrishna and George M. Woodwell, eds., *World Forests for the Future* (New Haven, Conn.: Yale University Press, 1993); replacement cost of forests' carbon storage function from Panayotou and Ashton, op. cit. note 7; U.S. Forest Service from O'Toole, op. cit. note 13.

33. Value of four products and of mushroom industry from Mater Engineering, Ltd., "Analysis and Development of a Conceptual Business Plan for Establishing a Special Forest Products Processing Plant," prepared for Sweet Home Ranger District, Sweet Home, Oreg., June 30, 1992; estimated value of nontimber forest products from Catherine Mater, vice president, Mater Engineering, Ltd., Corvallis, Oreg., private communication, September 7, 1993; 1992 value of solid wood from national forests from Randal O'Toole, "1992 TSPIRS Recalculations," *Forest Watch* (Cascade Holistic Economic Consultants, Oak Grove, Oreg.), April/May 1993.

34. W. Ed Whitelaw and Ernest G. Niemi, "Money: The Greening of the Economy," *Old Oregon*, Spring 1989.

35. Thomas Gladwin, Leonard N. Stern School of Business, New York University, New York, private communication, September 5, 1993; Center for Science and Environment, *The Price of Forests* (New Delhi: 1993).

36. FAO, *Forest Product Yearbook 1960* through *1991* (Rome: 1962 through 1993).

37. U.S. Department of Agriculture, Forest Service, *Patience and Patchcuts* (San Francisco, Calif.: 1974).

38. Loren Abraham, Anderson Windows, speech at First North American Conference on Trade in Sustainable Forest Products, Washington, D.C., May 26, 1993; TrusJoist International from Dori Jones Yang, "A Lumberman Goes Against the Grain," *Business Week*, March 29, 1993; Bob Johnston, Herman-Miller, Inc., speech at First North American Conference on Trade in Sustainable Forest Products, Washington, D.C., May 26, 1993.

39. Julie Titone, "Tomorrow's House," *American Forests*, March/April 1993.

40. U.S. house size from Michael Sumichrast, *The Real Estate Forecast Guide* (Gaithersburg, Md.: 1992), with historical information from National Association of Home Builders, Washington, D.C., private communication, August 28, 1993; residential floorspace per capita from Lee Schipper, staff senior scientist, Lawrence Berkeley Laboratory, Berkeley, Calif., private communication, November 6, 1991.

41. Figure 2–1 based on Pulp and Paper International, *PPI's International Fact and Price Book* (Brussels: 1993), on FAO, op. cit. note 36, on FAO, *European Timber Statistics 1913–1950* (Geneva: 1953), and on FAO, *World Forest Products Statistics 1946–1955* (Rome: 1957).

42. Photocopiers from Lynn Ritter, senior industry analyst, Dataquest Inc., San Jose, Calif., private communication, May 28, 1993; year of introduction of photocopiers from Xerox Corporation, *1993 Xerox Fact Book* (Stamford, Conn.: 1993); world printing and writing paper consumption from FAO, AGROSTAT-PC 1993, Forest Products Electronic Data Series (Rome: 1993); doubling of U.S. office paper consumption in eighties from "Leafing Through Europe," *The Economist*, August 25, 1990.

43. Share of paper from recycled fibers is Worldwatch Institute estimate based on wastepaper consumption from Pulp and Paper International, op. cit. note 41, and on world paper production from FAO, op. cit. note 36.

44. Keith Schneider, "U.S. Would End Cutting of Trees in Many Forests," *New York Times*, April 30, 1993.

45. O'Toole, op. cit. note 33.

46. Victor Mallet, "Rules Must Be Right—And Upheld," *Financial Times*, May 13, 1993; Robert Repetto and Malcolm Gillis, eds., *Public Policies and the Misuse of Forest Resources* (New York: Cambridge University Press, 1988).

47. Stan Sesser, "Logging the Rain Forest," *New Yorker*, May 27, 1991.

48. Ibid.

49. Indonesia from Charles Barber, Nels Johnson, and Emmy Hafild, *Breaking the Logjam: Obstacles to Forest Policy Reform in Indonesia and the United States* (Washington, D.C.: World Resources Institute, 1993); Philippines from Daniel Stiles, "Power and Patronage in the Philippines," *Cultural Survival Quarterly*, Summer 1991.

50. "Conflict-of-Interest Concerns Result in Probe of Clayoquot Logging Decision," *International Environment Reporter*, May 5, 1993.

51. Congressional contributions from Barber, Johnson, and Hafild, op cit. note 49; votes to increase harvest from Andy Stahl, forester, Sierra Club Legal Defense Fund, Seattle, Wash., private communication, October 5, 1993.

52. Commission of Inquiry into Aspects of the Timber Industry in Papua New Guinea, *Interim Report No. 4, Vol. 1* (Port Moresby, Papua New Guinea: Government of Papua New Guinea, 1989).

53. Indonesia from Mallet, op. cit. note 46; Philippines from Johnson and Cabarle, op cit. note 27.

54. Dietrich, op. cit. note 26.

55. SILDAP-Sidlakan, press release, Butuan City, Mindanao, Philippines, July 20, 1993.

56. Ansulang, op. cit. note 7.

57. "2000 Species of Fauna Protected" (advertisement), *Washington Post*, April 1, 1993; Mike Harcourt, premier, Province of British Columbia, speech to annual convention of the International Woodworkers' Union, Vancouver, B.C., October 26, 1992.

Chapter 3. Safeguarding Oceans

1. Marine fish supply and use as food source from U.N. Food and Agriculture Organization (FAO), "Marine Fisheries and the Law of the Sea: A Decade of Change," Fisheries Circular No. 853, Rome, 1993. At approximately 70 million tons and 52 million tons per year, respectively, pork and beef production are second and third to annual marine fish production of 80 million tons, from Lester R. Brown, Hal Kane, and Ed Ayres, *Vital Signs 1993* (New York: W.W. Norton & Company, 1993). Coastal tourism is a large but untallied percentage of the $1.9-trillion global tourism industry, from Enzo Paci, World Tourism Organization, Madrid, Spain, private communication, October 19, 1992.

2. Quote from the foreword of the 1961 edition, Rachel Carson, *The Sea Around Us* (New York: Oxford University Press, 1991).

3. Estimate of inhabited space from W. Jackson Davis, "Global Aspects of Marine Pollution Policy," *Marine Policy*, May 1990. This percentage of the biosphere is determined by calculating the volume of oceans, which are entirely occupied by life, and comparing it to the three-dimensional size of land and air occupied by life. Organisms live up to 500 feet in the air and down to several feet underground. Water statistics from Fits van der Leeden et al., *The Water Encyclopedia* (Chelsea, Mich.: Lewis Publishers, Inc., 1990).

4. Early ocean and atmosphere development from James F. Kasting, "Earth's Early Atmosphere," *Science*, February 12, 1993.

5. An example of possible regional climate change from Richard A. Kerr, "Even Warm Climates Get the Shivers," *Science*, July 16, 1993; higher global temperature from K. Rozanski, S.W. Fowler, and E.M. Scott, "Global Oceans Studies, the Greenhouse Effect, and Climate Change: Investigating Interconnections," *IAEA Bulletin*, February 1993.

6. Oxygen production from Davis, op. cit. note 3; alternatively, phytoplankton are estimated to account for nearly half of global photosynthesis, from Martin V. Angel, "Managing Biodiversity in the Oceans," in Melvin N.A. Peterson, ed., *Diversity of Oceanic Life* (Washington, D.C.: Center for Strategic and International Studies, 1992); figure of 1,000 years from Boyce Thorne-Miller, Ocean Advocates, Silver Spring, Md., private communication, September 28, 1993.

7. Carbon annually stored in oceans from P.D. Quay, B. Tilbrook, and C.S. Wong, "Oceanic Uptake of Fossil Fuel CO_2: Carbon-13 Evidence," *Science*, April 3, 1992; general discussion of carbon dioxide and annual release from Richard A. Kerr, "Fugitive Carbon Dioxide: It's Not Hiding in the Ocean," *Science*, April 3, 1992, and from Eric T. Sundquist, "The Global Carbon Dioxide Budget," *Science*, February 12, 1993.

8. Quantities of carbon stored in oceans and terrestrial biosphere from John A. McGowan, "The Role of Oceans in Global Change and the Ecosystem Effects of Change," in *National Forum on Ocean Conservation*, proceedings of November 19–21, 1991 conference (Washington, D.C.: Smithsonian Institution, 1991).

9. FAO, op. cit. note 1.

10. Boyce Thorne-Miller and John Catena, *The Living Ocean* (Washington, D.C.: Island Press, 1991).

11. Elliot A. Norse, ed., *Global Marine Biological Diversity: A Strategy for Building Conservation into Decision Making* (Washington, D.C.: Island Press, 1993).

12. Scientific and medical uses from Jon Kohl, "The Ocean's Bounty: Untapped Pharmacy," *Currents* (Woods Hole Oceanographic Institution, Woods Hole, Mass.), Spring 1993, from Gregor Hodgson, "Drugs from the Sea," *Far Eastern Economic Review*, April 11, 1991, from Lawrence K. Altman, "Sharks Yield Possible Weapon Against Infection," *New York Times*, February 15, 1993, and from "Sea is the New Frontier for Developing Drugs," *New York Times*, November 10, 1992.

13. Productivity of coastal waters from James J. McCarthy, "Marine Productivity," in *National Forum on Ocean Conservation*, op. cit. note 8, and from James J. McCarthy, Harvard University, Cambridge, Mass., private communications, October 4 and 13, 1993; width of continental shelf from Michael Allaby, ed., *The Oxford Dictionary of Natural History* (New York: Oxford University Press, 1985); productivity of estuaries and wetlands from Dale E. Ingmanson and William J. Wallace, *Oceanography: An Introduction* (Belmont, Calif.: Wadsworth Publishing Company, 1985).

14. FAO, op. cit. note 1.

15. Productivity from McCarthy, "Marine Productivity," op. cit. note 13, and from McCarthy, private communications, op. cit. note 13.

16. "Biodiversity: Whither the Ocean?" *Currents* (Woods Hole Oceanographic Institution, Woods Hole, Mass.), Spring 1993.

17. Charles R.C. Sheppard, *A Natural History of the Coral Reef* (Poole, U.K.: Blandford Press, 1983).

18. Table 3-3 based on the following: Joint Group of Experts on the Scientific Aspects of the Marine Pollution (GESAMP), *The State of the Marine Environment*, UNEP Regional Seas Reports and Studies No. 115 (Nairobi: 1990); nutrient sources from World Resources Institute (WRI), *World Resources 1992–93* (New York: Oxford University Press, 1992); oil pollution from National Research Council, *Oil in the Sea: Inputs, Fates, and*

Effects (Washington, D.C.: National Academy Press, 1985), and from "60% Drop in Oil Pollution Since 1981," *Marine Pollution Bulletin*, December 1990; species in transit from James T. Carlton and Jonathan B. Geller, "Ecological Roulette: The Global Transport of Nonindigenous Marine Organisms," *Science*, July 2, 1993; Paul E. Hagen, "The International Community Confronts Plastics Pollution from Ships: MARPOL Annex V and the Problem That Won't Go Away," *American University Journal of International Law and Policy*, Winter 1990.

19. Nutrient flow doubling from "Marine Pollution from Land-based Sources: Facts and Figures," *UNEP Industry and Environment*, January/June 1992.

20. Mark J. Costello and John C. Gamble, "Effects of Sewage Sludge on Marine Fish Embryos and Larvae," *Marine Environmental Research*, Vol. 33, 1992, pp. 49–74; sewage's contribution to nutrient load from WRI, op. cit. note 18.

21. Pollution and oyster catch from "The Chesapeake Bay: A Progress Report, 1990–91," Chesapeake Executive Council, Annapolis, Md., August 1991.

22. J.J. Cole et al., "Nitrogen Loading of Rivers as a Human-Driven Process," in M.G. McDonnell and S.T.A. Pickett, eds., *Humans as Components of Ecosystems: The Ecology of Subtle Human Effects and Population Areas* (New York: Springer-Verlag, 1993).

23. Pollution from GESAMP, op. cit. note 18; North Sea from "Marine Pollution from Land-based Sources," op. cit. note 19, and from Fred Pearce, "North Sea Crude," *Audubon*, May/June 1993; Gulf war information from S.W. Fowler, "Pollution in the Gulf: Monitoring the Marine Environment," *IAEA Bulletin*, February 1993, and from John Robinson, National Oceanic and Atmospheric Administration, Washington, D.C., private communication, October 13, 1993; global oil pollution from National Research Council, op. cit. note 18.

24. South Africa from "Experts Say Toxic, Alien Organisms in Ballast Water," transcript of Johannesburg Channel Africa Radio, March 24, 1993, as reprinted in *JPRS Report: Environmental Issues*, April 9, 1993; United States from James T. Carlton, Maritime Studies Program of Williams College, Mystic Seaport, Conn., private communication, September 30, 1993; species in transit from Carlton and Geller, op. cit. note 18.

25. Singapore from L.M. Chou, "Singapore," *ASEAN Marine Science* (newsletter of the ASEAN-Australia Marine Science Project, Townsville, Australia), April 1992; San Francisco Bay from Ingmanson and Wallace, op. cit. note 13, from Elliot Norse, Center for Marine Conservation, Redmond, Wash., private communication, April 23, 1993, and from Michael A. Rozengurt, "Alternation of Freshwater Inflows," in Richard H. Stroud, ed., *Stemming the Tide of Coastal Fish Habitat Loss* (Savannah, Ga.: National Coalition for Marine Conservation, 1992).

26. Wetland loss from WRI, *World Resources 1990–91* (New York: Oxford University Press, 1990); coral reef loss from Clive R. Wilkinson, "Coral Reefs Are Facing Widespread Extinctions: Can We Prevent These Through Sustainable Management Practices?" presented at the Seventh International Coral Reef Symposium, Guam, 1992 (proceedings in press); beach erosion from H. Jesse Walker, "The Coastal Zone," in B.L. Turner II et al., eds., *The Earth as Transformed by Human Action* (New York: Cambridge University Press, 1990).

27. Estimates of coastal populations vary, with 50 percent within 100 kilometers of the shoreline as a rough consensus; Southeast Asia from foreword of Chua Thia-Eng and Daniel Pauly, eds., *Coastal Area Management in Southeast Asia: Policies, Management Strategies and Case Studies* (Manila: International Center for Living Aquatic Resources Management, 1989); regions of high coastal population density from *The Times Atlas of the World* (New York: Times Books, 1985); largest cities from

Otto Johnson, ed., *The 1992 Information Please Almanac* (Boston, Mass.: Houghton Mifflin Company, 1992).

28. Rural migration from Eugene Robinson, "Worldwide Migration Nears Crisis," *Washington Post*, July 7, 1993.

29. Rural migration information from Don Hinrichsen, United Nations consultant, London, private communication, July 16, 1993; shrimp production from FAO, op. cit. note 1; general discussion in Peter Weber, "Missing Mangroves," *World Watch*, March/April 1993.

30. Marlise Simons, "A Dutch Reversal: Letting the Sea Back In," *New York Times*, March 7, 1993; rate of loss from Peggy Rooney, "Louisiana's Wetlands Calamity," *EPA Journal*, September/October 1989; area of Louisiana coastal wetlands from Ralph W. Tiner, Jr., *Wetlands of the United States: Current Status and Recent Trends* (Washington, D.C.: U.S. Fish and Wildlife Service, 1984).

31. Coastal dredging from GESAMP, op. cit. note 18; Anthony Hubbard, "Chemical War: Our Seabed Legacy," *Listener & TV Times* (New Zealand), January 16, 1993; Fredrik Laurin, "Scandinavia's Underwater Time Bomb," *Bulletin of the Atomic Scientists*, March 1991; Hal Bernton, "Russian Revelations Indicate Arctic Region is Awash in Contaminants," *Washington Post*, May 17, 1993; Davis, op. cit. note 3.

32. John T. Hardy, "Where the Sea Meets the Sky," *Natural History*, May 1991.

33. R.C. Smith et al., "Ozone Depletion: Ultraviolet Radiation and Phytoplankton Biology in Antarctic Waters," *Science*, February 12, 1992; John Hardy and Hermann Gucinski, "Stratospheric Ozone Depletion: Implications for Marine Ecosystems," *Oceanography*, November 1989.

34. Scientific consensus predictions for global warming from Intergovernmental Panel on Climate Change (IPCC), *Climate Change: The IPCC Scientific Assessment* (New York: Cambridge University Press, 1990),

updated in IPCC, *Climate Change 1992* (New York: Cambridge University Press, 1992); Peter W. Glynn, "Coral Reef Bleaching in the 1980s and Possible Connections with Global Warming," *Trends in Ecology and Evolution*, June 1991.

35. Maryland Sea Grant College, "Workshop on Coral Bleaching, Coral Reef Ecosystems and Global Change: Report of Proceedings," Miami, Fla., June 17–21, 1991.

36. Norse, op. cit. note 11.

37. J.W. Copland and J.S. Lucas, eds., *Giant Clams in Asia and the Pacific* (Canberra: Australian Centre for International Agricultural Research, 1988).

38. David E. Pitt, "Despite Gaps, Data Leave Little Doubt That Fish Are in Peril," *New York Times*, August 3, 1993.

39. Historical trend from Ray Hilborn, "Marine Biota," in Turner et al., op. cit. note 26; recent trends from M. Perotti, chief, Statistics Department, FAO Fisheries, Rome, private communication, November 3, 1993; Peruvian example from FAO, op. cit. note 1; population growth from U.N. Department of International Economic and Social Affairs, *World Population Prospects 1998* (New York: 1989); recent data from FAO, Fisheries Department, "Global Fish and Shellfish Production in 1991," COFI Support Document: Fishery Statistics, Rome, March 1993, and from John Madeley, "Law of Diminishing Returns Hits World Fish Catch," *Financial Times*, June 17, 1993.

40. FAO, op. cit. note 1.

41. Estimate of 100 million tons from the FAO-sponsored publication by J.A. Gulland, ed., *The Fish Resources of the Ocean* (West Byfleet, Surrey, U.K.: Fishing News (Books) Ltd., 1971). This estimate is meant to include traditional bony fish ranging from commonly eaten species such as cod and haddock to the small shoaling species such as the Peruvian anchovy. Current FAO projections from FAO, op. cit. note 1.

42. Driftnetting from Andy Palmer, American Oceans Campaign, Washington, D.C., private communication, September 27, 1993; shrimp bycatch from Basil Hinds, "The Economics of Fish Resources in Lesser Developed Countries: The Fish By-Catch and Externalities in Shrimp Fishery," PhD. dissertation, Howard University, 1981, cited in Lennox Hinds, "World Marine Fisheries," *Marine Policy*, September 1992; biomass fishing from FAO, op. cit. note 1.

43. Sand eel from Mark Avery and Rhys Green, "Not Enough Fish in the Sea," *New Scientist*, July 22, 1989; pollack from Natalia S. Mirovitskaya and J. Christopher Haney, "Fisheries Exploitation as a Threat to Environmental Security: The North Pacific Ocean," *Marine Policy*, July 1992; Tim MacClanahan, "Triggerfish: Coral Reef Keystone Predator," *Swara* (East African Wildlife Society, Nairobi, Kenya), May/June 1992.

44. Total employment from Hinds, "World Marine Fisheries," op. cit. note 42; 50,000 from Mark Clayton, "Hunt for Jobs Intensifies as Fishing Industry Implodes," *Christian Science Monitor*, August 25, 1993; "French Lose Out on Fish Ban," *Down to Earth*, May 15, 1993; conflict between trawlers and small-scale fishers from Hinrichsen, op. cit. note 29.

45. John Kurien, "Ruining the Commons and Responses of the Commoners: Coastal Overfishing and Fishermen's Actions in Kerala State, India," Discussion Paper 23, U.N. Research Institute for Social Development, Geneva, May 1991; J.M. Vakily, "Assessing and Managing the Marine Fish Resources of Sierra Leone, West Africa," *Naga, The ICLARM Quarterly* (Manila), January 1992.

46. Price from FAO, op. cit. note 1; fish consumption per capita from FAO, *1991 Yearbook of Fishery Statistics: Commodities* (Rome: 1993); Paul Reeves, "Fish Slips from the Poor Man's Table," *ICLARM Newsletter* (Manila), April 1985; Kelly Haggart, "Ex-porting More, Eating Less," *Panoscope*, November 1992.

47. "60% Drop in Oil Pollution Since 1981," op. cit. note 18; Davis, op. cit. note 3; "Agreement Reached on Dumping at Sea," *Journal of Commerce*, November 16, 1992.

48. U.N. negotiations from David E. Pitt, "U.N. Talks Combat Threat to Fishery," *New York Times*, July 25, 1993, and from Palmer, op. cit. note 42.

49. Sealing treaty from FAO, op. cit. note 1.

50. T.R. Reid, "World Whaling Body Riven by Dispute," *Washington Post*, May 15, 1993; Andrew Pollack, "They Eat Whales, Don't They? The Fight Resumes," *New York Times*, May 3, 1993; Karen Fossil, "Defiant Oslo Approves Whale Hunt," *Financial Times*, May 19, 1993; Norwegian whale kill from Rick Atkinson, "Oslo Stands Firm on Whales," *Washington Post*, October 1, 1993.

51. United Nations, *Agenda 21: The United Nations Programme of Action From Rio* (New York: U.N. Publications, 1992); Montreal Guidelines from "Marine Pollution from Land-based Sources," op. cit. note 19.

52. United Nations, *The Law of the Sea* (New York: 1983).

53. FAO, op. cit. note 1.

54. Australia example from ibid.

55. Ibid.

56. Vakily, op. cit. note 45.

57. Krill limit from Stephen Nicol and William de la Mare, "Ecosystem Management and the Antarctic Krill," *American Scientist*, January/February 1993; discussion of shortcomings of CCAMLR in Norse, op. cit. note 11; sustainability discussed by Donald Ludwig, Ray Hilborn, and Carl Walters, "Uncertainty, Resource Exploitation, and Conservation: Lessons from History," *Science*, April 2, 1993.

58. Netherlands from Simons, op. cit. note 30, and from Ministry of Transport and Pub-

lic Works, *A New Coastal Defence Policy for the Netherlands* (s-Gravenhage, Netherlands: 1990).

59. Predicted effects of global warming from IPCC, *Climate Change*, op. cit. note 34.

60. Donald D. Robadue, Jr., Coastal Resources Center, University of Rhode Island, private communication, September 27, 1993; Donald D. Robadue, Jr., and Luis Arriaga, "Ecuador's Coastal Resources Management Program," *Intercoast Network* (Narragansett, Rhode Island: Coastal Resources Center, University of Rhode Island), Spring 1993.

61. GESAMP, op. cit. note 18.

62. For further discussion of waste water and other water issues, see Sandra Postel, *Last Oasis: Facing Water Scarcity* (New York: W.W. Norton & Company, 1992).

63. For a discussion of the reduction of industrial waste water, see ibid.

64. Agreement provisions and progress from "The Chesapeake Bay," op. cit. note 21.

65. Regional Seas from Don Hinrichsen, *Our Common Seas: Coasts in Crisis* (London: Earthscan, 1990).

66. Agenda 21 from United Nations, op. cit. note 51; Global Environment Facility (GEF) involvement in the Black Sea from "Black Sea Nations Join Battle Against Pollution," *World Bank News*, July 22, 1993; GEF mission from Ian Johnson, "Cross-Sectorial Issues Affecting Land-Based Pollution," *Marine Policy*, January 1992.

67. "South Pacific Forum: Final Act of the Meeting on a Convention to Prohibit Driftnet Fishing in the South Pacific, Including Text of Convention for the Prohibition of Fishing with Long Driftnets in the South Pacific and its Protocols (November 24, 1989)," *International Legal Materials*, November 1990; first U.N. resolution against driftnets from "United Nations: General Assembly Resolution on *Large-Scale Pelagic Driftnet Fishing and* *Its Impact on Living Marine Resources of the World's Oceans and Seas* (passed December 22, 1989)," *International Legal Materials*, November 1990; 1990 and 1991 U.N. resolutions from Mike Hagler, Greenpeace International, Devonport, Auckland, Australia, private communication, October 1, 1993; status of driftnetting from Gerald Leape, Greenpeace, Washington, D.C., private communication, October 13, 1993.

Chapter 4. Reshaping the Power Industry

1. Richard Munson, *The Power Makers* (Emmaus, Pa.: Rodale Press, 1985).

2. Worldwatch Institute estimate based on United Nations, *1990 Energy Statistics Yearbook* (New York: 1992), and on Edison Electric Institute (EEI), *Statistical Yearbook of the Electric Utility Industry/1991* (Washington, D.C.: 1992); size of world auto industry is a Worldwatch Institute estimate based on Department of Commerce, Bureau of the Census, *Statistical Abstract of the United States 1992* (Washington, D.C.: 1992), on American Automobile Manufacturers Association, *World Motor Vehicle Data 1993* (Detroit, Mich.: 1993), and on Motor Vehicles Manufacturers Association of the United States, Inc., *Facts & Figures '90* (Detroit, Mich.: 1990).

3. Richard F. Hirsh, *Technology and Transformation in the American Electric Utility Industry* (New York: Cambridge University Press, 1989); Munson, op. cit. note 1.

4. Munson, op. cit. note 1.

5. Electricity costs are from Hirsh, op. cit. note 3, from EEI, "EEI Pocketbook of Electric Utility Industry Statistics," Washington, D.C., 1992, and from EEI, *Historical Statistics of the Electric Utility Industry Through 1970* (New York: 1973).

6. Figure 4–1 is from Hirsh, op. cit. note 3, and from *Electric Light and Power*, various issues.

7. Irvin C. Bupp and Jean-Claude Derian, *Light Water: How the Nuclear Dream Dissolved* (New York: Basic Books, Inc., 1978); International Atomic Energy Agency, *Nuclear Power Reactors in the World* (Vienna: 1993); Greenpeace International, WISE-Paris, and Worldwatch Institute, *World Nuclear Industry Status Report: 1992* (London: 1992).

8. Figure 4–2 is based on United Nations, *World Energy Supplies 1950–1975* (New York: 1976), on Organisation for Economic Co-operation and Development (OECD), International Energy Agency (IEA), *Energy Balances of OECD Countries 1960–1979* (Paris: 1991), on OECD, IEA, *Energy Balances of OECD Countries 1980–1989* (Paris: 1991), on OECD, IEA, *Energy Balances of OECD Countries 1990–1991* (Paris: 1993), on International Monetary Fund, *World Economic Outlook May 1993* (Washington, D.C.: 1993), on Robert Summers and Alan Heston, "The Penn World Table (Mark 5): An Expanded Set of International Comparisons, 1950-1988," *Quarterly Journal of Economics*, May 1991 (based on purchasing power parity), and on Yoko Takahashi, IEA, Paris, private communication, September 23, 1993; French debt from "EdF Getting Better All the Time as Investments Prove their Worth," *European Energy Report*, February 19, 1993; Richard Rudolph and Scott Ridley, *Power Struggle: The Hundred-Year War Over Electricity* (New York: Harper & Row, 1986).

9. Forty-five percent from Public Service Company of New Mexico, "San Juan Generating Station: Fact Sheet," February 20, 1992, in Charles Bensinger, "Solar Thermal Repowering: A Technical and Economic Pre-Feasibility Study" (draft revised version 2.0), The Energy Foundation, San Francisco, Calif., 1993; Barbara J. Cummings, *Dam the Rivers, Damn the People* (London: Earthscan Publications Ltd., 1990).

10. World Bank, *The World Bank's Role in the Electric Power Sector* (Washington, D.C.: 1993).

11. Ibid.

12. Policy Topic Committee of the Association of Demand Side Management Professionals, "Status Report: State Requirements for Considering Environmental Externalities in Electric Utility Decision-Making," Boca Raton, Fla., 1993; carbon dioxide emission percentage is a Worldwatch Institute estimate based on OECD, IEA, *World Energy Outlook to the Year 2010* (Paris: 1993), on Robert San Martin, U.S. Department of Energy (DOE), "Environmental Emissions from Energy Technology Systems: The Total Fuel Cycle," Washington, D.C., 1989, and on Gregg Marland, Oak Ridge National Laboratory, Oak Ridge, Tenn., private communication and electronic database, September 20, 1993.

13. Christopher Flavin, *Electricity's Future: The Shift to Efficiency and Small-Scale Power*, Worldwatch Paper 61 (Washington, D.C.: Worldwatch Institute, November 1984).

14. ABB and Texaco from Lester P. Silverman, McKinsey & Co., Inc., Washington, D.C., private communication, October 13, 1993; Figure 4–3 is based on DOE, Energy Information Administration (EIA), *Annual Electric Generator Report* (electronic database) (Washington, D.C.: 1993), and on EEI, *Capacity and Generation of Non-Utility Sources of Energy* (Washington, D.C.: various years), with 1992 data from Utility Data Institute, *UDI Directory of Selected U.S. Cogeneration, Small Power and Industrial Power Plants* (Washington, D.C.: 1993). Independent producer data through 1991 is the amount of capacity placed in operation each year and still operating in 1991; thus the data underestimate the total amount of new capacity that was installed annually by independent producers.

15. Ministry of Energy, Danish Energy Agency, *Energy Efficiency in Denmark* (Copenhagen: 1992); Sara Knight, "German Survey," *Windpower Monthly*, March 1993; "Germany," Country Profiles, *European Energy Report*, May 1992; Steven Strong, "An Overview of Worldwide Development Activity in Photovoltaics," Solar Design Associates,

Harvard, Mass., 1993; "Netherlands," Country Profiles, *European Energy Report*, March 1992; Matthew Parris, "The End of the Nuclear Affair," (London) *Times*, November 10, 1989; Andrew Holmes, "Electricity in Europe: Power and Profit," *Financial Times Management Report*, London, 1990; Sandy Hendry, "US, Europe Firms Look to Spark China Power Ventures," *Journal of Commerce*, June 2, 1993; U.S. Agency for International Development, Office of Energy and Infrastructure, "Country Profiles on India, Indonesia, and Pakistan," *Private Power Reporter*, March 1993; Andy Pasztor, "Power Plants in Mexico Cast Pall Over Nafta," *Wall Street Journal*, September 9, 1993.

16. DOE, op. cit. note 14; EEI, op. cit. note 14.

17. Robert H. Williams and Eric D. Larson, "Expanding Roles for Gas Turbines in Power Generation," in Thomas B. Johansson, Birgit Bodlund, and Robert H. Williams, eds., *Electricity: Efficient End-Use and New Generation Technologies, and Their Planning Implications* (Lund, Sweden: Lund University Press, 1989); Robert L. Bradley, Jr., "Reconsidering the Natural Gas Act," Southern Regulatory Policy Institute Issue Paper No. 5, Roswell, Ga., August 1991; "The Use of Natural Gas in Power Stations," *Energy in Europe* (Commission of the European Communities, Brussels), December 1990.

18. Eric Jeffs, "First 9F in Service with EdF," *Electricity International*, June/July 1993; Steven Collins, "Special Report: Gas Fired Powerplants," *Power Magazine*, February 1993; Bob Bjorge, General Electric, Schenectady, N.Y., private communication and printout, August 26, 1993; "For the Record," *Energy Economist*, April 1993; "For the Record," *Energy Economist*, September 1993; Neil Buckley, "Hurdles in the Path of the Dash for Gas," *Financial Times*, December 10, 1992; the Teeside station has eight gas turbines and two steam turbines, according to Kristin Rankin, Enron Corp, Houston, Tex., private communication, October 20, 1993.

19. Williams and Larson, op. cit. note 17; Bjorge, op. cit. note 18; William H. Day and Ashok D. Rao, "FT4000 HAT with Natural Gas Fuel," *Turbomachinery International*, January/February 1993; Steven Collins, "Small Gas Turbines Post Gains in Performance," *Power Magazine*, October 1992.

20. D.L. Chase, J.M. Kovacik, and H.G. Stoll, "The Economics of Repowering Steam Power Plants," General Electric Company, 1992; Douglas M. Todd and Robert M. Jones, General Electric, "Advanced Combined Cycles Provide Economic Balance for Improved Environmental Performance," presented at International Power Generation Conference, San Diego, Calif., October 6–10, 1991; William Keeling, "Indonesia's Power Scramble," *Financial Times*, August 10, 1993; GE Power Generation, "MS9001E Gas Turbines: Heavy-Duty 50 Hz Power Plant," Schenectady, N.Y., 1991; "Europe's Most Modern Combined-Cycle Plant," *Electricity International*, June/July 1993.

21. Worldwatch Institute estimate based on D.O. Hall et al., "Biomass for Energy: Supply Prospects," in Thomas B. Johansson et al., eds., *Renewable Energy: Sources for Fuels and Electricity* (Washington, D.C.: Island Press, 1993), on Population Reference Bureau, "World Population Estimates and Projections by Single Years: 1750–2100," Washington, D.C., 1992, and on United Nations, op. cit. note 2.

22. Thomas B. Johansson et al., "Renewable Fuels and Electricity for a Growing World Economy: Defining and Achieving the Potential," in Johansson et al., op. cit. note 21; Susan Hock, Robert Thresher, and Tom Williams, "The Future of Utility-Scale Wind Power," in S. Burley and M.E. Arden, eds., *Advances in Solar Energy: An Annual Review of Research and Development* (Boulder, Colo.: American Solar Energy Society, 1992); J.C. Chapman, *European Wind Technology* (Palo Alto, Calif.: EPRI, 1993).

23. The photovoltaic panels would actually cover just 15 percent of this land area;

John Schaefer and Edgar DeMeo, Electric Power Research Institute, "An Update on U.S. Experiences with Photovoltaic Power Generation," Proceedings of the American Power Conference, April 23, 1990; U.S. land area used by the military from Michael Renner, "Assessing the Military's War on the Environment," in Lester R. Brown et al., *State of the World 1991* (New York: W.W. Norton & Company, 1991); wind potential is based on wind resources above Class 3 wind, from D.L. Elliott, L.L. Wendell, and G.L. Gower, "An Assessment of the Available Windy Land Area and Wind Energy Potential in the Contiguous United States," Pacific Northwest Laboratory, Richland, Wash., August 1991. A more optimistic review of wind resources found that North Dakota alone could nearly meet current U.S. demand; see Michael C. Brower et al., *Powering the Midwest: Renewable Electricity for the Economy and the Environment* (Cambridge, Mass.: Union of Concerned Scientists, 1993).

24. Lawrence Flowers et al., "Utility-Scale Wind Energy Update," in Burley and Arden, op. cit. note 22; M.N. Schwartz, D.L. Elliott, and G.L. Gower, Pacific Northwest Laboratory, "Seasonal Variability of Wind Electric Potential in the United States," presented at the American Wind Energy Association's Windpower '93 Conference, San Francisco, Calif., July 12–16, 1993; Henry Kelly and Carl J. Weinberg, "Utility Strategies for Using Renewables," in Johansson et al., op. cit. note 21.

25. David Roe, *Dynamos and Virgins* (New York: Random House, 1984); Hirsh, op. cit note 3.

26. OECD, IEA, *Energy Policies of IEA Countries, 1991 Review* (Paris: 1992).

27. Amory B. Lovins, *Soft Energy Paths: Toward a Durable Peace* (Cambridge, Mass.: Ballinger Publishing Company, 1977); OECD, op. cit. note 26; Arnold P. Fickett, Clark W. Gellings, and Amory B. Lovins, "Efficient Use of Electricity," *Scientific American*, September 1990; Steven Nadel, Virendra Ko-

thari, and S. Gopinath, "Opportunities for Improving End-Use Electricity Efficiency in India," American Council for an Energy-Efficient Economy (ACEEE), Washington, D.C., November 1991; U.S. Congress, Office of Technology Assessment, *Energy Efficiency Technologies for Central and Eastern Europe* (Washington, D.C.: U.S. Government Printing Office, 1993).

28. Chris J. Calwell and Ralph C. Cavanagh, "The Decline of Conservation at California Utilities: Causes, Costs and Remedies," Natural Resources Defense Council, San Francisco, Calif., July 1989; David Moskovitz, "Profits and Progress Through Least-Cost Planning," National Association of Regulatory Commissioners, Washington, D.C., November 1989.

29. Rowe quote is found in EEI, *Washington Letter*, Washington, D.C., September 15, 1989; Moskovitz, op. cit. note 28; Stephen Wiel, "Making Utility Efficiency Profitable," *Public Utilities Fortnightly*, July 1989; Michael Smith, "An Island's Experience," *Financial Times*, September 8, 1993.

30. Cynthia Mitchell, consulting economist, Reno, Nev., private communication, June 24, 1993; Cynthia Mitchell, "Integrated Resource Planning Survey: Where the States Stand," *The Electricity Journal*, May 1992.

31. DOE, EIA, *Electric Power Annual 1991* (Washington, D.C.: 1993); Results study is from Ted Flanigan and June Weintraub, "The Most Successful DSM Programs in North America," *The Electricity Journal*, May 1993; Paul L. Joskow and Donald B. Marron, "What Does Utility-Subsidized Energy Efficiency Really Cost?" *Science*, April 16, 1993; Amory B. Lovins, "The Cost of Energy Efficiency" (letter to the editor), *Science*, August 20, 1993.

32. John Fox, Ontario Hydro, Toronto, Ont., Canada, private communication, September 29, 1993; Katrina van Bylandt, Power Smart Inc., Vancouver, B.C., private communication, January 28, 1993; Evan Mills, "Efficient Lighting Programs in Europe: Cost Ef-

fectiveness, Consumer Response, and Market Dynamics," *Energy—The International Journal*, Vol. 18, No. 2, 1993.

33. Evan Mills, Lawrence Berkeley Laboratory, Berkeley, Calif., private communication, June 15, 1993; Mills, op. cit. note 32; Wim Sliepenbeek, "Massive Programs Get the Dutch Market Moving," *IAEEL Newsletter* (International Association for Energy-Efficient Lighting, Stockholm), No. 1, 1993; Uwe Leprich, "German Giant Explores Its Demand-Side Resources," *IAEEL Newsletter*, No. 2, 1992; Reinhard Loske, Wuppertal Institute for Climate, Environment and Energy, Wuppertal, Germany, private communication, September 24, 1993.

34. Thailand from Peter du Pont, Terry Kraft-Oliver, and Peter Rumsey, International Institute for Energy Conservation (IIEC), Washington, D.C., private communication, June 23, 1993; Howard S. Geller and José Roberto Moreira, "Brazil Encourages Electricity Savings," *Forum for Applied Research and Public Policy*, University of Tennessee, Fall 1993; Mark D. Levine, Feng Liu, and Jonathan E. Sinton, "China's Energy System: Historical Evolution, Current Issues, and Prospects," in *Annual Review of Energy and the Environment 1992* (Palo Alto, Calif.: Annual Reviews Inc., 1992); Ignacio Rodriguez and David Wolcott, "Growth Through Conservation: DSM in Mexico," *Public Utilities Fortnightly*, August 1, 1993; Lawrence Berkeley Laboratory estimate is from Mark D. Levine et al., *Energy Efficiency, Developing Nations, and Eastern Europe*, A Report to the U.S. Working Group on Global Energy Efficiency (Washington, D.C.: IIEC, 1991), and from Charles Campbell, Lawrence Berkeley Laboratory, Berkeley, Calif, private communication and printout, June 19, 1992; Howard Geller, *Efficient Electricity Use: A Development Strategy for Brazil* (Washington, D.C.: ACEEE, 1991); Lee Schipper and Eric Martinot, "Decline and Rebirth: Energy Demand in the Former Soviet Union" (draft), Paper II: Towards Efficiency in 2010, Lawrence Berkeley Laboratory, Berkeley, Calif., September 1992; David

Wolcott, Jaroslaw Dybowski, and Ewaryst Hille, "Implementing Demand-Side Management Through Integrated Resource Planning in Poland," presented at the European Council for an Energy-Efficiency Economy Summer Study, Rungstedgaard, Denmark, May 1993.

35. Figure 4–4 is based on U.S. Bureau of the Census, *Statistical Abstract of the United States* (Washington, D.C.: various years), on State of California, Department of Finance, "Population Estimates for California Cities and Counties," Report 92 E-2, Sacramento, Calif., 1993, on DOE, EIA, *Annual Energy Review 1992* (Washington, D.C.: 1993), on DOE, EIA, *State Energy Data Report 1991: Consumption Estimates* (Washington, D.C.: 1993), on Population Reference Bureau, *1992 World Population Data Sheet* (Washington, D.C.: 1992), and on Daniel Nix, California Energy Commission, Sacramento, Calif., private communication, August 24, 1993; Electric Power Research Institute, *Drivers of Electricity Growth and the Role of Utility Demand-Side Management* (Palo Alto, Calif.: 1993); "Holland Turns the Tide," *IAEEL Newsletter*, No. 1, 1992; Greg M. Rueger, senior vice president and general manager, Pacific Gas and Electric Company, Testimony before the Subcommittee on Energy and Power, Committee on Commerce and Energy, U.S. House of Representatives, Washington, D.C., March 7, 1991; Eric Hirst, "Managing Demand for Electricity: Will It Pay Off?" *Forum for Applied Research and Public Policy*, Fall 1992.

36. Matthew L. Wald, "Utilities Offer $30 Million for a Better Refrigerator," *New York Times*, July 8, 1993.

37. Michael Philips, *The Least Cost Energy Path for Developing Countries: Energy Efficient Investments for the Multilateral Development Banks* (Washington, D.C.: IIEC, 1991); Michael Philips, IIEC, Washington, D.C., private communication, October 7, 1993.

38. Richard Stone, "Polarized Debate: EMFs and Cancer," *Science*, December 11, 1992.

39. Brooke Stoddard, "Fuel Cell Update," *American Gas*, June 1993.

40. Fuel Cell Commercialization Group, "What Is a Fuel Cell?" Washington, D.C., 1992; Philip H. Abelson, "Applications of Fuel Cells" (editorial), *Science*, June 22, 1990.

41. John Douglas, "Utility Fuel Cells in Japan," *EPRI Journal*, September 1991; "SoCalGas Inks First Commercial Fuel Cell Deal," *Oil & Gas Journal*, April 15, 1991.

42. Mark Hankins, *Solar Rural Electrification in the Developing World* (Washington, D.C.: Solar Electric Light Fund, 1993); Strong, op. cit. note 15.

43. Strong, op. cit. note 15; Ronal W. Larson, Frank Vignola, and Ron West, "Economics of Solar Energy Technologies," American Solar Energy Society, Boulder, Colo., December 1992; Paul Maycock, "Tenth Annual Survey—Worldwide Production of Photovoltaic Modules in 1992," *Photovoltaic News*, February 1993.

44. Tammie R. Candelario and Tim Townsend, "PVUSA—Progress and Plans," in Burley and Arden, op. cit. note 22; "Siemens Completes 500-Kilowatt (Peak) PV System at Kerman, Calif., for PG&E," *The Solar Letter*, May 14, 1993; Carl Weinberg, Joseph J. Iannucci, and Melissa M. Reading, "The Distributed Utility: Technology, Customer and Public Policy Changes Shaping the Electrical Utility of Tomorrow," PG&E Research and Development, San Ramon, Calif., December 1992; Utility PhotoVoltaic Group, "Electric Utilities Serving 40% of U.S. Consumers Propose $513 Million Program to Accelerate Use of Solar Photovoltaics," Washington, D.C., September 27, 1993.

45. Richard F. Post, "Flywheel Energy Storage," *Scientific American*, September 1973; John V. Coyner, "Flywheel Energy Storage and Power Electronics Program," Oak Ridge National Laboratory, 1993; Abacus Technology Corporation, *Technology Assessments of Advanced Energy Storage Systems for Electric and Hybrid Vehicles*, prepared for U.S. Department of Energy, April 30, 1993; Lawrence Livermore projections from Richard F. Post, Lawrence Livermore National Laboratory, Livermore, Calif., private communication, July 15, 1993.

46. Weinberg, Iannucci, and Reading, op. cit. note 44; Sara Knight, "Portrait of a Booming Market," *Windpower Monthly*, March 1993.

47. Figure 4–5 is based on EEI, "Pocketbook of Utility Statistics," op. cit. note 5, and on EEI, *Statistical Yearbook of the Electric Utility Industry* (Washington, D.C.: various years).

48. Kelly and Weinberg, op. cit. note 24.

49. Steven R. Rivkin, "Look Who's Wiring the Home Now," *New York Times Magazine*, September 26, 1993.

50. Carl J. Weinberg and Katie McCormack, "Toward a Sustainable Energy Future," speech to Consumer Federation of America, Washington, D.C., May 27, 1993; Leslie Lamarre, "The Vision of Distributed Generation," *EPRI Journal*, April/May 1993.

51. "Germany," op. cit. note 15; Jennifer S. Gitlitz, "The Relationship Between Primary Aluminum Production and the Damming of World Rivers," Energy and Resources Group, University of California, Berkeley, Calif., July 21, 1993; François Nectoux, *Crisis in the French Nuclear Industry* (Amsterdam: Greenpeace International, 1991).

52. U.S. Congress, "National Energy Policy Act of 1992," PL 102–486, Washington, D.C., October 24, 1992.

53. Cost spread from Silverman, op. cit. note 14; "Global Electricity Prices," *Energy Economist*, September 1993.

54. Ralph C. Cavanagh, "The Great 'Retail Wheeling' Illusion—And More Productive Energy Futures," Natural Resources Defense Council, San Francisco, Calif., draft, September 1993; Armond Cohen, senior attorney, Conservation Law Foundation, "Retail Wheeling and Rhode Island's Energy Fu-

ture: Issues, Problems, and Lessons from Europe," presented to the Retail Wheeling Subcommittee of the Rhode Island Energy Coordinating Council, July 22, 1993.

55. Paul Ward, Pacific Gas and Electric, San Francisco, Calif., private communication, August 10, 1993; Mark Ohrenschall, "Small Progressive Town Embraces Conservation," *Conservation Monitor*, November/December 1992; "German City Lashes Out at Global Climate Change," *Multinational Environmental Outlook*, September 18, 1990.

56. Sacramento Municipal Utility District (SMUD), *1992 Annual Report: Working for Sacramento* (Sacramento, Calif.: undated); transcript from "Living on Earth," National Public Radio, August 27, 1993; SMUD, "Official Statement Relating to Sacramento Municipal Utility District $498,410,000 Electric Revenue Refunding Bonds, 1993 Series D $75,-000,000 Electric Revenue Bonds, 1993 Series E," Sacramento, Calif., April 15, 1993.

57. David H. Moskovitz, "Cutting the Nation's Electric Bill," *Issues in Science and Technology*, Spring 1989.

58. Several new regulatory models are discussed in California Public Utilities Commission, Division of Strategic Planning, "California's Electric Services Industry: Perspectives on the Past, Strategies for the Future," San Francisco, Calif., February 3, 1993, though none conforms exactly to the model suggested here.

59. Cohen, op. cit. note 54; Don Bain, "New Northwest Resources: Gas, or Conservation and Renewables?" Oregon Department of Energy, Salem, Oreg., December 23, 1992; Kelly and Weinberg, op. cit. note 24.

60. Pace University Center for Environmental Legal Studies, *Environmental Costs of Electricity* (New York: Oceana Publications, 1990); Jan Hamrin and Nancy Rader, *Investing in the Future: A Regulator's Guide to Renewables* (Washington, D.C.: National Association of Regulatory Utility Commissioners, 1993); David H. Moskovitz, "Green Pricing:

Experience and Lessons Learned," The Regulatory Assistance Project, Gardiner, Maine, undated.

61. Silverman, op. cit. note 14.

62. Steven R. Rivkin and Jeremy D. Rosner, "Shortcut to the Information Superhighway: A Progressive Plan to Speed the Telecommunications Revolution," Progressive Policy Institute Policy Report No. 15, Washington, D.C., July 1992.

63. S. David Freeman, general manager and chief executive officer, Sacramento Municipal Utility District, Sacramento, Calif., private communication, October 13, 1993.

Chapter 5. Reinventing Transport

1. For a discussion of the environmental impacts of automobiles, see Michael Renner, *Rethinking the Role of the Automobile*, Worldwatch Paper 84 (Washington, D.C.: Worldwatch Institute, June 1988), Marcia D. Lowe, *The Bicycle: Vehicle for a Small Planet*, Worldwatch Paper 90 (Washington, D.C.: Worldwatch Institute, September 1989), and Marcia D. Lowe, *Alternatives to the Automobile: Transport for Livable Cities*, Worldwatch Paper 98 (Washington, D.C.: Worldwatch Institute, October 1990).

2. Renner, op. cit. note 1; current auto ownership from Motor Vehicle Manufacturers Association (MVMA) of the United States, Inc., *Facts & Figures '92* (Detroit, Mich.: 1992).

3. MVMA, *World Motor Vehicle Data, 1992 ed.* (Detroit, Mich.: 1992).

4. In this analysis, car travel refers to use of private motor vehicles including vans, light trucks, recreational vehicles, motorcycles, and mopeds; per capita car ownership from John Pucher, "Capitalism, Socialism, and Urban Transportation: Policies and Travel Behavior in the East and West," *APA Journal*, Summer 1990; MVMA, op. cit. note 2.

5. U.S. Federal Highway Administration (FHWA), *1990 Nationwide Personal Transportation Survey: Summary of Travel Trends* (Washington, D.C.: 1992).

6. Annual number of car trips from ibid.

7. U.S. average for household trips from FHWA, op. cit. note 5; Orlando estimate from Andres Duany and Elizabeth Plater-Zyberk, "The Second Coming of the American Small Town," *Wilson Quarterly*, Winter 1992.

8. Social isolation from Jeffrey R. Kenworthy, "Australian Cities: Beyond the Suburban Dream," *Habitat*, December 1987; restrictions on children's play from John Whitelegg, *Transport for a Sustainable Future: The Case for Europe* (New York: Belhaven Press, 1993); teenagers from Elmer W. Johnson, "Taming the Car *and* Its User: Should We Do Both?" *Bulletin of the American Academy of Arts and Sciences*, November 1992.

9. Whitelegg, op. cit. note 8.

10. Dan Beyers, "Not the Family Car, But the Family Fleet," *Washington Post*, April 4, 1993.

11. Whitelegg, op. cit. note 8; consistency of travel time also reported in A.N. Bleijenberg, *Transport, Economy and Environment* (Delft, Netherlands: Center for Energy Conservation and Environmental Technologies, 1992); comparison of work commuting times from Alan Thein Durning, *How Much is Enough? The Consumer Society and the Future of the Earth* (New York: W.W. Norton & Company, 1992).

12. U.S. Department of Transportation (DOT), *National Transportation Strategic Planning Study* (Washington, D.C.: 1990); Paris from Steve Nadis and James J. MacKenzie with Laura Ost, *Car Trouble* (Boston: Beacon Press, 1993); Jakarta from "Breaking Up the Jams," *Asiaweek*, February 28, 1992.

13. U.S. General Accounting Office (GAO), *Smart Highways: An Assessment of Their Potential to Improve Travel* (Washington, D.C.: 1991); Mia Layne Birk and P. Christopher Zegras, *Moving Toward Integrated Transport Planning: Energy, Environment, and Mobility in Four Asian Cities* (Washington, D.C.: International Institute for Energy Conservation, 1993).

14. Data from MVMA, op. cit. note 2.

15. Pucher, op. cit. note 4.

16. For a discussion of recent progress in reducing the environmental impacts of cars, see Christopher Flavin, "Jump Start: The New Automotive Revolution," *World Watch*, July/August 1993; for a discussion of alternative fuels, see Nicholas Lenssen and John E. Young, "Filling Up in the Future," *World Watch*, May/June 1990.

17. Paul B. MacCready, "Perspectives on Vehicle Energy Efficiency and Electric Vehicles," *ESD Technology*, November 1992.

18. Flavin, op. cit. note 16.

19. Ibid.

20. Volvo and fuel cell potential efficiency from ibid.; Amory B. Lovins, John W. Barnett, and L. Hunter Lovins, "Supercars: The Coming Light-Vehicle Revolution" (draft), Rocky Mountain Institute, Old Snowmass, Colo., unpublished, March 31, 1993.

21. Electric cars in Geneva from Urs Muntwyler, Förderprogramm Leicht-Elektromobile, Zollikofen, Switzerland, private communication with Nicholas Lenssen of Worldwatch Institute, October 21, 1993; cars in California from Bill Siuru, "Building the Infrastructure for EVs," *Public Power*, May/June 1993; hydrogen technologies from Lenssen and Young, op. cit. note 16.

22. Electric vehicle prices from "Overcoming EV Market Barriers," *Green Car Journal*, March 1993, and from "Could the 'Miata' of Electric Vehicles be Coming to the Market?" *Green Car Journal*, June 1993.

23. Intelligent Vehicle Highway Society of America (IVHS America), *Strategic Plan for In-*

telligent Vehicle-Highway Systems in the United States (Washington, D.C.: 1992).

24. IVHS could increase traffic flow three-to fivefold, according to Adib Kanafani, director of the University of California's Institute of Transportation Studies, as cited in Nadis and MacKenzie, op. cit. note 12; sevenfold figure from recent studies cited in David W. Freeman, "Street Smarts," *Popular Mechanics*, November 1991.

25. Moshe Ben-Akiva et al., "The Case for Smart Highways," *Technology Review*, July 1992.

26. For a detailed critique of IVHS, see Deborah Gordon, "Intelligent Vehicle/Highway Systems: An Environmental Perspective," in Jonathan L. Gifford, Thomas A. Horan, and Daniel Sperling, eds., *Transportation, Information Technology, and Public Policy: Institutional and Environmental Issues in IVHS*, proceedings of IVHS Policy: A Workshop on Institutional and Environmental Issues conference, George Mason University Institute of Public Policy, Fairfax, Va., and University of California Institute of Transportation Studies, Davis, Calif., April 26–28, 1992; concerns about the possible effects of IVHS are also raised in Nadis and MacKenzie, op. cit. note 12, in "Traffic Volume May Foil Smart Highways," *Wall Street Journal*, August 4, 1992, and in "Environmentalists Urge IVHS Players to Rethink Basic Assumptions," *Inside IVHS*, August 16, 1993.

27. For a discussion of this and related concerns, see Marcia D. Lowe, "Road to Nowhere," *World Watch*, May/June 1993.

28. Downtown Washington, D.C., has some 311,000 parking spaces in lots and garages, according to Stephen C. Fehr and D'Vera Cohn, "Subsidized Parking Fueling Area Traffic," *Washington Post*, April 18, 1991. At approximately 30 square meters per space (a standard figure that includes room for aisles and access lanes), this amounts to more than 9 million square meters. Parking costs average $10,000–15,000 per space for

above-ground structures and about $20,000 per space for underground parking, according to Elizabeth Deakin, "The United States," in Jean-Philippe Barde and Kenneth Button, *Transport Policy and the Environment: Six Case Studies* (London: Earthscan, 1990).

29. IVHS America, op. cit. note 23; fuel efficiency data from Stacy C. Davis and Melissa D. Morris, *Transportation Energy Data Book: Edition 12* (Oak Ridge, Tenn.: Oak Ridge National Laboratory, 1992).

30. IVHS field test results cited in GAO, op. cit. note 13; kilojoules per passenger-kilometer based on Deborah Gordon, *Steering a New Course: Transportation, Energy, and the Environment* (Washington, D.C.: Island Press, 1991).

31. Estimate of IVHS potential to save lives from FHWA, *A Public/Private Partnership: An Overview of the IVHS Program Through FY 1992* (Washington, D.C.: 1992); safety potential of switching car travel to buses is a Worldwatch Institute estimate based on an annual total of 2.3 trillion passenger-miles of automobile travel (the figure for 1991) and 1991 accident death rates (9.7 deaths per billion passenger-miles for automobiles versus 0.01–0.03 deaths per billion passenger-miles for transit and intercity buses), from National Safety Council, *Accident Facts 1993 Edition* (Itasca, Ill.: 1993).

32. Europe from Ben-Akiva et al., op. cit. note 25; Japan from U.S. Congress, Office of Technology Assessment (OTA), *Defense Conversion: Redirecting R&D* (Washington, D.C.: U.S. Government Printing Office, 1993).

33. Federal support to date from OTA, op. cit. note 32; future spending from IVHS America, op. cit. note 23.

34. U.S. Urban Mass Transportation Administration, *Assessment of Advanced Technologies for Transit and Rideshare Applications* (Washington, D.C.: 1991).

35. Transportation Research Board, *Assessment of Advanced Technologies for Relieving*

Urban Traffic Congestion (Washington, D.C.: National Academy of Sciences, 1991).

36. For a discussion of privacy concerns in relation to road pricing and other IVHS applications, see Brian Martin, "Computers on the Roads: The Social Implications of Automatic Vehicle Identification," *Current Affairs Bulletin*, October 1990.

37. Clifford Winston, "Efficient Transportation Infrastructure Policy," *Journal of Economic Perspectives*, Winter 1991; 1983 study cited is Philip A. Viton, "Pareto-Optimal Urban Transportation Equilibria," *Research in Transportation Economics*, No. 1, 1983; countries considering congestion pricing from Kenneth A. Small, "Urban Traffic Congestion: A New Approach to the Gordian Knot," *The Brookings Review*, Spring 1993, and from Kiran Bhatt, "Seminar Presentations and Discussions," in FHWA, *Exploring the Role of Pricing as a Congestion Management Tool*, proceedings of the Seminar on the Application of Pricing Principles to Congestion Management, Washington, D.C., July 23, 1991.

38. Martin, op. cit. note 36; computer model described in Charlene Rohr and Mike Salter, "Model Drivers?" *Transport Innovation*, Autumn 1992; John Whitelegg, Lancaster University Department of Geography, Lancaster, U.K., private communication, October 11, 1993.

39. Gordon, op. cit. note 26.

40. Bicycle Institute of America (BIA), *Bicycling Reference Book 1993–1994 Edition* (Washington, D.C.: 1993); tripling is a Worldwatch estimate based on ibid.; current number of regular bicycle commuters from 1992 Harris Poll cited in J.C. McCullagh, "The 50 State Solution," *Bicycling*, June 1992; police on bicycles from BIA, *Bicycling Reference Book 1992–1993 Edition* (Washington, D.C.: 1992).

41. India and Pakistan from Michael Replogle, *Non-Motorized Vehicles in Asian Cities* (Washington, D.C.: World Bank, 1992); Rob

Gallagher, *The Rickshaws of Bangladesh* (Dhaka: University Press Limited, 1992).

42. Gallagher, op. cit. note 41.

43. Electric van from "Electric Commuter Bus," *Green Car Journal*, January 1993; compressed natural gas bus from "NG Transit Bus Uses Topside Fuel Cylinders," *Green Car Journal*, February 1993; diesel retrofit from "Santa Barbara's Transit EV Made by Military Contractor," *Electric Vehicle Progress*, February 1993; hydrogen fuel cell bus from Marshall Miller, Union of Concerned Scientists, Berkeley, Calif., private communication, October 15, 1993.

44. Construction cost comparison from Alan Armstrong-Wright, *Urban Transit Systems: Guidlelines for Examining Options* (Washington, D.C.: World Bank, 1986); for a discussion of rail transport, see Marcia D. Lowe, "Rediscovering Rail," in Lester R. Brown et al., *State of the World 1993* (New York: W.W. Norton & Company, 1993).

45. Space comparison is Worldwatch Institute estimate based on American Public Transit Association, *Transit Fact Book*, 1991 ed. (Washington, D.C.: 1991).

46. Sacramento from Regional Plan Association, *The Renaissance of Rail Transit in America* (New York: 1991); Manila from "Breaking Up the Jams," op. cit. note 12.

47. Opening of Florida maglev line from Joseph Vranich, *Supertrains: Solutions to America's Transportation Gridlock* (New York: St. Martin's Press, 1991).

48. Pakistan from "Pakistan Rail Upgrade To Include 'Bullet Train,'" *Journal of Commerce*, September 8, 1992; all others from Vranich, op. cit. note 47.

49. In France and Germany, where government rail investments in recent years have been skewed toward high-speed rail, regular intercity service has been reduced, according to Jonathon Bray, *Transport: Policy Options*, Economic Alternatives for Eastern Europe Briefing No. 5 (London: New Economics Foundation, 1992); for a broader discussion

of this and related concerns, see John White-legg, Staffan Hultén, and Torbjörn Flink, eds., *High Speed Trains: Fast Tracks to the Future* (Hawes, North Yorkshire, U.K.: Leading Edge Press, 1992).

50. Developing countries' adoption of Western-style zoning described in UNCHS (Habitat), *Transportation Strategies for Human Settlements in Developing Countries* (Nairobi: 1984); for a broader discussion of urban land use and transportation, see Marcia D. Lowe, *Shaping Cities: The Environmental and Human Dimensions*, Worldwatch Paper 105 (Washington, D.C.: Worldwatch Institute, October 1991).

51. John Holtzclaw, "Explaining Urban Density and Transit Impacts on Auto Use," testimony presented to the State of California Energy Resources Conservation and Development Commission, January 15, 1991.

52. Ibid.

53. For more on reforming land use controls, see Duany and Plater-Zyberk, op. cit. note 7.

54. Conversion of commercial space in U.K. cities from Tim Elkin and Duncan McLaren with Mayer Hillman, *Reviving the City: Towards Sustainable Urban Development* (London: Friends of the Earth, 1991); U.S. estimate from Martin Gellen, *Accessory Apartments in Single-Family Housing* (New Brunswick, N.J.: Center for Urban Policy Research, 1985).

55. For recent information on land taxation to encourage full use of urban land, see Wallace Oates and Robert Schwab, "The Impact of Urban Land Taxation: The Pittsburgh Experience," Lincoln Institute of Land Policy, Cambridge, Mass., 1992, Kenneth M. Lusht, "The Site Value Tax and Residential Development," Lincoln Institute of Land Policy, Cambridge, Mass., 1992, and back issues of *Incentive Taxation*, the monthly bulletin of the Center for the Study of Economics, Columbia, Md.

56. Parking quotas from Deakin, op. cit. note 28.

57. Tridib Banerjee and William C. Baer, *Beyond the Neighborhood Unit* (New York: Plenum Press, 1984), as cited in Ray Oldenburg, *The Great Good Place* (New York: Paragon House, 1989).

58. Studies on overcrowding in rural versus urban settings cited in James E. Karas, "Resident Attitudes Toward Higher Residential Densities in Columbus, Ohio: Privatism Versus Public Advantage and the Acceptance of Urban Megastructures," masters thesis, Ohio State University, Columbus, Ohio, 1983.

59. Crime rates, measured in murders per 100,000 population, from Population Crisis Committee, *Cities: Life in the World's 100 Largest Metropolitan Areas* (Washington, D.C.: 1990); densities from Peter Newman and Jeffrey Kenworthy, *Cities and Automobile Dependence: An International Sourcebook* (Aldershot, U.K.: Gower, 1989).

60. Recent studies include Brian Ketchum and Charles Komanoff, "Win-Win Transportation: A No-Losers Approach to Financing Transport in New York City and the Region," presented at the American Association for the Advancement of Science Annual Meeting, Boston, February 12, 1993, and Donald Shoup, *Cashing Out Employer-Paid Parking* (Washington, D.C.: DOT, 1992); for a comprehensive overview of the results of several studies, see James J. MacKenzie, Roger C. Dower, and Donald D.T. Chen, *The Going Rate: What it Really Costs to Drive* (Washington, D.C.: World Resources Institute, 1992).

61. Per Kågeson, *Getting the Prices Right: A European Scheme for Making Transport Pay its True Costs* (Stockholm: European Federation for Transport and Environment, 1993).

62. Vukan R. Vuchic, "Cheap Gasoline: An American Addiction," *Moving People*, April/May 1993; Kågeson, op. cit. note 61.

63. Los Angeles example from Jeffrey Tumlin and Patrick Siegman, "The Cost of

Free Parking," *Urban Ecologist*, Summer 1993; see also Shoup, op. cit. note 60.

64. London estimate from Organisation for Economic Co-operation and Development, International Energy Agency, *Cars and Climate Change* (Paris: 1993).

65. Assuming a $1-per-gallon gasoline subsidy and using U.S. data for average annual gasoline expenditures and household income, Kirk R. Barrett has calculated that households in the highest income bracket receive a subsidy of $1,700 per year, compared with $300 per year for households in the lowest income bracket; Kirk R. Barrett, "Increased Gasoline Tax: It's Only Fair," Northwestern University, Evanston, Ill., unpublished paper, February 1993. See also Bleijenberg, op. cit. note 11.

66. For more on allocating public funds to IVHS projects, see Gordon, op. cit. note 26.

67. Integrated resource planning described in Birk and Zegras, op. cit. note 13; for a similar discussion, see Brian Ketchum and Charles Komanoff, "Win-Win Transportation: A No-Losers Approach to Financing Transport in New York City and the Region," Transportation Alternatives, New York, 1992; 30 states from Cynthia Mitchell, consulting economist, Reno, Nev., private communication, June 24, 1993, and from Cynthia Mitchell, "Integrated Resource Planning Survey: Where the States Stand," *The Electricity Journal*, May 1992.

68. Birk and Zegras, op. cit. note 13.

69. For an eloquent discussion of the social impacts of car-oriented sprawl in the United States, see James Howard Kunstler, *The Geography of Nowhere: The Rise and Decline of America's Man-Made Landscape* (New York: Simon and Schuster, 1993).

Chapter 6. Using Computers for the Environment

Many of the references for this chapter were obtained on-line. When possible, both on-line and print versions of documents are cited. Conferences of the Association for Progressive Communications (APC), which were reached through Econet—APC's U.S. system—are listed by name in brackets. Electronic mail addresses and ftp addresses (for documents obtained by Internet remote file transfer) are listed similarly.

1. For an illuminating discussion of the evolution of computers from data-processing machines to personal learning tools, see Howard Rheingold, *Tools for Thought: The People and Ideas Behind the Next Computer Revolution* (New York: Simon & Schuster, 1985).

2. Ibid.

3. Ibid.; figure for 1980 is a Worldwatch Institute estimate based on Karen Petska Juliussen and Egil Juliussen, *The 6th Annual Computer Industry Almanac* (Lake Tahoe, Nev.: Computer Industry Almanac, Inc., 1993); current and MIPS figures from Egil Juliussen, Computer Industry Almanac, Inc., Lake Tahoe, Nev., private communication, July 29, 1993.

4. Industry sales from Stratford Sherman, "The New Computer Revolution," *Fortune*, June 14, 1993.

5. Lenny Siegel, "Analysis of High-Tech Employment Patterns in Eight Leading U.S. High-Tech Centers—1990," Pacific Studies Center, Mountain View, Calif., September 1992.

6. Unionization from Michael Eisenscher, "Silicon Fist in a Velvet Glove," unpublished paper, Mattapan, Mass., December 1992.

7. Ted Smith, Silicon Valley Toxics Coalition, San Jose, Calif., private communication, August 21, 1993.

8. Edward O. Wilson, *The Diversity of Life* (Cambridge, Mass.: Harvard University Press, 1992).

9. U.S. Environmental Protection Agency (EPA), Office of Pollution Prevention and

Toxics, *1991 Toxics Release Inventory: Public Data Release* (Washington, D.C.: 1993).

10. Alair MacLean, OMB Watch, Washington, D.C., private communication, August 24, 1993.

11. United Nations, *Agenda 21: The United Nations Programme of Action from Rio* (New York: U.N. Publications, 1992); Paul Muldoon, Pollution Probe, Toronto, Canada, private communication, August 13, 1993; European Community information from Frances Irwin, World Wildlife Fund, Washington, D.C., private communication, August 13, 1993.

12. Eric Rodenburg, *Eyeless in Gaia: The State of Global Environmental Monitoring* (Washington, D.C.: World Resources Institute, 1992). Sampling equipment is commonly described and advertised in the environmental engineering trade press; see, for example, the product profiles in *Hazmat World*.

13. L. David Mech and Eric M. Gese, "Field Testing the Wildlink Capture Collar on Wolves," *Wildlife Society Bulletin*, Vol. 20, 1992, pp. 221–23; K.E. Kunkel et al., "Testing the Wildlink Activity-Detection System on Wolves and White-Tailed Deer," *Canadian Journal of Zoology*, Vol. 69, 1991, pp. 2466–69.

14. David Leversee, "Cooperative Forest Management: The Sierra Club of Western Canada and British Columbia Ministry of Forests Use Multiple GIS Data Sources to Assess Logging Effects on Vancouver Island," *Earth Observation Magazine*, July/August 1993.

15. Christopher Flavin, *Slowing Global Warming: A Worldwide Strategy*, Worldwatch Paper 91 (Washington, D.C.: Worldwatch Institute, October 1989).

16. J.T. Houghton, G.J. Jenkins, and J.J. Ephraums, *Climate Change: The IPCC Scientific Assessment* (Cambridge: Cambridge University Press, 1990).

17. John Freymann, The Futures Group, Washington, D.C., presentation at the World Wildlife Fund, Washington, D.C., April 20, 1993; U.S. Congress, Office of Technology Assessment, *Improving Automobile Fuel Economy: New Standards, New Approaches* (Washington, D.C.: U.S. Government Printing Office, 1991).

18. Alan Thein Durning, "Are You an Eco-Titan?" *World Watch*, March/April 1993; the Global Lab project is thoroughly documented in (and coordinated through) 14 different APC conferences.

19. For an excellent overview of the Internet and how to reach its information resources, see Ed Krol, *The Whole Internet: User's Guide and Catalog* (Sebastopol, Calif.: O'Reilly and Associates, Inc., 1992); for a general, although U.S.-centered, review of environmental networks, see Don Rittner, *Ecolinking: Everyone's Guide to Online Environmental Information* (Berkeley, Calif.: Peachpit Press, Inc., 1992).

20. Number of host computers and users from Michael Stein, San Francisco, Calif., private communication, August 23, 1993; rate of network growth from Howard Rheingold, *Whole Earth Review*, Sausalito, Calif., private communication, March 2, 1993.

21. Internet history from Rheingold, op. cit. note 1; international connections from Larry Landweber, "International Connectivity," University of Wisconsin, Madison, Wisc., April 15, 1993 (available from GNET archive, which can be reached on the Internet at the ftp address [dhvx20.csudh.edu], or from ftp at [ftp.cs.wisc.edu]); electronic journals from Michael Strangelove, *Directory of Electronic Journals and Newsletters*, July 1992 (available through ftp at [nisc.sri.com] or in print from Office of Scientific & Academic Publishing, Association of Research Libraries, Washington, D.C.). Special search programs available include Gopher, Archie, and WAIS, all of which are described in detail in Krol, op. cit. note 19.

22. APC, "Global Computer Communications for Environment, Human Rights, De-

velopment, and Peace," brochure (available from GNET archive or in the APC conference [standard]); number of APC users from Stein, op. cit. note 20; costs of APC access from International Institute for Sustainable Development (IISD), *Sourcebook on Sustainable Development* (Winnipeg, Man., Canada: 1992), the full text of which may be found in the APC conference [iisd.sourcebk].

23. The bulletins on the Yanomami and the Malaysian land rights battles were found in the APC's [rainfor.general] conference; the first bulletins on the Yanomami appeared on-line on August 18, 1993; James Brooke, "Miners Kill 20 Indians in the Amazon," *New York Times*, August 20, 1993; Jeb Blount, "40 Yanomami Indians Slain on Brazilian Reservation," *Washington Post*, August 21, 1993.

24. IISD, op. cit. note 22; Earth Summit documents can be found in the APC conference [en.unced.documents] (in English), [cnumad.documentos] (in Spanish), and [cnued.documents] (in French).

25. Greenpeace International, Waste Trade Project, *The International Trade in Wastes: A Greenpeace Inventory* (Washington, D.C.: 1990).

26. RTK Net is a joint project of the Unison Institute and OMB Watch; MacLean, op. cit. note 10; John Chelen, Unison Institute, testimony before the Subcommittee on Legislation and National Security and the Subcommittee on Environment, Energy, and Natural Resources, U.S. House of Representatives, Washington, D.C., May 6, 1993.

27. EPA, op. cit. note 9; John Chelen, Unison Institute, Washington, D.C., private communication, July 18, 1993.

28. The author serves as an unpaid editorial advisor to the GreenDisk.

29. Sheldon Annis, "Giving Voice to the Poor," *Foreign Policy*, Fall 1991.

30. Saul Hahn, "The Organization of American States Hemisphere-Wide Networking Intitiative," Organization of American States, Washington, D.C., 1992; Mayuri Odedra et al., "Information Technology in Sub-Saharan Africa," *Communications of the Association for Computing Machinery*, February 1993; both articles available from GNET archive.

31. Pascal Renaud and Monique Michaux, "RIO: An Operational Network in 6 Sub-Saharan Countries of Africa and Three Pacific Islands," presented at INET 92, Kobe, Japan, June 15–18, 1992; Randy Bush, "FidoNet: Use, Technology, and Tools," Pacific Systems Group, Portland, Ore., 1992; Mike Jensen and Geoff Sears, "Low Cost Global Electronic Communications Networks for Africa," presented at 34th Annual Meeting of the African Studies Association, St. Louis, Mo., November 1991; all three articles available from GNET archive.

32. Gary L. Garriott, "Packet Radio in Earth and Space Environments for Relief and Development," presented at 34th Annual Meeting of the African Studies Association, St. Louis, Mo., November 1991 (available from GNET archive); Motorola from Mark Bennett, University of Zambia, Lusaka, Zambia, private communication, August 18, 1993.

33. Stephen R. Ruth and R.R. Ronkin, "Aiming for the Elusive Payoff of User Networks: An NGO Perspective," presented at the annual meeting of the International Society for the Systems Sciences, Denver, Colo., July 12–17, 1992 (available from GNET archive); Garriott, op. cit. note 32.

34. Apple Community Affairs, "Apple in the Community: San Francisco Bay Area and National Programs," brochure, Cupertino, Calif., undated; Albert Langer, "Notes on Computer Communications in Developing Countries," 1991 (available from GNET archive).

35. Larry Press, "Strategies for Software Export," California State University at Dominguez Hills, Los Angeles, Calif., 1992 (available from GNET archive).

36. Odedra et al., op. cit. note 30.

37. Lenny Siegel and John Markoff, *The High Cost of High Tech* (New York: Harper and Row, 1985).

38. Ted Smith, Silicon Valley Toxics Coalition, San Jose, Calif., private communication, March 3, 1993; Tekla S. Perry, "Cleaning Up," *IEEE Spectrum* (Institute of Electrical and Electronics Engineers), February 1993; Silicon Valley Superfund sites from EPA, Hazardous Site Evaluation Division, "National Priorities List," Washington, D.C., June 1993. There have been as many as 29 Silicon Valley sites on the Superfund list at any given time; see California Regional Water Quality Control Board, "Alphabetical List of National Priority Cases," Oakland, Calif., October 25, 1991.

39. Siegel and Markoff, op. cit. note 37; Perry, op. cit. note 38; Terry Greene, "Motorola," *New Times* (Phoenix, Ariz.), May 6–12, 1992; Terry Greene, "Disaster Response," *New Times*, July 1–7, 1992; Terry Greene, "Here's How You'll Pay for Motorola's Contamination," *New Times*, August 19–25, 1992; Terry Greene, "Unanswered Prayers and Questions," *New Times*, October 7–13, 1992; Terry Greene, "A Year Inside the Motorola Mess," *New Times*, December 30-January 5, 1992–93 (*New Times* articles available in RTK Net's documents collection).

40. U.S. Department of Labor, Occupational Safety and Health Administration, "29 CFR Part 1910: Occupational Exposure to 2-Methoxyethanol, 2-Ethoxyethanol and Their Acetates (Glycol Ethers); Proposed Rule," *Federal Register*, March 23, 1993; Harris Pastides et al., "Spontaneous Abortion and General Illness Symptoms Among Semiconductor Manufacturers," *Journal of Occupational Medicine*, July 1988; Shanna H. Swann, "Reproductive Hazards in Semiconductor Manufacturing: The Semiconductor Industry Association Studies," presentation at OSHA's informal public hearing on glycol ethers, July 20–21, 1993; "Final Report: The Johns Hopkins University Retrospective and Prospective Studies of Reproductive Health Among IBM Employees in Semiconductor Manufacturing (Ronald Gray, M.D., MSc., principal investigator), Baltimore, Md., May 1993; Fairchild leak study cited in "New IBM Study Shows One-in-Three Semiconductor Workers Suffer Miscarriages," Campaign for Responsible Technology (CRT), Somerville, Mass., press release, October 12, 1992.

41. Phoenix from Greene, article series, op. cit. note 39; Japan from Kenmochi Kazumi, "High-Tech Pollution," *AMPO Japan-Asia Quarterly Review*, Vol. 23, No. 3, 1992; South Korea from David E. Sanger, "Chemical Leak in Korea Brings Forth a New Era," *New York Times*, April 16, 1991.

42. Perry, op. cit. note 38.

43. Siegel and Markoff, op. cit. note 37.

44. For Sematech, see Perry, op. cit. note 38.

45. Smith, op. cit. note 7; United Nations Environment Programme, *Montreal Protocol: 1993 Report of the Technology and Economic Assessment Panel* (New York: 1993).

46. "SEMATECH Gets Campaign Proposals," *The Bargaining Chip* (bulletin of the Electronics Industry Good Neighbor Campaign, a joint project of CRT, Somerville, Mass., and the Southwest Network for Environmental and Economic Justice, Albuquerque, N.M.), April 1993; Rand Wilson, "Bargaining for a New Industrial Policy," CRT, Somerville, Mass., undated.

47. Sharon M. Lipp, Gregory E. Pitts, and Francis D. Cassidy, eds., *Environmental Consciousness: A Strategic Competitiveness Issue for the Electronics and Computer Industry* (Austin, Tex.: Microelectronics and Computer Technology Corporation, 1993).

48. Steven Anzovin, *The Green PC: Making Choices That Make a Difference* (Toronto, Canada: McGraw-Hill, 1993).

49. EDI information from Ibid.

50. EPA, Office of Air and Radiation, "Introducing . . . EPA Energy Star Computers," Washington, D.C., November 1992; world computer electricity use is a Worldwatch Institute estimate, based on ibid., on Department of Energy, *Annual Energy Review 1991* (Washington, D.C.: 1992), on Juliussen and Juliussen, op. cit. note 3, on Juliussen, op. cit. note 3, on United Nations, *Energy Statistics Yearbook 1990* (New York: 1992), and on Brian Johnson, Energy Star Program, EPA, Washington, D.C., private communication, August 2, 1993.

51. John E. Young, "Asleep on the Job," *World Watch*, March/April 1993.

52. Johnson, op. cit. note 50.

53. Ibid.; Young, op. cit. note 51.

54. Lipp, Pitts, and Cassidy, op. cit. note 47; Federal Republic of Germany, Minister of the Environment, Nature Conservation, and Nuclear Reactor Safety, "Ordinance on the Avoidance, Reduction and Salvage of Waste from Used Electrical and Electronic Equipment," working paper, Bonn, October 15, 1992.

55. Alex Randall, East-West Education Development Foundation, Boston, Mass., private communication, August 10, 1993.

56. Hal Sackman, "Computer Workstations: The Occupational Hazard of the 21st Century," presented at DIAC-92 (Directions and Implications of Advanced Computing), Berkeley, Calif., May 2–3, 1992.

57. Rheingold, op. cit. note 1.

Chapter 7. Assessing Environmental Health Risks

1. J.M. Murray, corporate advertising manager, E.I. du Pont de Nemours and Co., Wilmington, Del., private communication, October 26, 1993; Carl Moskowitz, manager of public relations for chemical group, Monsanto Co., St. Louis, Mo., private communication, October 13, 1993; number of chemicals from National Research Council (NRC), *Toxicity Testing: Strategies to Determine Needs and Priorities* (Washington, D.C.: National Academy Press, 1984).

2. For information on benzene, see Marc Lappé, *Chemical Deception: The Toxic Threat to Health and the Environment* (San Francisco, Calif.: Sierra Club Books, 1991); for information on asbestos, see Paul Brodeur, *Outrageous Misconduct* (New York: Pantheon Books, 1985).

3. The studies conducted by the scientists at the Wingspread meeting have been collected in Theo Colborn and Coralie Clement, eds., *Chemically-Induced Alterations in Sexual and Functional Development: The Wildlife/Human Connection* (Princeton, N.J.: Princeton Scientific Publishing Co., Inc., 1992).

4. Ibid.

5. Hippocrates in C.D. Klaassen, M.O. Amdur, and J. Doull, eds., *Casarett and Doull's Toxicology* (New York: MacMillan Publishing Company, 1986); Charles Dickens, *The Uncommercial Traveller* (London: Chapman and Hall, 1893).

6. Information on PCBs supplied by J.W. Huismans, director of the International Register of Potentially Toxic Chemicals, U.N. Environment Programme (UNEP), January 8, 1993, and by David P. Rall, former director of the National Institute of Environmental Health Sciences and founder and former director of the National Toxicology Program, private communication, October 15, 1993; PCBs in people in UNEP, *The Contamination of Food* (Nairobi: 1992); Clyde H. Farnsworth, "For Arctic Data, Ask a Polar Bear," *New York Times*, November 24, 1992.

7. Chlorine production from Thomas Webster, research associate, Center for Biology of Natural Systems, Queens College, City University of New York, Flushing, N.Y., private communication, December 20, 1992.

8. Effects of DDT in birds from Rachel Carson, *Silent Spring* (Boston: Houghton Mifflen Company, reprint, 1987), and from Theo Colborn, "Epidemiology of Great Lakes Bald Eagles," *Journal of Toxicology and Environmental Health*, Vol. 33, 1991, pp. 395–453; Frank Falck, Jr. et al., "Pesticides and Polychlorinated Biphenyl Residues in Human Breast Lipids and Their Relation to Breast Cancer," *Archives of Environmental Health*, March/April 1992; Mary S. Wolff et al., "Blood Levels of Organochlorine Residues and Risk of Breast Cancer," *Journal of the National Cancer Institute*, April 21, 1993.

9. Sandra Postel, *Altering the Earth's Chemistry: Assessing the Risk*, Worldwatch Paper 71 (Washington, D.C.: Worldwatch Institute, July 1986); Jerome Nriagu et al., "Mercury Pollution in Brazil" (letter), *Nature*, April 2, 1992; mercury found in human blood samples in "The Price of Gold: Mercury Exposure in the Amazon Rain Forest," *Clinical Toxicology*, Vol. 31, No. 2, 1993; global emissions of mercury from Organisation for Economic Co-operation and Development (OECD), "OECD Cooperative Risk Reduction Activities for Certain Dangerous Chemicals—Mercury," paper presented at 16th Joint Meeting, Paris, May 1993, cited in Henry Cole, Amy Hitchcock, and Robert Collins, *Mercury Warning: the Fish You Catch May be Unsafe to Eat* (Washington, D.C.: Clean Water Fund/ Clean Water Action, 1992); neurotoxicity of cadmium, lead, and mercury in NRC, *Environmental Neurotoxicity* (Washington, D.C.: National Academy Press, 1992).

10. Percentage of chemicals that have been tested from NRC, op. cit. note 1; number of commercial substances that standards have been set for from Peter Breysse, School of Public Health and Community Medicine, University of Washington, Seattle, private communication, October 12, 1993.

11. Paul Campanella, Office of Pollution Prevention and Toxics, U.S. Environmental Protection Agency (EPA), Washington, D.C., private communication, November 5, 1993; Erik Olson, remarks made at annual meeting of the American Public Health Association, Washington, D.C., November 10, 1992.

12. Review of active ingredients of pesticides, to be accomplished by 1997, is stipulated by the 1988 amendments to the Federal Insecticide, Fungicide, and Rodenticide Act; information on law from U.S. Congress, Office of Technology Assessment (OTA), *Identifying and Controlling Immunotoxic Substances* (Washington, D.C.: U.S. Government Printing Office (GPO), 1991); share of pesticides without minimal toxicity information is estimated at 64 percent by NRC, op. cit. note 1.

13. W. Kent Anger, "Workplace Exposures," in Zoltan Annau, ed., *Neurobehavioral Toxicology* (Baltimore, Md.: Johns Hopkins University Press, 1986), as cited in NRC, op. cit. note 9.

14. OTA, op. cit. note 12; NRC, Committee on Biologic Markers, *Biologic Markers in Immunotoxicology* (Washington, D.C.: National Academy Press, 1992); effects of pollutants on reproduction and sex-linked behavior from Colborn and Clement, op. cit. note 3, and from NRC, Committee on Biologic Markers, *Biologic Markers in Reproductive Toxicology* (Washington, D.C.: National Academy Press, 1989); DDT use in developing countries from UNEP, op. cit. note 6.

15. Figure of 53 million Americans using herbicides from Colborn and Clement, op. cit. note 3; neurotoxic chemicals in consumer products from OTA, *Neurotoxicity* (Washington, D.C.: GPO, 1990), and from NRC, op. cit. note 9; hazardous waste sites containing neurotoxins from NRC, *Environmental Epidemiology: Public Health and Hazardous Waste*, Vol. I (Washington, D.C.: National Academy Press, 1991).

16. Richard Doll, "Health and the Environment in the 1990s," *American Journal of Public Health*, July 1992.

17. Howard M. Kipen and I. Bernard Weinstein, "The Role of Environmental

Chemicals in Human Cancer Causation," in Alyce Bezman Tarcher, ed., *Principles and Practice of Environmental Medicine* (New York: Plenum Publishing Company, 1992). The 7-percent figure results from counting exposure to industrial products, workplace chemicals, and environmental pollution; 20 percent is one of the higher estimates of cancer attributable to occupational exposures alone.

18. "Cancer rates" here refers both to rates of incidence, or new cases of cancer annually, and mortality rates. Debate over direction of cancer incidence from Hans-Olov Adami et al., "Increasing Cancer Risk in Younger Birth Cohorts in Sweden," *The Lancet*, March 27, 1993; share of malignancies attributable to smoking from Kipen and Weinstein, op. cit. note 17; impact of prevalence of smoking on overall rates of cancer from Alan D. Lopez, "Competing Causes of Death: A Review of Recent Trends in Mortality in Industrialized Countries with Special Reference to Cancer," in Devra Lee Davis and David Hoel, eds., "Trends in Cancer Mortality in Industrial Countries," *Annals of the New York Academy of Sciences*, Vol. 609, 1990; see also David Hoel et al., "Trends in Cancer Mortality in 15 Industrialized Countries, 1969–1986," *Journal of the National Cancer Institute*, March 4, 1992.

19. International trends in smoking-related lung cancer from Lopez, op. cit. note 18; drop in lung cancer deaths for U.S. males from Devra Davis et al., "International Trends in Cancer Mortality in France, West Germany, Italy, Japan, England and Wales, and the United States," *The Lancet*, August 25, 1990.

20. Ibid.; share of cancers that occur after the age of 60 from Rall, op. cit. note 6.

21. Richard Doll, "Progress Against Cancer: An Epidemiological Assessment," *American Journal of Public Health*, October 1, 1991.

22. Rises in incidence of testicular cancer in Europe from Niels Skakkebaek et al., "Evidence for Decreasing Quality of Semen Dur-

ing Past 50 Years," *British Medical Journal*, September 12, 1992; Connecticut study from Linda Morris Brown et al., "Testicular Cancer in the United States: Trends in Incidence and Mortality," *International Journal of Epidemiology*, Vol. 15, No. 2, 1986.

23. Variety of factors that could affect cancer mortality rates from Lopez, op. cit. note 18; impact of mammography on recorded breast cancer incidence from Wolff et al., op. cit. note 8.

24. Davis and Hoel, op. cit. note 18.

25. Ibid.; Devra Davis, senior scientific advisor to the Assistant Secretary for Health, U.S. Department of Health and Human Services, Washington, D.C., private communication, May 24, 1993.

26. Albert de la Chapelle et al., "Clues to the Pathogenesis of Familial Colorectal Cancer," *Science*, May 7, 1993; Albert de la Chapelle et al., "Genetic Mapping of a Locus Predisposing to Human Colorectal Cancer," *Science*, May 7, 1993; Jean Marx, "New Colon Cancer Gene Discovered," *Science*, May 7, 1993; role of oncogenes and tumor suppressor genes in cancer from Kipen and Weinstein, op. cit. note 17.

27. Kipen and Weinstein, op. cit. note 17; Davis et al., op. cit. note 19.

28. Estimate of the proportion of cancer due to environmental factors from Kipen and Weinstein, op. cit. note 17; oral and stomach cancers' link to food preservation from Lappé, op. cit. note 2; role of fruits and vegetables in staving off cancer from NRC, Committee on Diet, Nutrition, and Cancer, *Diet, Nutrition, and Cancer* (Washington, D.C.: National Academy Press, 1982).

29. Fat as a tumor promoter from Philip Abelson, "Diet and Cancer in Humans and Rodents" (editorial), *Science*, January 10, 1992, and from Kipen and Weinstein, op. cit. note 17; role of fat in colon cancer from Walter Willet et al., "Relation of Meat, Fat, and Fiber Intake to the Risk of Colon Cancer in

a Prospective Study Among Women," *New England Journal of Medicine*, December 13, 1990; average levels of fat in American diet and its possible role in female breast cancer from Ann Misch, "Rich Diets Risk Breast Cancer," *World Watch*, November/December 1992.

30. Few substances tested from International Agency for Research on Cancer (IARC)/World Health Organization, IARC Monographs on the Evaluation of Carcinogenic Risks to Humans, "Preamble" and "Lists of IARC Evaluations," IARC, Lyons, France, May 1993; few mouse and rat carcinogens regulated from David P. Rall, Testimony before Environment and Public Works Committee, U.S. Senate, Washington, D.C., March 24, 1993.

31. Kipen and Weinstein, op. cit. note 17; Devra Davis, Aaron Blair, and David Hoel, "Agricultural Exposures and Cancer Trends in Developed Countries," *Environmental Health Perspectives*, Vol. 100, 1992, pp. 39–44; OTA, op. cit. note 12; Aaron Blair et al., "Clues to Cancer Etiology from Studies of Farmers," *Scandinavian Journal of Work, Environment and Health*, Vol. 18, 1992, pp. 209–15.

32. Effects of DES in laboratory animals from Retha R. Newbold and John A. McLachlan, "Diethylstilbestrol Associated Defects in Murine Genital Tract Development," in John McLachlan, ed., *Estrogens in the Environment* (New York: Elsevier Science Publishing Co., 1985); outcome of DES exposure in children of women who took the drug from ibid. and from A.L. Herbst, H. Ulfelder, and D.C. Poskanzer, "Adenocarcinoma of the Vagina: Association of Maternal Stilbestrol Therapy With Tumor Appearance in Young Women," *New England Journal of Medicine*, April 15, 1971; possible effects of environmental pollutants on the endocrine system from Colborn and Clement, op. cit. note 3.

33. Alyce Bezman Tarcher and Edward J. Calabrese, "Enhanced Susceptibility to Environmental Chemicals," in Tarcher, op. cit. note 17.

34. Aaron Blair et al., "Cancer Among Farmers: A Review," *Scandinavian Journal of Work, Environment and Health*, Vol. 11, 1985; Table 7–1 includes information adapted from Aaron Blair and Sheila Hoar Zahm, "Cancer Among Farmers," *Occupational Medicine: State of the Art Reviews*, July/September 1991, with information on prostate cancer from R. Santti et al., "Developmental Oestrogenization and Prostatic Neoplasia" (editorial), *International Journal of Andrology*, April 1990; Davis, Blair, and Hoel, op. cit. note 31.

35. Davis, Blair, and Hoel, op. cit. note 31; NRC, *Biologic Markers in Immunotoxicology*, op. cit. note 14; Blair and Zahm, op. cit. note 34.

36. Extra sensitivity of nervous system from Kaye Kilburn, "Is the Human Nervous System Most Sensitive to Environmental Toxins?" *Archives of Environmental Health*, No. 440, 1989, pp. 343–44, and from OTA, *Neurotoxicity: Identifying and Controlling Poisons of the Nervous System* (Washington, D.C.: GPO, 1990); natural loss of neurons and effects of accelerating that loss from Bernard Weiss, "Neurobehavioral Toxicity as a Basis for Risk Assessment," *Trends in Pharmacological Sciences*, February 1988, from NRC, op. cit. note 9, and from Bernard Weiss and William Simon, "Quantitative Perspectives on the Long-term Toxicity of Methylmercury and Similar Poisons," in Bernard Weiss and V.G. Laties, eds., *Behavioral Toxicology* (New York: Plenum Press, 1975).

37. Number of U.S. workers exposed to neurotoxic chemicals from David Hartman, Stephen Hessl, and Alyce Bezman Tarcher, "Neurobehavioral Disorders," in Tarcher, op. cit. note 17; number of chemicals tested for neurotoxicity from NRC, *Toxicity Testing: Strategies to Determine Needs and Priorities* (Washington, D.C.: National Academy Press, 1984); Table 7–2 based on number of workers exposed to chemicals, excluding mercury, toluene, and xylene, from John L. O'Donoghue, ed. *Neurotoxicity of Industrial and Commercial Chemicals* (Boca Raton, Fla.: CRC Press, 1985), on number of workers exposed to

mercury and industries/products requiring mercury from Cole, Hitchcock, and Collins, op. cit. note 9; on information about processes and products incorporating lead from Dean M. Merke, research associate, Center for Clean Products and Clean Technologies, Knoxville, Tenn., private communication, September 27, 1993, and on estimates of chemicals to which 1 million or more U.S. workers are exposed that have the potential to harm the nervous system from Anger, op. cit. note 13; workers exposed to toluene and xylene from ibid.

38. Philip Landrigan, "Lead in the Modern Workplace," *American Journal of Public Health*, August 1990; Neil Maizlish et al., "Elevated Blood Lead in California Adults, 1987: Results of a Statewide Surveillance Program Based on Laboratory Reports," *American Journal of Public Health*, August 1990; lead in Greenland snow in M. Murozumi et al., *Geochem. cosmochim Acta*, Vol. 33, 1969, pp. 1247–94, cited in K.J.R. Rosman, "Isotopic Evidence for the Source of Lead in Greenland Snows Since the Late 1960s," *Nature*, March 25, 1993.

39. Changing federal standards for unsafe lead exposure from Herbert Needleman, "Childhood Lead Poisoning: Manmade and Eradicable," *The Physicians for Social Responsibility Quarterly*, September 1992; revised U.S. standards for lead exposure from Centers for Disease Control and Prevention, "Preventing Lead Poisoning in Young Children," Atlanta, Ga., October 1991.

40. Relationship between lead in gasoline and blood lead levels in the United States from OTA, op. cit. note 36; information on date of complete phaseout of lead from U.S. gasoline from Jim Caldwell, Office of Air and Radiation, EPA, Washington, D.C., private communication, August 30, 1993.

41. Estimate of 10 million workers from OTA, op. cit. note 36; German estimate from G. Triebig et al., "International Working Group on the Epidemiology of the Chronic Neurobehavioral Effects of Organic Solvents: Congress Report," *International Archives of Occupational and Environmental Health*, Vol. 61, 1989, pp. 423-24.

42. For a review of solvent neurotoxicity, see P. Arlien-Soborg, *Solvent Neurotoxicity* (Boca Raton, Fla.: CRC Press, 1992), Edward L. Baker, "The Neurotoxicity of Industrial Solvents: A Review of the Literature," *American Journal of Industrial Medicine*, Vol. 8, 1985, pp. 207–17, and Hartman, Hessl, and Tarcher, op. cit. note 37; adverse effects of solvents at permissible levels from National Institute of Occupational Safety and Health, "Organic Solvent Neurotoxicity," *Current Intelligence Bulletin*, March 31, 1987, and from Stif-Arne Elofsson, "Exposure to Organic Solvents," *Scandinavian Journal of Work, Environment and Health*, Vol. 6, 1980, pp. 239–73; car and industrial spray painters from ibid.; compensation for disabled workers in Ulf Flodin et al., "Clinical Studies of Psychoorganic Syndromes Among Workers with Exposure to Solvents," *American Journal of Industrial Medicine*, Vol. 5, 1984, pp. 287–95.

43. Judith S. Schreiber et al., "An Investigation of Indoor Air Contamination in Residences Above Dry Cleaners," *Risk Analysis*, Vol. 13, No. 3, 1993; Judith Schreiber, toxicologist, New York State Department of Health, private communications, July 27–28, 1993.

44. Schreiber, private communications, op. cit. note 43.

45. Kaye H. Kilburn and Raphael H. Warshaw, "Effects on Neurobehavioral Performance of Chronic Exposure to Chemically Contaminated Well Water," *Toxicology and Industrial Health*, Vol. 9, No. 3, 1993; Kaye Kilburn, M.D., University of Southern California School of Medicine, private communication, August 19, 1993; Kaye Kilburn, remarks at Annual Meeting of the American Public Health Association, Washington, D.C., November 11, 1992.

46. NRC, op. cit. note 9; role of dopamine from Solomon Snyder and Robert D'Amato,

"Predicting Parkinson's Disease," *Nature*, September 19, 1985.

47. William Langston et al., "Chronic Parkinsonism in Humans Due to a Product of Meperidine-Analog Synthesis," *Science*, February 25, 1983.

48. Pesticides and Parkinson's disease from André Barbeau et al., "Comparative Behavioral, Biochemical and Pigmentary Effects of MPTP, MPP+, and Paraquat in Rana Pipiens," *Life.Sciences*, October 21, 1985; Snyder and D'Amato, op. cit. note 46; Karen Semchuk, "Parkinson's Disease and Exposure to Agricultural Work and Pesticide Chemicals," *Neurology*, July 1992; see also Patricia Butterfield, "Environmental Antecedents of Young-Onset Parkinson's Disease," *Neurology*, June 1993, and A. Bocchetta, "MPTP Model: Renewed Interest in Environmental Factors in Parkinson's Disease," in Guiseppe Nappi et al., eds., *Neurodegenerative Disorders: The Role Played By Endotoxins and Xenobiotics* (New York: Raven Press, 1988); Parkinson's-like conditions in workers from Edward L. Baker, Jr., "Neurologic and Behavioral Disorders," in Barry S. Levy and David Wegman, eds., *Occupational Health: Recognizing and Preventing Work-Related Disease* (Boston: Little, Brown and Company, 2nd ed., 1988).

49. André Barbeau et al., "Ecogenetics of Parkinson's Disease: Prevalence and Environmental Aspects in Rural Areas," *Canadian Journal of Neurological Sciences*, Vol. 14, pp. 36–41, 1987; André Barbeau, "Etiology of Parkinson's Disease: A Research Strategy," *Canadian Journal of Neurological Sciences*, Vol. 11, pp. 24–28, 1984; D.B. Calne et al., "Alzheimer's Disease, Parkinson's Disease, and Motoneurone Disease: Abiotrophic Interaction between Ageing and Environment?" *The Lancet*, November 8, 1986; Susan Calne et al., "Familial Parkinson's Disease: Possible Role of Environmental Factors," *Canadian Journal of Neurological Sciences*, Vol. 14, 1987, pp. 303–05.

50. NRC, *Biologic Markers in Reproductive Toxicology*, op. cit. note 14; OTA, *Infertility: Medical and Social Choices* (Washington, D.C.: GPO, 1988).

51. Uses of glycol ethers from Radha Krishnan, senior chemical engineer, ITT Corporation, Cincinnati, Ohio, from comments at informal public hearing on proposed rule for occupational exposure to 2-methoxyethanol, 2-ethoxyethanol, and their acetates (glycol ethers), Occupational Health and Safety Administration (OSHA), U.S. Department of Labor, Washington, D.C., July 21, 1993, and from OSHA, proposed rulemaking, "Occupational Exposure to 2-Methoxyethanol, 2-Ethoxyethanol and Their Acetates (Glycol Ethers)," *Federal Register* 29 CFR Part 1910 (Docket no. H-044), March 23, 1993; chemicals tested for reproductive or developmental tests from NRC, op. cit. note 37, and from General Accounting Office (GAO), *Reproductive and Developmental Toxicants: Regulatory Actions Provide Uncertain Protection* (Gaithersburg, Md.: 1991); epidemiological studies of semiconductor workers from Harris Pastides et al., "Spontaneous Abortion and General Illness Symptoms Among Semiconductor Workers," *Journal of Occupational Medicine*, July 1988, from Shanna H. Swann, "Reproductive Hazards in Semiconductor Manufacturing: The Semiconductor Industry Association Studies," presentation at OSHA's informal public hearing on glycol ethers, July 20–21, 1993, and from "Final Report: The Johns Hopkins University Retrospective and Prospective Studies of Reproductive Health Among IBM Employees in Semiconductor Manufacturing (Ronald Gray, M.D., MSc., principal investigator), Baltimore, Md., May 1993; similarity in estimates of increased risk associated with photolithography from Ronald Gray, professor of epidemiology, School of Hygiene and Public Health, Johns Hopkins University, Baltimore, Md., private communication, September 2, 1993.

52. OSHA proposal discussed at public hearing, op. cit. note 51.

53. Jon Luoma, "New Effects of Pollutants: Hormone Mayhem," *New York Times*, March 24, 1992; Colborn and Clement, op. cit. note 3.

54. New research on effects of hormonally active pollutants from Colborn and Clement, op. cit. note 3, from Ann Misch, "Chemical Reaction," *World Watch*, March/April 1993, and from Ann Misch, "Chemical Reaction in the Animal Kingdom," *World Watch*, July/August 1992; Mertice M. Clark et al., "Hormonally Mediated Inheritance of Acquired Characteristics in Mongolian Gerbils," and John B. Vandenbergh, "And Brother Begat Nephew," both in *Nature*, August 19, 1993; Natalie Angier, "Female Gerbil Born With Males is Found to Be Begetter of Sons," *New York Times*, August 24, 1993.

55. For overview of effects of estrogens and other "endocrine disruptors," see Colborn and Clement, op. cit. note 3; John McLachlan, *Estrogens in the Environment II: Influences on Development*, Proceedings of the Symposium on Estrogens in the Environment—Influences on Development, Raleigh, N.C., April 10–12, 1985 (New York: Elsevier Publishing, 1985); effects of DES on development of reproductive organs and sexual function from ibid., from Leon Early Gray, Jr., "Delayed Effects on Reproduction Following Exposure to Toxic Chemicals During Critical Periods of Development," in Ralph Cooper, Jerome Goldman, and Thomas Harbin, eds., *Aging and Environmental Toxicology* (Baltimore, Md.: Johns Hopkins University Press, 1991), and from Richard M. Sharpe and Niels Skakkebaek, "Are Oestrogens Involved in Falling Sperm Counts and Disorders of the Male Reproductive Tract?" *The Lancet*, May 29, 1993.

56. Effects of estrogens in men exposed in utero from Sharpe and Skakkebaek, op. cit. note 55; Skakkebaek et al., op. cit. note 22; Santti et al., op. cit. note 34; Brian Henderson et al., "Risk Factors for Cancer of the Testis in Young Men," *International Journal of Cancer*, Vol. 23, 1979, pp. 598–602; potential influence of DES on the sexual orientation of women exposed in utero from Melissa Hines, "Estrogen and Human Neurobehavioral Development," in Colborn and Clement, op. cit. note 3.

57. Role of plant estrogens, dietary fiber, and high-fat diets from Sharpe and Skakkebaek, op. cit. note 55; latest findings on estrogenic effects of various environmental agents, including light, from Janet Raloff, "Ecocancers," *Science News*, July 3, 1993; possible impact of environmental estrogens in people from Skakkebaek et al., op. cit. note 56; industrial substances that act like estrogen and other hormones from Colborn and Clement, op. cit. note 3, from McLachlan, op. cit. note 55, and from Gray, op. cit. note 55; plastics containing estrogenic chemicals from Kenneth Korach, "Surprising Places of Estrogenic Activity" (editorial), *Endocrinology*, Vol. 132, No. 6, 1993, from Aruna V. Krishnan, "Bisphenol-A: An Estrogenic Substance is Released from Polycarbonate Flasks During Autoclaving," *Endocrinology*, Vol. 132, No. 6, 1993, and from Ana M. Soto et al., "*p*-Nonyl-Phenol: An Estrogenic Xenobiotic Released from 'Modified' Polysytrene," *Environmental Health Perspectives*, Vol. 92, 1991, pp. 167–93.

58. Skakkebaek et al., op. cit. note 56; Sharpe and Skakkebaek, op. cit. note 55; "Testicular Descent Revisited," *The Lancet*, February 18, 1989; "An Increasing Incidence of Cryptorchidism and Hypospadias?" *The Lancet*, June 8, 1985.

59. Lack of information on relative potency in vivo of different environmental estrogens from Patricia Whitten, professor of anthropology, Emory University, Atlanta, Ga., private communication, October 14, 1993.

60. Strength of foreign estrogens compared to estradiol, the sex hormone, from John McLachlan et al., "Environmental Estrogens: Orphan Receptors and Genetic Imprinting," in Colborn and Clement, op. cit.

note 3, and from Raloff, op. cit. note 57; relative importance of natural estrogens to estrogenic effects in wildlife and people, in addition to other sources provided, from Whitten, op. cit. note 59, and from John McLachlan, remarks at "Women's Health and the Environment," Society for the Advancement of Women's Health Research, Washington, D.C., June 14, 1993; perturbations in wildlife communities exposed to environmental pollutants that act like hormones from "International Joint Commission Workshop on Cause-Effect Linkages" (Special Issue), *Journal of Toxicology and Environmental Health*, August 1991, and from Theodora Colborn, testimony before U.S. Senate, Committee on Governmental Affairs, Washington, D.C., April 7, 1992; hormonally active chemicals in the Great Lakes from Joe Thornton, "The Product is the Poison: The Case for a Chlorine Phase-out," Greenpeace USA, Washington, D.C., 1991.

61. John McLachlan, scientific director, U.S. National Institute of Environmental Health Sciences, Research Triangle Park, N.C., private communication, November 20, 1992.

62. Higher rates of cancer among transplant patients and unanswered questions in field of immunotoxicology from OTA, op. cit. note 12, and from National Research Council, *Biologic Markers in Immunotoxicology*, op. cit. note 14; Loren Koller, dean, School of Veterinary Medicine, Oregon State University, Corvallis, Oreg., private communication, December 20, 1992.

63. OTA, op. cit. note 12; NRC, *Biologic Markers in Immunotoxicology*, op. cit. note 14; see also, "Brain-Immune System Connection," *Environmental Health Perspectives*, August 22, 1993; immunotoxic effects of chemical mixtures from Dori Germolec et al., "Toxicology Studies of a Chemical Mixture of 25 Groundwater Contaminants," *Fundamental and Applied Toxicology*, Vol. 13, 1989, pp. 377–87; absence of conclusive evidence linking immune alterations to poorer health

from references in OTA and NRC studies and from NRC, op. cit. note 15.

64. Asthma as evidence for link between immune dysfunction and pollution from Alf Fischbein and Alyce Bezman Tarcher, "Disorders of the Immune System," in Tarcher, op. cit. note 17; discussion of the increases of asthma in various countries, including Australia, in R. Michael Sly, "Increases in Deaths from Asthma," *Annals of Allergy*, July 1984; increasing prevalence in Britain in P.G.J. Burney, S. Chinn, and R.L.J. Rona, "Has the Prevalence of Asthma Increased in Children? Evidence from the National Study of Health and Growth 1973–1986," *British Medical Journal*, May 19, 1990; rising prevalence in the United States from Kevin B. Weiss and Diane K. Wagener, "Changing Patterns of Asthma Mortality: Identifying Target Populations at High Risk," *Journal of the American Medical Association*, October 3, 1990, and from Epidemiology and Statistics Unit, "Trends in Asthma Morbidity and Mortality," American Lung Association, Washington, D.C., June 1993; children fastest growing group entering hospital due to asthma attacks from Weiss and Wagener, op. cit. in this note.

65. Hypersensitivity versus immune suppression from OTA, op. cit. note 12.

66. Effects of air pollutants on exercising asthmatics from Jonathan M. Samet and Mark J. Utell, "The Environment and the Lung: Changing Perspectives," *Journal of the American Medical Association*, August 7, 1991; Frederick Lipfert, "Acid Aerosols: The Next Criteria Air Pollutant," *Environmental Science and Technology*, Vol. 23, No. 11, 1989; criteria air pollutants in EPA, *National Air Quality and Emissions Trends Report, 1991* (Research Triangle Park, N.C.: 1992).

67. Joel Schwartz et al., "Particulate Air Pollution and Hospital Emergency Room Visits for Asthma in Seattle," *American Review of Respiratory Disease*, Vol. 147, 1993, pp. 826–31.

68. Poor understanding of asthma from OTA, *Identifying and Controlling Pulmonary Tox-*

icants (Washington, D.C.: GPO, 1992); role of bronchodilators in rising asthma deaths from Robin Marantz Henig, "Asthma Kills," *New York Times Sunday Magazine*, March 28, 1993; other factors in asthma deaths from Lawrence K. Altman, "Rise in Asthma Deaths is Tied to Ignorance of Many Physicians," *New York Times*, May 4, 1993; air pollution exacerbation of preexistent asthma from Dean Sheppard, "Disorders of the Lungs," in Tarcher, op. cit. note 17; WHO/UNEP, *Urban Air Pollution in Megacities of the World* (Oxford: Blackwell Publishers, 1992).

69. The International Agency for Research on Cancer classifies substances as Group 1 (definitely carcinogenic in humans) if there is "sufficient evidence of carcinogenicity in humans," and on rare occasions when there is "sufficient evidence of carcinogenicity in experimental animals and strong evidence in exposed humans that the agent (mixture) acts through a relevant mechanism of carcinogenicity"; IARC/World Health Organization, op. cit. note 30. The Environmental Protection Agency generally follows the IARC's classification scheme for carcinogens; EPA, Office of Health and Environmental Assessment, *The Risk Assessment Guidelines of 1986* (Washington, D.C.: 1987).

70. Marvin S. Legator and Sabrina F. Strawn, "Public Health Policies Regarding Hazardous Waste Sites and Cigarette Smoking: An Argument by Analogy" (commentary), *Environmental Health Perspectives*, April 22, 1993.

71. Cancer latency from Kipen and Weinstein, op. cit. note 17, and Rall, op. cit. note 6.

72. Minimum increase in risk detected through epidemiological studies from Kipen and Weinstein, op. cit. note 17, and Rall, op. cit. note 6.

73. Effects of low levels of PCBs from Joseph Jacobson et al., "Effects of In Utero Exposure to Polychlorinated Biphenyls and Related Contaminants on Cognitive Func-

tioning in Young Children," *Journal of Pediatrics*, Vol. 116, 1990, pp. 38–45, and from Joseph Jacobson and Sandra Jacobson, "Effects of Exposure to PCBs and Related Compounds in Growth and Activity in Children," *Neurotoxicology and Teratology*, Vol. 12, 1990, pp. 319–26; effects of low levels of lead from David Bellinger et al., "Low-level Lead Exposure, Intelligence and Academic Achievement: A Long-term Follow-up Study," *Pediatrics*, December 1992, and from P.A. Baghurst et al., "Environmental Exposure to Lead and Children's Intelligence at the Age of Seven Years—The Port Pirie Cohort Study," *New England Journal of Medicine*, October 29, 1992.

74. Exposure to solvent mixtures in Hartman, Hessl, and Tarcher, op. cit. note 37; alcohol's interaction with organic solvents in Edward Calabrese, *Multiple Chemical Interactions* (Chelsea, Mich.: Lewis Publishers, 1991).

75. NRC, *Pesticides in the Diets of Infants and Children* (Washington, D.C.: National Academy Press, 1993); EPN cancellation from EPA, *Status of Pesticides in Reregistration and Special Review* (Washington, D.C.: GPO, 1992).

76. Workshop on Multiple Chemical Sensitivity, Annapolis, Md., April 13–14, 1993.

77. Bellinger et al., op. cit. note 73; Elizabeth Bowen, M.D., Department of Family Medicine, Morehouse School of Medicine, Remarks at Human Health and the Environment Symposium, sponsored by Harvard School of Public Health, MIT, and Physicians for Social Responsibility, Cambridge, Mass., October 11, 1992.

78. One good example of this is the current controversy (and attendant confusion among the public) over the real health risks posed by environmental exposure to dioxin; see Karen Schmidt, "Dioxin's Other Face: Portrait of an Environmental Hormone," *Science News*, January 11, 1992, and Ann Misch, "Chemical Reaction," *World Watch*, March/April 1993. Critics of EPA's strict regulation of dioxin in the past have pointed to the ab-

sence of data supporting elevations in rates of cancer following high exposures to dioxin, such as after a major industrial accident in Seveso, Italy, in 1976. Recent assessments of the prevalence of specific cancers in Seveso, however, have in fact found elevated risk; Richard Stone, "New Seveso Findings Point to Cancer," *Science*, September 10, 1993.

79. Failure of U.S. regulations on pesticides in food to assess adequately differences in metabolism, among other things, between adults and children from NRC, op. cit. note 75; inadequate protection against reproductive and developmental toxins from GAO, op. cit. note 51.

80. Higher levels of risk allowed among workers in C. Mark Smith, Karl Kelsey, and David Christiani, "Risk Assessment and Occupational Health," *New Solutions*, Winter 1993; inadequate protection in developing countries from David C. Christiani, professor of occupational medicine, Harvard School of Public Health, Cambridge, Mass., private communication, October 20, 1993.

81. Neil A. Lewis, "Man in the News: Benjamin Franklin Chavis, Jr.: Seasoned by Civil Rights Struggle," *New York Times*, April 11, 1993; Roberto Suro, "Pollution-Weary Minorities Try Civil Rights Tack," *New York Times*, January 11, 1993; United Church of Christ, Commission for Racial Justice, *Toxic Wastes and Race in the United States: A National Report on the Racial and Socio-Economic Characteristics of Communities with Hazardous Waste Sites* (New York: Public Data Access, 1987); Needleman, op. cit. note 39.

82. Need to look at cancer rates among fellow migrant farmworkers from Sheila Zahm, occupational studies section, National Cancer Institute, remarks at annual meeting of the American Public Health Association, November 9, 1992; neurotoxicity among migrant farmworkers and share of pesticide-related illnesses from OTA, op. cit. note 36. Diagnosing an acute poisoning is difficult, since few emergency room physicians have been trained to recognize such effects when

they occur or to distinguish them from other conditions, such as the flu; Howard Freed, M.D., remarks at Annual Meeting of American Public Health Association, Washington, D.C., November 9, 1992.

83. Bellinger et al., op. cit. note 73.

84. Robert Ginsburg, environmental health consultant, Chicago, Ill., private communication, October 15, 1993.

85. Keith Schneider, "Pesticide Plan Could Uproot U.S. Farming," *New York Times*, October 10, 1993.

86. Sharon M. Lipp, Gregory E. Pitts, and Francis D. Cassidy, eds., *Environmental Consciousness: A Strategic Competitiveness Issue for the Electronics and Computer Industry* (Austin, Tex.: Microelectronics and Computer Technology Corporation, 1993); mercury belatedly removed from interior latex paint in Cole, Hitchcock, and Collins, op. cit. note 9.

Chapter 8. Cleaning Up After the Arms Race

1. Susan E. Davis, "The Battle Over Johnston Atoll," *Washington Post*, April 9, 1991.

2. William J. Broad, "A Soviet Company Offers Nuclear Blasts for Sale to Anyone with the Cash," *New York Times*, November 7, 1991; Defense Nuclear Agency proposal from David Clark, "Chemical Weapons Disposal," letter to the editor, *Science*, July 3, 1992; other suggestions reported by Karen Elliott House and Philip Revzin, "Arsenal of Poison Gas Languishes as Russia is Unable to Destroy it," *Wall Street Journal*, February 25, 1993.

3. Michael Renner, "Assessing the Military's War on the Environment," in Lester R. Brown et al., *State of the World 1991* (New York: W.W. Norton & Company, 1991).

4. Ruth Leger Sivard, *World Military and Social Expenditures 1989* (Washington, D.C.: World Priorities, 1989).

5. Robert S. Norris et al., "Nuclear Weapons," in Stockholm International Peace Research Institute (SIPRI), *SIPRI Yearbook 1991: World Armaments and Disarmament* (Oxford: Oxford University Press, 1991); United Nations Department for Disarmament Affairs, *Disarmament Facts No. 77: Comprehensive Study on Nuclear Weapons. Summary of a U.N. Study* (New York: United Nations, 1991); International Institute for Strategic Studies, *The Military Balance 1992–1993* (London: Brassey's, 1992).

6. The treaties include agreements between the United States and the former Soviet Union—the 1988 Intermediate-Range Nuclear Forces (INF) Treaty, 1991 and 1993 Strategic Arms Reduction Treaties (START I and II); an agreement covering the European continent—the 1990 Conventional Forces in Europe (CFE) Treaty; and an international agreement—the 1993 Chemical Weapons Convention (CWC).

7. "Arms Controllers V. Greenpeace," *Bulletin of the Atomic Scientists*, November 1990.

8. For post-Soviet politics affecting the prospects for disarmament, see Christoph Bluth, "What Do You Do with a Nuclear Arsenal?" *New Scientist*, July 18, 1992, Sergei Kiselyov, "Ukraine: Stuck with the Goods," *Bulletin of the Atomic Scientists*, March 1993, and Elaine Sciolino, "Russian Chaos Stalls Disarmament, Senate is Told," *New York Times*, March 10, 1993.

9. Norris et al., op. cit. note 5; projection over next decade from William J. Broad, "Nuclear Accords Bring New Fears on Arms Disposal," *New York Times*, July 6, 1992; warheads in storage from "Nuclear Weapons After the Cold War: Too Many, Too Costly, Too Dangerous," *The Defense Monitor*, Vol. 22, No. 1, 1993. The other self-acknowledged nuclear powers—China, France, and the United Kingdom—are not party to the START treaties, and their warhead numbers may actually rise; Michael Renner, "Nuclear Arsenal Decline on Hold," in Lester R. Brown, Hal Kane, and Ed Ayres, *Vital Signs 1993* (New York: W.W. Norton & Company, 1993).

10. David Albright, Frans Berkhout, and William Walker, *World Inventory of Plutonium and Highly Enriched Uranium 1992* (Oxford: SIPRI and Oxford University Press, 1993); William J. Broad, "Russian Says Soviet Atom Arsenal Was Larger Than West Estimated," *New York Times*, September 26, 1993; lung cancer from Scott Saleska et al., "Nuclear Legacy: An Overview of the Places, Problems, and Politics of Radioactive Waste in the U.S.," Public Citizen, Washington, D.C., September 1989; non-nuclear components from "Breaking up (a Bomb) is Hard to Do," *Science*, September 24, 1993.

11. Difficulty of dismantling from U.S. Congress, Office of Technology Assessment (OTA), *Dismantling the Bomb and Managing the Nuclear Materials* (Washington, D.C.: U.S. Government Printing Office (GPO), 1993); dismantlement challenge in former Soviet Union from John Rettie, "Soviet Nuclear Nightmare," *The Guardian* (London), January 29, 1992.

12. Previous "recycling" practices from Albright, Berkhout, and Walker, op. cit. note 10; Russian pledge and lack of U.S. reciprocation from Frans Berkhout et al., "Disposition of Separated Plutonium," prepared for Workshops on Disposal of Plutonium in Bonn, June 15–16, 1992, and in London, June 18, 1992, Center for Energy and Environmental Studies, Princeton University, revised version, July 8, 1992, and from Tom A. Zamora, "Nuclear Warhead Dismantlement: Faster, More Open," in The Tides Foundation, *Facing Reality: The Future of the U.S. Nuclear Weapons Complex* (Seattle, Wash.: Nuclear Safety Campaign, 1992).

13. C.H. Bloomster et al., "Options and Regulatory Issues Related to Disposition of Fissile Materials from Arms Reduction," Pacific Northwest Laboratory, Richland, Wash., December 1990, prepared for the U.S. Department of Energy, presented at the

Annual Meeting of the American Association for the Advancement of Science, Washington, D.C., February 18, 1991; OTA, op. cit. note 11.

14. Frans Berkhout et al., "Plutonium: True Separation Anxiety," *Bulletin of the Atomic Scientists*, October 1992.

15. Institute for Defense and Disarmament Studies (IDDS), *Arms Control Reporter 1992* (Cambridge, Mass.: 1992), sheets 611.E-3.40 and .44; IDDS, *The Arms Control Reporter 1993* (Cambridge, Mass.: 1993), sheet 611.E-3.55; William J. Broad, "Russians Offering Nuclear Arms Fuel for U.S. Reactors," *New York Times*, July 22, 1992; William J. Broad, "Deal With Russia is Said to Involve More Uranium Than Believed," *New York Times*, September 5, 1992; value of deal from "Uranium, Plutonium, Pandemonium," *The Economist*, June 5, 1993; U.S. government from OTA, op. cit. note 11.

16. Ashton B. Carter and Owen Coté, "Transport, Storage, and Dismantlement of Nuclear Weapons," and Ashton B. Carter and Owen Coté, "Disposition of Fissile Materials," both in Graham Allison et al., eds., *Cooperative Denuclearization: From Pledges to Deeds*, CSIA Studies in International Security No. 2 (Cambridge, Mass.: Harvard University, Center for Science and International Affairs: 1993); Berkhout et al., op. cit. note 12.

17. Arjun Makhijani, "Options for Plutonium from Dismantled Nuclear Weapons," *Science for Democratic Action*, Winter 1992; Bloomster et al., op. cit. note 13; Paul Rogers, "Ploughshare Option for Warheads," *The Guardian* (London), February 1, 1992; need for rigorous evaluation from Albright, Berkhout, and Walker, op. cit. note 10.

18. T.R. Reid, "Japan Proposes to Tame Soviet Plutonium," *Washington Post*, July 26, 1992; David Swinbanks, "Japan Plans Furnace Reactor to Consume Soviet Plutonium," *Nature*, July 30, 1992; William J.

Broad, "A Plutonium Pact Will Aid Disposal," *New York Times*, April 6, 1993.

19. Many nations are highly uncomfortable with the idea of transporting even limited amounts of plutonium, as Japan realized when its shipment of 1 ton of reprocessed civilian plutonium from France was greeted with a torrent of protest; David E. Sanger, "Japan's Plan to Ship Plutonium Has Big and Little Lands Roaring," *New York Times*, October 5, 1992; possibility of theft from Berkhout et al., op. cit. note 12.

20. "World Status Report: Plutonium," *Financial Times Energy Economist*, May 1992; Berkhout et al., op. cit. note 12; William Walker and Frans Berkhout, "The Problem of Plutonium," *Financial Times*, February 13, 1992; reactor design and MOX uses from "Uranium, Plutonium, Pandemonium," op. cit. note 15.

21. Berkhout et al., op. cit. note 12; Makhijani, op. cit. note 17.

22. Berkhout et al., op. cit. note 12; Roger D. Harrison, *The Ultimate Disposal of Fissile Materials from Nuclear Warheads* (London: Scientists Against Nuclear Arms, 1991).

23. Adequacy of planned capacities from James D. Werner, "An Eternal Pile of Bomb Relics," (Cleveland) *Plain Dealer*, April 6, 1992, and from Berkhout et al., op. cit. note 14; difficulties at Hanford and Savannah River from Matthew L. Wald, "At Old A-Plant, One Sure Thing is the Volatility," *New York Times*, June 21, 1993, and from IDDS, *Arms Control Reporter 1993*, op. cit. note 15, sheets 611.E-0.5 and 611.E-3.61.

24. Konrad B. Krauskopf, "Disposal of High-Level Nuclear Waste: Is It Possible?," *Science*, September 14, 1990; Matthew L. Wald, "Judge Sets Up New Hurdles for U.S. Plutonium Dump," *New York Times*, February 4, 1992; for a general discussion of problems of nuclear waste disposal, see Nicholas Lenssen, *Nuclear Waste: The Problem That Won't Go Away*, Worldwatch Paper 106 (Washing-

ton, D.C.: Worldwatch Institute, December 1991).

25. Fact Sheet on the START II Treaty issued by Office of the Press Secretary, White House, January 1, 1993, and "Treaty Between the United States of America and the Russian Federation on Further Reduction and Limitation of Strategic Offensive Arms," Official Text, January 3, 1993, both provided by the U.S. Arms Control and Disarmament Agency, Washington, D.C.; Jack Mendelsohn, "Next Steps in Nuclear Arms Control," *Issues in Science and Technology*, Spring 1993; total number of missiles affected by the START treaties from U.S. Library of Congress, Congressional Research Service, "START II: Central Limits and Force Structure Implications," Washington, D.C., January 8, 1993.

26. Robert Darst, "Disposal of Liquid Missile Propellants," in Allison et al., op. cit. note 16; Robert J. Esher, DeLisle Environmental Laboratory, Mississippi State University Research Center, Waveland, Miss., private communication, July 29, 1993; William Broad, "New Methods Sought to Dispose of Rockets With No Harm to Earth," *New York Times*, September 17, 1991; Steven Aftergood, "Environmental Impacts of Solid Rocket Propellants," *F.A.S. Public Interest Report* (Journal of the Federation of American Scientists), September/October 1991; Steven Aftergood, "Poisoned Plumes," *New Scientist*, September 7, 1991.

27. W. Jackson Davis and John M. Van Dyke, "Dumping of Decommissioned Nuclear Submarines at Sea," *Marine Policy*, November 1990; Joshua Handler, "No Sleep in the Deep for Russian Subs," *Bulletin of the Atomic Scientists*, April 1993; Joshua Handler, "Trip Report: Greenpeace Visit to Moscow and Russian Far East July–November 1992. Subject: Russian Navy Nuclear Submarine Safety, Construction, Defense Conversion, Decommissioning, and Nuclear Waste Disposal Problems," Greenpeace Nuclear Free Seas Campaign, Washington, D.C., February

15, 1993; Sergei Leskov, "Lies and Incompetence," *Bulletin of the Atomic Scientists*, June 1993; Thomas Nilsen, "The Nuclear Threat from the Russian Northern Fleet," Bellona Working Paper No. 2, The Environmental Foundation Bellona, Oslo, Norway, March 10, 1993.

28. Lenny Siegel, *Chemical Weapons Disposal: The Threat at Home* (Boston: National Toxics Campaign, Military Toxics Network, 1991).

29. Ibid.; Stephen I. Schwartz, Greenpeace USA, "The Impact of Military Operations on the Environment," prepared for the SANE/Freeze Campaign for Global Security International Working Conference on the Arms Trade, November 1, 1991; "White Sea Chemical Munitions Burial Sites Revealed," *Komsomolskaya Pravda*, June 20, 1991, as reprinted in *JPRS Report: Environmental Issues*, September 13, 1991; S.J. Lundin and Thomas Stock, "Chemical and Biological Warfare: Developments in 1990," in SIPRI, op. cit. note 5; S.J. Lundin and Thomas Stock, "Chemical and Biological Warfare and Arms Control Developments in 1991," in SIPRI, *SIPRI Yearbook 1992: World Armaments and Disarmament* (Oxford: Oxford University Press, 1992); IDDS, *Arms Control Reporter 1992*, and *Arms Control Reporter 1993*, both op. cit. note 15, and IDDS, *Arms Control Reporter 1991* (Cambridge, Mass.: 1991), sections 704.E-0 and 704.E-2.

30. Stephen J. Ledogar, "Destruction of Weapons Systems Under Multilateral Arms Control Agreements," *Disarmament*, Vol. 14, No. 4, 1991; potential chemical weapons possessor states from OTA, *Disposal of Chemical Weapons: Alternative Technologies—Background Paper* (Washington, D.C.: GPO, 1992); U.S. and Russian stocks from IDDS, *Arms Control Reporter 1992*, op. cit. note 15, sheets 704.E-1.19 and 704.E-0.6.

31. Jozef Goldblat and Thomas Bernauer, "The US-Soviet Chemical Weapons Agreement of June 1990: Its Advantages and Shortcomings," *Bulletin of Peace Proposals*,

Vol. 21, No. 4, 1990; Joachim Badelt, Eric Chauvistré, and Peter Lock, "Disposing of Chemical Weapons: A Common Heritage Calls for a Cooperative Approach," *Bulletin of Peace Proposals*, Vol. 23, No. 1, 1992; time requirements from National Research Council (NRC), *Alternative Technologies for the Destruction of Chemical Agents and Munitions* (Washington, D.C.: National Academy Press, 1993), and from Ledogar, op. cit. note 30.

32. IDDS, *Arms Control Reporter 1992*, op. cit. note 15, sheet 704.E-2.58; Chapayevsk from House and Revzin, op. cit. note 2.

33. Government plan from IDDS, *Arms Control Reporter 1993*, op. cit. note 15, sheets 704.E-2.86 and -2.87; IDDS, *Arms Control Reporter 1992*, op. cit. note 15, sheets 704.E-2.68 and -2.73; opposition from Jay Brin, "Handle With Care: The Destruction of Chemical Weapons," *Technology Review*, April 1993, and from House and Revzin, op. cit. note 2; promises of amenities from Amy E. Smithson, "Chemicals Destruction: The Work Begins," *Bulletin of the Atomic Scientists*, April 1993.

34. John J. Fialka, "Russia Seeks to Include a Recycling Plan in its Chemical-Weapons Dismantling," *Wall Street Journal*, September 2, 1992; Brin, op. cit. note 33; "Udmurtia Discusses Ways to Dispose of Chemical Weapons," *ITAR-TASS*, April 1, 1992, as reprinted in *JPRS Report: Environmental Issues*, May 22, 1992; IDDS, *Arms Control Reporter 1992*, op. cit. note 15, sheet 704.E-2.59.

35. NRC, op. cit. note 31.

36. Ibid.; Lundin and Stock, "Developments in 1991," and "Developments in 1990," both op. cit. note 29; Badelt, Chauvistré and Lock, op. cit. note 31; IDDS, *Arms Control Reporter 1992*, and *Arms Control Reporter 1993*, both op. cit. note 15, sections 704.E-2.

37. IDDS, *Arms Control Reporter 1992*, op. cit. note 15, sheet 704.E-0.3; Ledogar, op. cit. note 30; NRC, op. cit. note 31.

38. Siegel, op. cit. note 28; OTA, op. cit. note 30.

39. Siegel, op. cit. note 28; Alfred Picardi, "Greenpeace Review of Johnston Atoll Chemical Agent Disposal System. Draft Second Supplemental Environmental Impact Statement," Greenpeace International Pacific Campaign, Washington, D.C., February 1990.

40. Picardi, op. cit note 39; OTA, op. cit. note 30.

41. IDDS, *Arms Control Reporter 1992*, op. cit. note 15, sections 704.E-0 and 704.E-1.

42. Siegel, op. cit. note 28; David Clark Scott, "US Plan to Incinerate Chemical-Arms Stocks Rouses Opposition," *Christian Science Monitor*, September 26, 1989; Keith Schneider, "U.S. Plan to Burn Chemical Weapons Stirs Public Fear," *New York Times*, April 29, 1991; IDDS, op. cit. note 15 and 1991 volume, sections 704.E-1; Smithson, op. cit. note 33.

43. TheNational Research Council formed two panels, the Committee on Alternative Chemical Demilitarization Technologies and the Committee on Review and Evaluation of the Army Chemical Stockpile Disposal Program (to reevaluate the status of incineration); the first committee published its report in June 1993: NRC, op. cit. note 31.

44. Siegel, op. cit. note 28; Alfred Picardi, "Greenpeace Review of Johnston Atoll Chemical Agent Disposal System. Final Second Supplemental Environmental Impact Statement (June 1990) for the Storage and Ultimate Disposal of the European Chemical Munition Stockpile," Greenpeace International Pacific Campaign, Washington, D.C., July 9, 1990; "Arms Controllers v. Greenpeace," op. cit. note 7; disassembly and detoxification option from NRC, op. cit. note 31.

45. NRC, op. cit. note 31; Alfred Picardi, Paul Johnston, and Ruth Stringer, *Alternative*

Technologies for the Detoxification of Chemical Weapons: An Information Document (Washington, D.C.: Greenpeace International Pacific Campaign, 1991).

46. NRC, op. cit. note 31; OTA, op. cit. note 30.

47. OTA, op. cit. note 30; NRC, op. cit. note 31.

48. Ledogar, op. cit. note 30; Picardi, op. cit. note 44; NRC, op. cit. note 31.

49. Reductions calculated from IDDS, *Arms Control Reporter 1991*, op. cit. note 29, section 407; 90 percent share of Warsaw Pact from IDDS, *Arms Control Reporter 1992*, op. cit. note 15, sheet 407.B.477; options exercised other than destruction from Jane M.O. Sharp, "Conventional Arms Control in Europe," in SIPRI, op. cit. note 5, from Michael R. Gordon, "Soviets Shift Many Tanks to Siberia," *New York Times*, November 15, 1990, and from Ian Anthony, Agnes Courades Allebeck, and Herbert Wulf, *West European Arms Production. Structural Changes in the New Political Environment* (Stockholm: SIPRI, 1990).

50. Artur Volmerig, "Die Materielle Hinterlassenschaft der NVA," *Wehrtechnik Spezial*, May 1993; "Weapons Recycling Begins at Two Firms, But Cleanup of Military Sites Difficult," *International Environment Reporter*, August 12, 1992; Hans-Joachim Giessmann, "Utilization of Hardware—Options and Constraints. The NVA Case," in Anke Brunn, Lutz Baehr, and Hans-Jürgen Karpe, eds., *Conversion: Opportunities for Development and Environment* (Berlin and Heidelberg: Springer Verlag, 1992).

51. Giessmann, op. cit. note 50; Richard Schütz, "Weapons Destruction and Disposal: Technical and Economical Aspects of Armament Reduction," Industrieanlagen-Betriebsgesellschaft Gmbh, Ottobrunn, Germany, February 18, 1992; Ledogar, op. cit. note 30; IDDS, *Arms Control Reporter 1993*, op. cit. note 15, sheet 407.E-1.117.

52. Giessmann, op. cit. note 50; Ledogar, op. cit. note 30; Schütz, op. cit. note 51.

53. Giessmann, op. cit. note 50.

54. Ammunition in Soviet successor states from Steve Malevich, Alliant Techsystems, Inc., Edina, Minn., private communication, September 14, 1993; East Germany from Volmerig, op. cit. note 50, and from Werner Hänsel and Heinz Michael, "Rüstungskonversion in den Neuen Bundesländern," *Informationsdienst Wissenschaft und Frieden*, December 1990.

55. "Dumping of Arms at Sea Accelerated as January 1993 Restrictions Draw Near," *International Environment Reporter*, September 23, 1992; "Defense Ministry Confirms Dumping of Munitions in Atlantic," (London) *Daily Telegraph*, September 8, 1992, as reprinted in *JPRS Report: Environmental Issues*, October 2, 1992.

56. Giessmann, op. cit. note 50.

57. Bernd Niemeyer and Theodor Rosendorfer, "Conversion and Disposal of Explosives and Propellants," in Brunn, Baehr, and Karpe, op. cit. note 50; Vladimir V. Kalashnykov, Vladimir N. Postnov, and Boris V. Roumiantsev, "A Technique for Environmentally Clean Conversion of Ammunition," in Nils Petter Gleditsch, ed., *Conversion and the Environment* (Proceedings of a Seminar in Perm, Russia, 24–27 November 1991), PRIO Report No. 2 (Oslo, Norway: Peace Research Institute Oslo, 1992).

58. Barry Meier, "Breaking Down an Arms Buildup," *New York Times*, October 15, 1993; Lenny Siegel, "Smoking Guns," National Toxics Campaign Fund Fact Sheet, Mountainview, Calif., March 9, 1993; increased capacities from Giessmann, op. cit. note 50; open-air burning and incineration in Germany from "Munitionsvernichtung auf Kaltem oder Heißem Wege," *Ökologische Briefe*, September 16, 1992, from Bernd Niemeyer, Deutsche Aerospace, Schrobenhausen, Germany, private communication, August 9, 1993, and from Entsorgungs- und Sanie-

rungstechnik GmbH, "Kurzbeschreibung der Munitionsentsorgungsanlage am Standort Steinbach," Schrobenhausen, Germany, 1993.

59. Ukraine from Eric Schmitt, "Selling the Shreds of the Cold War," *New York Times*, July 28, 1993; Kalashnykov, Postnov, and Roumiantsev, op. cit. note 57.

60. Current U.S. chemical disposal estimate from IDDS, *Arms Control Reporter 1992*, op. cit. note 15, sheet 704.E-1.19; 1985 from Smithson, op. cit. note 33; Russian chemical weapons cost estimates from Walter Goodman, "The Special Horror of Chemical War," *New York Times*, October 23, 1990, and from Smithson, op. cit. note 33; comparison of chemical weapon destruction and production costs from J.P. Perry Robinson, Thomas Stock, and Ronald G. Sutherland, "The Chemical Weapons Convention: The Success of Chemical Disarmament Negotiations," in SIPRI, *SIPRI Yearbook 1993: World Armaments and Disarmament* (Oxford: Oxford University Press, 1993); U.S. nuclear warhead dismantling cost from OTA, op. cit. note 11; U.S. submarine decommissioning costs from Handler, "No Sleep in the Deep," op. cit. note 27; ammunition and tanks from Giessmann, op. cit. note 50, from Petra Opitz, "Disarmament Economy—A New Industrial Activity?" in Brunn, Baehr, and Karpe, op. cit. note 50, and from "If You Can't Build Weapons, Destroy 'em," *Business Week*, March 9, 1992.

61. Western pledges of assistance to Russia from IDDS, *Arms Control Reporter 1992* and *Arms Control Reporter 1993*, both op. cit. note 15, sections 611.E-3 (nuclear weapons) and 704.E-2 (chemical weapons), from Dunbar Lockwood, "Dribbling Aid to Russia," *Bulletin of the Atomic Scientists*, July/August 1993, and from John J. Fialka, "U.S. is Studying Ways to Help Russia Dispose of Aging Nuclear Submarines," *Wall Street Journal*, April 2, 1993; discrepancy between chemical weapons aid and aid request from Smithson, op. cit. note 33, and from IDDS, *Arms Control*

Reporter 1993, op. cit. note 15, sheet 704.E-2.91.

62. Steven Pearlstein, "The Big Bucks in Dirty Weapons," *Washington Post*, May 19, 1991; "If You Can't Build Weapons, Destroy 'em," op. cit. note 60; Martin Dickson, "Disarmament Company Formed," *Financial Times*, January 31, 1992; Adam Bryant, "Venture Hopes to Cash in on Military Cutbacks," *New York Times*, June 23, 1992; Katie Hickox, "Swords Into Bankshares," *Washington Monthly*, March 1992.

63. Triana Silton, "Out of the Frying Pan . . . Chemical Weapons Incineration in the United States," *The Ecologist*, January/February 1993; advisory commissions from "Chemical Weapons: The Winds Are Shifting," *Touching Bases*, November/December 1992. The commissions are to be created in Kentucky, Maryland, and Indiana, and at any of the other five designated sites if requested by the governor.

64. For an overview of constraints imposed on production and other aspects of weapons by international arms treaties, see Michael Renner, *Critical Juncture: The Future of Peacekeeping*, Worldwatch Paper 114 (Washington, D.C.: Worldwatch Institute, May 1993).

65. U.S. procurement figures are from Center for Defense Information, direct mail letter to supporters, August 1993; NATO from Saadet Deger, "World Military Expenditure," in SIPRI, op. cit. note 60.

66. Michael Renner, "Nuclear Arsenal Shrinking," in Lester R. Brown, Christopher Flavin, and Hal Kane, *Vital Signs 1992* (New York: W.W. Norton & Company, 1992); "Russian (C.I.S.) Strategic Nuclear Forces, End of 1992," *Bulletin of the Atomic Scientists*, March 1993; "Estimated CIS (Soviet) Nuclear Stockpile (July 1992)," *Bulletin of the Atomic Scientists*, July/August 1992; John J. Fialka, "Russia to Halt Submarine Output Over 2 to 3 Years," *Wall Street Journal*, November 20, 1992; IDDS, *Arms Control Reporter 1993*, op. cit. note 15, sheet 407.E-1.134.

Chapter 9. Rebuilding the World Bank

1. For a description of the Bretton Woods Conference, see Bruce Rich, *Mortgaging the Earth: The World Bank, Environmental Impoverishment, and the Crisis of Development* (Boston, Mass.: Beacon Press, forthcoming).

2. Quoted in ibid.

3. World economic growth and international trade growth based on International Monetary Fund data in Lester R. Brown, Hal Kane, and Ed Ayres, *Vital Signs 1993* (New York: W.W. Norton & Company, 1993).

4. United Nations, *Agenda 21: The United Nations Programme of Action From Rio* (New York: U.N. Publications, 1992).

5. Lending at the regional development banks added up to $15 billion in 1992. Inter-American Development Bank, *Annual Report 1992* (Washington, D.C.: 1993); Asian Development Bank, *Annual Report 1992* (Manila: 1993); African Development Bank, *Annual Report 1992* (Abidjan: 1993); European Bank for Reconstruction and Development, *Annual Report 1992* (London: 1993); Rich, op. cit. note 1; Michael Philips, *The Least Cost Energy Path For Developing Countries: Energy Efficient Investments for the Multilateral Development Banks* (Washington, D.C.: International Institute for Energy Conservation (IIEC), 1991); Maurice J. Williams and Patti L. Petesch, *Sustaining the Earth: Role of Multilateral Development Institutions*, Policy Essay No. 9 (Washington, D.C.: Overseas Development Council, 1993).

6. Some countries that are just above the cutoff point for IDA credit receive mixed loan packages that include funds from both sources. Organisation for Economic Co-operation and Development, *Development Co-operation 1992 Report* (Paris: 1992); World Bank, *Annual Report 1993* (Washington, D.C.: 1993); World Bank, "The World Bank Group," World Bank Information Briefs, April 1993; Marjorie Messiter, Department of Information and Public Affairs, World Bank, Washington, D.C., private communication, October 12, 1993. Figure 9–1 is a Worldwatch estimate based on raw calendar year data (not fiscal year) from World Bank, Financial Information Center, September 28, 1993, adjusted for inflation using a manufactures unit value index for exports from France, Germany, Japan, the United Kingdom, and the United States, weighted proportionately to the countries' exports to developing countries, supplied by World Bank, International Economics Department, "Revision of Primary Commodity Price Forecasts," August 20, 1993.

7. World Bank, "IDA and Economic Reform," World Bank Information Briefs, April 1993; original plans for adjustment lending to equal only 10 percent of total lending from Robert Paarlberg and Michael Lipton, "Changing Missions at the World Bank," *World Policy Journal*, Summer 1991; historical adjustment lending data from the World Bank, Financial Information Center, Washington, D.C., data base and printout, September 28, 1993.

8. Global Environment Facility, brochure, Washington,D.C., December 1991; U.N. Environment Programme (UNEP), U.N. Development Programme (UNDP), and World Bank, "Interim Report of the Independent Evaluation of the Global Environment Facility—Pilot Phase" (draft), Washington, D.C., August 26, 1993.

9. Global Environment Facility, op. cit. note 8; Global Environment Facility, "The Pilot Phase and Beyond," Working Paper Series Number 1, Washington, D.C., May 1992; Global Environment Facility, "Bulletin & Quarterly Operational Summary," Washington, D.C., September 1993.

10. World Bank, *Annual Report 1993*, op. cit. note 6; Dean Kline, assistant to the U.S. executive director, World Bank, Washington, D.C., private communication, October 13, 1993.

11. Rich, op. cit. note 1.

12. World Bank, "The World Bank Group," op. cit. note 6; field staff from Wil-

liam Silverman, Human Resource Information Services Division, World Bank, Washington, D.C., private communication, October 18, 1993; World Bank, *Annual Report 1993*, op. cit. note 6.

13. Rich, op. cit. note 1; Lori Udall, Environmental Defense Fund, Testimony before the Committee on Foreign Relations, U.S. Senate, Washington, D.C., May 27, 1993.

14. Rich, op. cit. note 1; Bruce Rich, Environmental Defense Fund, Washington, D.C., private communication, October 6, 1993. For other examples of bank-financed projects damaging to the environment, see Sierra Club, *Bankrolling Disasters: International Development Banks and the Global Environment* (San Francisco, Calif.: 1986).

15. Jeremy Warford and David Pearce, *World Without End* (New York: Oxford University Press, Inc., 1993); David Reed, ed., *Structural Adjustment and the Environment* (Boulder, Colo.: Westview Press, 1992); Wilfredo Cruz and Robert Repetto, *The Environmental Effects of Stabilization and Structural Adjustment Programs: The Philippines Case* (Washington, D.C.: World Resources Institute, 1992).

16. Rich, op. cit. note 1; Address of Barber B. Conable, President, World Bank and International Finance Corporation, to the World Resources Institute, Washington, D.C., May 5, 1987.

17. World Bank, *The World Bank and the Environment, Fiscal 1993* (Washington, D.C.: 1993); "World Bank Demands Environment Action: The Story of NEAPs," Panos Media Briefing No. 6, Panos Institute, London, undated.

18. World Bank, op. cit. note 17; World Bank, "The World Bank Group," op. cit. note 6; World Bank, Pollution and Environmental Economics Division, "The Evolution of Environmental Concerns in Adjustment Lending: A Review," *CIDIE Workshop on Environmental Impacts of Economywide Policies in Developing Countries*, Washington, D.C., February 23–25, 1993; Reed, op. cit. note 15; Rich, op. cit. note 1.

19. World Bank, *World Development Report 1992* (New York: Oxford University Press, 1992); Williams and Petesch, op. cit. note 5; World Bank, op. cit. note 17.

20. Sheldon Annis, "The Shifting Grounds of Poverty Lending at the World Bank," in Richard E. Feinberg et al., *Between Two Worlds: The World Bank's Next Decade* (New Brunswick, N.J.: Transaction Books, for Overseas Development Council, 1986).

21. The critics include Harvard University economist Jeffrey Sachs and U.S. Congressman David Obey, among others, according to Rich, op. cit. note 1.

22. Giovanni Andrea Cornia, Richard Jolly, and Frances Stewart, eds., *Adjustment With a Human Face* (New York: Oxford University Press, 1989); Alan B. Durning, *Poverty and the Environment: Reversing the Downward Spiral*, Worldwatch Paper 92 (Washington, D.C.: Worldwatch Institute, November 1989).

23. Importance of participatory approaches to project success from Operations Evaluation Department, *Evaluation Results for 1991* (Washington, D.C.: World Bank, 1993), and from Bhuvan Bhatnagar and Aubrey C. Williams, eds., *Participatory Development and the World Bank: Potential Directions for Change* (Washington, D.C.: World Bank Discussion Papers, 1992); failure of bank project to be participatory from William J. Nagle and Sanjoy Ghose, "Community Participation in World Bank Supported Projects," Strategic Planning and Review, Discussion Paper No. 8, World Bank, June 1990, and from Steve Coll, "A Plan to Save the Globe Dies in a Village," *Washington Post*, May 24, 1992.

24. "Learning process" on participation from Bhatnagar and Williams, op. cit. note 23; NGO involvement from External Affairs Department, International Economic Relations Division, "Cooperation Between the World Bank and NGOs: 1991 Progress Re-

port," World Bank, Washington, D.C., April 1, 1992; World Bank, op. cit. note 17; Sheldon Annis, "The Next World Bank? Financing Development from the Bottom Up," *Grassroots Development*, Vol. 11, No. 1, 1987.

25. Bradford Morse, Chairman, *Sardar Sarovar: Report of the Independent Review* (Ottawa: Resource Futures International, 1992); Udall, op. cit. note 13.

26. Portfolio Management Task Force, "Effective Implementation: Key to Development Impact," World Bank, Washington, D.C., November 3, 1992.

27. Rich, op. cit. note 1.

28. Portfolio Management Task Force, op. cit. note 26.

29. UNEP, UNDP, and the World Bank, op. cit. note 8; "Official GEF Review Panel Confirms Deep-Set Problems," *Early Warning* (Bank Information Center), September 1993; see also, Glenn T. Prickett, Natural Resources Defense Council, Testimony on Behalf of Bank Information Center, Conservation International, and Environmental Defense Fund, before the Subcommittee on International Development, Finance, Trade and Monetary Policy, Committee on Banking, Finance and Urban Affairs, U.S. House of Representatives, Washington, D.C., August 3, 1993.

30. World Bank, *Getting Results: The World Bank's Agenda for Improving Development Effectiveness* (Washington, D.C.: 1993); Nancy Alexander, Bread for the World, Lori Udall, Environmental Defense Fund, and Barbara Bramble, National Wildlife Federation, Memorandum to Mark Collins, alternate U.S. executive director, World Bank, Washington, D.C., July 7, 1993.

31. "New Policy Guidelines May Weaken Accountability," *Early Warning* (Bank Information Center), June 1993.

32. Rich, op. cit. note 14; George Graham, "Panel to Review Rules Complaints," *Financial Times*, September 27, 1993; "New World Bank Policies Set on Information and Appeals," *Early Warning* (Bank Information Center), September 1993.

33. Nicholas Lenssen, *Empowering Development: The New Energy Equation*, Worldwatch Paper 111 (Washington, D.C.: Worldwatch Institute, November 1992); Marcia D. Lowe, *Alternatives to the Automobile: Transport for Livable Cities*, Worldwatch Paper 98 (Washington, D.C.: Worldwatch Institute, October 1990).

34. Annis, op. cit. note 20; World Bank, *Annual Report 1993*, op. cit. note 6.

35. World Bank, *The World Bank's Role in the Electric Power Sector* (Washington, D.C.: 1993); Philips, op. cit. note 5; U.S. expenditures on demand-side management are a Worldwatch Institute estimate based on Edison Electric Institute (EEI), *Statistical Yearbook of the Electric Utility Industry 1992* (Washington, D.C.: 1993), and on Thomas Devlin, Science Applications International Corp., Arlington, Va., private communication, June 15, 1993.

36. Projection to 1995 from Energy Development Division, "FY91 Annual Sector Review: Energy," World Bank, Washington, D.C., October 23, 1991.

37. Transport Division, "FY92 Transport Sector Review," World Bank, Washington, D.C., October 1992; Philips, op. cit. note 5.

38. World Bank, op. cit. note 35; World Bank, *Energy Efficiency and Conservation in the Developing World* (Washington, D.C.: 1993); "Revised Energy Policy Papers Approved by World Bank Board," *BankNote* (IIEC), December 1992; "COMMENTARY: New MDB Energy Policies Raise Hopes," *BankNote*, June 1993; Paul Guitink, World Bank, Washington, D.C., private communication, October 6, 1993.

39. Michael Philips, IIEC, Washington, D.C., private communication, October 7, 1993; Karan Capoor and Glenn Prickett, *The World Bank's Energy Efficiency Policy: An Assess-*

ment of Recent Experience in the Electric Power Sector (Washington, D.C.: Environmental Defense Fund, 1993); World Bank, op. cit. note 17; Kim Coghill, "Bank to Factor in Environmental Costs When Assessing Asian Power Projects," *Journal of Commerce*, September 22, 1993.

40. Energy Development Division, op. cit. note 36; World Bank, op. cit. note 17.

41. Philips, op. cit. note 5; "MDB Urban Transport Projects Look Beyond Roads and Cars," *Banknote*, June 1993; Guitink, op. cit. note 38; Jenny S. Testino, "Program of Popular Transport of Non-Motorized Vehicles (Peru)," in Proceedings from the 1992 Global Forum on Sustainable Transportation Strategies and Development, Rio de Janeiro, June 2–4, 1992.

42. Walter Hook, "Towards Sustainable and Equitable Transportation and Human Settlements Investments Which Put People First," Institute for Transportation and Development Policy (ITDP), Washington, D.C., August 1993; Walter Hook, ITDP, Washington, D.C., private communication, September 24, 1993.

43. Todd Goldman and Karan Capoor, "Soot in the Pipeline," *ECO* (NGO Newsletter, Climate Change Negotiations), August 25, 1993; Susan B. Levine, deputy assistant secretary, Department of the Treasury, memo to Bruce Rich, director, international program, Environmental Defense Fund, July 15, 1993; Steven Nadel, S. Gopinath, and Virendra Kothari, "Opportunities for Improving End-Use Electricity Efficiency in India," U.S. Agency for International Development, Washington, D.C., November 1991. Conversion of rupees to dollars as of mid-November 1993.

44. World Bank, *Annual Report 1993*, op. cit. note 6.

45. World Bank time series agricultural lending and total lending data from World Bank, data base, op. cit. note 7; Paarlberg and Lipton, op. cit. note 7.

46. Paarlberg and Lipton, op. cit. note 7; Michael Lipton and Robert Paarlberg, *The Role of the World Bank in Agricultural Development in the 1990s* (Washington, D.C.: International Food Policy Research Institute, 1990).

47. Paarlberg and Lipton, op. cit. note 7.

48. Ibid.; Robert L. Ayres, *Banking on the Poor* (Cambridge, Mass.: The MIT Press, 1984); Rich, op. cit. note 1; Jodi L. Jacobson, *Gender Bias: Roadblock to Sustainable Development*, Worldwatch Paper 110 (Washington, D.C.: Worldwatch Institute, September 1992).

49. Paarlberg and Lipton, op. cit. note 7; Ayres, op. cit. note 48; Annis, op. cit. note 20.

50. Rich, op. cit. note 1.

51. World Bank, op. cit. note 17; World Bank, *Water Resources Management* (Washington, D.C.: 1993); Deborah Moore, Environmental Defense Fund, and Leonard Sklar, International Rivers Network, "Reforming the World Bank's Lending for Water: NGO Comments on the World Bank's Water Resources Management Policy Paper," Washington, D.C., February 25, 1993.

52. Ibrahim F. I. Shihata, Vice-President and General Counsel, World Bank, "The World Bank and the Environment—A Legal Perspective," in American Bar Association, *International Environmental Law: Recent Developments and Implications*, Report on a Conference held in Washington, D.C., October 31-November 1, 1991; Patti Petesch, "Tropical Forests: Conservation with Development?" Policy Focus No. 4, Overseas Development Council, Washington, D.C., 1990; World Bank, *The World Bank and the Environment, Fiscal 1991* (Washington, D.C.: 1991).

53. Tropical Forestry Action Plan, "Report of the Independent Review," Kuala Lumpur, Malaysia, May 1990; Omar Sattaur, "Last Chance for the Rainforest Plan?" *New Scientist*, March 2, 1991; Rich, op. cit. note 1.

54. Rich, op. cit. note 1; Keith Bradsher, "Rain Forest Project in Africa Stirs Debate at

World Bank," *New York Times*, October 14, 1991.

55. Rich, op. cit. note 1; World Bank, *The Forest Sector* (Washington, D.C.: 1991).

56. World Bank, "Operational Directive 4.20: Indigenous Peoples," Washington, D.C., September 17, 1991; World Bank, "Operational Directive 4.30: Involuntary Resettlement," Washington, D.C., June 29, 1990; wildlands policy summarized in Raymond F. Mikesell and Lawrence F. Williams, *International Banks and the Environment: From Growth to Sustainability—An Unfinished Agenda* (San Francisco: Sierra Club Books, 1992).

57. Rich, op. cit. note 1; Friends of the Earth Ltd. and Environmental Defense Fund, "The World Bank's 'Forestry and Environment Project' for Gabon: A Test Case for the World Bank's New Forest Policy," Special Briefing, Washington, D.C., September 1992; "Forest Policy Undermined in Gabon," *BankCheck Quarterly* (International Rivers Network), November 1992.

58. Raymond Colitt, "When Conservation Efforts Fail to Protect," *Financial Times*, September 1, 1993; "Ecuador: GEF Cancels Project," *Early Warning* (Bank Information Center), June 1993.

59. Rich, op. cit. note 1; "Laos: Forestry Reform Controversy," *Early Warning* (Bank Information Center), June 1993; World Rainforest Movement, "Notes for NGO/GEF/World Bank Consultation on 'Lao PDR: Forest Management and Conservation Project,'" Washington, D.C., April 2, 1993.

60. Durning, op. cit. note 22; Cameron Duncan, "Internal Report Card Looks Bad for Structural Adjustments," *BankCheck Quarterly* (International Rivers Network), November 1992.

61. World Bank, *Implementing the World Bank's Strategy to Reduce Poverty: Progress and Challenges* (Washington, D.C.: 1993); Lawrence Summers, under secretary for international affairs, U.S. Department of Treasury, Statement before the International Development Subcommittee of the House Committee on Banking and Urban Affairs, U.S. Congress, May 5, 1993.

62. World Bank, op. cit. note 61; Nancy Alexander, "Response to Jerome Levinson," Conference on Human Rights, Public Finance, and the Development Process, *The American University Journal of International Law and Policy*, Fall 1992.

63. World Bank, *World Development Report 1990* (New York: Oxford University Press, 1990); World Bank, op. cit. note 61; Carol Capps, Church World Service/Lutheran World Relief, "The International Development Association: Flawed but Essential," Statement before the Subcommittee on International Development, Finance, Trade, and Monetary Policy, Banking Committee, U.S. House of Representatives, Washington, D.C., May 5, 1993.

64. World Bank, op. cit. note 61; Sven Sandstrom, managing director, World Bank, "An Effective Strategy for Poverty Reduction," Address to the International Development Conference, Washington, D.C., January 12, 1993; Lawrence H. Summers, "Investing in *All* the People," World Bank Working Paper, Washington, D.C., May 1992.

65. Augusta Molnar and Gotz Schreiber, "Women and Forestry: Operational Issues," World Bank Working Paper, Washington, D.C., May 1989; Jacobson, op. cit. note 48.

66. World Bank, *Women in Development: A Progress Report on the World Bank Initiative* (Washington, D.C.: 1990); Inge Khoury, "The World Bank and the Feminization of Poverty," *BankCheck* (International Rivers Network), July 1992.

67. Foundation for the Philippine Environment described in John C. Ryan, *Life Support: Conserving Biological Diversity*, Worldwatch Paper 108 (Washington, D.C.: Worldwatch Institute, April 1992); Marnie Stetson, "Giving Credit Where It's Due,"

World Watch, March/April 1991; Rich, op. cit. note 1; Anna Savage, Office of General Counsel, Inter-American Development Foundation, Washington, D.C., private communication, October 22, 1993.

68. World Bank *Annual Report 1993*, op. cit. note 6; Inter-American Development Bank, "Microenterprise and the IDB: Credit Where it's Due," Washington, D.C., brochure; Dan Martin, Inter-American Development Bank, Washington, D.C., private communication, October 20, 1993; John Clark, World Bank, Washington, D.C., private communication, October 20, 1993.

69. For an analysis of this chain of events in the Philippines, see Frances F. Korten, "The High Costs of Environmental Loans," *Asia Pacific Issues* (East-West Center), September 1993; Rich, op. cit. note 1.

70. World Bank, *Annual Report 1993*, op. cit. note 6; Jonathan E. Sanford, "African Debt: Recent Initiatives and Policy Options for Multilateral Bank Debt," Congressional Research Service, U.S. Library of Congress, Washington, D.C., July 9, 1993.

71. Alexander, Udall, and Bramble, op. cit. note 30.

72. John Kellenberg and Herman Daly, "Counting User Cost in Evaluating Projects Involving Depletion of Natural Capital: World Bank Best Practice and Beyond," World Bank Environment Department, Washington, D.C., October 1993.

73. Williams and Petesch, op. cit. note 5; Robert Repetto, remarks at "Valuing the Environment," First Annual Conference on Environmentally Sustainable Development, World Bank, September 30-October 1, 1993.

Chapter 10. Facing Food Insecurity

1. See Lester R. Brown, Hal Kane, and Ed Ayres, *Vital Signs 1993* (New York: W.W. Norton & Company, 1993), which cites U.S. Department of Agriculture (USDA), *World Grain Database* (unpublished printout) (Washington, D.C.: 1992); U.N. Food and Agriculture Organization (FAO), *Yearbook of Fishery Statistics: Catches and Landings* (Rome: various years), with updates for 1991 and 1992 data from FAO, Rome, private communication, April 29, 1993.

2. USDA, op. cit. note 1; FAO, op. cit. note 1.

3. U.S. Bureau of the Census population projections, published in Francis Urban and Ray Nightingale, *World Population by Country and Region, 1950–90 and Projections to 2050* (Washington, D.C.: USDA, Economic Research Service (ERS), 1993).

4. FAO and World Health Organization (WHO), *Nutrition and Development—A Global Assessment* (Rome: 1992).

5. Ibid.

6. Population growth from Bureau of the Census, op. cit. note 3.

7. FAO, op. cit. note 1; World Resources Institute, *World Resources 1990–91* (New York: Oxford University Press, 1991). The maximum sustainable yield in Figure 10-1 of 100 million tons, which includes aquacultural output as well as the oceanic and inland catches, is the author's estimate based on recent FAO reports indicating that all 17 of the world's major fishing areas have either reached or exceeded their limits. If rapid growth in world grain production can be reestablished, it might be possible to expand fish farming greatly, thus ameliorating the projected worldwide decline in per capita seafood supplies. Similarly, improved management of oceanic fisheries, which is theoretically possible, could ameliorate the decline. But short of a dramatic near-term slowdown in world population growth, a substantial decline in seafood supply per person appears inevitable.

8. FAO, *1948–1985 World Crop and Livestock Statistics* (Rome: 1987); FAO, *FAO Production Yearbooks* (Rome: 1988 through 1991); USDA, *World Agricultural Production*, August

1992 and March 1993; Worldwatch estimates.

9. USDA, op. cit. note 1; USDA, *World Grain Situation and Outlook*, Washington, D.C., March 1993.

10. Table 10–1 based on World Bank, unpublished printout, Washington, D.C., February 1992, on gross world product data for 1950 and 1955 from Herbert R. Block, *The Planetary Product in 1980: A Creative Pause?* (Washington, D.C.: U.S. Department of State, 1981), on U.S. Bureau of the Census, Center for International Research, Washington, D.C., private communication, March 26, 1993, and on International Monetary Fund, *World Economic Outlook: Interim Assessment* (Washington, D.C.: 1993).

11. World Bank, *World Development Report 1992* (New York: Oxford University Press, 1992); USDA, ERS, *Former USSR, Situation and Outlook Series*, Washington, D.C., May 1993; USDA, *World Grain Situation and Outlook*, Washington, D.C., September 1993.

12. These trends are documented throughout the chapter.

13. Worldwatch projection, based on a 100-million-ton world fish catch and on population projections from Bureau of the Census, op. cit. note 3.

14. "Soil Loss Accelerating Worldwide: Hinders Effort to Feed Earth's Growing Population," FAO, Rome, press release, July 13, 1993.

15. Fish conversion rate from Ross Garnaut and Guonan Ma, East Asia Analytical Unit, Department of Foreign Affairs and Trade, *Grain In China* (Canberra: Australian Government Publishing Service, 1992); conversion ratio for grain to beef from Allen Baker, Feed Situation and Outlook Staff, ERS, USDA, Washington, D.C., private communication, April 27, 1992.

16. USDA, op. cit. note 1; USDA, *World Grain Situation and Outlook*, Washington, D.C., April 1993.

17. USDA, op. cit. note 1; USDA, op. cit. note 16; Soviet area from USDA, *Former USSR*, op. cit. note 11; U.S. Conservation Reserve Program land area from USDA, ERS, Resources and Technology Division, *RTD UPDATES: 1993 Cropland Use*, Washington, D.C., September 1993.

18. USDA, op. cit. note 17; European land set-aside from Dan Plunckett, USDA, Washington, D.C., private communication, October 20, 1993.

19. Figure 10–3 from historical data in USDA, *Agricultural Statistics* (Washington, D.C.: various years), and from data since 1950 in USDA, op. cit. note 1.

20. USDA, op. cit. note 19; USDA, op. cit. note 1.

21. Figure 10–4 from USDA, op. cit. note 1.

22. Figure 10–5 from USDA, op. cit. note 1; irrigated area figures from "Thirsty Fields: Asia's Rice Lands," *AsiaWeek*, May 26, 1993.

23. World grain yields from USDA, op. cit. note 1.

24. FAO, *Fertilizer Yearbook* (Rome: various years); International Fertilizer Industry Association, *Fertilizer Consumption Report* (Paris: 1992); USDA, op. cit. note 1.

25. FAO, *Production Yearbook* (Rome: various years); Bill Quimby, USDA, ERS, Washington, D.C., private communication, March 20, 1992.

26. Donald O. Mitchell and Merlinda D. Ingco, International Economics Department, *The World Food Outlook: Malthus Must Wait* (Washington, D.C.,: World Bank, July 1993 (draft)); USDA, op. cit. note 1.

27. Donald L. Plucknett, "Science and Agricultural Transformation," International Food Policy Research Institute Lecture Series, No. 1, Washington, D.C., September 1993; USDA, op. cit. note 1.

28. USDA, op. cit. note 1.

29. Figure 10–6 from USDA, op. cit. note 1, with Worldwatch projections based on USDA and on population projections by Bureau of the Census, op. cit. note 3.

30. "Justus von Liebig," *Encyclopaedia Britannica* (Cambridge: Encyclopaedia Britannica, Inc., 1976); "Gregor Mendel," ibid.; Joseph A. Tainter, *The Collapse of Complex Societies* (Cambridge: Cambridge University Press, 1988).

31. G. Thottappilly et al., eds., *Biotechnology: Enhancing Research on Tropical Crops in Africa* (Ibadan, Nigeria: International Institute of Tropical Agriculture and Technical Centre for Agricultural and Rural Cooperation, 1992).

32. Royal Society of London and the U.S. National Academy of Sciences (NAS), *Population Growth, Resource Consumption, and a Sustainable World* (London and Washington, D.C.: 1992).

33. Gabrielle J. Persley, *Beyond Mendel's Garden: Biotechnology in the Service of World Agriculture* (Wallingford, U.K.: CAB International, 1990); D.O. Hall et al., "Biomass for Energy: Supply Prospects," in Thomas B. Johansson et al., eds., *Renewable Energy: Sources for Fuels and Electricity* (Washington, D.C.: Island Press, 1993); Vernon W. Ruttan, ed., *Agriculture, Environment, and Health* (Minneapolis: University of Minnesota Press, 1993).

34. Irrigation from Sandra Postel, *Last Oasis: Facing Water Scarcity* (New York: W.W. Norton & Company, 1993).

35. Rice yields from USDA, op. cit. note 1.

36. Growth in China from International Monetary Fund (IMF), *World Economic Outlook*, May 1993.

37. Garnaut and Ma, op. cit. note 15; USDA, *World Grain Situation and Outlook*, August 1993.

38. Grain yields from USDA, op. cit. note 1.

39. Ibid.

40. Grain deficit from ibid.

41. Environment and Urban Affairs Division, Government of Pakistan, and IUCN–The World Conservation Union, *The Pakistan National Conservation Strategy* (Karachi: 1992).

42. USDA, Foreign Agricultural Service, *World Grain Situation and Outlook*, Washington, D.C., various editions during 1993.

43. FAO, *FAO Production Yearbook 1990* (Rome: 1991).

44. Grain projection based on data from USDA, op. cit. note 1, and on population from Bureau of the Census, op. cit. note 3; FAO and WHO, op. cit. note 4.

45. Nicholas D. Kristof, "Riddle of China: Repression as Standard of Living Soars," *New York Times*, September 7, 1993.

46. FAO, op. cit. note 43.

47. Ibid.

48. Ibid.

49. Production data, more readily available than consumption data, are used here. In reality, there are slight differences when the small trade in livestock products is taken into account, but these differences, where they exist, are typically so small that they are lost in the rounding to kilograms. Life expectancies from Population Reference Bureau, *1993 World Population Data Sheet* (Washington, D.C.: 1993).

50. Feed-to-poultry conversion ratio derived from data in Robert V. Bishop et al., *The World Poultry Market—Government Intervention and Multilateral Policy Reform* (Washington, D.C.: USDA, 1990); conversion ratio for grain to beef based on Baker, op. cit. note 15; pork data from Leland Southard, Livestock and Poultry Situation and Outlook Staff, ERS, USDA, Washington, D.C., private communication, April 27, 1992; fish conversion ratio from Garnaut and Ma, op. cit. note 15;

eggs and cheese conversion ratios from Alan Durning and Holly Brough, *Taking Stock: Animal Farming and the Environment*, Worldwatch Paper 103 (Washington, D.C.: Worldwatch Institute, July 1991).

51. Figure 10–7 from USDA, op. cit. note 1, from FAO, *Food Outlook*, March 1993, and from IMF, *World Economic Outlook*, January 1993.

52. USDA, op. cit. note 1.

53. Ibid.

54. FAO, *1991 Food Aid in Figures, Vol. 9* (Rome: 1992).

55. John Bongaarts, "The KAP-Gap and the Unmet Need for Contraception," *Population and Development Review*, June 1991; Karen Rindge, National Wildlife Federation, private communication, October 19, 1993; Foreign Operations Bill HR 2295 appropriated the money to the U.N. Population Fund for FY 94. It became law on September 30, 1993.

56. United Nations, *International Transmission of Population Policy Experience* (New York: 1990); Stanley K. Henshaw, "Induced Abortion: A World Review, 1990," *Family Planning Perspectives*, March/April 1990.

57. Jodi L. Jacobson, *Planning the Global Family*, Worldwatch Paper 80 (Washington, D.C.: Worldwatch Institute, December 1987); Jodi L. Jacobson, *Gender Bias: Roadblock to Sustainable Development*, Worldwatch Paper 110 (Washington, D.C.: Worldwatch Institute, September 1992).

58. Edward O. Wilson, *The Diversity of Life* (Cambridge, Mass.: Harvard University Press, 1992).

59. Royal Society and NAS, op. cit. note 32.

60. Union of Concerned Scientists, "World's Leading Scientists Issue Urgent Warning to Humanity," Washington, D.C., press release, November 18, 1992.

61. Lawrence H. Summers, "Investing in *All* the People," World Bank Working Paper, Washington, D.C., 1992.

62. Meeting with Global Legislators Organization for a Balanced Environment of Japanese Parliament, Nagano, Japan, September 21, 1993.

63. Ruth Marcus, "U.S. to Sign Earth Pact," *Washington Post*, April 22, 1993; Bongaarts, op. cit. note 55; support for international family planning from Rindge, op. cit. note 55.

Index